Actresses of a
Certain Character

Actresses of a Certain Character

Forty Familiar Hollywood Faces from the Thirties to the Fifties

AXEL NISSEN

Foreword by Olivia de Havilland

McFarland & Company, Inc., Publishers
Jefferson, North Carolina, and London

The present work is a reprint of the illustrated case bound edition of Actresses of a Certain Character: Forty Familiar Hollywood Faces from the Thirties to the Fifties, *first published in 2007 by McFarland.*

Extract from "Memoirs" by Tennessee Williams
copyright © 1975, renewed 2003 the University of the South.
Reprinted by permission of Georges Borchardt, Inc.,
for the Tennessee Williams Estate.

Photographs are from the author's collection
unless otherwise credited

LIBRARY OF CONGRESS CATALOGUING-IN-PUBLICATION DATA

Nissen, Axel.
Actresses of a certain character : forty familiar Hollywood faces
from the thirties to the fifties / Axel Nissen ; foreword by Olivia de Havilland.
         p.   cm.
Includes bibliographical references and index.

ISBN 978-0-7864-6110-3
softcover : 50# alkaline paper ∞

1. Motion picture actors and actresses—United States—Biography.
2. Actresses—United States—Biography.   3. Character actors
and actresses—United States—Biography.   I. Title.
PN1998.2.N57   2011
791.4302'80922—dc22   2006029052

BRITISH LIBRARY CATALOGUING DATA ARE AVAILABLE

© 2007 Axel Nissen. All rights reserved

*No part of this book may be reproduced or transmitted in any form
or by any means, electronic or mechanical, including photocopying
or recording, or by any information storage and retrieval system,
without permission in writing from the publisher.*

Cover photograph: Agnes Moorehead

Manufactured in the United States of America

*McFarland & Company, Inc., Publishers
Box 611, Jefferson, North Carolina 28640
www.mcfarlandpub.com*

To Siân Phillips

ACKNOWLEDGMENTS

I've worked on this book in three cities and during some of the happiest and some of the saddest times of my life. Writing it, though, has been an unalloyed joy.

My first, heartfelt thanks must go to a woman whose name is synonymous in our culture with grace, beauty, and boundless talent: Olivia de Havilland. Her support for this project has meant much to me.

My parents, Liv and Nils Axel Nissen, have always been among my closest friends and staunchest allies. To them, many thanks.

The following have aided me in my research or in the publication of the book: Adi I. Bar, Michael Cooper, the late Kasey Rogers, Fredrick Tucker.

I want to thank those of my friends and colleagues who have sustained me during the four years I've been involved in this project: Hunter M. Cole, Sheila Coulson, Richard Currier, the late Espen Flølo, Vibeke Flølo, Ingrid Haug, Edward Hibbert, Olav Lausund, Orm Øverland, Ivan Raykoff, Catherine Roberts, Pål N. Somdalen, and Bob Tobin.

This book is dedicated to a woman of character, my fairy godmother Siân Phillips, with love and sincere admiration.

Last but not least, I want to thank my former partner and ever fond friend, Mark Hildebrandt; and Jonas Bjørnødegård, with whom I spent a charmed time as I was completing this book.

TABLE OF CONTENTS

Acknowledgments   vi
Foreword by Olivia de Havilland   1
Introduction: A Character Actress Is Born   3

The Actresses

That Morgan Woman SARA ALLGOOD (1879–1950)	9	*Earth Mother* JANE DARWELL (1879–1967)	76
Classic Dame JUDITH ANDERSON (1897–1992)	13	*Not So Big Mama* MILDRED DUNNOCK (1901–1991)	80
Mother of the Year FAY BAINTER (1893–1968)	19	*The Star That Wasn't* GLADYS GEORGE (1900–1954)	84
How the Mighty Have Fallen ETHEL BARRYMORE (1879–1959)	23	*Bride of Laughton* ELSA LANCHESTER (1902–1986)	88
Not So Nice to Come Home To FLORENCE BATES (1888–1954)	29	*Mother Hen* JESSIE ROYCE LANDIS (1904–1972)	95
Leave It to Beavers LOUISE BEAVERS (1902–1962)	33	*The Magnificent Mammy* HATTIE MCDANIEL (1893–1952)	100
Glamour and L'Amour MARY BOLAND (1882–1965)	38	*Butterflies Are Free* BUTTERFLY MCQUEEN (1911–1995)	106
Miss Bondi Goes to Hollywood BEULAH BONDI (1888–1981)	43	*Ma Kettle* MARJORIE MAIN (1890–1975)	110
The Gay Divorcée ALICE BRADY (1892–1939)	49	*Lavender Lady* AGNES MOOREHEAD (1900–1974)	117
The Professional Tweetybird BILLIE BURKE (1884–1970)	54	*Blithe Spirit* MILDRED NATWICK (1905–1994)	128
Mother for Metro SPRING BYINGTON (1886–1971)	61	*A Real Scream* UNA O'CONNOR (1880–1959)	132
Doyenne of Dowagers GLADYS COOPER (1888–1971)	66	*A Real Nutter* EDNA MAY OLIVER (1883–1942)	137
Aunt Pittypat LAURA HOPE CREWS (1879–1942)	72	*Russian Gargoyle* MARIA OUSPENSKAYA (1876–1949)	141

What a Pal
  LEE PATRICK (1901–1982)   146

The Eternal Aunt
  ELIZABETH PATTERSON (1875–1966)   152

Chinless Wonder
  ALICE PEARCE (1917–1966)   156

Duchesses and Domestics
  JESSIE RALPH (1864–1944)   159

Mother Courage
  ANNE REVERE (1903–1990)   163

The Forgotten Woman
  ELISABETH RISDON (1887–1958)   167

The Last Character Actress
  THELMA RITTER (1905–1969)   170

La Belle Laide
  FLORA ROBSON (1902–1984)   178

Star for a Day, Grandmother for a Decade
  MAY ROBSON (1858–1942)   184

The Duchess
  ALISON SKIPWORTH (1863–1952)   189

Cat Woman
  GALE SONDERGAARD (1899–1985)   196

Grand Dame
  LUCILE WATSON (1879–1962)   202

A Real Dame
  MAY WHITTY (1865–1948)   208

Libeled Lady
  CORA WITHERSPOON (1890–1957)   212

Notes   217
Bibliography   231
Index   235

FOREWORD
by
Olivia de Havilland

Actresses of a Certain Character is a remarkable work and its author, Professor Axel Nissen, is a remarkable man.

With his encyclopedic knowledge of, and his love for, the films of the Golden Era and the supporting actresses whose performances embellished them, he has given us an astonishing collection of mini-biographies of these gifted women whose lives were often even more dramatic than the films in which they played.

What is striking about the compilation is that Professor Nissen, a scholar, has written his perceptive vignettes in a lively, intimate, and often humorous style. *Actresses of a Certain Character* is not only a wonderful tribute to its subjects, but is also wonderful reading. I found it irresistibly interesting—addictive, in fact.

INTRODUCTION: A CHARACTER ACTRESS IS BORN

"Hello everybody, I'm Mrs. Norman Maine." Many old film buffs will recall this final line from the classic movie about the movies, *A Star Is Born*. In the original, 1937 version, Janet Gaynor as Vicki Lester addresses these words to her fans the world over via an international radio hook-up at the gala premiere of her latest film. Shortly beforehand, Vicki's proud septuagenarian grandmother speaks the following words to listeners with a dream of coming to Hollywood: "It took me over seventy ... *sixty* years to get here, but I am here and here I mean to stay."

Less well remembered than the film's final line, these words and the actress who speaks them are an appropriate starting point for a book on Hollywood character actresses. Do you recall who played Grandma Lettie? It was the earliest born actress to have a major film career in the sound era, May Robson, born in Australia in 1858. Indeed, it took Robson nearly seventy years to get to Hollywood, a place that did not even exist until she was in her fifties. She arrived in 1927 and, yes, she came to stay. *A Star Is Born*, which provides an indirect yet telling commentary on Robson's own life and that of many a Hollywood character actress, was her thirty-third sound film. She would make movies till her death in 1942 at age eighty-four.

Decked out in first night finery, in the final scene of *A Star Is Born* Robson looks the way we imagine she would have looked at the premiere of one of her own films. Oscar-nominated in the Best Actress category in 1934 for *Lady for a Day*, May Robson was one of the rare character actress stars. After Marie Dressler's death in 1934, she was the grandest of Hollywood's grand old ladies until her own death. As such, "Muzzy," as she was affectionately known in the business, was not representative of the typical Hollywood character actress: uncredited, unrecognized, unawarded if not unrewarded, appearing in maybe a dozen or more films a year, the first to end up on the cutting room floor, the last to be photographed or interviewed.

In *A Star Is Born* we also find a character actress of average rank, Clara Blandick, remembered today, if at all, as Dorothy's Auntie Em in *The Wizard of Oz* (1939). For more than twenty years, Blandick worked in the movie industry, lending her sour-pussed, bespectacled, spinsterish presence to more than a hundred films. She retired in 1950 and twelve years later, in poor health, nearly blind, she had her hair done, arranged mementos of her career around her bed, and took her own life by swallowing a dose of sleeping pills.[1]

In *A Star Is Born*, Blandick has one good scene—the opening scene—in which, as Gaynor's termagant Aunt Mattie, she ridicules her niece's aspirations for a movie career. Her job done, she disappears from the film. It is up to Robson as the grandmother to provide the advice and the emotional sustenance Gaynor needs to pursue her dreams. She teaches her granddaughter, "For every dream of yours you make come true, you pay the price in heartbreak." Their scenes together are among the most touching in the film. Grandma Lettie is allowed to make a dramatic return to the film towards the end, when squawking imperiously in classic Robson fashion she demands to see her granddaughter, now the famous movie star Vicki Lester. She reminds Gaynor that she has known all along that she might have to sacrifice her personal happiness for success. She does not want her granddaughter to be a quitter.

As the spiritual center of the film, Robson's performance shows some of the significant qualities an experienced character actress could contribute. Looking back on her career and "the perfectly marvelous characters actors" she had worked with, Joan Crawford tried to say something about their contribution to the film industry: "I don't know how to describe it, but words like 'character' and 'depth' crop up. Also a matter of identity—people who saw movies must have loved them."[2]

* * *

They were the mothers, grandmothers, and maiden aunts to the stars. They were their best friends, maids, teachers, landladies, nurses, and nannies. One might say they were the *real* women in the movies. They certainly had real talent. Tall and short, large and small, old and not so old, ugly and not so ugly, they were ever-present, greasing the machinery of the plot, providing the necessary help and hindrance. Often in the background, they were no less beloved for being part of the furniture. Familiar faces, they gave a picture its distinctive depth and flavor.

We've all seen them and from time to time we've wondered: "Who's that woman?" Who *is* that amazing old broad who just bellowed her way through a scene or wheedled her way, silver cord in hand? Who is that pert, wisecracking best friend or that peppery spinster? Who is that dizzy dame or that hilarious eccentric? The credits give only their names and sometimes not even that. The questions remain: Who was Alison Skipworth? Laura Hope Crews? Lee Patrick? Edna May Oliver? Billie Burke? Elsa Lanchester? Where did they come from? Where did they learn their trade? How did they get into the movies? What kinds of roles did they play?

Actresses of a Certain Character tells you all these things and more, as it documents in detail the lives and careers of two score of Hollywood's most talented character actresses from the early days of sound till the end of the studio era. The book provides not just the information easy to come by—births, deaths, film credits, prizes—but the less tangible but no less important reckoning of these players' unique talents, signature roles, and overall career development.

The book covers a representative range of backgrounds, character types, career experiences, and reputations, from the rare character actress stars, such as Marjorie Main, Agnes Moorehead, and Thelma Ritter; via A-list actresses, such as Fay Bainter, Beulah Bondi, and Lucile Watson; through to less easily recognized but no less important film presences, such as Sara Allgood, Lee Patrick, and Jessie Ralph. Forty actresses rate individual profiles, while dozens more are discussed as points of comparison and contrast.

The book includes all the most beloved and familiar female faces one step behind the stars in Hollywood films of the 1930s, '40s, and '50s from Sara Allgood to Cora Witherspoon; from May Robson, born before the Civil War, to Alice Pearce, born during the First World War; from homegrown, rural types, such as Jane Darwell and Marjorie Main, to dignified British dowagers, such as Gladys Cooper and May Whitty. Here are the tallest and the smallest; the gracefully aging beauties, the indestructible profiles, and the plain Janes; the massive chins and the chinless wonders; the great eccentrics and all the dizzy dames. Here are the success stories, the tragedies, and the careers destroyed by the Red Scare. Here are the working class women and the grande dames; the decade-long troupers and the one- or two-hit wonders; the little old ladies and the best friends; and last but not least, mothers, grandmothers, and aunts of every age, size, and description.

About the character actress, we might use the well worn adage "Always a bridesmaid, never a bride." Come to think of it, though, a character actress was more likely to play a housemaid than a bridesmaid. Yet there were compensations for not taking center stage, beyond the opportunity for privacy and avoiding studio control over every aspect of one's life. While many a screen star saw her career peter out when she hit the forty mark or chose to end it herself, like Garbo and Norma Shearer, a character actress had no expiration date.[3] Some retired in their sixties, but others worked at their chosen profession in their seventies and even into their eighties.

To revert to our initial example: While Janet Gaynor was finished in the movies only a year after *A Star Is Born*, May Robson worked steadily until her death in 1942. Clara Blandick worked for another thirteen years, until she was seventy. Some other examples: Adeline De Walt Reynolds made her last film when she was ninety-four; Estelle Winwood when she was ninety-three; Ethel Griffies and Dame Judith Anderson when they were eighty-seven. Judging from the longevity of most character actresses, their quality of life and job satisfaction must have been high.

While a movie star might be "discovered" sipping a soda at the counter at Schwab's Drug Store, in legend at least, a character actress inevitably had a long stage career behind her. For many of the actresses who got a new lease on life on the big screen, their films were merely a parenthetical aside in the long sentence of their acting careers. Some had been stage stars, others character players from the beginning. For all, Hollywood was the great leveler. Stage stardom seldom transferred to the screen. You left your past, however stellar, at the studio door. Gladys Cooper? No one in Hollywood had ever heard of her when she arrived there in '39. The same went for Flora Robson. All they saw was a woman of a certain age, shape, appearance, and, not least of all, accent. Bette Davis, arguably the greatest character actress of them all, would never get used to the fact that the stage stars of her youth—Cooper, Fay Bainter, Jane Cowl, Laura Hope Crews—were cast in supporting roles in her films.[4]

Hollywood character actresses came from all four corners of the English-speaking world and from a few more exotic places. But mostly they came from Broadway. The introduction of cinematic sound in the late twenties put a premium on actors who could emote *and* enunciate. As in all things, the Hollywood movie moguls sought the best money could buy. The best properties to film often came from Broadway. The same went for actresses of a certain age. Thus many a seasoned stage actress found herself making her cinematic debut reprising her role in a stage hit. Beulah Bondi started that way in 1931 when she repeated her role in Elmer Rice's *Street Scene*, Maria Ouspenskaya did likewise in *Dodsworth* in 1936, and Mildred Dunnock got her first chance at film work reprising her role in *The Corn Is Green* in 1945.

Other actresses had been paying their dues for years in stock and repertory companies and, through a lucky break, got a chance at a film role. This was the case for Thelma Ritter, a housewife with two children, semi-retired after fifteen years worth of a less than stellar stage career. She happened to be a friend of director George Seaton and his wife, Phyllis. Seaton needed someone to play a weary Christmas shopper at Macy's in *Miracle on 34th Street*. Could Ritter do it? You bet she could. Ritter went on to become one of the most prominent second leads of the fifties and sixties. Florence Bates was "discovered" strutting her stuff at the Pasadena Playhouse. Yet Bates, Jane Darwell, Louise Beavers, and Hattie McDaniel were among the few major Hollywood character actresses to have no Broadway credits.

For African American actresses, though, the career path was often different. A black performer like Beavers might go from being a maid to playing a maid. Hattie McDaniel said famously when she was criticized for contributing to Hollywood stereotyping of African Americans: "Why should I complain about making $7,000 a week playing a maid? If I didn't, I'd be making $7 a week being one."[5] A black film actress found herself *back* being a maid, too, if Central Casting could no longer find work for her.

For the most sought-after actresses, there was the chance of a long-term contract. The terms were basically the same as for leading players. Contractees were guaranteed work forty weeks out of the year, just like the stars.[6] At the bigger studios, character actors made B movies between more prestigious assignments.[7] Or they might be loaned out to another studio, again just like the stars, while their home studio pocketed the difference.

Every self-respecting studio had one or more resident character women. During the first half of the 1930s, Alison Skipworth reigned supreme at Paramount, Edna May Oliver at RKO, and May Robson at MGM. Paramount also appears to have had Mary Boland and Elizabeth Patterson under contract in the thirties. Fox Films and later Twentieth Century–Fox had Jane Darwell, Sara Allgood, Anne Revere, and Thelma Ritter. Warner Bros. had May Robson in the late 1930s and early '40s and RKO Elisabeth Risdon in the same period. In the '40s and early '50s, MGM had Fay Bainter, Ethel Barrymore, Spring Byington, Gladys Cooper, Agnes Moorehead, and Dame May Whitty on their payroll. Marjorie Main completed two consecutive seven-year contracts at Metro between 1940 and 1954, but her biggest hit was in *The Egg and I* at Universal, and she would go on to finish her career there.

Not all character actresses wished to be under contract. Beulah Bondi, for example, had a highly successful, three-decade film career as a freelancer. As a freelancer, you had more control over what films you acted in, limited of course by what was offered you. A studio contract player might well be chosen over a freelance actress, as the former would be less expensive to use. Bondi felt she had lost the coveted role of Ma Joad in *The Grapes of Wrath* (1940) to Jane Darwell because Darwell was a contract player at Twentieth Century–Fox.[8]

Hollywood character actresses are a vastly undervalued group of performers. The contribution they made to the film industry, starting in the early days of the talkies and extending into the 1940s and early 1950s, was unparalleled. Never before or since have there been more opportunities for actresses of a certain age and their impact has never been greater than it was in the classic Hollywood era.

The gradual but irrevocable dismantling of the studio system in the wake of the Supreme Court order for the studios to divest themselves of their movie theaters meant the demise of the traditional character actress. The last generation of these actresses, born during the first decade of the twentieth century, found themselves in the same situation as their star contemporaries, either forced into retirement or competing for ever-fewer roles for older women as fewer and fewer films were being made. The sixties and early seventies was a period when more first-rate actresses performed in third-rate films than at any time before or since. The trouble started, though, in the 1950s. Symptomatically, when *A Star Is Born* was remade in 1954 as a comeback vehicle for Judy Garland, both May Robson's and Clara Blandick's parts had been excised from the script.

The degeneration of the Hollywood film industry was also due to an increasingly youthful audience and the competition of television. The most energetic, youthful, and adaptable actresses transferred their allegiance to the new medium in the course of the fifties and sixties. Actresses like Spring Byington, Agnes Moorehead, Mildred Natwick, Elizabeth Patterson, and Alice Pearce went on to new fame and fortune in television; some even starred in their own series. Ironically, these actresses are now best remembered for their work on the small rather than the big screen. Today one might claim that the character actress lives on in television drama series, situation comedies, and soap operas.

THE ACTRESSES

That Morgan Woman
SARA ALLGOOD (1879–1950)

Sara Allgood was the most prominent Irish actress to come to Hollywood in the studio era. Her stage career began in her native city of Dublin in 1904, while her screen career dated back to 1918, when she made her one and only silent film in Sydney. In 1929 she was in the first British sound film, Alfred Hitchcock's *Blackmail*, where she played the mother of the killer and blackmail victim. Hitchcock made two further films with her—*Juno and the Paycock* (1930), where she reprised her celebrated stage role as Mrs. "Juno" Boyle, and *Sabotage* (1936)—and she racked up no less than twenty British screen credits before transplanting herself to the United States.

Today Allgood's contemporary actress and fellow Irishwoman, Universal horror queen Una O'Connor, is probably better remembered. Yet compared with Allgood's stature and reputation at home, O'Connor was no more than a midget. Granted O'Connor had also treaded the boards at the legendary Abbey Theatre in Dublin, but Sara Allgood *was* the Abbey Theatre, as a founding member of the company and one of its brightest stars for the first nine years of its existence. During those years she had taken part in practically every production the theater put on: *Spreading the News*, *Riders to the Sea*, *The Playboy of the Western World*, *The Shewing Up of Blanco Posnet*, *Kathleen Ni Houlihan*, to name but a few. Even fifty years on, oldtimers remembering the early days of the Abbey spoke of her with awe. Allgood was known particularly for her marvelous voice. One fellow actress recalled that "Sara's voice had a range, a depth, a clarity impossible to describe. It was gold and silver and, if so she wished, iron."[9]

Despite Allgood's pre-eminence in the legitimate theater, Una O'Connor had the more successful American screen career, making sixty films between 1933 and 1948, including such thirties classics as *The Invisible Man*, *The Informer*, *Bride of Frankenstein*, *David Copperfield*, and *The Adventures of Robin Hood*. Allgood arrived in California eight years after her countrywoman, missing the innovative and experimental thirties entirely; she made only half the number of films, and she did not find her niche in movieland the way O'Connor had.

The circumstances of Allgood's early life in Ireland are somewhat cloudy. She claimed to have been born in Dublin on October 31, 1883, yet her true birth date—recorded in the Social Security Death Index and on her grave—was October 15, 1879 (which, incidentally, was also Jane Darwell's birth date). Allgood's father, George, was an upholsterer and her mother, Margaret (born Harold), was by all accounts an uncommonly high-minded upholsterer's wife.[10] At least she was touted in Allgood's *New York Times* obituary as the friend of William Butler Yeats, J.M. Synge, George Moore, and Lady Gregory.[11] Allgood had three sisters and two brothers.[12] Her sister, Maire O'Neill (1885–1952), was also a celebrated actress in Ireland.[13]

Allgood went to Marlborough Street Training College in Dublin and was apprenticed to an upholsterer.[14] Thus, she could "support her habit" when around the turn of the twentieth century she was bitten by the acting bug. Veteran actor Frank J. Fay trained her and Lady Gregory encouraged her.[15] In February 1904, she made her professional stage debut in a one-act play with the Irish National Theatre Society of which she was a founding member.[16] Thirty-six years and countless roles later, and many miles away from her native land, she took her final stage bow in 1940. During the last decade of her life and career, she was exclusively a Hollywood movie (and TV) actress.

In her personal life, Allgood knew tragedy. In 1916, she married fellow actor and leading man, Gerald Henson, only to lose him and their infant daughter to influenza within the space of a year. Her daughter died in 1917, her husband in November 1918, while Allgood and her family were on an extended tour of Australia with *Peg o' My Heart*.[17] During her absence, both her brothers were killed in World War I.[18] Allgood soldiered on for another twenty years, until she joined the second wave of British, Irish, and Australian actresses to come to Hollywood, including Flora Robson, Gladys Cooper, Moyna MacGill, Dame May Whitty, and Judith Anderson.

It appears that Allgood was on tour in Los Angeles, when she decided that she'd had enough—of touring, that is.[19] She had spent four years in Australia, had made frequent trips to the United States with the Abbey Theatre's touring company in the teens and twenties, and this most recent tour was yet another revival of *Juno and the Paycock*, which had made a hit on Broadway in early 1940.[20] Brooks Atkinson wrote that Allgood was "inspired."[21] Most likely the offer of a role in an

The likeness between mother and daughter is not striking in this photo from *That Hamilton Woman* (United Artists, 1941), where Vivien Leigh played Emma Lady Hamilton and Sara Allgood her mother, Mrs. Cadogan-Lyon. The beautiful costumes were by René Hubert. Allgood had been waiting for years for a chance to dress up. Unfortunately, Hollywood would not offer her many other opportunities to frolic in finery.

American movie also influenced her decision to relocate to Los Angeles. Producer-director Alexander Korda was making his first Hollywood film, re-pairing his two young stars from *Fire Over England* (1937), Vivien Leigh and Laurence Olivier. Korda needed someone to play Leigh's mother in a film about Lord Nelson and Lady Hamilton that would be entitled *That Hamilton Woman*.

Leigh and Allgood had filmed together before. In 1936 they had both starred in a feathery light satire on Scottish local politics called *Storm in a Teacup* (I. Dalrymple, V. Saville), where Allgood played a woman of the people who goes all-out to save her beloved dog from the clutches of the local authorities. Leigh portrayed the hoity toity daughter of a local pundit. *That Hamilton Woman* (aka *Lady Hamilton*, A. Korda, 1941) was more solid fare, giving both actresses something to chew on. Allgood played Leigh's folksy, Liverpudlian mother, Mrs. Cadogan-Lyon, who takes to the high life with style and aplomb after her daughter Emma marries up and becomes Lady Hamilton. As far back as 1909, when she was still in her twenties, Allgood had written with a sigh: "I will admit to you that I would like a long part with plenty of fine clothes, in which it would not be necessary to make up 100 years old."[22] Here finally was her chance.

But the opportunities to frolic in finery, even in Hollywood, would for Allgood be severely limited. Upper-class dowager roles were not for her, nor solid middle-class mother roles either. At a glance, it looks as if the low social status of Irish immigrants to the United States generally was reflected in the types of roles offered to older Irish actresses in Hollywood. The bonny young lasses—Greer Garson, Maureen O'Hara, Geraldine Fitzgerald—could "pass," but a mature Irish woman was almost by definition cast as a domestic both on screen and off. Even donning the dignity of a nun's habit was not a frequent film alternative for the Catholic Allgood. Her only nun role in Hollywood was a modest part playing Sister Martha in Fox's answer to MGM's *Goodbye, Mr. Chips* (1939), *The Keys to the Kingdom* (J.M. Stahl, 1944). The film starred Gregory Peck in the role of an aged Catholic priest and missionary in China looking back on the vagaries of his long life.

In Ireland, Allgood had been known as the most talented and versatile actress of her generation. Comedies by Lady Gregory, straight plays by Synge and O'Casey, old parts and young parts, star turns or character roles, she could do them all. In tinseltown you had to look the part, so to speak, both in life and art. When producers looked at Sara Allgood, all they saw was a trusted family servant, a landlady, or a working-class mother. In a society that took appearances for realities, Allgood's lack of conventional beauty or physical distinction counted against her, even in character roles.

By any standard, she was not attractive. Her large, moon-shaped face, like a bun with two black currants for eyes, was so flat it had the air of being permanently pressed against a window, her hair was stringy, and her body was short, stout, and fairly formless.[23] What little evidence remains of her character seems to indicate that her determined chin was symbolic of a general disposition for belligerence and quarrelsomeness. Several members of the cast of *How Green Was My Valley* remembered that Allgood loved to argue, even with the godlike director John Ford.[24] Evidently she was not imbued with any great respect for this new class of professionals. She considered Hitchcock cheap and second-rate.[25]

Yet Allgood had gotten off to a flying start in Hollywood in 1941. *That Hamilton Woman* was followed by the role of the wife of a mental patient in *Dr. Jekyll and Mr. Hyde* (V. Fleming, MGM), starring Spencer Tracy and Ingrid Bergman, and a modest but striking part as an Irish slum mother in *Lydia* (J. Duvivier, 1941), another of Korda's films, starring his wife, Merle Oberon, Joseph Cotten, and Edna May Oliver. In the latter film, Allgood has an amusing scene when she threatens patrician do-gooder Oberon with a slop bucket if she does not leave the premises at once.

Allgood's fourth and final film in '41, and her first for Twentieth Century Fox, was *How Green Was My Valley*. Any character actress is fortunate if she is allowed one iconic role in her career. For Jane Darwell it was Ma Joad, for Hattie McDaniel "Mammy," for Judith Anderson Mrs. Danvers, for Margaret Hamilton the Wicked Witch of the West, for Elsa Lanchester the Bride of Frankenstein. For Allgood, her signature role was Beth Morgan, wife of Gwylim Morgan (Donald Crisp), and the mother of six sons (including the child star Roddy McDowall) and a daughter, Angharad (Maureen O'Hara). If she had done nothing else in Hollywood, Sara Allgood would still be remembered for her classic interpretation of a Welsh matriarch, the wife and mother of coal miners, struggling to keep her family together in trying times.

Allgood's performance in *How Green Was My Valley* got her an Oscar nomination for Best Actress in a Supporting Role and a seven-year contract at Twentieth Century Fox. She lost the Oscar to Mary Astor in *The Great Lie* and, artistically speaking, the contract was a loss as well. Though Allgood made most films and her best films for Fox, that isn't saying much. Like other actresses who scored a resounding hit early in their film careers—Blanche Yurka, Gale Sondergaard, Margaret Dumont, Elsa Lanchester, Butterfly McQueen, even Judith Anderson and Agnes Moorehead to some extent—the years following Allgood's celebrated performance in *How Green Was My Valley* were a long, drawn-out anticlimax.

That is not to say there weren't bright spots here and there. One of them was *Roxie Hart* (W.A. Wellman, Twentieth Century–Fox, 1942), starring Ginger Rogers in the title role and Allgood as a prison matron, who becomes a sort of maid and confidante to the jailbird played by Rogers. In her first scene, Allgood stops the cat fight between Rogers and another prisoner by knocking their heads together, before returning sedately to her newspaper. One would have liked to know what she thought of dancing the "big black bottom" with Rogers, Spring Byington and the boys in prison with a moronic grin on her face.

Next to Beth Morgan, Allgood's performance as Bessie in the second sound version of Charlotte Brontë's classic novel is probably her best remembered role. *Jane Eyre* (R. Stevenson, Twentieth Century–Fox, 1944) had Joan Fontaine in the title role and Orson Welles as Edward Rochester. Bessie is employed as a maid at the home of Jane Eyre's evil aunt, Mrs. Reed (Agnes Moorehead), and is the only one who treats Jane with kindness during her childhood, giving her a pin that she wears always. For someone of Allgood's grit and gall, though, the part wasn't much to write home about.

The Strange Affair of Uncle Harry

This double portrait of Sara Allgood and her four-time fellow player in film, Donald Crisp, shows them as Beth and Gwylim Morgan in *How Green Was My Valley* (Twentieth Century–Fox, 1941). The role of the matriarch of the Morgan clan was Allgood's most showy part during her decade in Hollywood and garnered her an Academy Award nomination for Best Actress in a Supporting Role.

(R. Siodmak, Universal, 1945), starring Geraldine Fitzgerald, Ella Raines, and George Sanders as Uncle Harry, was a strange affair indeed. Allgood plays the faithful but bellicose cook for a prominent New England family that has fallen on hard times. Nona, as she is called, is in constant conflict with one of her three employers, Hester (played by fellow Irish actress Moyna MacGill), about who has precedence in the kitchen. The film at least allowed Allgood to get into some good scraps. Finally, in *Cluny Brown* (E. Lubitsch, Twentieth Century–Fox, 1946), Allgood had a marvelous part as a snooty housekeeper, Mrs. Maile, who tries to teach star Jennifer Jones her proper place as second parlor maid. Allgood's interaction with the equally snobbish butler, played by Ernest Cossart, is hilarious, as they form a kind of mutual admiration society. Like no other, this film shows what Allgood could do as a comedienne.

Sara Allgood stayed with Twentieth Century–Fox till the end of her life. Her eleventh and last film for the studio was *Cheaper by the Dozen* (W. Lang, 1950) with Myrna Loy and Clifton Webb. As the Gilbreth family's devoted housekeeper, Mrs. Monohan, she was given eighth billing, but only had five lines to speak. Allgood died from a heart attack at the Motion Picture Country Home and Hospital in Woodland Hills, California on September 13, 1950. Her grave marker in Holy Cross Cemetery, Culver City, Los Angeles, reads "Sara Allgood—Abbey Theater."

Classic Dame
JUDITH ANDERSON (1897–1992)

Dame Judith Anderson was one of the most celebrated actresses of the twentieth or any other century. I would also venture the assertion that her acting career contained more variety and contrast than any other actress in the English-speaking world. For what can we say of a woman who built her stellar reputation on a series of startling, innovative interpretations of some of the heftiest women's roles in the classical and modern stage repertoire, while all along taking parts large and small in westerns, thrillers, and film noir, and ultimately in television daytime drama?

Anderson had her first hit on Broadway as a flamboyant vamp in 1924 and broke into films as an obsessive, British, lesbian housekeeper more than fifteen years later. The year after she played the cold, vengeful Lavinia Mannon in Eugene O'Neill's *Mourning Becomes Electra* (1932), she played a warm, sexy temptress in her first film *Blood Money* (1933). The same year she played Lady Macbeth to Maurice Evans's Macbeth, she portrayed a Chicago gangster queen in a low-budget crime comedy at RKO. The year she triumphed as the definitive modern Medea in a Tony Award–winning performance at the National Theatre on West 41st Street in New York, she played an adulterous rancher's wife in the first noir western. If that were not enough, the woman who had given the world O'Neill's Nina Leeds and Lavinia Mannon, Shakespeare's Gertrude, Lady Macbeth *and* Hamlet, Chekhov's Olga, and Euripedes' Medea on stage; and Herodias, Lady Macbeth (twice), Medea (twice), and Tennessee Williams's Big Mama on the large and small screens, ended her record-long, seventy-two-year acting career as an ancient Sioux crone, a high priestess in *Star Trek*, and a matriarch in the soap opera *Santa Barbara*!

It would be reassuring to say that Judith Anderson was always good no matter how bad the part or the film. Well, frankly, she wasn't. Often she was no better than the material and there are probably a greater proportion of stinkers in her film repertoire than any other actress in this book. By any conventional criteria of excellence in acting, precious few of her film roles would qualify as great or even good. However excellent and preeminent she was on the stage, on the silver screen Anderson was transferred into the queen of camp, dishing out performances that are literally awfully good. Camp is something that is so bad it becomes good. It must be said too, that camp is in the eye of the beholder. There may be fans who value Anderson chiefly for her realistic, down-to-earth portrayals of average humanity in the trials and tribulations of their daily lives, but I'm not one of them. I tend to think that, on film at least, Anderson is often at her best when she is at her worst. We can only ask ourselves what she thought she was doing in films like *Lady Scarface*, *The Red House*, and *The Furies*.

Though she was only 5' 4" tall,[26] there was something larger than life about Judith Anderson. She looked like someone you would not want to meet in a dark alley. Vincent Price spoke of her, Tallulah Bankhead, and Laurette Taylor as having "that magnificent beauty that is ugly in a funny way.... They came off as being the most beautiful women in the world through an illumination of their own personality."[27] Alabaster, marble, plaster, Anderson's face is often compared to something cold, pale, and hard. It was indeed a most unusual and unsettling face and one that, even if she had arrived in Hollywood twenty years earlier, would have disqualified her from screen stardom. As it happens, she did arrive in Hollywood for the first time as early as 1918, when she was twenty-one. With her mother in tow, she came hoping to make an indelible impression on the film capital. She left four months later, minus a few illusions and with no offers forthcoming.[28] Who was this enterprising young woman who had taken herself halfway around the world to further her acting career?

Judith Anderson was born Frances Margaret Anderson-Anderson in Adelaide, Australia, the fourth child and second daughter of the Scottish silver mine owner James Anderson-Anderson and English-born Jessie Margaret Saltmarsh. Her father lost his money and abandoned the family when Frances was five. Her enterprising mother opened a grocery store to provide for herself and her children, and sent them to private schools. Frances Anderson made her first stage appearance in 1915 at the Royal Theatre in Sydney as Stephanie in *A Royal Divorce*.[29]

According to Eric Johns, she had to leave Australia to progress in her career, as all the starring roles on the Australian stage were being played by British and American actors.[30] After getting no response in Hollywood, she was engaged by the stock company at the 14th Street Theatre in New York and toured with William Gillette in *Dear Brutus* in 1920.[31] She changed her name to Judith Anderson after her first Broadway show, *On the Stairs* (1922), and would rack up twenty-five credits on the Great White Way in the ensuing sixty years, including the Unknown One in Pirandello's *As You Desire Me* (1931), playing Lavinia Mannon to Florence Reed's Christine in *Mourning Becomes Electra* (1932), Gertrude to John Gielgud's Hamlet in 1936–37, Olga in *The Three Sisters* (1942–43) with Katharine Cornell and Ruth Gordon (which got them on the cover of *Time*), and her landmark interpretation of Medea in Robinson Jeffers' adaptation of Euripedes' classic during the 1947–48 season.[32] Anderson is the only actor to have won an Emmy twice for playing the same role in two separate productions, in her case of *Macbeth* (1954 and 1960). She was created a Dame Commander of the British Empire in 1960, only the second Australian performer so honored.[33]

The films of Judith Anderson—all twenty-seven of them—may be divided into four categories, according to the size of the role and the status of the film: 1) Major roles in major films; 2) Major roles in minor films; 3) Minor roles in major films; and 4) Minor roles in minor films. In the first category, we find *Rebecca*, *Pursued*, *Salome*, *Cat on a Hot Tin Roof*, and *A Man Called Horse*; in the second, *Lady Scarface*, *The Red House*, and *The Furies*; and in the third category, *Laura*, *The Ten Commandments*, and *Star Trek III*.

The fourth and final category shall not greatly concern us here, but examples are *Kings Row*, *Edge of Darkness*, *And Then There Were None*,

In this iconic still photograph from *Rebecca* (United Artists, 1940), Joan Fontaine and Judith Anderson are all dressed up for the costume ball at Manderley. At Mrs. Danvers's diabolical suggestion, the second Mrs. de Winter has worn the same costume as Rebecca, the first Mrs. de Winter, once did on a similar occasion. Mrs. Danvers has allowed herself the luxury of a little lace around her alabaster neck. One wonders what they are looking at with such rapt attention.

and *The Diary of a Chambermaid*. In *Kings Row* (S. Wood, Warner Bros., 1942), Anderson plays the wife of a dangerously inept physician, Charles Coburn, and is only interested in keeping up appearances and avoiding scandal at any cost. *Edge of Darkness* (L. Milestone, Warner Bros., 1943) was one of Hollywood's attempts to follow President Roosevelt's appeal to "look to Norway" and allow Americans to be inspired by the fighting spirit of the descendants of the Vikings. As Gerd Blarnesen (there is no such Norwegian surname), Anderson played an innkeeper in the coastal village of Trollnes whose father is shot as a hostage when the Germans occupy the village. In René Clair's *And Then There Were None* (1945), based on a murder mystery by Agatha Christie, she joined a cast considerably more talented than the resulting film, as the cliché-spouting, purse-lipped, obsessively knitting spinster Emily Brent. In Jean Renoir's *The Diary of a Chambermaid* (1946), she plays Madame Lanlaire, who tries to keep her wayward son, Hurd Hatfield, at home by hiring an attractive maid, Paulette Goddard.

Alfred Hitchcock's first American film, *Rebecca* (Selznick Int., 1940), was as showy a film as a character actress could hope for. By the time Anderson got a new chance in Hollywood, seven years after her false start in *Blood Money* (R. Brown, 1933), she was forty-three years old.[34] The years had done nothing to soften her recalcitrant features so important to her overall sinister impression as the housekeeper of Manderley. Mrs. Danvers is the kind of part that does not so much require acting as being. Anderson's classic portrayal was a combination of her unique look—the impassive, plaster of Paris face with its characteristic mole, the close-set, dark, hooded eyes with their faraway expression—and the accoutrements of the classic film villainess and housekeeper—the hair in a braided twist, the poker-stiff back and clasped hands, and the plain, foot-length black gown. As Nigel Bruce says of "Danny": "She's not exactly an oil painting, is she." Anderson had her only stab at an Oscar in 1941, but lost to veteran character actress Jane Darwell for *The Grapes of Wrath*. Had she won, she would have joined the exclusive company of those actors who have won an Academy Award, a Tony, and an Emmy.

Martin Scorsese no less has called *Pursued* (1947) the first noir western.[35] Helmed by veteran Warner Bros. director Raoul Walsh, the screenplay was by Niven Busch, bestselling author of the novel on which *Duel in the Sun* was based the previous year and an Oscar-nominee for the original story for *In Old Chicago* (1937). Three years later, another of Busch's novels would form the basis for the Thanksgiving-size Anderson turkey *The Furies*. The noir element in *Pursued*, set in turn-of-the-century New Mexico, is chiefly linked to a recurring dream of a tragic event from his childhood, which haunts the hero, Jeb Rand (Robert Mitchum). We are supposed to believe that Jeb is able to find out nothing about his past and his dead relatives, even though their old homestead is within easy riding distance and he is surrounded on all sides by people who knew his family, including his adoptive mother, Medora Callum. Ma Callum is portrayed by a suitably rustic, top-knotted, plaid-shawled and calico-clad Judith Anderson, who only looks truly ludicrous in the few scenes where we see her as her younger, long-tressed, adulterous self. I leave to the reader to discover who she was being adulterous with....

Charles Higham and Joel Greenberg found Anderson to be "excellent" in this film.[36] I would say she takes about as naturally to playing maternal and nurturing, as Mae West would take to acting prudish and morally indignant. This is the woman who, the same year *Pursued* was released, made it look convincing that, as Medea, she would kill her own children solely to spite her faithless husband.

Anderson's regal bearing and imperial profile made her an obvious choice to play Queen Herodias when Columbia filmed the story of Salome in 1953 with William Dieterle as director. There are many versions of the story of Salome, of course; Oscar Wilde's being one modern, well-known version, which clearly was not the basis for the film. To adjust the original fable of Salome to the requirements of the star system and the need for a happy ending, Anderson *qua* Herodias was made John the Baptist's chief opponent and the one indirectly responsible for his decapitation. Rita Hayworth's Salome is too busy being beautiful and in love with wimpy Christian convert Stewart Granger in one of his many ancient action hero roles (though here there isn't much action) to concern herself with anything quite so common as a dirty, smelly prophet (Alan Badel). Well, that's not entirely true. We are to believe that she actually dances for her lascivious stepfather, King Herod (Charles Laughton), so as to be able to plead for the prophet's life afterwards. The inefficacy of this scheme becomes brutally evident when John's head suddenly appears on a silver salver. Anderson looks suitably imposing even with pneumatic "Joan Crawford lips" and gets to wear a lot of gold baubles and bangles. Sad to say, there isn't much more to her performance than a kind of soap opera villainess quality, as if *Santa Barbara*'s Minx Lockridge had been transported to Galilee in biblical times.

One would have liked to have known the rationale behind casting Anderson as Ida "Big Mama" Pollitt in the filmatization of Tennessee Williams's hit play, *Cat on a Hot Tin Roof* (R. Brooks, MGM, 1958). A more unlikely candidate to play the fifties version of the dizzy dame so common in the thirties, one can hardly imagine. Alice Brady was long dead, Mary Boland had retired, but surely Spring Byington and Billie Burke were still around? Truth to tell, Anderson is not quite as bad as one might have expected, however painful it is to see her flirting with Deacon Davis (Vaughn Taylor), clucking over her hubby, Burl Ives (in a peerless portrayal of Big Daddy), doting on her troubled son, Brick (Paul Newman), and trying to give well-intentioned marital advice to her daughter-in-law, Maggie (Elizabeth Taylor). One would have welcomed a chance to compare Anderson with the creator of the role on Broadway, Mildred Dunnock, so small and spare the nickname "Big Mama" must have taken on an ironic coloring. It is hard to imagine any actress, though, playing the part better than Kim Stanley in the 1985 TV version with Tommy Lee Jones, Jessica Lange, and Rip Torn. It was Stanley's final role and she deservedly won an Emmy for it.

Finally, I wonder if I don't think Anderson's aged squaw, Buffalo Cow Head, in *A Man Called Horse* (E. Silverstein, 1970) is not one of her most convincing portrayals. It goes to show that her range encompassed even the consciously comic (as opposed to camp, which is unconsciously so). Anderson was billed second after Richard Harris as the kidnapped Brit, whom she is given as a mixture of slave and pet. Again, the film makes a highly ironic commentary on Anderson's nurturing qualities, as she does not know quite what to make of the funny-looking, white-skinned creature who has landed in her care. The film touchingly and convincingly portrays the "rapprochement" and even budding affection between two human beings who might as well have been from different planets. This is one of the very few times we are tempted to say that Anderson looks cute. She was nominated for a Golden Laurel Award for her pig-tailed portrayal.

Anderson's major roles in minor films can be dealt with more summarily, with the exception of *The Furies* (A. Mann, 1950), which must be one of the campiest film she ever made. Based on yet another Niven Busch "lust in the

Very few people photograph well from this nearly dead-on angle, but here it serves somewhat to soften Judith Anderson's characteristically severe features and we find her both glamourous and uncustomarily feminine in this portrait from *The Diary of a Chambermaid* (United Artists, 1946). The chambermaid was Paulette Goddard. Anderson played her employer, Madame Lanlaire, in Jean Renoir's dull domestic drama.

dust" type novel, "The Furies" of the title is a vast cattle ranch in the Southwest, owned by the Rabelaisian Walter Huston as T.C. Jeffords and run by his only daughter, Vance (Barbara Stanwyck), until the machinations of her father's lady friend, Flo Burnett, wrest it out of her hands. The lady friend is Judith Anderson, this time corseted and ringleted in Gilded Age splendor. However nonsensical the film as a whole, this was a wonderful opportunity for Anderson to use all her feminine wiles and make convincing the fact that Huston would suddenly choose to break his word to his own daughter and deliver his ranch lock, stock, and barrel into the grasping hands of a penniless, middle-aged adventuress. For some reason, though, Anderson seems most intent on starting and ending every sentence with "My dear," which becomes fairly distracting after a while, not to say annoying. Suitably indignant at her potential stepmother's meddling, which includes the threat to evict Stanwyck's childhood friend, Juan Herrera (played by the ridiculously good-looking Gilbert Roland), and having a textbook Electra complex, Stanwyck flings a nasty pair of scissors at Anderson's head, permanently disfiguring the right side of her face.[37]

Those who have also seen Anderson's second starring vehicle, Lady Scarface (F. Woodruff, RKO, 1941) will see the cunning connection with The Furies, as the lady mobster Slade in this pallid feminine copy of Scarface with Paul Muni was also deeply scarred (though on the left-hand side). Though she plays "Lady Scarface," Anderson is actually precious little in evidence, as this intricately plotted crime comedy centers around the blonde police investigator played by Dennis O'Keefe and his "Girl Friday," a journalist played by Frances E. Neal (who was soon to retire to become Mrs. Van Heflin). At any rate, the film has "B" written all over it, unless one wants venture further along in the alphabet.

The Red House (1947) must have had its talented director, Delmer Daves, and stars Edward G. Robinson and Judith Anderson tearing their hair and wondering: "How the hell did I get myself into this?" Daves must bear chief responsibility for the debacle, as in addition to directing the film, he had also written the absurd screenplay based on a novel by George Agnew Chamberlain. Robinson plays a farmer with a wooden leg, Anderson his live-in spinster sister. Together they have raised an orphan, Meg, played by Allene Roberts. The plot begins to thicken when Meg and her beau, Nath (Lon McAllister), are warned by Robinson not to go near the red house in the woods. "You Dare Not Even Guess the Strange Love Story of The Red House" was one tagline. Who would want to, one might well ask. The unmitigated boredom of this noir murder mystery thriller is only alleviated by dishy Rory Calhoun as a welcome threat to the young heroine's virtue.

As already mentioned, Anderson had smaller roles in three film classics. In Laura (O. Preminger, Twentieth Century–Fox, 1944), she was fifth-billed as the titular heroine's dubious aunt, Ann Treadwell, who is enamored of her niece's fiancé, a pleasantly plump, very young-looking Vincent Price ("a male beauty in distress," as Clifton Webb quips). In The Ten Commandments (C.B. DeMille, Paramount, 1956), Anderson played Memnet, nurse to the pharaoh's sister Bithia (Nina Foch) and daughter Nefertiri (Anne Baxter); a "puckered old persimmon" who knows the secret of Moses' Jewish ancestry and reveals it before Baxter pushes her off a balcony to her death. Fittingly, one might say, Star Trek III: The Quest for Spock (L. Nimoy, Paramount, 1984) was out-of-this-world Judith Anderson's final feature film. At age eighty-seven, she made a "Special Appearance" as the High Priestess of the Vulcans, her voice still resonant and strong, her incomparable face remarkably unlined even in close-up, her function in the film to give Mr. Spock "refusion," returning him to his own body and to life. In case you were wondering: yes, she too has pointy ears.

In real life, Anderson was as quick-witted and individualistic as one could hope for. When Claire Trevor once said to her, "I simply can't find the words to tell you how superb you were," Anderson answered: "Try."[38] When interviewed late in life by the entertainment writer Boze Hadleigh, she described her film career as a "mutual love-hate relationship." She found that, "the older I get, the more immaterial other people's convictions and suggestions are for me." Hadleigh, as was his wont, pressed her about her "romantic orientation." She responded: "I am no romantic! *That* is my orientation." She added: "I'm for everyone's rights, mostly my own. I do not associate myself with anyone—group or individual."[39]

According to Anderson, "Most people aren't strong enough to be an *I*. They have to join another person, or group or church or organization, and be a *we*. I always wanted to be an *I*."[40] She was married for only seven out of her ninety-five years on earth. She would probably have said herself that that was seven years too many. The year she turned forty, she married Benjamin Harrison Lehman, a professor of English at the University of California. That marriage was dissolved in August of 1939. Seven years later, she tried again with the theatrical producer Luther Greene. They were divorced in 1951.

The inimitable "I" that was Dame Judith Anderson passed out of life on January 3, 1992, at her home in Santa Barbara, California.[41]

Mother of the Year
FAY BAINTER (1893–1968)

Fay Bainter belongs to that small, exclusive coterie of "star" character actresses that includes her contemporaries Beulah Bondi and Marjorie Main, the older Marie Dressler and the younger Agnes Moorehead. Unlike these others, though, Bainter had also been a star in the legitimate theater, starting in 1916 and up until the time she abandoned the stage for the screen. When she went into films in 1934, it was straight into a top-billed role. She would frequently receive top billing during the next ten years and, symbolizing her special status, her own star on the Walk of Fame at 7021 Hollywood Boulevard.

Fay Okell Bainter was born in Los Angeles on December 7, 1893. She made her stage debut as a child in Oliver Morosco's production of *The Jewess*, starring the legendary Nance O'Neil, and remained with Morosco's company until she was fourteen, when she started playing ingénue roles in a variety of stock companies. Her Broadway debut was in a musical opera at Daly's Theatre in early 1912, followed by a highly instructive tour with Minnie Maddern Fiske in *Mrs. Bumpstead-Leigh*. Bainter's breakthrough came upon her return to New York, in a newly written play called *Arms and the Girl*, which premiered at the Fulton Theatre on September 27, 1916. During the teens and twenties, Bainter starred in several other long-forgotten dramas: *The Willow Tree* (1917), *The Kiss Burglar* (1918), *The Other Rose* (1923–24), *The Dream Girl* (1924), and her biggest hit by far, *East Is West*, which opened on Christmas Day 1918 and ran for no fewer than 680 performances.[42]

In addition to her expressive, dark eyes and liquid features, Bainter was graced with what David Ragan has called "one of the screen's most uniquely appealing speaking voices."[43] To another observer, she was "pure poetry."[44]

Bainter starred in the Broadway production of Noël Coward's comedy of marital ennui, *Fallen Angels*, with Estelle Winwood in 1927–28. This was followed by unsuccessful revivals of Oliver Goldsmith's *She Stoops to Conquer* and George Farquhar's *The Beaux Stratagem* (both 1928). By the early 1930s, Bainter badly needed a hit. She didn't get it with the fifth and final Broadway revival of that old chestnut *Uncle Tom's Cabin* (1933), in which Bainter, now fast approaching forty, played Topsy! The show to put her back on top was Sidney Howard's *Dodsworth* (1934), based on the novel by Sinclair Lewis. This hit was probably instrumental in bringing Bainter to the attention of the powers that be in Hollywood, though her creation of the role of the wayward wife, Fran Dodsworth, did not secure her the part in the 1936 film version (that went to Ruth Chatterton). Bainter had also lost the lead role in the original 1931 version of *Cimarron* to Irene Dunne, who made her film debut in Wesley Ruggles's epic Western.[45]

Bainter's debut film was *This Side of Heaven* (W.K. Howard, MGM, 1934), a drama in which she starred with Lionel Barrymore, but her film career did not begin in earnest until 1937 with *Quality Street* (G. Stevens, RKO) and *Make Way for Tomorrow* (L. McCarey, Paramount). The latter film was one of the handful of excellent en-

Spring Byington, Fay Bainter, and Horace (later Stephen) McNally in a scene from *The War Against Mrs. Hadley* (Metro-Goldwyn-Mayer, 1942). Bainter starred as Stella Hadley, a cosseted society woman who must learn that in a world at war the rules are no longer the same (McNally was her chauffeur).

semble productions Bainter lent her considerable talents to during the course of her film career. In *Make Way* she played Anita Cooper, the not-unsympathetic wife of Thomas Mitchell who is in the difficult position of having to take her garrulous, aged mother-in-law (Beulah Bondi) into the house. In one of the best domestic dramas ever filmed, Bainter was perfect casting as a shabby, genteel wife, mother, daughter-in-law (and bridge instructor) torn between conflicting claims on her time, love, and loyalty.

In *Quality Street* Bainter supported Katharine Hepburn and—many would say—upstaged her with the understated repose of her performance as the always volatile Hepburn's spinster sister. Bainter was reunited with her *Fallen Angels* co-star, Estelle Winwood, who had a small but amusing role as a nosy neighbor. George Stevens directed this interpretation of J.M. Barrie's novel of English village life during the Napoleonic Wars. Stevens would go on to direct two other films with Bainter: *Vivacious Lady* (RKO, 1938; the only film in which her scenes were deleted) and, most famously, *Woman of the Year* (MGM, 1942). In the latter film, Bainter gave one of her classic performances as Ellen Whitcomb, level-headed and sympathetic spinster aunt and confidante to the strong-willed career-woman, Tess Harding, played by Hepburn in her first film with Spencer Tracy.

Bainter was a supremely versatile actress. To the extent that she can be typed, though, one might say that she tended to play mothers (from homespun to haute couture) and maiden aunts like Ellen Whitcomb. By the time *Woman of the Year* premiered on January 19, 1942, Bainter was well established as one of the leading "Mothers for Metro," as Mary Astor famously called herself and fellow film matrons like Bainter, Fay Holden, Spring Byington, and Selena Royle. Fine performances in films such as *Mother Carey's Chickens* (R.V. Lee, RKO, 1938), *Yes, My Darling Daughter* (W. Keighley, Warner Bros., 1939), and *Daughters Courageous* (M. Curtiz, Warner Bros., 1939) had finally brought Bainter to the mother of all Hollywood studios. She was not the most long-lived of screen moms at Metro, but in the four years of her MGM contract during the early 1940s she was arguably the most widely recognized of them, playing the mother of Mickey Rooney in *Young Tom Edison* (N. Taurog, 1940), the mother of Rooney, Van Johnson, Donna Reed, and Jackie "Butch" Jenkins in *The Human Comedy* (C. Brown, 1943), and the mother of Van Heflin in *Presenting Lily Mars* (N. Taurog, 1943).

Bainter was also loaned out for significant maternal roles at other studios. These included a 1940 remake of *A Bill of Divorcement* (J. Farrow, RKO), where she took up Billie Burke's role as Meg Fairfield, who agonizes over whether to stay with her mentally ill husband (Adolphe Menjou) or to start a new life with Herbert Marshall, while her daughter is equally torn by divided loyalties (Maureen O'Hara). Bainter played Mrs. Julia Gibbs, the doctor's wife who dies of pneumonia, in a very faithful and innovative first filmatization of Thornton Wilder's classic play *Our Town* (S. Wood, 1940) by an independent production company. Her own favorite maternal role was Charlotte Danfield in *Maryland* (H. King, Twentieth Century–Fox, 1940), where she was given top billing with Walter Brennan as an overprotective mother who fears her son (John Payne) will be killed in a riding accident, as was her husband.

Bainter varied her repertoire while at Metro by playing the sympathetic director of an orphanage in *Journey for Margaret* (W.S. Van Dyke, 1942), an astrologer in *The Heavenly Body* (A. Hall, 1943), a WWII army nurse in *Cry "Havoc"* (R. Thorpe, 1943), and an imposter aunt to Merle Oberon in the "unthriller" *Dark Waters* (A. De Toth, 1944). Her film career was also considerably enlivened both for her fans and no

Fay Bainter as Mrs. Macauley in *The Human Comedy* (Metro-Goldwyn-Mayer, 1943), based on a story by William Saroyan. Like *The War Against Mrs. Hadley*, this was a film about the "home front." Bainter's real-life husband, Commander Reginald Venable, was a navy man. When the United States joined the war in 1941, they had been married twenty years and had a sixteen-year-old son (roughly the age of Mickey Rooney's character, Homer Macauley, in *The Human Comedy*).

doubt for herself by the few but important unsympathetic roles she played on screen. The first of these was Hannah Linden, Melvyn Douglas's snooty, unmarried sister and Joan Crawford's sister-in-law from hell in the claustrophobic melodrama *The Shining Hour* (F. Borzage, MGM, 1938), which also starred Robert Young and Margaret Sullavan in a characteristically breathless performance. It is questionable whether the film was Bainter's "shining hour," though, as her fall into madness seems too abrupt and her recovery likewise. One suspects some of her scenes ended up on the cutting room floor.

A more significant, one could even say *magnificent* entry in this high and mighty category is a largely forgotten classic of the "home front" from 1942, entitled *The War Against Mrs. Hadley* (H.S. Bucquet, MGM). This film is simply a dream come true for any lover of character actresses as, in addition to Bainter, the movie contains standout performances by Sara Allgood, Spring Byington, and Isobel Elsom, in addition to Connie Gilchrist in a smaller role. Bainter stars as the stunningly elegant widow of a Washington, D.C. newspaper editor, who must learn that war is more than a personal inconvenience. The story opens as the Japanese attack Pearl Harbor in the middle of Stella Hadley's birthday celebration. She goes on as if nothing has happened, keeping her spoiled, wastrel son (Richard Ney) and sensible daughter (Jean Rogers) in line with emotional blackmail the likes of which film audiences had not seen since Laura Hope Crews in *The Silver Cord* almost a decade before. The original screenplay by George Oppenheimer was nominated for an Academy Award and Bainter should have been as well.

Compared to most other character actresses, though, Bainter was amply rewarded by the Academy for her efforts. She was the first actress to be nominated both in the Supporting Actress and Leading Actress category in the same year. The year was 1939 and Bainter was nominated for her supporting role in *Jezebel* (W. Wyler, 1938), Warner Bros.' attempt to preempt *Gone with the Wind*, and for her starring role in the melodrama *White Banners* (E. Goulding, Warner Bros., 1938). In *Jezebel*, Bainter played the strong-willed Bette Davis's sympathetic aunt, while in *White Banners* she was a homeless woman who seeks out the illegitimate son she had to abandon years before. Both Bainter and Davis won for *Jezebel*, which is to say that Bainter lost for *White Banners*. Years later, Davis recalled her "inspired" co-star: "Miss Bainter's contribution to the film and to my performance was immeasurable. It just wouldn't have been the same picture without her."[46] Among Bainter's fellow nominees for Best Supporting Actress in a very competitive year were Beulah Bondi for *Of Human Hearts*, Billie Burke for *Merrily We Live*, and Spring Byington for *You Can't Take It with You*. None of these three fine actresses would ever win an Oscar. Bainter had been director Frank Capra's first choice for the artistically inclined mother in *You Can't Take It With You*, but she had been unavailable.[47]

Bainter would play Davis's sidekick again a decade later in *June Bride* (B. Windust, 1948), a witty comedy in which Davis stars as a ladies' journal editor willing to go to any length for a good story and Bainter as her able assistant, who struggles to turn the Brinker family (including Marjorie Bennett as the portly mother) into the stuff of magazine readers' dreams. Another of her more notable late '40s films is *The Secret Life of Walter Mitty* (N.Z. McLeod, Samuel Goldwyn, 1947), where we find a slim and trim Bainter playing Danny Kaye's nagging but lovable live-in mom in glorious Technicolor.

Bainter retired from films after her role in a biopic about Andrew Jackson's early years, *The President's Lady* (H. Levin, Twentieth Century-Fox, 1953), though she made a dozen or so guest appearances in television dramas between 1948 and 1965 and went on tour with productions of Tennessee Williams's *A Glass Menagerie* and Eugene O'Neill's *Long Day's Journey Into Night*. She came out of retirement in 1961 to play one final role on the big screen, Mrs. Amelia Tilford, the formidable grandmother in Lillian Hellman's *The Children's Hour*. William Wyler had also directed the first version, *These Three* (1936), with the venerable character actress Alma Kruger as Mrs. Tilford and starring Merle Oberon and Miriam Hopkins (who now took up the part of the obnoxious ex-thespian aunt, Lily Mortar). Opinions have been divided on the 1961 version as a whole. Bosley Crowther called it "a cultural antique."[48] Yet Bainter's interpretation of the self-righteous, upper-class woman who must confront her own prejudices and moral responsibility was powerful and memorable. The scene where her granddaughter's mendacity is finally revealed and Bainter falls dramatically to the floor, stays in the mind. She was nominated for an Oscar, but lost out to Rita Moreno for *West Side Story*.

Fay Bainter died at home of pneumonia on April 16, 1968. She was buried next to her husband of forty-two years, Lt. Commander Reginald S.H. Venable of the U.S. Navy, in Arlington National Cemetery.

How the Mighty Have Fallen
ETHEL BARRYMORE (1879–1959)

In MGM's famous group photo from the twenty-fifth anniversary celebration of the studio in the spring of 1949, Ethel Barrymore sits front and center with a faraway expression in her legendary, soulful, dark eyes. She is nearly seventy years old. She has been on the wagon for a decade and has a decade left to live. She has made her home in California since 1946 and given up the stage, her real home for half a century.[49] She has already made the best films of her career, save one. Barrymore had originally been lured to Hollywood to make a film for RKO during the height of her spectacular success in Emlyn Williams's play, *The Corn Is Green*, and for the sake of her health and her bank book, she had remained.[50] In January 1949, she signed a one-year contract with MGM with a forty-week guarantee at $2,000 a week.[51] One wonders what she is thinking, as she sits surrounded by the stars of the "Studio of the Stars," new faces, young faces, strangers to her, except her brother, Lionel, old and decrepit at the end of the front row. One wonders what the others were thinking to have the "First Lady of the American Stage" among them, a star before many of them had been born.

Ethel Barrymore was the most prestigious American actress to lend her talents to the big screen in the Studio Era. We can be glad she did or we should have had no audio-visual record of her acting. The total effect of her regal bearing, her patrician profile, her melting eyes, and not least of all, her legendary voice, would have been lost to us. We have no record of her Madame Trentoni in *Captain Jinks of the Horse Marines*, or Lady Helen Haden in *Déclassée*, or Constance Middleton in *The Constant Wife*, or of her one-act sensation *The Twelve Pound Look*, but we do have Mary Herries in *Kind Lady*, Miss Em in *Pinky*, and Agatha Morley in *The Farmer's Daughter*. That is something to be grateful for, especially as Barrymore was famous for her beauty even in her seventies.[52] Her fabulous voice remains "between a cello and a delicious caramel sauce"[53]; a voice that prompted critic Ashton Stevens to dub her "Ethel Barrytone" and that was described in her *New York Times* obituary as "The echo of an inexhaustible wealth of experience."[54] Mark Twain called her the "water sprite."[55] Henry James said she reminded him of a cornice on a Gothic building.[56] The camera did not always treat her kindly, but in her best films we can understand something of what her magic spell was all about. As she once said to a young actor who was afraid that he would upstage her: "Oh, my dear, don't worry about me. Wherever I am is center stage."[57]

The plainly and darkly clad, quietly distinguished, elderly lady who sits between Mary Astor and Spring Byington in the MGM photograph had been at the center of American cultural life since her breakthrough at the age of twenty-one in Clyde Fitch's comedy *Captain Jinks of the Horse Marines*. Three days after the premiere at the Garrick Theatre on February 18, 1907, producer Charles Frohman put her name in lights and so it would remain for the rest of her acting days.[58] During the first three decades of the twentieth century, Barrymore went from hit to hit. For a more detailed account of these glory days of her career, I refer you to her notoriously reticent autobiography and Margot Peters's fine biography.[59] Suffice it here to mention plays like *Sunday* (1904–05), *A Doll's House* (1905), *The Twelve Pound Look* (1911), *The Lady of the Camellias* (1917–18), *Déclassée* (1919–20), *Romeo and Juliet* (1922–23), *The Second Mrs. Tanqueray* (1924), *Hamlet* (1925), *The Constant Wife* (1926–27), and *The Kingdom of God* (1928–29). Barrymore also starred in fourteen silent films during the years 1914–19, including filmatizations of her hit plays *The Awakening of Helena Ritchie* and *Our Mrs. McChesney*.

Then, as Barrymore entered her fifties, things began to slow down. Her disastrous marriage to an abusive husband, Russell Griswold

Colt (of the revolver dynasty and Providence, R.I.), had taken its toll and finally ended in divorce in 1923, leaving her with three children to support. Never very good with money, she was plagued by financial difficulties. Barrymore was by this time an alcoholic and it was beginning to affect her both personally and professionally.[60] The years between 1930, when she started drinking again on tour with Louis Calhern, and 1939, when she went on the wagon for good, were the low point of her life and career.[61] She was reduced to doing J. M. Barrie's *The Twelve Pound Look* as an overture to a feature film.[62] She worked in radio.[63] She talked about retiring from the stage and starting a drama school.[64] Finally, things began to look up when she had a critical and commercial success with *Whiteoaks* in 1938. That Barrymore was back was confirmed once and for all when she scored the biggest hit of her career as Miss Moffat in *The Corn Is Green* (1940–43). Both Helen Hayes and Katharine Cornell had turned it down.[65] The play ran for 533 performances at the National, Royale, and Martin Beck theaters in New York before a national tour. It had the longest run of any of Ethel, Lionel, and John Barrymore's shows.[66]

RKO approached Barrymore in 1944 with a proposal. If she took a break from the tour of *The Corn Is Green* to play Cary Grant's Cockney, shopkeeper mother in *None But the Lonely Heart* (1944), the studio would pay the actors' and crew's salaries until she was ready to return.[67] Clifford Odets would be making his directing debut and writing his first screenplay based on a novel by Richard Llewellyn.[68] Barrymore said yes. She was billed second as Ma Mott, mother of the "Tramp of the Universe," Ernie Mott (Grant), whom she says is "like a breath of homeless wind." Barrymore looks pinched and worn as mortally cancer-ridden "Ma," who sells stolen goods through her second-hand store, so as to leave her son more money when she dies. She is caught, of course, and passes from life in the prison infirmary with Grant at her side in the film's only affecting scene. Charles Higham and Roy Moseley call this "Cary Grant's finest moment on the screen" and add, "It was also Miss Barrymore's."[69] The latter judgment, at least, seems hasty. As part of their working-class London drag, Grant and Barrymore are equipped with quaint Cockney accents. Given Grant's background, one might have thought he would have done a more convincing job. Maybe the film struck too close to home for Archie Leach. At any rate, it flopped at the box office.[70] Grant never again attempted a dramatic role or a cinematic return to his working-class roots. Barrymore, on the other hand, won an Oscar for what was only her second role in a sound film and her first

As Agatha Morley, matriarch of a powerful political family in *The Farmer's Daughter* (RKO, 1947), Ethel Barrymore prepares to deliver a campaign speech on radio looking like a mixture of Eleanor Roosevelt and Barbara Bush, if such a thing can be imagined. In real life, Barrymore was rarely photographed with glasses covering her famous, soulful eyes.

film in a dozen years. She was set for the final stage of her long acting career.

All told, Ethel Barrymore only made twenty-one films between 1944 and 1957. She made her best films before she signed with MGM in 1949. These include *The Spiral Staircase* (1946), *The Farmer's Daughter* (1947), *The Paradine Case* (1947), *Portrait of Jennie* (1948), and *Pinky* (1949). Once she'd learned the special techniques and requirements of film acting, Barrymore could have played most of the parts she was offered with one hand tied behind her back.[71] Or rather, it would be more accurate to say she could play them with both hands under a coverlet, and she did, as she was destined to spend a substantial amount of her on-screen time in bed. One wonders sometimes what she's thinking lying there. Perhaps: "Ho hum, here I am bedridden again, looking soulful and ever so wise. At least I can have a little nap while I'm waiting and nobody will notice if I have to pass wind..."

Her first horizontal role was in her second film, also for RKO, *The Spiral Staircase* (R. Siodmak, 1946). In this serial killer thriller, Barrymore plays George Brent's suspicious, seemingly addle-pated stepmother, who despite her invalid condition has to try to save her mute nurse, Dorothy McGuire, from falling victim to Brent's depredations. Named above the title with the two younger stars, Barrymore turns out to have been a big game hunter with her husband in her prime and finally rises from her sickbed and polishes off the killer with a shotgun, before expiring on the spiral staircase. The critic for the *New York Times* found her part "hardly deserving of her vast talents."[72] Yet she was again nominated for an Academy Award. That year the Oscar for Best Actress in a Supporting Role went to Anne Baxter for *The Razor's Edge* (1946).

The Farmer's Daughter from the following year, directed by H.C. Potter, gave Barrymore more to work with. Granted she was movement-impaired also this time, though far from bedridden. She has her own stair-lift in the ancestral halls of the Morley family of which she is the undisputed head. Into this patrician setting comes young, wholesome Swedish-American Katrin Holstrom (Loretta Young) as a maid. As fate and Hollywood would have it, she moves up in the world and wins both a husband (Joseph Cotten) and a political career. Again Barrymore was given star billing, in this Capraesque romantic comedy with sinister undertones. After watching the film one understands both where the Princess Leia hairdo and the jogging craze originated. The plot is not dissimilar to Loretta Young's 1936 film *Private Number*. *The Farmer's Daughter* garnered Young her only Oscar.

Alfred Hitchcock's *The Paradine Case* (Selznick Releasing Organization, 1947) was the first of two Barrymore films produced under the aegis of David O. Selznick, with whom Barrymore was at the time under personal contract. She plays Charles Laughton's sensitive, high-strung wife, Lady Sophie Horfield, with a jade collection and exquisite taste. Apparently, Selznick opted to cut most of her part.[73] She is left with only two substantial scenes in this courtroom drama where Laughton plays a sadistic judge and husband, who calls his wife a "silly woman" and is determined to see Alida Valli hang for the purported murder of her husband. For the third time, Barrymore was Oscar-nominated. She lost out to Celeste Holm for *Gentleman's Agreement*, which was fair enough in a lackluster year for the Supporting Actress category.

To say that *Portrait of Jennie* (W. Dieterle, 1948) is haunting is a bit like saying *GWTW* is epic. Barrymore plays the sympathetic spinster Miss Spinney ("I am an old maid and nobody knows more about love than an old maid"), who tries to help struggling artist Joseph Cotten make sense of his encounters in 1934 with the ghost of a young girl who died in a storm on Cape Cod in the 1920s. Producer Selznick's wife, Jennifer Jones, is the Jennie of the title and the ghost.

Finally, Barrymore rounded off the forties with a terrific part in the socially and racially conscious drama, *Pinky* (Twentieth Century-Fox, 1949), starring Jeanne Crain as a young nurse with mixed black and white ancestry, who decides to reclaim her black racial heritage symbolized by her grandmother, Ethel Waters. Given star billing yet again, Barrymore plays the

In this photo from Ethel Barrymore's seventieth birthday celebration on August 15, 1949, the actress is seated between her host and longtime friend, director George Cukor, and her brother, Lionel Barrymore. Ethel and Cukor had been fast friends since he stage managed the original American production of Somerset Maugham's *The Constant Wife* in 1926. Because Barrymore was having trouble remembering her lines, Cukor hid in the fireplace to prompt her.

childless Southern gentlewoman, Miss Em, waiting to die in marble halls with rapacious relatives waiting with her, personified by Evelyn Varden in one of her finest roles. Though Barrymore gives almost her entire performance in bed, her spirit and verve come through in lines like: "It's all I ever wanted. To have my own way." Forty years later, replacement director Elia Kazan remembered her fondly. While he had trouble with Waters, as John Ford had had before he quit the film, Barrymore was his favorite:

> She had a way of kidding me I enjoyed; she mocked my seriousness. Like many old-timers, she had patience for only one take of a scene. And no heavy Actors Studio-type directorial analyses beforehand, please. When I'd ask her for another take, she'd ask, "Why? I can't do it better, boy." And if I still pushed her, she'd come out with: "What do you want it for, your collection?"[74]

All three female leads were Oscar-nominated; all lost, Barrymore and Waters to Mercedes McCambridge for *All the King's Men* (1949).

When Barrymore's seven-year contract with Selznick was cancelled by mutual consent,[75] she signed with MGM. This one-year contract, which was not renewed,[76] would result in *The Great Sinner* (R. Siodmak, 1949), *The Red Danube* (G. Sidney, 1949), and *That Midnight Kiss* (M. Taurog, 1949). The last was the most interesting of the three, though that is not saying a lot. Barrymore was billed third as Abigail Trent Budell, a patron of the arts in her native Philadelphia, in a film that is best known for introducing the singing sensation Mario Lanza. After funding a symphony orchestra, Mrs. Budell decides to start a civic opera company to showcase her granddaughter Kathryn Grayson's talents. Mrs. Budell wants her granddaughter to have the singing career her own grandmother had prevented her from having by refusing to let her sing in public. We never really find out what *Grayson* wants, apart from Lanza. Famous Spanish conductor José Iturbi plays himself, Lanza almost plays himself (he too was a native of Philadelphia), and José Iturbi's sister, Amparo, even has a scene playing herself. Despite the garish Technicolor, Barrymore looks better in this film than usual.

Barrymore would later make *It's a Big Country*, *Kind Lady*, *The Story of Three Loves*, and *Main Street to Broadway* at Metro, where she had also made her first, disastrous sound film, *Rasputin and the Empress* (R. Boleslawski), in 1932. The story of the doomed Russian royal family and particularly its relations with the religious mystic Rasputin, it was the only film to star all three Barrymores and ultimately lost the studio a lot of money.[77] Ethel Barrymore had the original director, Charles Brabin, fired after she and "Mr. Theda Bara," as she called him (he was married to the silent screen star), had several run-ins.[78] Everyone speaks in capital letters in this stagey dud. Ethel spends most of the film looking regal and long-suffering as the Empress Alexandra. As the Russian nobleman who ultimately kills Rasputin, John wears enough makeup to make Julian Eltinge jealous. Margot Peters is right in observing that this is "Lionel's film from beginning to end" as Rasputin.[79] Ethel Barrymore would make $57,500 from the movie.[80] It was money she badly needed. She didn't see the film herself until it appeared on television in the 1950s.[81]

The legendary Broadway star Ethel Barrymore is seventy-one in this portrait in costume for her starring role in *Kind Lady* (Metro-Goldwyn-Mayer, 1951). Her hair has been sculpted by MGM's legendary hair stylist, Sydney Guilaroff. The lace tablecloth she is wearing was designed by Walter Plunkett. No wonder she looks pensive. *Kind Lady* is Barrymore's finest film. Regrettably, it has never been released on video or DVD.

If nothing else, Metro-Goldwyn-Mayer did give Barrymore the finest role of her screen career in the remake of Edward Chodorov's psychological thriller *Kind Lady* (J. Sturges, 1951). The play, based on a short story by Hugh Walpole, had opened on Broadway on April 23, 1935 with Grace George playing the patrician art collector and lady bountiful, Mary Herries. It was first filmed by MGM in 1935 with Aline MacMahon in the lead. Miss Herries falls victim to a charlatan painter, played in the 1951 film version by the noted Shakespearean actor Maurice Evans; he keeps her a prisoner in her own home and almost succeeds in murdering her and appropriating her entire estate for himself. The excellent supporting cast includes Betsy Blair (no longer

Mrs. Gene Kelly) as Evans's long-suffering wife, Angela Lansbury and Keenan Wynn as married partners in crime, and Doris Lloyd as Barrymore's trusty maid, who is finally strangled by Wynn when she tries to escape. As Miss Herries, Barrymore is plain-spoken, broad in her sympathies, and a mite eccentric, which lends credence to the lie Evans puts about that she has gone around the bend. For one thing, she has a genuine Benvenuto Cellini doorknocker on the front door of her London townhouse. In her drawing room full of priceless antiques, the walls are covered with paintings by El Greco, Whistler, and Rembrandt. The dénouement is ingenious, but to reveal it would spoil the fun for those who have not yet seen this miniature masterpiece most deserving of re-release on DVD. Unfortunately, the studio did not promote the film on its original release on June 20, 1951.[82]

The glory days of the film dowager were on the wane by the early 1950s. Barrymore's friend, two-time Broadway co-star, and contemporary, Lucile Watson, hung on till 1951, though she survived Barrymore by three years. The almost ten-years-younger Gladys Cooper captured some of the meatier parts in forties films such as *Now, Voyager* (1942), *The Song of Bernadette* (1943), and *The Bishop's Wife* (1947), but by the 1950s her opportunities were almost non-existent. Among other actresses born in the 1880s, only Isobel Elsom and Florence Bates were really able to base a steady film career on playing matrons, grand dames, and upper-class ladies in the final decade of the studio era. Among younger character actresses, only Judith Anderson and Agnes Moorehead would play a substantial number of dowager roles.

Barrymore's eight films after *Kind Lady* are clearly of inferior quality to those of the preceding decade. The most interesting for a Barrymore fan is probably *Main Street to Broadway* (T. Garnett, MGM, 1953), for there she plays herself. With her in this quasi-documentary venture, she has her brother Lionel in what would prove his final screen appearance. They share a scene with Louis Calhern in a dressing room, where they hear on the radio about a troubled playwright, who has been incarcerated on suspicion of wanting to do away with himself. After freeing the unfortunate man, there is a scene in a cab where they listen to his tribulations, including his rejection by the Broadway star and Ethel's old friend, Tallulah Bankhead. At the opening of the film, we also see Ethel contemplating her own portrait in the lobby of the doomed Empire Theatre. There she had made her New York debut as Julia in *The Rivals* on January 25, 1894[83] and had starred in many of her great plays for her "Svengali," legendary producer Charles Frohman, from 1907 until he went down with the *Lusitania* in 1915. The Empire, on Broadway between 40th and 41st Street, was razed in 1953 to make room for an office building.[84]

Barrymore herself appears to have particularly enjoyed making *Just for You* (E. Nugent, Paramount, 1952) with Jane Wyman and Bing Crosby. At least she writes in her autobiography, which was published in 1956, that, "when I played in a picture with Bing it was one of the most charming experiences I have had in the movies."[85] Barrymore portrayed Alida De Bronkhart, the headmistress of a posh girls school that entertainer Bing is anxious to get his daughter, fourteen-year-old Natalie Wood, into. Barrymore was still billed above the title with the younger stars.

Barrymore's final film appearance and acting job was playing the lead, Katherine Chandler, in the drama *Johnny Trouble* (J.H. Auer, 1957). Margot Peters observes that this "cheap production was a sad way to end a long and distinguished acting career."[86] Barrymore made her last public appearance on television during a testimonial on her seventy-eighth birthday.[87] She died quietly in her sleep on June 18, 1959 in her modest Beverly Hills apartment with her son, Samuel Colt, and her nurse and companion, Anna Albert, at her side.[88] She was buried in the Main Mausoleum of Calvary Cemetery, Los Angeles, where her brother Lionel had been laid to rest in 1954. To conclude with Barrymore's famous line from her hit play, *Sunday*: "That's all there is, there isn't any more."

Not So Nice to Come Home To
FLORENCE BATES (1888–1954)

Florence Bates gave a whole new meaning to the word awful. She was awfully ugly, awfully obnoxious, awfully bossy, and awfully, awfully talented. Despite the many fine actresses in this book, Bates is the only one I can say categorically was one of a kind, *sui generis*, a law unto herself. Only if you combined the overripe coquettishness of Laura Hope Crews with the neckless avoirdupois of Alison Skipworth, the earthy folksiness of Jessie Ralph, the frosty hauteur of Isobel Elsom, the vulgar rapaciousness of Evelyn Varden, and the barely subdued, butch malevolence of Judith Anderson might you approach the multi-faceted *monstre sacré* that was Florence Bates in her prime.

All these qualities were in place from her very first film role. What a debut it was! Frank S. Nugent of the *New York Times* wrote that Bates's Mrs. Edythe Van Hopper was "a magnificent specimen of the ill-bred, moneyed, resort-infesting, servant-abusing dowager."[89] Ironically, her first film role in Hitchcock's *Rebecca* (United Artists, 1940) remains her best known performance, though she deserves to be remembered for many other portrayals large and small. If you needed a demanding customer in a department store scene, you called Bates. If you needed a henpecking, upper-middle-class matron, you called Bates. If you needed a nouveau riche dowager dripping with ill-gotten gains, you called Bates. A sycophantic, dyspeptic domestic? Call Bates. An unctuous, inquisitive landlady in a down-at-heel boarding house? Why not call Bates? And they did call, producers at Warner Bros., MGM, RKO, Twentieth Century-Fox, Universal, Republic, Columbia, and Paramount. There wasn't a studio or major independent producer, who didn't use her talents during her fifteen years in movieland, where she racked up a total of sixty-six feature films. That's an average of more than four films a year.

From her auspicious beginnings in *Rebecca*, Bates appeared almost exclusively in named, credited parts. The only exception to this rule is the small group of "customer" roles she played in the early 1940s. One of these was in *Kitty Foyle* (RKO, 1940), where star Ginger Rogers sold her an expensive bottle of perfume in a boutique run by Odette Myrtil. Rogers won her Oscar for this role, though the scene with Bates didn't necessarily clinch it for her. The temperamental Sam Wood directed. He must have liked Bates's performance, because he used her again the following year in *The Devil and Miss Jones* (1941), which you will recall is largely set in the shoe department of a large department store. Here Bates's part was built up so that she was not just a regular customer, but a professional "store shopper" trying to catch the employees breaking the rules or giving bad service. She accuses Charles Coburn of chewing gum. What she doesn't know is that he is in fact the owner of the store, J.P. Merrick, undercover himself.

Throughout her career Bates was unsurpassed in a variety of dowdy dowager roles, taking over from the likes of Alison Skipworth and Jessie Ralph in this highly amusing category. Mrs. Van Hopper was the first, but special mention must also be made of Mrs. Cooper in *Love Crazy* (J. Conway, MGM, 1941), Mrs. Griswold in *The Secret Life of Walter Mitty* (N.Z. McLeod, Samuel Goldwyn, 1947), Mrs. Manleigh in *A Letter to Three Wives* (J.L. Mankiewicz, Twentieth Century-Fox, 1949), and Mrs. Sullivan in *Paris Model* (A.E. Green, Columbia, 1953).

Love Crazy was yet another vehicle for the comic couple Myrna Loy and William Powell, best known for the popular "Thin Man" series. Bates was billed fifth, after the stars, Gail Patrick and Jack Carson, as Loy's doting mother and Powell's perpetually present mother-in-law, who invites herself to the couple's fourth wedding anniversary. She gives them a horrendous

Laurence Olivier, Joan Fontaine, and Florence Bates in Alfred Hitchcock's *Rebecca* (United Artists, 1940). At this very moment Bates's grasping, invidious character, Edythe Van Hopper, has just been informed that her paid companion (Fontaine) is marrying the wealthy proprietor of the estate Manderley, Maxim de Winter (Olivier). In a split second, Mrs. Van Hopper must decide whether she should be visibly pleased or appalled at this highly unexpected news.

hall carpet, only to trip on it and sprain her ankle, necessitating her continued, irritating presence. When she ultimately gets pushed into a swimming pool, the original audience cheered.[90]

In *The Secret Life of Walter Mitty* six years later, Bates played a *potential* mother-in-law, to Danny Kaye. Her daughter was played by Ann Rutherford. The following exchange with Kay gives something of the flavor of her role:

> BATES: Walter, what's that awful smell?
> KAYE: It's that cologne you gave me for Christmas.
> BATES: It's lovely, isn't it?

A Letter to Three Wives would surely rate as director Joseph L. Mankiewicz's finest film, if it weren't for the fact that he made *All About Eve* the following year. Bates's performance as Mrs. Manleigh, the dragonic wife of a mousy radio advertising executive (and Ann Sothern's boss), is so meticulously chilling that it should be studied by anyone who wants to act before the camera. With Bates it is all about the details. Few could use a prop like her. In *Rebecca* it was a long strain of cigarettes. One ends up in the cold cream. In *Letter*, it was a lorgnette. There are few dinner parties on film as disastrous as the one Sothern and her husband, Kirk Douglas, throw in the Manleighs' honor.

In this roster of Bates's most notable dowager roles, final mention must be made of *Paris Model*, a very slight film fare about how a French designer dress plays a role in the lives of four different women (Eva Gabor, Paulette Goddard, Marilyn Maxwell, and Barbara Lawrence). Bates is solid as always, though, as the self-important, Irish-inflected wife of a retiring company director (Cecil Kellaway), who prevents him from nominating Maxwell's husband for the job after she suspects there has been hanky panky going on. Bates is noticeably thinner and more drawn in this her final film.

Some of Bates's dowagers were more benign or even at times downright sympathetic, for example Mrs. Van Every in *Mr. Lucky* (H.C. Potter, RKO, 1943), Sophie Bellop in *Saratoga Trunk* (Warner Bros., 1945), Florence Dana Moorhead in *I Remember Mama* (G. Stevens, RKO, 1948), and Amelia Foster in *The Second Woman* (J.V. Kern, 1951). Bates's characteristically dimpled cheeks and vulpine leer are amply in evidence in *Mr. Lucky*, where as a volunteer at the Welfare Relief Society run by Gladys Cooper she teaches Cary Grant to knit while evincing every evidence of climacteric upheaval. Her friend DeWitt Bodeen recalls that Bates was forever knitting when she had time on her hands.[91]

In her third film for Sam Wood, her most frequent director, she played a nineteenth-century Elsa Maxwell at the resort of Saratoga, who reveals a softer side when she takes Ingrid Bergman under her wing and defends her against the female forces massed by the formidable Ethel Griffies. "Hang on to your jewelry," Bates counsels her new protégée, "It's a woman's best friend." In a classic Bates scene from

(*From left*) John Warburton, Ingrid Bergman, Florence Bates, Gary Cooper (smoking a cigar in the background), Ethel Griffies (seated), and Sarah Edwards on the piazza of a Saratoga hotel in Sam Wood's extravaganza, *Saratoga Trunk* (Warner Bros., 1945), based on a novel by Edna Ferber. Bates as Sophie Bellop is about to give the dubious "Countess" impersonated by Bergman her stamp of approval and hence smooth the way for Bergman's advantageous marriage to Bart Van Steed (Warburton). Griffies, as Bergman's potential mother-in-law, is visibly unimpressed.

Saratoga Trunk, she demolishes a bowl of cherries, while telling Bergman that life isn't one. Apparently she loved playing this particular part and it shows.[92]

Bates's part in *I Remember Mama* is short but sweet. She plays an author-celebrity who gives budding writer Barbara Bel Geddes some advice on her stories in return for "Mama" Irene Dunne's recipe for Norwegian (*not* Swedish) meatballs. In *The Second Woman*, a film that resembles *Rebecca*, Bates plays a genial, concerned, perpetually knitting aunt to Betsy Drake, who gives her niece (and us) the lowdown on the film's troubled, Byronic hero, Robert Young, and his fabled house Hilltop.

Bates played plenty of maids, dressers, lady companions, and landladies in her time. In Risë Stevens's appalling film debut, *The Chocolate Soldier* (R. Del Ruth, MGM, 1941), a remake of Lunt and Fontanne's famous Broadway hit *The Guardsman* (also filmed none too successfully by MGM in 1931), Bates was billed fourth as the heroine's dresser, Madame Helene (nicknamed "Pugsy"). She lives vicariously through Stevens's pseudo-affair with a handsome officer (Stevens's husband in disguise). Bates is at daggers drawn with the master of the house, Nelson Eddy, who refers to her as an "old blimp" and remarks that "I never hit a woman bigger than myself."

In the 1944 version of *Kismet* (W. Dieterle, MGM), starring Marlene Dietrich and Ronald Colman, Bates plays Karsha, an ancient, mean-spirited servant in the household of the "Beggar King" Colman, who refers to her as an "unblossoming cactus." Her favorite expression in the film is "Bah!" Her role in *The Diary of a Chambermaid* (J. Renoir, 1946) is more entertaining, though the film as a whole is not. Bates reaches new levels of abjection in her doggish devotion to her master and lover, Burgess Meredith, who abandons her when he becomes enamored of the chambermaid of the title, played by Paulette Goddard. The added presence of Judith Anderson as Goddard's austere employer and a young Irene Ryan (of *Beverly Hillbillies* fame) as a homely scullery maid cannot save this chamber pot of a film. As if Bates's encounter with the future Miss Ellie in *I Remember Mama* was not enough, we find her cooking breakfast for Miss Ellie's husband, Jock Ewing (that is to say the young Jim Davis) in *Winter Meeting* (B. Windust, Warner Bros., 1948). Bates plays Bette Davis's homely housekeeper, Mrs. Castle, in a subtle performance that shows her ability to mingle amusement and disapproval.

In *Portrait of Jennie* (W. Dieterle, 1948) and *My Dear Secretary* (C. Martin, 1949), Bates played landladies, though widely differing on the social scale. Mrs. Jekes, Joseph Cotten's landlady in *Portrait*, is a nosy, gossipy old soul who runs a modest rooming house, while Kirk Douglas's landlady in the second film, Mrs. Reeve (nicknamed "Horrible Hannah"), runs a much more upscale establishment and ends up marrying Douglas's buddy, Keenan Wynn.

Bates's most famous musicals (though she didn't sing in them) were *On the Town* (S. Donen, G. Kelly, MGM, 1949), in which she played Vera-Ellen's Russian dance instructor, Madame Dilyovska, who is a bit too fond of the bottle; and *Lullaby of Broadway* (D. Butler, Warner Bros., 1951), where she played her frequent co-star, S.Z. Sakall's steel-dimpled, mink-infested, diamond-studded wife.

Coincidentally, one of Bates's factotum parts was in a dull as dust Western set in her hometown of San Antonio, Texas in its early days. Called simply *San Antonio* (D. Butler, Warner Bros., 1945), the film starred Errol Flynn and Alexis Smith. Bates played Henrietta, the heroine's clucking, "mother hen" wardrobe woman and traveling companion. The exteriors were done in Calabasas, California, so Bates didn't get anywhere near the town where she was born Florence Raby on April 15, 1888. Other actresses to come out of San Antonio are Lily Cahill (1885–1955), Joan Crawford (1904–77), and Carol Burnett (b. 1933).

Bates stayed in San Antonio longer than the others. She was a musical prodigy as a child, until an injury to her hand put a stop to plans for a concert pianist career and she started teaching piano instead. In 1909 she married her first husband and had a daughter, Ann. The couple divorced and in 1914 Florence Raby became the first female attorney in Texas when she passed the bar exam after only six months of study. She worked as a lawyer for four years, before she and her sister took over their deceased parents' antiques business.

Fast forward to the 1930s and we find Bates in Los Angeles, the owner with her second husband, Will Jacoby, of a bakery on Washington Boulevard. In the mid–30s, Bates embarked on what would be her seventh and final career, acting, and soon became one of the most popular players at the Pasadena Playhouse. Her first hit was as Miss Bates in a dramatization of Jane Austen's *Emma*. With the success of this role, Florence Raby Jacoby became known professionally as Florence Bates.[93]

Florence Bates was never nominated for an Oscar, nor did she win any other film or theatrical award. Maybe she took comfort in the fact that contemporaries like Elisabeth Risdon, Rafaela Ottiano, Margaret Dumont, and Cora Witherspoon went similarly unrewarded. Yet Bates worked continuously and relentlessly in the movie industry from 1940 till her death from a heart attack on January 31, 1954, at the age of sixty-five. In a highly competitive business, working steadily was of course its own form of recognition and, when you loved the work as Bates did, its own reward.

Leave It to Beavers
LOUISE BEAVERS (1902–1962)

Had Hattie McDaniel not been Hattie McDaniel, Louise Beavers might have been Hattie McDaniel. Or to put it another way: Louise Beavers was Hattie McDaniel before Hattie McDaniel was Hattie McDaniel. Confused? Let me set you straight.

Louise Beavers was the most prominent African American actress in the first decade of sound films. She was given what amounted to starring roles, in screen time if not in billing, in movies such as *Imitation of Life* (1934) and *Rainbow on the River* (1936). Before Beavers, claims Donald Bogle, "there had been no distinctive mammy figure."[94] Furthermore:

> The studios realized Beavers was a perfect foil and background flavor for such Depression heroines as Jean Harlow, Mae West, and Claudette Colbert—women forced by the times to be on their own, yet needing someone in their corner to cheer them up when things looked too rough, to advise them when personal problems overwhelmed them.[95]

Beavers's unique status changed on that night in December 1939 when *Gone with the Wind* premiered and Hattie McDaniel nailed the role of Mammy.

Beavers had been a major contender for the part of Mammy, but according to legend lost it by dressing up too much for her audition with producer David O. Selznick.[96] It is as likely that the beaming and benevolent, meek and mild screen persona she had established after a decade of steady work in the movies was not quite what Selznick was looking for in the actress to portray Margaret Mitchell's feisty, belligerent, and bossy O'Hara family retainer. As Bogle points out: "Beavers's cheerful, naïve maids and companions were always there to soothe, never to rock the boat."[97] McDaniel went on to glory and was, as we recall, the first African American actress to win an Academy Award. Beavers was never even nominated for an Oscar, though certainly she had deserved to be in 1935 for her standout performance in *Imitation of Life*. There was not yet a Supporting Actress category, though, and it was impossible to imagine a black actress being nominated for an Oscar in a leading role.

It was her justly famous performance as the golden-hearted Delilah Johnson that would prove Louise Beavers's most important role and "the first dramatic, starring role ever created by a white studio for an African-American actress."[98] Bogle calls *Imitation of Life* (J.M. Stahl, Universal, 1934): "the slickest and possibly the best made tear-jerker of all time."[99] He credits the film with establishing Beavers's unique "humanized domesticity": a quality of being morally superior to most of the other characters in the film, which would make her "for a time the most important black actress working in films."[100] As "the essence of Christian stoicism and passivity,"[101] Beavers's Delilah is endlessly devoted to her friend, employer, and later business partner, Bea Pullman (Claudette Colbert). Even when she receives 20 percent of the pancake business and becomes economically independent, she desires only to remain with Colbert and continue to serve her. Selfless, grateful, and undemanding, Beavers as Delilah became the "black angel"[102] in Hollywood; an African American who lives up to the highest American ideals, but poses no threat to white supremacy. She lives the American Dream, but it does not fundamentally change her reassuringly dependent and self-effacing attitude. Though clearly the star of *Imitation of Life*, Beavers continues to play a literally supporting role. While Warren William and Colbert were given star billing, Beavers was billed fifth, after the stars, Rochelle Hudson (as Colbert's daughter), and Ned Sparks.

Despite its sentimental ideology, it needs to be remembered that *Imitation of Life* was "The only Hollywood movie of its era that even suggested the existence of such a thing as a race problem in America."[103] According to James Robert Parish and William T. Leonard, Beavers lobbied successfully with the help of the NAACP to have the word "nigger" removed from the script.[104] *Variety* wrote of her performance: "It is one of the most unprecedented personal triumphs for an obscure performer in the annals of a crazy business."[105] Ironically enough, in real life Beavers hated cooking and avoided the kitchen whenever possible. "On movie sets," writes Jill Watts, "she made clear her disdain for cooking and cleaning and refused to participate in any kind of preparation whatsoever for kitchen scenes."[106]

Fortunately for Beavers, after being a maid in her youth, she grew affluent enough to be able to hire household help. According to film historian Thomas Cripps, Beavers was one of the "grandes dames of the ghetto": "a social elite who gave without stint to help the race while at the same time supporting their style of life by playing traditional roles as domestic servants."[107] These distinguished ladies were among the most prominent African American actresses in Hollywood. In addition to Beavers, there was her good friend Hattie McDaniel, Theresa Harris, Libby Taylor, Lillian Yarbo, and Marietta Canty.[108]

Theresa Harris (1909–85) only made about seventy films compared with Beavers's approximately 160. Harris was Ginger Rogers's musical maid in *Professional Sweetheart* (1933), Billie Burke's long-suffering maid in *Finishing School* (1934), Bette Davis's maid in *Jezebel* (1938), Marlene Dietrich's maid in *The Flame of New Orleans* (1941), Maureen O'Hara's maid in *Miracle on 34th Street* (1947), the list goes on. Libby Taylor (dates unknown) played mostly maids in more than fifty films between 1931 and 1953, including *I'm No Angel* (1933), *Belle of the Nineties* (1934), *Ruggles of Red Gap* (1935), *Reckless* (1935), *Shanghai* (1935), *The Howards of Virginia* (1940), *The Hard Way* (1942), and *Another Part of the Forest* (1948). Lillian Yarbo (dates unknown) was, like Butterfly McQueen, innately comic, particularly in films like *Rainbow on the River* (1936), her first, where she had what was for her a substantial role as Beavers's fried chicken vendor friend; the little known *Café Society* (1939), where as Mattie Harriett, she was a minor Mata Hari paid by a gossip columnist to spy on stars Fred MacMurray and Madeleine Carroll; and *Destry Rides Again* (1939), where she was Marlene Dietrich's gun-shy maid. Finally, Marietta Canty (1905–86), like Butterfly McQueen again, was a late arrival in Hollywood. She only made roughly forty films between 1940 and 1955, but they included familiar titles like *Boom Town* (1940), *The Lady Is Willing* (1942), *Father of the Bride* (1950), *The Bad and the Beautiful* (1952), and *Rebel Without a Cause* (1955).

Louise Beavers was born in Cincinnati, Ohio on March 2, 1902, making her the contemporary of Mildred Dunnock, Lee Patrick, Flora Robson, Elsa Lanchester, and Anne Revere. According to her *New York Times* obituary, she moved to California with her family as a young girl and attended Pasadena High School.[109] She is known to have worked as a maid for silent screen siren Leatrice Joy in the early 1920s and possibly also for Lilyan Tashman, whose maid she played on screen in *Gold Diggers of Broadway* (R. Del Ruth, Warner Bros., 1929).[110] Beavers began working as an extra in the 1923 film *The Gold Diggers* (H. Beaumont, Warner Bros.). Her first sound film was *Coquette* (S. Taylor, 1929), where she played Mary Pickford's maid. She had her film breakthrough in *Imitation of Life* in 1934, which was only one of seventeen of her films released that year.

Imitation of Life was, of course, more the exception than the rule with regard to the types of roles Beavers customarily played on film. In *The Negro in Films* (1952), Peter Noble called her "a striking example of wasted talent."[111] Yet she was fortunate in being given several other unique screen opportunities during her thirty-seven years in Hollywood, even if nothing could compare with the exposure of her 1934 hit. In films like *Bullets or Ballots*, *Rainbow on the River*, *Make Way for Tomorrow*, *Made for Each Other*, *Holiday Inn*, *The Big Street*, and *The Jackie Robinson Story*, we again find Beavers in roles that in various ways would showcase her unique talents, both comic and dramatic.

In *Bullets or Ballots* (W. Keighley, Warner Bros., 1936), Beavers was surprisingly cast against type as the "Numbers Queen," Nellie LaFleur. Cripps calls the part "her most dramatic departure from her bread-and-butter roles playing maids."[112] In a parallel to *Imitation of Life*, Beavers has had the business idea, but her friend, business partner, and former employer, Joan Blondell (as Lee Morgan), is the one chiefly reaping the rewards. No sooner is Beavers inside Blondell's office, than she shoos off Blondell's new maid and begins to fix her hair herself. At least she gets to dress up for a change.

Beavers's role in *Rainbow on the River* (a.k.a. *It Happened in New Orleans*; K. Neumann, 1936) is arguably the second most important of her career, though the film is much less well known than *Imitation of Life* and has never been released on video or DVD. Here Beavers plays Toinette, an interesting variation on the mammy figure in that she becomes the foster mother of a white boy and provides for him and herself by selling flowers in the New Orleans market. The film has an unusual focus on the African American actress's emotional life. She remains a presence in the story till the end, being reunited with her adoptive son and carried off to the North. For her efforts, Beavers was this time billed seventh.

Make Way for Tomorrow (Paramount, 1937) is arguably director Leo McCarey's masterpiece, though he is better known for *The Awful Truth* (1937) and *Love Affair* (1939). Beavers plays Mamie, the maid of the borderline genteel big city couple played by Fay Bainter and Thomas Mitchell. Beavers, Bainter, and Mitchell, and the latter's daughter, played by Barbara Read, all have their lives disrupted when they must take in Mitchell's aged mother, stunningly well played in all her exasperating old biddy sweetness by Beulah Bondi. Beavers has a hilarious scene where she has to carry Bondi's rocking chair into the living room in the middle of a bridge party. Later she threatens to quit, because staying home to take care of granny is interfering with her love life.

In *Made for Each Other* (J. Cromwell, Selznick Int., 1939), Beavers plays newlyweds Carole Lombard and James Stewart's third cook and good fairy, Lily, who tries to give Lombard some homespun advice: "Never let the seeds stop you from enjoying the watermelons." This part in another of producer David O. Selznick's 1939 pictures must have been a poor comfort for losing the role of Mammy in *GWTW*. Selznick had also cast Beavers in *What Price Hollywood?* (1932) and *Hell's Highway* (1932).

Beavers's favorite part was the cook and mother of two, Mamie, in *Holiday Inn* (M. Sandrich, Paramount, 1942),[113] probably because she got to sing the duet "Abraham" with Bing Crosby and set him straight too on what women need (Marjorie Reynolds in this case): "You could melt her heart to butter, if you'd only turn

Louise Beavers had one of the most dazzling smiles in Hollywood and used it often in her many devoted domestic roles. As the maid Chloe, she is seen with her employers, Sam and Lu Clayton, portrayed by Gary Cooper and Ann Sheridan, in *Good Sam* (RKO, 1948). The talented director of this film, Leo McCarey, had directed Beavers eleven years earlier in his little-known classic *Make Way for Tomorrow*.

on the heat." Beavers's sixth billing was highly respectable. All the more surprising, then, that her next role as Rudy, Lucille Ball's ever-devoted, outspoken maid in *The Big Street* (I. Reis, RKO, 1942), was uncredited. Beavers does all she can to help Ball after her accident, but finally has to think of her own family and leaves her employer and friend in the hands of the chivalrous Henry Fonda.

Finally, *The Jackie Robinson Story* (A.E. Green, 1950) is often mentioned in surveys of Beavers's career both for the film's significance in the history of films about African Americans and because, for once, she did not play a maid but a mother. As Mrs. Robinson, Beavers was billed fourth, after Jackie Robinson playing himself, Ruby Dee, and Minor Watson. A jovial and none too bright woman, Mrs. Robinson tells her son to trust in God, seek out a minister when in doubt, and talk to his brother about baseball, as he knows more about it than she does.

Despite these several interesting roles, the vast majority of the approximately 160 parts Beavers played on film were run-of-the mill domestics. Despite her prominence, these might even be non-speaking or virtually non-speaking parts and she would sometimes appear uncredited. Among her more prominent, non-prominent maid, mammy, and cook roles, we find Constance Bennett's maid Bonita in *What Price Hollywood?* (G. Cukor, RKO, 1932); Mae West's maid Pearl in *She Done Him Wrong* (L. Sherman, Paramount, 1933)[114]; Jean Harlow's

Louise Beavers looks mournfully down on her friend and employer, Lucille Ball, who is prostrate after being attacked by a jealous lover in *The Big Street* (RKO, 1942). In the 1930s, no African American actress enjoyed a more sterling reputation in Hollywood than Beavers and no screen maid offered more devoted service. Among the concerned onlookers are Henry Fonda and Ball's Pekinese.

maid Loretta in *Bombshell* (V. Fleming, MGM, 1933); Myrna Loy and William Powell's maid Estrellita in *Shadow of the Thin Man* (W.S. Van Dyke, MGM, 1941); Gene Tierney's mammy, Mammy Lou, in *Belle Starr* (I. Cummings, Twentieth Century-Fox, 1941); Paulette Goddard's mammy, Maum Maria, in *Reap the Wild Wind* (C.B. DeMille, Paramount, 1942)[115]; and Myrna Loy and Cary Grant's maid, Gussie, in *Mr. Blanding Builds His Dream House* (H.C. Potter, RKO, 1948). Gussie, incidentally, comes up with the advertising slogan beleaguered Grant needs: "If you ain't eatin' Wham, you ain't eatin' ham."

Beavers's five final films were a sad commentary on how little her own career had progressed from her beginnings thirty years before. If possible, opportunities for older African American actresses were even more limited in the film industry in the late 1950s than when she'd started. Beavers was reunited with Ginger Rogers for the first time in twenty-three years in *Teenage Rebel* (E. Goulding, Twentieth Century-Fox, 1956), where she plays the Fallon family's maid, Willamay. She is referred to by Rogers as "my very good friend," but the spraying with a garden hose she gets from the son of the house is sadly reminiscent of her being pulled into the pool in *What Price Hollywood?* twenty-four years earlier.

Tammy and the Bachelor (J. Pevney, Universal, 1957) is an even sadder commentary on how little things had changed for African American actors in the film industry. Beavers plays Fay Wray and Sidney Blackmer's temperamental cook, Osia, but really only has one scene where she does more than beam inanely at the family's antics. Noticeably older and thinner here, the now grey-haired, fifty-five-year-old Beavers complains to heroine Debbie Reynolds that she has to wear a headscarf for the open house historical tour and later shows up, symbolically enough, in complete mammy costume. If Beavers thought she'd played her last mammy, she was wrong. In Kim Stanley's greatest film, the Paddy Chayefsky–authored drama, *The Goddess* (J. Cromwell, Columbia, 1958), Beavers is only glimpsed briefly as an unnamed cook in the kitchen of Hunter's Hollywood home. In *All the Fine Young Cannibals* (M. Anderson, MGM 1960), she plays Rose, the proprietress of a honky tonk and friend of Jack Wagner at the beginning of the film and a mourner at Pearl Bailey's funeral at the end. In her final screen appearance, she has a small part as Bob Hope and Lucille Ball's maid, Gussie, in *The Facts of Life* (M. Frank, United Artists 1960) with only two practically one-line scenes.

Louise Beavers was only 5'4" tall, but weighed 190 lbs. in her prime.[116] "She was heavy and hearty," writes Bogle, "but not heavy and hearty enough. [S]he went on force-feed diets, compelling herself to eat beyond her normal appetite."[117] After years of suffering with diabetes, no doubt caused by her overeating, Beavers entered a Hollywood hospital on October 25, 1962.[118] She died of a heart attack the next day. Beavers was survived by her husband, Leroy Moore, whom she had married in the late 1950s.[119] She had lived quietly with her mother, a choir director at various studios, Ernestine Monroe Beavers, until the latter's death in 1938.[120] Mother and daughter share a grave in Evergreen Cemetery, Los Angeles. Louise Beavers was inducted posthumously into the Black Filmmakers Hall of Fame on February 17, 1976.[121]

Glamour and L'amour
MARY BOLAND (1882–1965)

Mary Boland was like a meringue: light, rich, sweet, and addictive. She was also a born diva. Even in a cotton housedress, there was something grand about her. She had a beautiful, heart-shaped face, fine skin, and large, expressive eyes, in addition to a Rubensesque curvaceousness at a time when big could still be beautiful and Mae West was a sex symbol. This cream puff of a woman wheedled, commandeered, and sometimes downright nagged her way through numerous thirties comedies that required a regal or daffy female presence. Yet, don't let these culinary comparisons mislead you. Above and beyond her ample physical charms, Boland was a consummate comedienne and a tough businesswoman. She knew exactly what she was doing. Having found her niche in the movie industry at a time of life when good parts were at a premium, Boland played it for what it was worth.

There is some confusion about the year in which Marie Anne Boland was born, which she no doubt herself contributed to. If she was born in 1880, as some sources claim, she arrived in this world the day before her future co-star W.C. Fields and in the same place, Philadelphia. The year 1882, though, is given on her sepulcher in Forest Lawn Cemetery and in most contemporary sources, including her obituary in the *New York Times*. At any rate, she was the daughter of William Augustus Boland, a minor stock actor on tour in Philadelphia at the time of her birth, and Maria Cecilia (*née* Hatton). Boland grew up in her father's native city of Detroit, where she went to school at the Sacred Heart Convent, as it behooved an Irish Catholic girl, and had her stage debut with a local stock company in 1901, as it did not.[122]

Boland's film career is intimately tied up

with the development of a particular female character type, first on stage in the late teens and '20s and in the movies from the start of the sound era. That type is the "dizzy dame," the flibbertigibbet, the scatterbrain, and other even less politically correct designations for a type of middle- or upper-class matron characterized by her ability to speak before she thinks, to lose her power of concentration without a moment's notice, and to say just the wrong thing at the right time (or was it the right thing at the wrong time?). This was great material for stage and film comedy alike; for women's liberation, maybe less so. At any rate, dizzy dames dominated thirties comedies, particularly of the screwball variety, and proved once and for all that women could be funny.

Among the several actresses who lent their comic talents to dizzy damehood, Mary Boland had the most solid pedigree. This was by virtue of her creating the mold (if not breaking it) in a Booth Tarkington play called *Clarence*, which opened at the Hudson Theatre in New York on September 20, 1919 and ran for 300 performances. Boland played Mrs. Wheeler, the spoiled, addlebrained wife of a rich businessman—and suspects him of infidelity. A young Helen Hayes played her lovesick daughter, Cora, and Alfred Lunt played the eponymous hero, a veteran of World War I who in addition to being a handyman has to fix the Wheeler family's many interpersonal problems.

By the time *Clarence* came along, Boland had been a star on Broadway for a dozen years. She made both her New York debut in 1905 and her London debut in 1907 in a play called *Strongheart* by Cecil B. De Mille's brother, William. Under Charles Frohman's management, she became the leading lady of the legendary leading man John Drew (uncle of Ethel, Lionel, and John Barrymore) through a series of nine plays at the Empire Theatre between 1908 and 1914. Boland continued to be a highly successful comedienne into the 1920s in plays like *The Torch Bearers* (1922–23), George Kelly's first hit, and *Cradle Snatchers* (1925–26), which ran for 332 performances and also starred Edna May Oliver and a young Humphrey Bogart as the "Spanish lover," Jose Vallejo.

Boland's Broadway credentials, then, were impeccable by the time she transferred her allegiance to Hollywood in the early 1930s and signed a contract with Paramount, where she would make over half her forty-four sound films. The only comedienne whose star shone more brightly was Billie Burke, another of Charles Frohman's leading ladies, but then Burke had the added luster of being married to Flo Ziegfeld for the last twenty years of that genius showman's life. Boland never married anyone, very unlike her signature role as the nuptially inclined Countess in *The Women*. She said herself that "maybe I'm one of the few people who don't mind being alone."[123] Looking back on her friend and co-star's life a decade after Boland's death, Rosalind Russell would tell another story in her memoirs *Life Is a Banquet* (1977). According to Russell, Boland had been in love with John Drew (twenty-seven years her senior), but her widowed mother had actively discouraged her from marrying him (or anyone else): "Mary was too good a meal ticket." Boland advised Russell not to go through life "without someone." Within a short time, the younger actress was both married and pregnant. Russell and her husband, Freddie Brisson (known as "the Lizard of Roz"), ended up buying the house in Beverly Hills at 706 N. Beverly Drive that Boland had built for herself in 1940, but only lived in for a year. "Poor soul," writes Russell, "she was lonely."[124] L'amour, l'amour, how it can let you down...

Russell's physical presence and style of comic acting could hardly have been more different from Boland's, but the younger actress no doubt picked up a few tricks watching the old pro at work. Mary Astor recalled in her memoirs that Boland had told her: "'Comedy is the *last* thing you learn.' Because it's the toughest."[125] Another star of the screen who remembered her fondly was Katharine Hepburn. In 1928 Boland had the lead role in the production of *The Czarina* in Baltimore in which Hepburn got her first professional acting job as a lady in waiting.[126]

Perpetually single in real life, Boland was usually married on screen, most frequently to the dapper, wavy-haired ditherer Charles Ruggles. The pair was well matched, Ruggles being quite the dizzy dude himself, though the two never socialized off the set.[127] Their fourteen films together made them one of the strongest comic duos in the 1930s, together with Marie Dressler and Wallace Beery, Billie Burke and Roland Young, Alison Skipworth and W.C. Fields, and George Burns and Gracie Allen. In fact, in *Six of a Kind* (Leo McCarey, Paramount, 1934) they teamed up with the latter two pairs. No film was better named. In this early road movie, Boland and Ruggles try to save money on their second honeymoon by sharing their car with Burns and Allen (and their uninvited Great Dane). The running gag is that whenever Boland and Ruggles want to rekindle their marital fires, Burns and Allen interrupt them. Boland's *Torch Bearers* co-star Alison Skipworth played "The Duchess," a sticky-fingered innkeeper, and Fields an absent-minded local marshal encountered on the way. This film was, according to Parish and Leonard, Boland's "closest brush with slapstick,"[128] as she dangles from a tree over Grand Canyon, while her husband tries to save her and Gracie Allen makes not-very-helpful suggestions.

Boland and Ruggles were also with Skipworth and Fields in another classic thirties comedy, *If I Had a Million* (various directors, Paramount, 1932), though *with* is not exactly correct, as they appeared in different segments of the film. The picture consisted of eight sketches by different writers and directors based on the same premise that a dying multimillionaire picks eight people at random out of the telephone book

Mary Boland in one of her classic screen portrayals as the new rich Effie Floud of Red Gap, Washington, with delusions of grandeur and a hat that looks as if it ready to take flight. On her left is her frequent screen husband, Charles Ruggles, as Egbert Floud. As the "bery British" butler Ruggles (no relation), whom Mr. Floud has won in a card game, Charles Laughton stands far right in this group photo from *Ruggles of Red Gap* (Paramount, 1935), which also includes Maude Eburne (far left).

and gives them one million dollars each. Ruggles plays Henry Peabody, the quintessential "little man," who is driven round the bend by his relentlessly nagging wife (Boland) and ends up acting literally like a bull in a china shop. This film set a pattern for their comic collaboration. The classic Rip Van Winkle combination of downtrodden husband and harridan wife here found a modern, middle-class incarnation that has retained its popularity to this very day. Clearly, Patricia Routledge's and Clive Swift's impersonations of Hyacinth and Richard Bucket in the classic TV sitcom *Keeping Up Appearances* (1990–95) are very much in the spirit of the 1930s Boland-Ruggles comedies. The high point of their work together was reached in the delightful pseudo–Western *Ruggles of Red Gap* (L. McCarey, Paramount, 1935), which was Oscar-nominated for Best Film. Boland is simply hilarious as the snooty, nouveau riche Effie Floud of Red Gap, Washington, decked out in terrific "Belle of the Nineties" costumes and pulling out all the stops in her scenes with her "bery British" butler, Ruggles (Charles Laughton).

Throughout the 1930s, Boland and Billie Burke would be in competition for many of the same screen roles. In addition, they both had to reckon with Spring Byington and Alice Brady. Physically, though, these four ace dizzy dames were all quite different, as were their voices and acting styles. Billie Burke, apart from her kewpie doll cuteness and downy blonde hair, was chiefly distinguished by her famous tweetiebird voice. Spring Byington, pug-nosed and warm-eyed, had a broader range of screen personas, excelling too in unsympathetic roles. The same might be said for Alice Brady, who brought to the screen her broad stage experience in both dramatic and comic roles and in the latter was given to fast talk and wild gesticulation.

The division of the spoils in the 1930s went something like this: Byington nabbed Boland's role of Mrs. Wheeler in Paramount's 1937 filmatization of *Clarence* and Penny Sycamore in *You Can't Take It with You* (1938). Alice Brady got to play Bridgie Drake in *When Ladies Meet* (1933), Aunt Hortense in *The Gay Divorcee* (1934), and, most famously, Angelica Bullock in *My Man Godfrey* (1936). Burke captured plum dizzy dame parts in *Dinner at Eight* (1933), *Forsaking All Others* (1934), *Doubting Thomas* (1935), *Merrily We Live*, and the "Topper" films. The loss of the part of Paula in *Doubting Thomas* must have been particularly galling to Boland, as the film was based on her big stage success, *The Torch Bearers*. Boland was often left with lesser known vehicles, such as *Wives Never Know* (E. Nugent, Paramount, 1936), but she evened

Mary Boland in her only starring, dramatic film role as Mary Grady in *A Son Comes Home* (Paramount Pictures, 1936). The owner of a chowder house on Fisherman's Wharf in San Francisco, she sets out to prove that her son is not a murderer.

the score with two or three really showy parts towards the end of the 1930s, that we shall soon consider. *Wives Never Know* was a kind of precursor of Kaufman and Hart's hit play (and film), *The Man Who Came to Dinner* (1939/1942). Adolphe Menjou plays a "progressive" author who has written a book against marriage and tries to get Boland and her typically henpecked husband Ruggles "to live again. To live and suffer!" Boland's Marcia Bigelow responds: "I'm sure you must have loved in a way we've never even heard of in Topeka."

In their fascinating book *They Had Faces Then*, John Springer and Jack Hamilton observe, "Since the Boland roles were almost all the same, the success of her performance depended on the pictures. When *they* were good, she *was* wonderful."[129] Among her most wonderful and best remembered films are *The Women* (1939), based on the hit play by Clare Boothe Luce, and *Pride and Prejudice* (R.Z. Leonard, MGM, 1940), the first and still the finest filmatization of Jane Austen's classic novel. When George Cukor set about filming Luce's play at MGM, he retained only two of the principal players from the Broadway production, his friend Phyllis Povah and Majorie Main. The part of the countess went to Boland, who had been born to play it. Choked with diamonds and pearls, dressed to the nines, and coiffed to within an inch of her life, she uttered immortal lines like "Where love leads, I always follow" and, in relation to her soon-to-be husband Buck Winston: "Have you noticed the play of his muscles? Musical! Musical!" In conversation with Roy Newquist, Boland's co-star Joan Crawford recalled that "all the supporting players, including Mary Boland, or especially Mary Boland, were perfectly cast."[130]

In *Pride and Prejudice*, Boland played the benevolently obtuse matriarch of the Bennet clan, which included husband Edmund Gwenn and daughters Greer Garson, Maureen O'Sullivan, Ann Rutherford, Heather Angel, and Marsha Hunt. According to Bosley Crowther of the *New York Times*, Boland was "a completely overpowering Mrs. Bennet" and the film "the most deliciously pert comedy of old manners, the most crisp and crackling satire in costume that we in this corner remember ever having seen on the screen."[131] Boland would also support Greer Garson in *Julia Misbehaves* (J. Conway, MGM, 1948), which was Boland's penultimate film. Noticeably older, she played Garson's potential mother-in-law, Mrs. Gheneccio, part of a mother-and-son acrobatic act, "The Flying Gheneccios," and a delightful old soak (though Boland's attempt at a Cockney accent was an abject failure).

Two of my personal favorites among Boland's roles are to be found in the Eddy-MacDonald musical *New Moon* (R.Z. Leonard, MGM, 1940) and the 1944 melodrama *In Our Time* (V. Sherman, Warner Bros.). The latter film was clearly an attempt to capitalize on the success of *Rebecca* and Boland's part at the beginning of the picture bears a striking resemblance to Florence Bates's Mrs. Van Hopper in Hitchcock's 1940 thriller. Boland plays a grasping, self-centered antique dealer on a buying trip to Poland with Ida Lupino in the Joan Fontaine role as her downtrodden, mousy assistant. In this film, Paul Henreid rather than Olivier comes to Lupino's rescue, whisking her off to his castle, where she must confront not a forbidding housekeeper, but an aristocratic mother-in-law in the figure of Alla Nazimova. *New Moon* was a lavish, tropical, rococo extravaganza—*Les Miserables* meets *Mutiny on the Bounty*—in which Boland portrayed Jeanette MacDonald's worldly, gossipy aunt and uttered deathless lines like "No handsome man should ever have his head chopped off" and, with reference to the "natives": "Are they eating anyone yet?"

Boland had the kind of florid beauty that was well suited to seventeenth-century dress. Naturally, she was a big hit in early 1942 as Mrs. Malaprop, the mother of all dizzy dames, in Richard Brinsley Sheridan's play *The Rivals*. Boland did not get on, though, with actress-turned-director Eva Le Gallienne and was ultimately fined $500 by Actors Equity for refusing to submit to a doctor's examination before abruptly quitting the show.[132] It was one of the last of her thirty-two shows on Broadway.

Boland retired from the movies in 1950 and from the stage a few years later. In a survey for Daniel Blum's 1952 book *Great Stars of the American Stage*, she responded that her dislikes were "trashy novels, rich foods, petunias, champagne, poker, and the color red." Her likes, on the other hand, were "autobiographies, George Bernard Shaw, Helen Hayes, gardening, simple home-cooked food, carnations, Pekinese dogs, any drink served at parties, bridge, and the color rose."[133] According to the *New York Times*, her final years were "serene."[134] Mary Boland died as she had lived, alone, and was found dead from an apparent heart attack in her suite at the Essex House in New York on the morning of June 23, 1965. She had outlived all her contemporaries. Only thirty people attended her funeral service.[135]

Miss Bondi Goes to Hollywood
BEULAH BONDI (1888–1981)

Was Beulah Bondi the quintessential character actress? According to James Robert Parish, she was "Perhaps the most consummate of all character players."[136] Jordan R. Young has written more recently, "Her reputation as Hollywood's preeminent character actress remains unchallenged."[137] She was, certainly, the most distinguished screen actress of the talented generation born during the late 1880s that included Elisabeth Risdon, Blanche Yurka, Gladys Cooper, Florence Bates, and Margaret Dumont. Today Bondi is most frequently remembered as Jimmy Stewart's mother in *Mr. Smith Goes to Washington* (1939) and *It's a Wonderful Life* (1946), films that are often shown on television. Like so many of her sister actresses, though, she deserves to be remembered for a much broader range of roles. She did not always play little old ladies or the mother of the Prince of Dullness.

Beulah Bondy was born in Chicago on May 3, 1888 (not 1892, as frequently given). Her father was Abram O. Bondy and her mother Eva Suzanna Marble Bondy. Like Agnes Moorehead, Bondi was highly educated, culminating in 1918 in an MA in Oratory from Valparaiso University in Valparaiso, Indiana, where the family had moved when she was three. Her mother had trained her in elocution from an early age and sent her to study dance and diction under Maurice Browne at the Chicago Little Theatre. Even so, Young claims that the change in the final vowel of her surname was due to opposition in her family to her choice of profession.[138] Bondi made her stage debut as a child in the title role of *Little Lord Fauntleroy* and after college went on to join Stuart Walker's famous stock company. She made her New York debut in 1925, when she was asked to play an eighty-year-old, though only thirty-seven! It would not be the last time the makeup artist would have to work his wonders. The play was a hit and during the next eight years Bondi was singularly lucky in her choice of roles on Broadway. She was in *Saturday's Children* (1927–28) with Humphrey Bogart and Ruth Gordon, which ran for 326 performances; Elmer Rice's Pulitzer Prize–winning *Street Scene* (1929–30), which ran for 601 performances; and *The Late Christopher Bean* (1932–33), which starred Pauline Lord and ran for 224 performances.

Her role as the nefarious, narrow-minded Emma Jones in Elmer Rice's classic about the goings on in an average New York tenement brought Bondi to Hollywood and Sam Goldwyn's independent production company. The reprise of a Broadway role on film was, of course, a not uncommon route for character actresses making their way from theatreland to movieland and would be followed by actresses as diverse as Marjorie Main, Una O'Connor, and Maria Ouspenskaya. We can be grateful that wonderful stage performances, such as that given by Bondi in *Street Scene*, have been preserved for posterity (while, ironically, those of the stars of these productions have not), while marveling at the ease and rapidity with which these actresses adapted to the requirements of a new medium. Bondi's performance as Emma Jones is a miracle of restraint, unlike Main's performance in a somewhat similar part in *Dead End* six years later (both films starred the perpetually weepy Sylvia Sidney). Watch how the top-knotted Bondi uses the gesture of trying to keep her back hair in place as part of her characterization.

For *Street Scene* Bondi was paid $500 a week. Goldwyn wanted to sign her to a long-term contract on the same terms. Surprisingly, she declined the offer, though she played a small, uncredited role as Helen Hayes's disapproving mother in another Goldwyn film, *Arrowsmith* (J. Ford, United Artists, 1931), before going on to bigger and better things. During her more than three-decade-long film career, Bondi would never be under contract to a studio, giving her greater freedom to pick and choose roles (limited, of course, by what was offered). She made a total of sixty-four feature films in thirty-two years. Had she been a contract player, she might have made twice as many, as did actresses like Jane Darwell, Elizabeth Patterson, and Elisabeth Risdon, but many of the parts would have been of negligible interest and she would have had little control over her screen image.

The central feature of that image was strength. One can say of every substantial part Bondi played, whether it was a poor, rural grandmother or an upper-class dowager, whether benevolent or downright evil, that the character always had vast resources of inner strength to draw upon, particularly in hard times. There was something spiritual about Beulah Bondi. One imagines her as a vestal virgin in Ancient Greece (albeit a mature one). She worshipped all her life at the altar of Thespis, remaining unmarried throughout her near ninety-three years on earth. Half a century after he first became her friend on the set of *Track of the Cat*, Tab Hunter recalled: "When she spoke to you, you knew she was speaking from her soul."[139]

The majority of Bondi's films were dramas, often costume dramas. Like Moorehead, Bondi wore her fair share of bonnets and calico. We would no sooner expect to see her in a screwball comedy, than Mary Boland in a Western or Billie Burke in a melodrama. But, then again, Boland did make one pseudo-Western at least (*Ruggles of Red Gap*), and Burke started out in melodrama (*A Bill of Divorcement* and *Christopher Strong*). As it turns out, Bondi lent her talents to a couple of screwball comedies during the 1930s: *The Moon's Our Home* (W.A. Seiter, Paramount, 1936) and *Vivacious Lady* (G. Stevens, RKO, 1938). In the former, she was the lady companion to a temperamental movie star, played by Margaret Sullavan; and in the latter she played Jimmy Stewart's mother for the second time that year and the second of five times.[140]

This being said, the classic Bondi role was an old, often rural grandmother; a distinguished, though often unsympathetic, dowager; a mild-mannered, middle-class mother; or an unmarried working woman. Bondi rarely, if ever, played a maid, cook, or housekeeper, nor did she play other character actress staples, such as nuns, nurses, or governesses. In the little old lady category, mention must be made of films like *The Gorgeous Hussy*, *The Captain Is a Lady*, *The Shepherd of the Hills*, and *The Southerner*. Bondi's older women were often rural, or at least homespun, and in that regard, her part in *The Gorgeous Hussy* (C. Brown, MGM, 1936) was typical, though Rachel Jackson was not the ancient, withered crone we would encounter in other films. Bondi was nominated for her portrayal of "the Backwoods Belle," the folksy, pipe-smoking wife of President Andrew Jackson (Lionel Barrymore, Bondi's frequent co-star) in a biopic about the years leading up to his presidency, starring Joan Crawford in her only period costume drama; her then husband, Franchot Tone; and dashing Robert Taylor. With lines like "Don't get foamed up, general," it was a miracle Bondi even got nominated. She lost to Gale Sondergaard for her debut role in *Anthony Adverse*, as did Alice Brady, Maria Ouspenskaya, and Bonita Granville. This was the first year a separate Oscar was awarded in the supporting role category.

The Captain Is a Lady (R.B. Sinclair, MGM, 1940) was a character actress extravaganza set in an old ladies' home into which Bondi's husband (Charles Coburn) is allowed to move as "Old Lady 31." The film was a variant on two other Bondi classics, *Make Way for Tomorrow* and *On Borrowed Time* (H.S. Bucquet, MGM, 1939), in being concerned with the fading years of an old married couple. Benefiting from the talents of actresses as various as Helen Broderick, Billie Burke, Cecil Cunningham, Marjorie Main, and Helen Westley, *The Captain Is a Lady* had a happy ending.

In *The Shepherd of the Hills* (H. Hathaway, Paramount, 1941) and *The Southerner* (J. Renoir, 1945), Bondi's roles were considerably less benign. In the first mentioned film, she plays the hard-hearted, superstitious, and ignorant matriarch of the Mathews clan, who tirelessly tries to place the blame on others for her own misdeeds and ceaselessly spurs her menfolk on to avenge the wrong done to her sister and thus lift the curse on the family. According to blind Grandma Becky (Marjorie Main in one of her more ludicrous roles, which is saying a lot): "Her soul's et up with hate." In *The Southerner*, a cotton-pickers' *Grapes of Wrath*, which like *The Shepherd* starred multi-talented Betty Field, Bondi was even older and more sour than formerly, displaying more mean spirits as Granny Tucker than even May Robson at her worst could muster. Bondi was fifty-seven when she gave this convincing portrayal of ancient decrepitude. Part of her secret was her naturally dry, quivery voice. Speaking of *Grapes of Wrath*: It was the major disappointment of Bondi's career that she didn't bag the plum role of Ma Joad. She had been told she would get it by producer Darryl F. Zanuck, and had even gone to talk to the migrant workers in five separate camps. As it turned out, the role went to portly Jane Darwell, and an Oscar as well.[141] Bondi's part in *The Southerner* could hardly have been much of a consolation.

Bondi played her share of unpleasant parts, particularly as that long-vanished breed of dusty, fusty dowager that graced, if that is the word, so many '30s comedies and dramas alike. Bondi's first significant entry in this category was her Mrs. Davidson in *Rain*, but there was also Miss Van Alstyne in *Finishing School*, Mrs. Livingstone Ames in *The Case Against Mrs. Ames*, and Mrs. Lydia Sandow in *One Foot in Heaven*.

In *Rain* (L. Milestone, 1932), she played the pious, straight-laced wife of fire and brimstone preacher Walter Huston, who eggs him on in his ongoing spiritual (and fleshly) struggle with Joan Crawford's dissolute Sadie Thompson, ultimately contributing to his "sin" and suicide. The final shot of the film is of Bondi weeping, as she realizes her complicity in the tragic outcome. In *Finishing School* (G. Nichols Jr., RKO, 1934), she was the haughty headmistress of a school for girls where appearances are more important than realities. In *The Case*

Beulah Bondi plays one of the most ornery, evil-minded, exasperating old grannies on celluloid in the cotton-picking *Grapes of Wrath* called *The Southerner* (United Artists, 1945). Losing the role of Ma Joad in *Grapes of Wrath* to Jane Darwell was the biggest disappointment of Bondi's career. She was only fifty-six when this photo was taken, but had been playing ancient crones since she was in her late thirties.

Against Mrs. Ames (W.A. Seiter, Paramount, 1936), she played a pillar of San Francisco society, who after her son's death fights to gain custody of her grandson and tries to turn him against his mother (Madeleine Carroll). Last but not least, Mrs. Sandow in *One Foot in Heaven* (I. Rapper, Warner Bros., 1941) was a self-righteous, selfish, and resplendently wealthy parishioner at Fredric March's Methodist church, who objects to her pastor taking tea with her chauffeur. March's scenes with Bondi and with Harry Davenport as the chauffeur are two of the few bright spots in this drawn-out saga of the trials and tribulations of March and his ever-devoted wife, Martha Scott. Incredibly, this pious claptrap was nominated for Best Picture in 1942. There were ten nominees, though, and *How Green Was My Valley* won.

That many of Bondi's most familiar and beloved roles were playing mothers is ironic considering the fact that she never had any children of her own. We find her in important or familiar mother roles in *Of Human Hearts, Mr. Smith Goes to Washington, Remember the Night, Our Town,* and *It's a Wonderful Life.* Ironically again, the mother roles for which she is best known are the least interesting, that is to say Ma Smith in *Mr. Smith Goes to Washington* (F. Capra, Columbia, 1939), practically a nonspeaking part, and Ma Bailey in *It's a Wonderful Life* (F. Capra, 1946). Granted, the latter, a Christmas classic, allows her to show both the sunny and the sour side of her maternal screen persona, but if you primarily want to watch Bondi at work rather than James Stewart, a film such as *Of Human Hearts* (C. Brown, MGM, 1938) is much more interesting. In this drama set in the antebellum, pioneering community of Pine Hill, Ohio, Bondi plays the hard-tried wife of a fundamentalist preacher (Walter Huston again), who has clearly married down. Despite the romantic plot line, involving Bondi's self-satisfied prat of a son (Stewart) and Ann Rutherford, Bondi is the unquestionable star of the film, which garnered her her second Oscar nomination. This time, she lost to Fay Bainter (for *Jezebel*), whom Bondi replaced that same year in *Vivacious Lady*, when James Stewart fell ill and filming had to be delayed.

In *Remember the Night* (M. Leisen, Paramount, 1940), Bondi plays the doting, down-home Hoosier Indiana mother of Fred MacMurray, who worries when he brings home a woman with a past, played by Barbara Stanwyck, as his future wife. Bondi manages to retain our sympathy while trying to convince Stanwyck to move on. No mean feat. Finally, in the first, highly successful, filmatization of Thornton Wilder's classic play of New England village life at the turn of the last century, *Our Town* (S. Wood, 1940), Bondi plays Myrtle Webb, the stern but basically good-hearted wife of the local newspaper editor (Guy Kibbee) and the mother of Martha Scott. When Scott harps on the question of whether or not she is pretty, Bondi answers: "You're pretty enough for all normal purposes."

In the spinster and/or professional woman category, we find Bondi films like *Penny Serenade, Watch on the Rhine,* and *Back to Bataan.* Among these, my personal favorite is *Penny Serenade* (G. Stevens, Columbia, 1941), starring Irene Dunne and Cary Grant as a small-town newspaper editor and his wife, who desperately want a child. Bondi plays Miss Oliver, a worker at an adoption agency, who helps them find one, and the film records the trials and tribulations of the hopeful parents, often as told through letters to Bondi. She is luminous in the part of a woman who dedicates her life to helping childless couples, while remaining herself both uncoupled and childless.

Bondi was less successful in *Watch on the Rhine* (H. Shumlin, Warner Bros., 1943), a World War II homefront drama based on a play by Lillian Hellman. Lucile Watson reprised her hit Broadway role as Fanny Farrelly, a wealthy Washington widow who is "shaken out of the magnolias" and has the hard truths of war brought vividly home to her when her resistance fighter son-in-law (and Bette Davis's film husband), Paul Lukas, is threatened in her own, seemingly secure home. Bondi plays her companion, Anise, of ostensibly French origins and even more doubtful accent. Where was the speech coach? In *Back to Bataan* (E. Dmytryk, RKO, 1945), another war drama, this time from the battlefront rather than the home front,

Bondi was one of only two women in the cast, which included stars John Wayne and Anthony Quinn. Third-billed Bondi plays Bertha Barnes, a bossy, brave, and imperious Yankee schoolteacher in the Philippines, who becomes a witness to and near-victim of Japanese atrocities. She joins the American forces under the commando of Wayne's Col. Joseph Madden, to the latter's decidedly mixed delight.

I've yet to discuss what is arguably the standout role of Bondi's career: Lucy Cooper in Leo McCarey's little-known masterpiece *Make Way for Tomorrow* (Paramount, 1937). As an elderly couple who lose their home and are thrown on the mercies of their five children, Bondi and Victor Moore head an outstanding ensemble cast that includes Thomas Mitchell, Fay Bainter, Porter Hall, Minna Gombell, Elisabeth Risdon, and Louise Beavers. Bondi and her husband are separated after half a century of marriage, because none of the children are willing or able to take both their parents. The complications that ensue, particularly when Bondi must make her home with her sympathetic but spineless son (Mitchell) and his uptight, bridge instructor wife (Bainter), are hilarious, but also very sad. The scene where Bondi tries to communicate with her husband on the phone before Bainter's entire bridge class is heartrending: "her flat, slightly deaf voice trying to say intimate things in public communicates utter despair."[142] Bondi manages to make Ma Cooper both lovable and incredibly irritating at the same time. A fine screenplay by a couple that wrote under the wife's name, Viña Delmar, seems to foreshadow the powerful realism of Arthur Miller's *Death of a Salesman*, while having its fantastic, wish-fulfilling, Capraesque moments. Delicately the storyline balances the different, reasonable, and perpetually conflicting claims of the various family members. McCarey insisted on keeping the unhappy ending, despite the protests of Paramount's new studio head, Adolph Zukor, leading him to limit the film's publicity campaign. It flopped at the box office and McCarey left Paramount in a tizzy, but the film remained his favorite.[143] This is one of the films of the thirties most deserving of restoration and being made available on DVD.

Sadly, Bondi's film career went into a decline both in quantity and quality during the 1950s. Though she had small but interesting

In *The Snake Pit* (Twentieth Century–Fox, 1948), Beulah Bondi had a cameo role as Mrs. Green, an asylum inmate with delusions of grandeur, in a typical comic relief scene in an otherwise dour film. Olivia de Havilland played the troubled heroine in a movie that took the scenic route through every available postwar psychiatric treatment from shock treatment and hypnotic injections, via hydrotherapy and steam baths to occupational therapy and psychotherapy.

parts in films like *The Furies* (A. Mann, 1950) and *Lone Star* (V. Sherman, MGM, 1952) early in the decade, these ten years also contain some of the biggest clunkers of her career. Even as talented an actress as Bondi could not always rise above the material. For some reason, her most ill-considered parts were often of a backwoods, mountain folk or hillbilly variety (i.e. *The Shepherd of the Hills*). A signal example of this is *Track of the Cat* (W.A. Wellman, 1954), a ridiculous melodrama with a nonsensical script. Bondi plays Ma Letty Bridges, matriarch and ruler of her Colorado ranch kingdom with Robert Mitchum as her henchman son. Another son, Arthur, is killed by a panther—forgive me, "painter"—and Bondi finally repents of her proud, sinful ways: "All the things I could say, seems to me I could have said them when he was alive." Of all the patent absurdities: Carl "Alfalfa" Switzer of *Our Gang* fame plays a Native American farmhand![144] Tab Hunter fans will be the only ones to enjoy this inept, snowbound, noir Western, and even they should probably turn off the sound.

As the biggest turkey in the Bondi canon, though, I would nominate *The Unholy Wife* (J. Farrow, 1957), which might well have been entitled "The Unholy Mess." The plot of this stinker is so incredible it is worth retelling, especially as Bondi has a central role. She plays the aged, nervous old mother of winegrower Rod Steiger and mother-in-law to bombshell Diana Dors and spends most of the film wandering around in an old housedress complaining of "noises" and worrying about prowlers. Bondi has a stroke towards the end of the film when she discovers Dors has framed Steiger for the murder of a neighboring winegrower, whom Dors herself has shot. Bondi loses the ability to speak, but manages to revenge herself on her daughter-in-law by taking an extra pill right before Dors gives her one, making it look as if Dors has killed her. Hoist

Beulah Bondi was sixty-two when this lovely picture was taken of her in costume for her small but significant role in director Anthony Mann's second Western, *The Furies* (Paramount Pictures, 1950). She played Mrs. Anaheim, a long-suffering yet resilient banker's wife who helps the film's star, Barbara Stanwyck. It was ten years since Bondi supported Stanwyck in another memorable film, *Remember the Night*.

by her own petard! Dors is tried and convicted for the murder of her mother-in-law. If this film alone didn't put the studio into receivership, it is nevertheless a historical fact that it was one of the last films made at RKO.

It is symbolic of the state of Hollywood cinema in the early 1960s that such a signally talented actress as Bondi should close out her distinguished film career in—wait for it—*Tammy and the Doctor* (H. Keller, Universal, 1963), the third in that classic trilogy of nubile movie masterpieces starring first Debbie Reynolds and later Sandra Dee in the title role. Bondi was bedridden during most of the film, in which as Tammy's adopted grandmother, Annie Call, she landed in a hospital, her illness facilitating the heroine's scintillating encounters with, you guessed it, a doctor (Peter Fonda). Dare I say that this was Bondi's second venture into Tammyland? Yes, indeed. She had also featured in the second of the series, *Tammy Tell Me True* (H. Keller, Universal, 1961). For shame, Beulah, for shame.

Beulah Bondi never officially retired. Starting in the early 1950s, she made several guest appearances on television, where her presence on the set always generated excitement. Even the stars of the new medium asked for permission to "watch Bondi work."[145] The capstone of her long and varied career was her performance on an episode of *The Waltons* entitled "The Pony Cart," that originally aired December 2, 1976 and that will live forever in memory (and reruns). Bondi played Martha Corinne Tyler Walton, the widowed ninety-year-old aunt of Zeb Walton, who makes a visit of indeterminate length to the Walton family on their idyllic mountain in the summer of 1937. The idyll does not last long, as Bondi's meddling presence upsets the family's routines and sets the house on its head, much as it had almost forty years before in the 1937 classic *Make Way for Tomorrow*. The old woman's dignity and creativity, though, are symbolized by her decorative painting of a newly built pony cart, which becomes her final testament to the Waltons. She dies at the end of this beautifully written episode, which showed to the full what levels of excellence television drama could attain. Bondi was eighty-eight when she gave this outstanding performance, which was duly recognized by her being awarded an Emmy in 1977.

Bondi's final years were filled with world travels, including a two-month safari to Africa when she was eighty-three. She was awarded an honorary doctorate from her alma mater, Valparaiso University, in 1978, sixty years after she completed her master's degree.

Bondi attributed her good health and open-mindedness to her mother: "She believed in raising and expanding consciousness—letting go of the past, planning for the future, and living in the now."[146] Bondi might well have lived to be a hundred had she not tripped over her cat on January 2, 1981, breaking several ribs. She was rushed from her lovely, Spanish Colonial home in Hollywood's Whitley Heights, where she had lived for nearly forty years, to the Motion Picture Country Home and Hospital in Woodland Hills. Pulmonary complications set in and she died ten days later.[147] Beulah Bondi was cremated and her ashes scattered at sea.

The Gay Divorcée
ALICE BRADY (1892–1939)

The 1930s was the decade when scores of aging female thesps were reborn as Hollywood character actresses. More rarely, it was the decade in which great character actress talents also died. Marie Dressler is the most famous casualty during this decade, losing her bout with cancer in 1934. Less stellar but no less talented, Louise Closser Hale died in mysterious circumstances following an operation in 1933. And then there was Alice Brady, so rare a thing as a character actress who died young. As an actress, Brady immortalized the social x-ray on screen half a century before *Bonfire of the Vanities*, when Nan Kempner was still in designer diapers.

On the surface of things, Alice Brady seemed about as unlikely to become a star of the stage as Norma Shearer of the screen. She was not conventionally beautiful, she was nearsighted, and she even had a slight speech impediment.[148] Yet equally like Shearer, her success cannot be put down entirely, or even primarily, to her "family connections." Shearer, of course, was married to MGM crown prince, Irving Thalberg, while Brady was the only daughter of Broadway powerhouse producer, William A. Brady. No, what both Shearer and Brady had in spades was talent, both acting talent and a talent for success, whatever that is. Brady, in addition, had a talent to amuse. It is this quality that would dominate her work in film, despite a few high-profile dramatic roles.

Like Mary Boland and Lucile Watson, Alice Brady was convent-educated. As a compromise between a daughter who wanted to become an actress and a father who wanted her to stay off the stage, Brady was allowed to study grand opera at the Conservatory of Music in Boston under Theodora Irvine.[149] To hear DeWitt Bodeen tell it, the story of how Brady got a start in show business sounds like the plot of *Stage Door*. She landed her first parts with no help from her father and appeared under a stage name. When an observant critic noticed that the actress appearing as "Marie Rose" was none other than William Brady's daughter, she was forced to fess up.[150] The difference from *Stage Door* was that Brady's father was not a rich industrialist like Terry Randall's, but rather an influential Broadway producer, who could smooth the way for his child, if he so should wish. Brady reluctantly gave his strong-willed daughter her Broadway debut role in the musical *The Balkan Princess* (1911) and was pleasantly surprised to discover she had talent.[151] She appeared in several Gilbert and Sullivan operettas on Broadway during the next few years. Her first dramatic role was as Meg in Jessie Bonstelle's highly successful original 1912 production of Marian De Forest's dramatization of *Little Women*.

Among Brady's biggest hits on Broadway were Owen Davis's *Forever After* (1918–19), produced by her father; *Zander the Great* (1923); and *Bride of the Lamb* (1926), which she produced herself at the Greenwich Village Theatre. Yet Brady was to be best remembered for one of her final stage roles. She had been slated to create the part of Nina Leeds in the original, Theatre Guild production of Eugene O'Neill's *Strange Interlude*, but had to withdraw from the part after she suffered a nervous breakdown.[152] It was her second stab at an O'Neill play that carried her to glory, when she created the role of the vengeful Lavinia Mannon in O'Neill's classic trilogy, *Mourning Becomes Electra* (1931–32) with Nazimova as her adulterous mother, Christine. Pioneering theater historian, Arthur Hobson Quinn, writes: "Alice Brady's performance of Lavinia was superb ... [T]hose who were privileged to see her knew they were present at one of the supreme moments in the history of the theatre of the world."[153] The last of her more than thirty plays on Broadway was *Mademoiselle* (1932–33), adopted from the French by and co-starring her stepmother, Grace George, and produced at William Brady's famous Playhouse Theatre. Alice Brady retired from the stage in 1934 after playing the bohemian artist, Marion Froude (Ina Claire's celebrated role), in a Los Angeles production of S.N. Behrman's *Biography*.

Like character actress colleagues Elisabeth Risdon and Isobel Elsom, Brady had a solid background in silent films. In fact, she made twice as many silent films between 1914 and 1923, as she made sound films between 1933 and 1939. Among the best of her silents were *Bought and Paid For* and *The Gilded Cage* (both 1916). Brady's sound film debut in the original filmatization of Rachel Crothers's hit play, *When Ladies Meet* (H. Beaumont, MGM, 1933), was less than spectacular. Brady played Bridgie Drake, a professional gossip, social butterfly, and arbiter of taste, in whose country home in Connecticut most of the film is set. Spring Byington had created the role with great success on Broadway in 1932. In the film version, which starred Myrna Loy, Ann Harding, and Robert Montgomery, Brady's performance is stilted, artificial, and not very funny, yet it set her stage persona as the epitome of the sophisticated, elegant, thoughtless, and scatterbrained upper-class woman.

Among the many dizzy dame roles in Hollywood films of the 1930s, Brady often played the "heavies." A heavy dizzy dame may be something of a contradiction in terms, but there is no doubt that Brady's dames often had more of an edge to them than those of her competitors Billie Burke, Mary Boland, and Spring Byington.

The Gay Divorcée: Alice Brady (1892–1939)

In 1926 Alice Brady was voted the best dressed woman on the New York stage. Her extreme elegance on screen and off is evident in this still photo from *Three Smart Girls* (Universal Pictures, 1936) with her two-time co-star Charles Winninger. In the film, which introduced the soon-to-be singing sensation Deanna Durbin to moviegoers, Brady schemes to pry millionaire Winninger away from his wife and three daughters and into, not her own arms, but those of her dazzlingly blonde daughter, Donna "Precious" Lyons, played with customary aplomb by Binnie Barnes.

I'm thinking primarily of what is surely her best remembered role, the decadent, irresponsible, and thoroughly unpleasant Angelica Bullock in *My Man Godfrey* (G. La Cava, Universal, 1936), but also of roles like Binnie Barnes' grasping and scheming mother in *Three Smart Girls* (H. Koster, Universal, 1936), and Gloria Stuart's imperious, rich, yet miserly mother in the Busby Berkeley musical *Gold Diggers of 1935* (Warner Bros., 1935).

Rather than these hard-hearted, high-maintenance society women, I have a soft spot in my heart for one of Brady's more benign comic creations: Hortense, Ginger Roger's many-times-married, flibbertigibbet aunt in the Astaire-Rogers musical comedy *The Gay Divorcée* (M. Sandrich, RKO, 1934). For one thing, Brady is funnier here than she is in *My Man Godfrey*, and what the film lacks in searching social critique it makes up for in high spirits and deft situation comedy. The excellent cast includes Edward Everett Horton as Brady's former beau and Rogers's divorce lawyer, who gets sung to by a young Betty Grable while only wearing a bathing costume (the song is "Let's Knock Knees"); and Eric Blore, as a dizzy headwaiter at the resort where Rogers goes, Brady in tow, to give her husband cause for divorce. Brady is at her best when turning the world verbally on its head. She genially exclaims to Horton, "Divorces make me so sentimental. Don't you wish it were

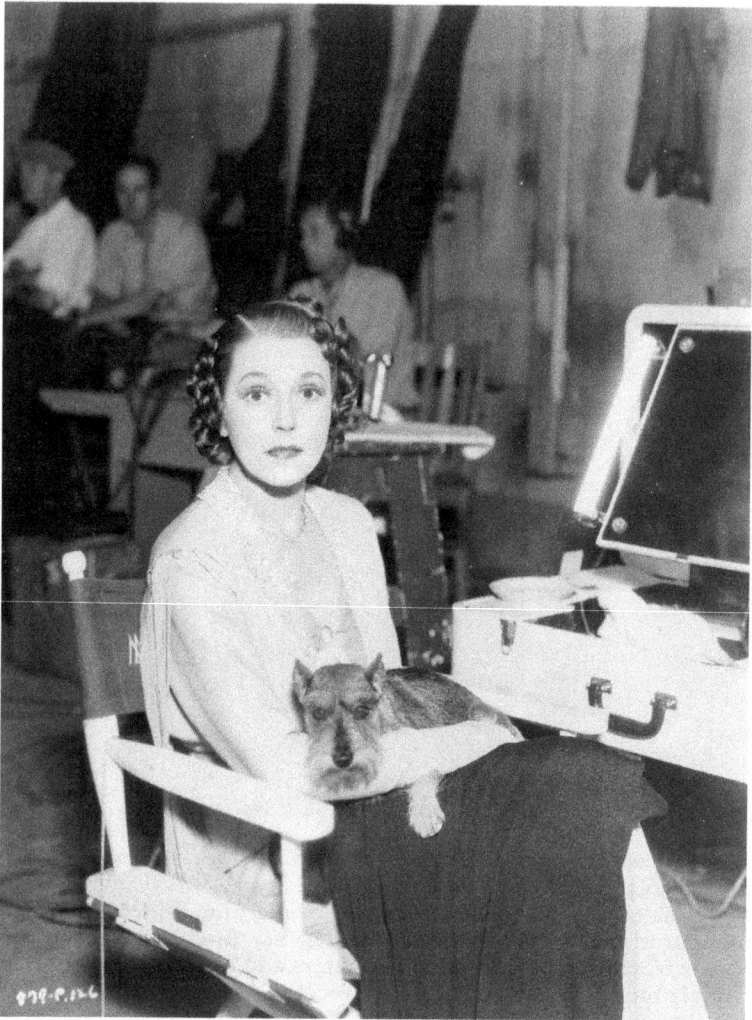

Alice Brady was crazy about dogs and never had fewer than five of them at a time. She was president of the Tailwaggers Club in Los Angeles. Here we see her with one of her canine friends on the set of *One Hundred Men and a Girl* (Universal Pictures, 1937), which was Brady's second film with Deanna Durbin. Both dog and owner have more or less the same slightly quizzical expression.

have a tête-à-tête where Brady admits that, like her philandering husband, she too is getting something on the side. Muriel diets by eating a lot between meals (in one amusing scene she drops her entire lunch tray on the floor during a theatrical matinee) and exclaims characteristically outside a boutique window: "I should adore to be naked with a check book!" All this is vintage Brady decadence, self-centeredness, and moral myopia without too many of the by now familiar Brady mannerisms.

Brady claimed herself that when she first started playing comic roles on stage, she had no idea how to be funny. "I didn't know what on earth to do," she recalled, "I just thought I'd flap my hands about even more than normally and 'talk silly.'"[154] An unsympathetic observer might remark that this is a pretty apt description of her comic technique on film as well. No one flutters her arms around more or speaks more rapidly and nonsensically than Brady. More than most of the dizzy dames, then, there is reason to believe Brady used elements of her own personality in her performance. Her *When Ladies Meet* co-star, Myrna Loy, remembered her almost half a century after her death as "charming, funny, and wonderful."[155] Her screen persona might best be described as a human exclamation point.

Repeating her transition from light comedy

ours?" or responds to Rogers, who claims a man tried to rip her clothes off: "Anyone we know?"

Another interesting Brady role is found in the long-forgotten marital comedy *Call It a Day* (A. Mayo, Warner Bros., 1937), starring Olivia de Havilland as a young girl in love with love. Brady plays Muriel West, the wicked friend of de Havilland's straight-laced mother, Frieda Inescort. In one scene the two women friends to drama in the course of her stage career, Brady moved into so-called serious roles in two films at the end of her film career: In Old Chicago (H. King, Twentieth Century-Fox, 1937) and Young Mr. Lincoln (J. Ford, Twentieth Century-Fox, 1939). She had to fight for the role of Molly O'Leary, the intrepid laundress, matriarch of the O'Leary clan, and owner of the cow that caused the disastrous Chicago fire of 1871, which is the historical context for a not unexciting family saga of Cain-and-Abel brotherly rivalry and working-class Paddy resilience. The producers were afraid of a repeat of what had happened when ZaSu Pitts assayed a straight part in 1930's All Quiet on the Western Front (the audience broke out in peals of laughter and her scenes had to be reshot with Beryl Mercer taking over the role).[156] No such mishap occurred at the previews of In Old Chicago. Very likely most filmgoers did not recognize the customarily chic, worldly, social register–accented Brady in the homely, pious, Irish-broguish woman they saw In Old Chicago, who might well have been played at a slightly later date by the likes of Sara Allgood, Jane Darwell, or Connie Gilchrist. As the prudish and proud Mrs. O'Leary, Brady utters lines like: "We O'Learys are a strange tribe, but there's strength in us and what we set out to do we finish." They certainly finished Chicago...

Brady's performance in In Old Chicago garnered her an Oscar in 1938, when she beat out Claire Trevor (Dead End) and Dame May Whitty (Night Must Fall), among others. (This was her second nomination. The first was for My Man Godfrey the previous year, when the first-ever Academy Award for Best Supporting Actress went to Gale Sondergaard for Anthony Adverse.) Brady was unable to receive her Oscar in person, as she had broken her ankle on the set of Goodbye Broadway (R. McCarey, Universal, 1938).

Brady would be equally unrecognizable in what would prove her final film, Young Mr. Lincoln. This was yet another lower-class mother role for Brady, this time portraying Abigail Clay, devoted mater to prettyboy (and Angela Lansbury's gay first husband), Richard Cromwell, and a passel of other fatherless Clays. Henry Fonda as Abraham Lincoln takes up the defense of two of Brady's sons, who have been falsely accused of murder by the true perpetrator, Ward Bond. The film as a whole is dull as prairie dust. Yet DeWitt Bodeen, author of one of the longest considerations of Brady's career, calls her scene in the witness box "one of the profoundest manifestations of humanity's frightened bafflement before an inexplicable universe ever recorded by the camera."[157] This is maybe somewhat overstated. In my opinion, Brady's dramatic film performances have not aged as well as her comic ones. But then, I may be just a little too gay to be able to accept Brady in a straight part.

Apart from her own long battle with cancer and early death, Brady's brief life was punctuated by tragedy. Her mother, the French dancer Rose Marie René, died in 1896, when little Alice was only four. Brady would be very close to her stepmother, the actress Grace George, and her half-brother, William Brady Jr., but he burned himself to death in 1935 when he fell asleep with a lighted cigarette.[158] Brady's husband, the actor James Lyon Crane, turned out to be an alcoholic.[159] They had starred in three silent films together and married in 1919, only to divorce three years later, after the birth of their only child, Donald. The child was sickly as a result of being born prematurely when Brady was involved in a car accident in which her chauffeur was killed.[160] Hard tried, Brady found comfort in her many pets and in her faith.

Alice Brady died of cancer five days short of her forty-seventh birthday, making her the shortest-lived among the character actresses profiled in this book. When William Brady realized the gravity of his daughter's condition, he had her brought from California to the LeRoy Sanatorium in New York. She died there alone late Saturday night, October 28, 1939, her father and stepmother arriving just a few minutes after she had passed from life. Alice Brady was buried in a private ceremony at Sleepy Hollow Cemetery, North Tarrytown (now re-named Sleepy Hollow), New York.[161]

The Professional Tweetybird
BILLIE BURKE (1884–1970)

Billie Burke is the only actress in this volume who lived to see herself and her life portrayed in a major Hollywood film.[162] The film was *The Great Ziegfeld* and the year 1936. William Powell played the famous showman of the title; his frequent co-star, Myrna Loy, played Burke; and Luise Rainer won her second Oscar playing Ziegfeld's first wife, Anna Held. Burke, on the other hand, won the gratitude of MGM for her collaboration and a standard contract with the prestigious studio where she had already made four films, starting with *Dinner at Eight* in 1933.[163] Myrna Loy recalled that she had felt self-conscious about playing Burke, who was still "very much alive": "Ziegfeld and Anna Held were gone, but here was Billie, bless her heart, trotting around Hollywood playing all kinds of parts." Yet Burke couldn't have been more pleased by it all, by Loy's account. She insisted on having their picture taken together and kept bringing friends on the set to meet Loy.[164] Rosalind Russell, who starred with Burke in *Craig's Wife* the same year, recalled in her memoirs that when Burke came on the lot "great trumpets sounded": "First you'd see an awful lot of dogs on leashes, and then the maid, and then the makeup man, and then some guys carrying a big tray with a potty on it. A potty all covered in satin, and monogrammed; that impressed the hell out of me.... Billie would follow in the wake of this entourage."[165]

Burke was an actress for the greater part of her long life; first on stage on both sides of the Atlantic, and then from 1932 on, mainly in the movies. Her career can be divided into several clear stages: Her early training and years on the English stage between the late 1890s and her permanent removal to the United States in 1907; her period as a Broadway star and one of producer Charles Frohman's leading ladies at the Empire Theatre from her debut there on August 31, 1907 with legendary leading man John Drew until her marriage to Florenz Ziegfeld in 1914; her continued stage and new silent film career (1916–21), under her husband's management until his death in 1932; and finally, her long and productive sound film career until her retirement in 1960.

The importance of Burke's contribution to the films of Hollywood's Golden Age has never been adequately assessed. On her death in 1970, her front page *New York Times* obituary did not mention her sound film career at all.[166] It is possible that she herself did not realize the significance of her film work within the arc of her own career and within American film history. At any rate, she gives her movies scant attention in her 1949 autobiography and regrets that she did not return to Broadway after Ziegfeld's death.[167] This seems remarkable considering the steady and remunerative work she found in Hollywood for the better part of two decades and the many wonderful parts she was given at most of Hollywood's major studios, including first and foremost "The Studio of the Stars," MGM: "[W]ith Metro geared to turning out gilt-edged society dramas and comedies, a Billie Burke was an invaluable piece of equipment."[168]

Billie Burke was more than an actress, she was a phenomenon. She was Society, she was celebrity, she was fantasy. She was yet another testament to the power of mind over matter; a seemingly hyperfeminine, powerless, helpless woman, who nevertheless managed to make her own living for most of her adult life. Maybe because of this hyperfemininity and unworldliness, she also managed to hook one of the most eligible bachelors in America (and the most infamous Casanovas) and stay married to him for eighteen years. She once described herself as a "clinging vine" and added: "I'm not an enterprising woman. I *enjoy* clinging."[169] Yet, after Ziegfeld's death in bankruptcy, his widow kept her head held high, paying off his considerable debts and supporting herself, if not entirely in

The Professional Tweetybird: Billie Burke (1884-1970)

the style to which she'd grown accustomed, at least in style. For Billie Burke was the essence of style.

The woman who became Billie Burke was born Mary William Ethelbert Appleton Burke in Washington, DC, on August 7, 1884. She would claim to have been born in 1886, admit to 1885, but in fact the year *was* 1884, when her father, the famous singing clown Billy Burke, was on tour in the United States.[170] Burke's mother was the former Blanche Beatty Hodkinson, a New Orleans widow with four children from her first marriage. It was Mrs. Burke who steered her daughter towards the stage.[171]

Apart from her parents, Burke's life and career would be shaped by the two legendary producers, Charles Frohman and Florenz Ziegfeld, and by her friend and sometime director, George Cukor. It was Burke's marriage to Ziegfeld that caused a breach with Frohman, who preferred his leading ladies to be unwed and out of the public eye. The breach was still not healed when Frohman went down on the *Lusitania* in 1915.[172] The Ziegfelds lived in great style at their upstate New York estate Burkely Crest, where they raised their only child, Patricia, who was born in 1916. Ziegfeld was hard hit by the stock market crash of 1929; what Burke referred to characteristically as "the Wall Street unpleasantness."[173] In dire economic straights, the family sought refuge in California in the early 1930s, where there was in Burke's words "a wonderful climate for geraniums and actresses."[174] George Cukor was instrumental in securing Burke her first and well-paid film role in *A Bill of Divorcement* and she was filming when her husband died on July 22, 1932. After recouping for two weeks at her friend Will Rogers's ranch, the trooper Burke returned to work. She would later regret not remarrying and was destined to remain a widow for thirty-eight years.[175]

More than any other actress, Billie Burke created and defined a type of female character predominant in the film comedies of the 1930s and known as the "dizzy dame." The dizzy dame was a stunning contrast to most parts for older women in Hollywood at this time. In an era of self-sacrificing mothers, devoted grandmothers, retiring spinsters, and faithful domestics, the dizzy dame was one of the few types of roles for older women where they might put themselves front and center and demand not just the attention, but the obedience both of men and of other women. In contrast to the dowager or matriarch (the other main category of empowered women in 1930s Hollywood movies), the dizzy dame or flibbertigibbet ruled over others not through fear,

This undated photograph of Billie Burke is probably from the mid-1930s. A star on Broadway in the teens and twenties, Mrs. Florenz Ziegfeld Jr. from 1914, Burke was known for her beauty, style, and panache. This portrait makes it clear why.

financial coercion, or brute force, but through a kind of charming self-centeredness, a moral obtuseness, and an altogether stylish eccentricity that could not fail to have its effect. In the screwball comedies and social satires of the 1930s, dizzy dames were positively Wildean in their inversion of all known value systems. Daily they recreated the world in their own image and insisted that in a conflict between appearances and reality, reality would have to give way.

We need seek no further for corroboration of the delightful egocentricity of the dizzy dame than Burke's first entry in this category: Millicent Jordan in *Dinner at Eight* (G. Cukor, 1933). An ensemble film with a cast the likes of which even MGM had seldom seen, it places Burke right at the center of the action as the boundlessly self-centered New York hostess, Mrs. Oliver Jordan. It is her dinner that is taking placing at eight. It is her dinner and her home that all the various plots and players in the evolving drama are converging on. And she herself has no doubt that her myriad problems with servants who have been stabbed or arrested, with guests of honor who cancel at the last moment, with finding a spare man for Carlotta Vance, or replacing the ruined aspic at the twelfth hour are of more earth-shattering significance than anything her husband, daughter, in-laws, or friends could be going through. This is brilliantly expressed by Burke in a major monologue towards the end of the film, which might be seen as the manifesto of all dizzy dames. Burke is directing her diatribe in an increasingly hysterical and distinctively fluttery voice to her daughter, Paula (Madge Evans), who is torn between her young, eminently suitable fiancé and an older, increasingly disreputable lover (John Barrymore); and to her husband, Oliver (Lionel Barrymore), who is facing the imminent demise of the family's business and his own certain death from heart disease. Yet Burke concludes her impromptu speech with the words: "*I'm* the one who ought to be in bed. *I'm* the one who's in trouble. You don't even know what trouble *is*, either of you." She is at least partially relieved of her illusions by the end of the film and suitably chastened, but her egotism sure is fun while it lasts. In many of her films, this shining of a little light of self-awareness and contrition into the darkest corners of her dizzy mind thankfully never occurs.

Donald Spoto writes of Burke: "In almost eighty movies, she was a pixie with a canny charm. Her bubbly, breathless tremolo and her fluttery delicacy were endearing rather than exasperating. There really was no one like her."[176] Despite portraying dozens of dizzy dames and the competition of such eminent comediennes as Mary Boland and Spring Byington, Burke brought a unique style, quality, and freshness to most all of her excursions into this genre. Let us remind ourselves of some of the highlights of this important part of her film repertoire. They are *Forsaking All Others* (1934), *Doubting Thomas* (1935), *Merrily We Live* (1938), *The Wizard of Oz* (1939), and *They All Kissed the Bride* (1942).

Burke's second film for MGM, *Forsaking All Others* (W.S. Van Dyke, 1934), was based on a recent Broadway play that had starred Tallulah Bankhead. Joan Crawford took over the lead role of the "Runaway Bride," Mary Clay, in the film version, while Burke played her addlebrained Aunt Paula, a role created in New York by Cora Witherspoon. Burke's costumes merit separate attention here, as she appears at Crawford's wedding in an explosion of bows, flounces, and tulle, only to materialize later in the film in rugged flannel in the log cabin sequence. The gowns were by MGM's legendary, Adrian, who designed costumes for eight of Burke's films and who also designed a dining room table and chairs for her first Hollywood home.[177]

Doubting Thomas was a very funny film based on a play by George Kelly called *The Torch Bearers* about everything that can possibly go wrong when a middle-aged, middle-class matron gets involved in amateur theatricals. The play had been a hit on Broadway back in 1922 with Mary Boland and Alison Skipworth in the lead. Skipworth reprised her signature role as the pompous amateur director Mrs. Pampinelli in Fox Films' 1935 filmatization, directed by David Butler, and Burke took over Boland's role as Paula. In her performance in the play within the play, Burke gives an amusing imitation of Mae West. The "Doubting Thomas" of the title

Billie Burke was nominated for an Oscar for her portrayal of the fluttery philanthropist, Emily Kilbourne, in the classic screwball comedy *Merrily We Live* (Metro-Goldwyn-Mayer, 1938), in which Clarence Kolb played her husband, Bonita Granville and Constance Bennett her daughters, and Tom Brown her son. Here we see the Kilbourne clan at breakfast in their palatial Long Island home after all the silverware has been stolen.

was Burke's film husband, a no-nonsense sausage factory owner played by Will Rogers. As Thomas Brown, Rogers is locked in a battle of wills with Mrs. Pampinelli over his wife's and, indeed, his marriage's future. Rogers died in a plane crash only a month after the film was released.

Merrily We Live (N.Z. McLeod, 1938) is very much the Hal Roach Studios' somewhat lighter, Long Island version of Universal's classic screwball comedy, *My Man Godfrey* (1936). Here Brian Aherne plays the gentleman tramp and Billie Burke the ditzy, reformist society woman, Emily Kilbourne, a more benevolent counterpart of Alice Brady's acidulous airhead, Angelica Bullock. Burke thinks she is going to reform Aherne by making him her chauffeur. Both Brady and Burke were Oscar-nominated for their efforts, though neither won. It was Burke's only nomination and she lost the Oscar to Fay Bainter for *Jezebel*. Burke has a star on the Walk of Fame at 6617 Hollywood Boulevard.

What is Glinda the Good Witch of the North, but the dizziest dame of them all? Burke was all of fifty-five years old when she created this classic portrayal, but who could tell? She would write twenty-one years later that she knew "darn well" that she didn't look her age and that she had been working at it for years.[178] She began every morning by standing on her head, turning somersaults, and taking a cold shower. In 1941, she became a vegetarian.[179] Burke claimed that Glinda was her favorite role. "I never played such a being on stage," she said, "but this role is as close as I have come in motion pictures to the kind of parts I did in the theater."[180] Apparently there was no serious competition for the role of Dorothy's good fairy in *The Wizard of Oz* (V. Fleming, 1939). According to film historian Aljean Harmetz, Burke was the clear favorite ahead of other MGM contract players like Fanny Brice, Constance Collier, Gracie Fields, Una Merkel, Edna May Oliver, and Cora Witherspoon. She certainly had a fairer face than these many classic battle-axes.[181] Burke was paid $766.67 per week for her most famous role,[182] which was quite a bit down from the salary of $2,500 per week which Cukor has secured for her seven years earlier when she first started in movies.[183] Then she was a fresh face with the glamour of Broadway still clinging to her and not yet a widow.

In *They All Kissed the Bride* (A. Hall, Columbia, 1942), Burke played Mrs. Drew, the snooty, upper-class mother of career woman Joan Crawford. She is instrumental in teaching her daughter how to become a "true woman" and win her man, Melvyn Douglas, in what must be one of the most sexist films produced in the 1940s. The tagline says it all: "There's Never Anything Wrong With a Woman That a Man's Lips Won't Cure!" In this connection, it is maybe worth asking how much of Burke's own personality and attitudes went into her creation of the classic Hollywood dizzy dame in general and Mrs. Drew in particular. She admitted herself that "I am not always saner than I seem" and added that she was prone to "*always* chatter."[184]

Burke's second book is particularly revealing of some of her attitudes, as she blithely jumps feet first into the "woman question." In

This delightful still is from *Topper Returns* (United Artists, 1941), the last of the three "Topper" films in which Billie Burke played Mrs. Clara Topper. Her put-upon husband and the Topper of the title was Burke's frequent screen partner, Roland Young. With Burke in this photograph are Patsy Kelly as her maid and Eddie "Rochester" Anderson as her fur-clad chauffeur.

With Powder on My Nose (1960), a kind of beauty-guide-cum-autobiography published on the brink of second wave feminism, Burke emerges as a champion of "Femininity" with a capital F, as if Mrs. Drew had written the book herself. Here we are told that "every woman should consider herself 'on' wherever she is—in a steaming kitchen, in a bedroom, or behind the footlights"; "She should at all times put her best foot forward. That is, if her foot is her best feature. If not, put something else forward." Burke wants "women to be women and accept their God-given role." If this were not enough, women are admonished, "You have to get up early to make sure you look kissable." Women mustn't "dare, ever, to get caught in the morning with messy hair or with last night's stale rouge on your mouth." One must "Always look accessible, morning, noon, and night," Burke concludes.[185] This is heady stuff indeed!

In *Father of the Bride* (V. Minnelli, MGM, 1950) and *Father's Little Dividend* (V. Minnelli, MGM, 1951), Burke delivered a version of her by-now standard hoity-toity, fluttery, fluty-voiced matron as Doris Dunstan, mother-in-law of the bride, Elizabeth Taylor, and grandmother of the "little dividend." With *Small Town Girl* (L. Kardos, 1953), these were the last three of Burke's twenty-two films at MGM. By this time, her film roles had become few and far between. She would not make another film until 1959. Returning to the stage after two short-running Broadway plays in 1943 and 1944, Burke was nearly burned to death in the Shubert Theatre fire in Washington, DC on January 28, 1959. She was starring with Eva le Gallienne and Una Merkel in *Listen to the Mocking Bird*. The show had to close.[186]

My focus on Burke's portrayal of the dizzy dame is not meant to suggest that she could not also portray other kinds of women, be it in comedies or dramas. Burke also specialized in straight-laced, uptight society women and had a sideline in neurotic or neglectful mothers. Notable entries in the former category are to be found in the films *Christopher Strong* (1933), *Becky Sharp* (1935), *The Bride Wore Red* (1937), and the three "Topper" films (1937–41). In *Christopher Strong*, Katharine Hepburn starred as pioneering aviatrix Lady Cynthia Darrington and Burke was the wronged, weepy-eyed wife of Hepburn's lover, played by that notorious old soak, Colin Clive. Burke makes her first entrance in a rabbit-skin robe and it's basically downhill from there, as she gives an over-the-top performance as a pious, sniveling wet blanket with a quavering little old lady voice. Thankfully, she would soon find her feet in her third film, *Dinner at Eight* (1933). Her parts in *Becky Sharp* (R. Mamoulian, RKO, 1935) and *The Bride Wore Red* (D. Arzner, MGM, 1937) were, like her Lady Elaine Strong in *Christopher Strong*, titled ladies who try to create trouble for the heroine, Miriam Hopkins and Joan Crawford respectively. As the snooty, domineering Mrs. Clara Topper in *Topper* (N.Z. McLeod, Hal Roach, 1937), *Topper Takes a Trip* (N.Z. McLeod, Hal Roach, 1939), and *Topper Returns* (R. Del Ruth, Hal Roach, 1941), Burke embarked on her most enduring comic collaboration, with Roland Young, who played her henpecked husband and the titular anti-hero. They had first acted together in the Broadway play *The Rescuing Angel* twenty years before. They made seven films together between 1937 and 1942, which in addition to the Topper films included *The Young in Heart* (R. Wallace, Selznick Int., 1938), *Dulcy* (S.S. Simon, MGM, 1940), *Irene* (H. Wilcox, 1940), and *They All Kissed the Bride* (1942). Their pairing was not unlike that of fellow dizzy dame Mary Boland and Charles Ruggles.

Among Burke's bad mothers, we find Mrs. Helen Crawford Radcliff in *Finishing School* (G. Nichols Jr., Wanda Tuchock, RKO, 1934) and Lavinia Timberlake in *In This Our Life* (J. Huston, Warner Bros., 1942). Burke is simply outrageous as Frances Dee's vain, vulgar, and stupid Mrs. Skeffington–like mother in the former film about the unfinished aspect of finishing school life. She received top billing despite her relatively few scenes in what was her fifth and last film for RKO in the early 1930s. Her scenes are all memorable, though, as she tries to impress hyper-genteel school principal and former classmate, Miss Van Alstyne (Beulah Bondi), or rattles on about the challenges of maintaining her immaculate appearance to her hard tried and apathetic maid, Evelyn (Theresa Harris). In *In This Our Life*, the second of her four films for Warner Bros., she was the neurotic and invalid wife of milksop Frank Craven, mother of dastardly Bette Davis and saintly Olivia de Havilland, and sister of classic curmudgeon and business tycoon Charles Coburn. She tries to give her daughter an alibi when Davis kills a child in a hit-and-run car accident and puts the blame on the son of the family's African American cook.

It is also worth remembering that Burke got her start in the movies in a dramatic role, playing a mature, modern woman confronting the challenges of modern life. What is an upper middle-class wife and mother to do when her husband has been around the bend for fifteen years and she has fallen in love with someone else? *A Bill of Divorcement* (RKO, 1932) was based on a hit Broadway play starring Katharine Cornell, with Janet Beecher in Burke's role as Meg Fairfield. The film version reunited director George Cukor with two of his friends from his days running the Cukor-Kondolf Stock Company in Rochester, New York: Burke and Elizabeth Patterson as Aunt Hester Fairfield. Katharine Hepburn made her movie debut as the daughter of the house, Sydney Fairfield.[187] For Burke, it was not an auspicious sound film debut. We don't have her reaction on seeing herself for the first time in middle-age on the big screen, but we may well imagine she might have been as appalled as was another former stage beauty and Burke's near contemporary, Gladys Cooper, when eight years later she viewed herself in her first Hollywood film, *Rebecca*. Apart from the fact that Burke looks her age (forty-eight) and plays her first scene draped in something closely resembling a fringed tablecloth, she has yet to adjust herself to the demands of the new medium and has a tendency to overact. Mordaunt Hall of the *New York Times*, though, found "Miss Burke as Margaret most gratifying. She has a pleasing enunciation and the ability to express herself in a serious and difficult role."[188]

Burke played unmarried women with their own romantic interests in the films *Only Yesterday*, *Craig's Wife*, and *The Captain Is a Lady*. Though far from being one of her more popular or familiar films, *Only Yesterday* (J.M. Stahl, 1933), her fourth film and her first of five for Universal, gave Burke one of the most intriguing roles of her career. The film has a flashback structure and features young lovers thwarted by war, John Boles and film debutante Margaret Sullavan (not unlike the 1946 film *To Each His Own* for which Olivia de Havilland won an Oscar for Best Actress). What we nowadays would call a one-night stand results in pregnancy for Sullavan, whose despairing Southern mother, Jane Darwell, sends her to her sister (and Sullavan's aunt) in New York. The film is remarkable for its frank portrayal of homosexuality (Franklin Pangborn finally gets a boyfriend), pre-marital sex, unwed mothers, and open marriages, though naturally it is pre–Code, having premiered on November 1, 1933. Fourth billed as Sullavan's "terribly broadminded" aunt, Julia Warren, Burke is a former suffragette, an unmarried and childless career woman with a younger lover (Reginald Denny in one of his seven films with Burke), and a thoroughly liberated, modern woman. She welcomes her wayward niece with open arms and puts her to work in her dress shop. We even get treated to Burke's somewhat flat rendition of "Shine On Harvest Moon" to her boyfriend's accompaniment. *Only Yesterday* was remade as *Letter from an Unknown Woman* in 1948 and starred Joan Fontaine and Louis Jourdan.

In *Craig's Wife* (Columbia, 1936), the second film version of George Kelly's hit play, starring Rosalind Russell as the controlling, obsessive housewife, Harriet Craig, Burke played Mrs. Frazier, Mrs. Craig's feminine and beguiling counterpart next door with a propensity for gardening. Russell's jealousy is supposedly revealed as absurd when Burke turns out to be a grandmother (albeit a well preserved one), though why that would rule her out as a potential rival for John Boles's affections is hard for a modern viewer to fathom. The film was directed by Burke's close friend and three-time director, Dorothy Arzner. Finally, in the character actress extravaganza *The Captain Is a Lady* (R.B. Sinclair, MGM, 1940), Burke plays Blossy Stort, another youthful pensioner and the unlikely resident of an old age home with the more suitably aged Cecil Cunningham, Beulah Bondi, Helen Broderick, cook Marjorie Main, and directress Helen Westley. In the film, Burke's paramour of twenty years standing is a toupee-challenged fishmonger portrayed by Clem Bevans. Needless to say, this is one of Burke's most uncharacteristically down-to-earth roles.

Yet, her several types of roles aside, Billie Burke remained an ace dizzy dame until the end of her career. Her last two roles, in *The Young Philadelphians* (V. Sherman, Warner Bros., 1959) and *Sergeant Rutledge* (J. Ford, Warner Bros., 1960), were both amusing and substantial. In the first mentioned film, Burke plays Mrs. J. Arthur Allen, the slightly eccentric but not unsympathetic, multi-millionaire owner of the Allen Oil Co., who gets Paul Newman started on his corporate law career when she transfers her business from her old law firm to his. This mutually beneficial alliance begins with her desire to provide for her Chihuahua Carlos. The Chihuahua and, one assumes, Burke's millions are to go to her niece, Barbara Rush, who also happens to be Newman's long lost love.

Burke's Mrs. Cordelia Fosgate in *Sergeant Rutledge* is the charmingly unfocused and malapropos wife of the fortress commander, Colonel Otis Fosgate (Willis Bouchey), and a witness at the murder trial of the African American First Sergeant Braxton Rutledge (Woody Strode), where her husband is the presiding judge. From the moment of her entry into the courtroom at the head of a party of ladies that she's brought as chaperones due to the presence of "all these men," seventy-six-year-old Burke captivates us, insisting that "I don't swear on anything but the King James version of the Bible." It is an end to a fine film career that many an actress might have envied her.

Sadly, the last decade of Burke's life was not so blessed. She had been plagued by financial difficulties since the late 1940s. Old friends like George Cukor increasingly had to come to her aid.[189] She was never reconciled to the natural aging process, remaining marvelously vain till the end and refusing to allow even her own family to refer to her as a great-grandmother.[190] Burke lived next door to her married daughter in Brentwood, until she was moved to an old age home in the San Fernando Valley.[191] She was confined to her bed during the final years of her life.[192] Billie Burke Ziegfeld died on May 14, 1970, at the age of eighty-five. She was laid to rest next to her husband in Kensico Cemetery, Westchester County, New York.

Mother for Metro
SPRING BYINGTON (1886–1971)

In the late thirties and early forties, Spring Byington was the most powerful symbol of middle-class motherhood at the most powerful studio in America. Maybe powerful is the wrong word for the kind of hyperfeminine wives and mothers she commonly portrayed, yet they say the hand that rocks the cradle rules the world. Byington was dubbed "the Queen of Homey Matriarchs" and comforted, advised, and admonished her way through dozens of movies between 1933 and 1960.

Spring Byington was born in Colorado Springs, Colorado, on October 17, 1886. Both her parents came from Port Hope in Ontario, Canada. Her father, the educator Edwin Lee Byington, died when she was five. Her widowed mother, Helene, became a doctor, but passed away not long after Byington went on stage for the first time at age fourteen with the Elitch Garden Stock Company in Denver. At age eighteen, she married the stage manager of her touring company, Roy Carey Chandler, and the couple spent the four years of their married life in Buenos Aires, Argentina, where they had two daughters, Lois Irene and Phyllis Helene.[193] After the couple's divorce, Byington returned to New York and the stage, making her Broadway debut in 1924 supporting Roland Young in a play called *Beggar on Horseback*. Byington took part in some twenty Broadway productions, including a hit as a Louella Parsons–like Hollywood gossip columnist in *Once in a Lifetime* (1930), before removing to California and abandoning the stage for good in 1934.

Byington's film career started with an adaptation of a nineteenth-century classic, Louisa May Alcott's *Little Women* (RKO, 1933). This was the third time the novel was filmed (the first time with sound) and the cast was impressive, including Katharine Hepburn as Jo March (fresh from her Oscar-winning role in *Morning Glory*); Paul Lukas as her scholarly paramour, Professor Bhaer; and star character actress Edna May Oliver in a definitive interpretation of Aunt March. Byington landed the role of the brood hen, Marmee March. According to the film's director, George Cukor, it was not an auspicious beginning. Forty years after the film's premiere, he stated in an interview with Gavin Lambert that he couldn't remember why he had cast her, as she wasn't at all like Alcott's description of Mrs. March.[194] In Cukor's opinion she was "too one-dimensional" and played at loving her children in the wrong way.[195] By the time he voiced this opinion, Byington had been three years in the grave. Seeing the film today, it is easy to agree with her three-time director (*The Adventures of Tom Sawyer, I'll Be Seeing You*). Byington's Marmee has none of the whimsy that would later become her trademark. In fact, she is a contender for biggest killjoy in film history with the strained and anxious expression of one suffering from permanent indigestion.

Though she was freelance throughout her near thirty-year film career and worked for all the major studios, Byington would be most closely associated with Fox and Metro-Goldwyn-Mayer. Altogether she would make more than half her total of ninety-seven movies for these two studios. Among her most important films for MGM are *Ah, Wilderness!* (1935), *When Ladies Meet* (1941), *The War Against Mrs. Hadley* (1942), and *Presenting Lily Mars* (1943), though arguably she scored bigger hits at other studios, such as Universal and Columbia.

Byington's first part at Metro was a small one as Franchot Tone's anxious mother at the beginning of *Mutiny on the Bounty* (the Charles Laughton–Clark Gable version; Frank Lloyd, 1935). The same year she played in a more recent classic, Eugene O'Neill's *Ah, Wilderness!* (C. Brown, MGM). Here she was married to idealistic newspaper editor, Lionel Barrymore, sister to spinster Aline MacMahon, sister-in-law to inebriate Wallace Beery, and mother to Frank Albertson, Eric Linden, Mickey Rooney, and Bonita Granville. In this film Byington fortified her position with the public as a figure of sweetness and light, an angel in the house, yet one that could wield the silken cord when necessary. When she discovers her would-be radical son reading *The Picture of Dorian Gray*, for example, we are told that Oscar Wilde was an "awful man they put in jail." MGM would remake the film thirteen years later as the musical *Summer Holiday* with Selena Royle in Byington's part.

Two of her sons in *Ah, Wilderness!*, Eric Linden and Mickey Rooney, also played her sons in *A Family Affair* (G.B. Seitz, 1937), the first entry in what would become the "Andy Hardy" series at MGM. When it was decided to make more Andy Hardy films, Lionel Barrymore was replaced as Mr. Hardy by Lewis Stone and Byington as Mrs. Hardy by Fay Holden. Part of the reason for the latter change was surely that Byington was already the maternal focal point of a B-movie series at a rival studio, the "Jones Family" series at Twentieth Century–Fox. The first of this series was *Educating Father* (J. Tingling, 1936) and the last was *On Their Own* (O. Brower, 1940), making up seventeen out of the twenty-seven films Byington made at Fox.

Some of her more familiar films at Fox were *The Story of Alexander Graham Bell*, *The Blue Bird*, and *Heaven Can Wait*. Her roles in *Alexander Graham Bell* (I. Cummings, 1939) and *Heaven Can Wait* (E. Lubitsch, 1943) were typical run-of-the-mill costume drama fare in which she lent staunch and sympathetic support to her potential son-in-law, Alexander Graham Bell, in the first case and to her wayward son, Henry Van Cleve, in the latter. As it happened, both roles were played by Don Ameche, a long-term contractee at Fox making two of his finer film efforts. Byington could also be palsy-walsy with her screen daughters. In her second Frank Capra film, *Meet John Doe* (1941), for example, she lent support to her independent, journalist daughter, Barbara Stanwyck, in the latter's quest to make a folk hero of Gary Cooper.

The Blue Bird (W. Lang, 1940) is a more interesting case, as it gives us a rare example of a character actress playing a role *younger* than her true years. When she played Shirley Temple's mother for the first of two times, Byington was all of fifty-six years old and, truth to tell, she does seem a mite long in the tooth to be the mama of a twelve-year-old. Maybe there is some foundation to the story that Byington claimed to have been born in 1893.[196] Forty-seven would have been closer to the mark for playing Maeterlinck's Mama Tyl.

Byington's biggest screen success was in a film for Columbia, playing Penny Sycamore, the absent-minded, whimsical, artistic mother of Jean Arthur, potential mother-in-law of James Stewart, wife of Samuel S. Hinds, and daughter of Lionel Barrymore in Frank Capra's classic *You Can't Take It with You* (1938). As the story goes, Capra originally wanted Byington's chief rival, Fay Bainter, but she was otherwise engaged (probably with *Mother Carey's Chickens* or *The Shining Hour*). The part went to Byington ("Bainter and water," some would say), who had already done *Love Me Forever* (V. Schertzinger, 1935) and *Theodora Goes Wild* (R. Boleslawski,

In *The Devil and Miss Jones* (RKO, 1941), department store boss Charles Coburn infiltrates his own shoe department to find out what is afoot, so to speak. There he meets fellow workers Spring Byington and Jean Arthur.

1936) for boss Harry Cohn at Columbia. Her part in the latter film was particularly choice and her first important village gossip role. As Rebecca Perry, the president of the Lynnwood Literary Society, Byington leads the female forces against progress in general and Theodora Lynn (Irene Dunne) in particular, when it is revealed that she is the shocking romantic novelist Caroline Adams.

Another of Byington's high-profile films of the '30s was *Dodsworth* (W. Wyler, 1936) for Sam Goldwyn's independent production company. Here she played Matey Pearson, the sympathetic wife of Walter Huston's oldest friend, whom he asks for marital advice when his own wife, devastatingly well played by Ruth Chatterton, refuses to return from her dalliance in Europe.

All this is not to suggest that Byington was constitutionally incapable of playing unsympathetic or downright evil women. Far from it. Despite claiming in an interview that "Lady Macbeth and I aren't friends,"[197] she did a convincing job as Robert Young's cruel, unthinking mother in *The Enchanted Cottage* (J. Cromwell, RKO, 1945) and had a sideline in snooty gossip columnists, bird-brained society women, and sharp-tongued tattletales as a carryover from her stage career.

Byington had created the role of the inquisitive and malapropos society woman and gossip Bridgie Drake in the Broadway production of Rachel Crothers's hit play *When Ladies Meet* in 1932–33, but the role had gone to Alice Brady in the original film from 1933. When MGM decided to remake the film and star Joan Crawford, Greer Garson, Robert Taylor, and Herbert Marshall, Byington finally had the chance to show what she could do with the part on film. She is billed fifth, but steals every scene she is in. With a voice of pure saccharine, she is always saying the wrong thing, as when she introduces her decorator-lover, Walter Del Canto (Rafael Storm), to Taylor with the words: "Walter is my decorator. He is doing me over. I mean, he's doing over my place in the country." The costumes and hair deserve separate mention. Crawford starts with a sheet on her head courtesy of Adrian and continues in a poodle cut courtesy of Sydney Guilaroff. Garson is in her most irritating palsy-walsy, "hail, fellow, well met" mode and is dressed in something that looks like a flag. George Cukor was quite right when he noted that fashion-wise the early forties was "a tacky period."[198]

Byington's roles in *Roxie Hart* (W.A. Wellman, Twentieth Century–Fox, 1942) and *The War Against Mrs. Hadley* (H.S. Bucquet, MGM, 1942) were variations on the same theme. In the former she was Mary Sunshine, a sympathetic, ditsy newspaper feature writer who comes to interview Ginger Rogers in prison. In the latter, she was Cecilia Talbot, Fay Bainter's deliciously malapropos friend, who can always be counted on to say the wrong thing and has all her information from her elevator boy (he turns out to be a septuagenarian). *Dragonwyck* (J.L. Mankiewicz, Twentieth Century–Fox, 1946) was a departure, though, in the role of Magda, the eerie housekeeper at Dragonwyck. She lets heroine and mistress of the estate, Gene Tierney, in on some of the family secrets in what is a kind of American, Upper Hudson, Dutch patroon version of *Jane Eyre*. Byington prophecies that Tierney will bitterly regret coming to Dragonwyck.

Byington could also do a good job with mothers and matriarchs further up the social scale than her customary comfortable, middle-class matrons. Two good examples from opposite ends of her career are *The Charge of the Light Brigade* (M. Curtiz, Warner Bros., 1936) and *Please Believe Me* (N. Taurog, MGM, 1950). In the former film, she plays an Anglo-Indian viceroy's wife, Lady Octavia Warrenton. Her regimented husband (played by Nigel Bruce) is also her child this time and sighs resignedly that "Life with you is just one pill after another!" In *Please Believe Me*, Byington makes the most of a short scene as Mrs. Milwright, a snobbish, matchmaking dowager seated at the captain's table with her daughter and Deborah Kerr on the latter's first transatlantic crossing.

One might claim the last major film of Byington's maternal phase was *Presenting Lily Mars* (N. Taurog, MGM, 1943). Here she played a dithery, daffy mother of five not unlike Penelope Sycamore, though widowed this time and without Penelope's artistic pretensions. Judy

Garland plays Byington's star-struck daughter, who will do anything to get on the stage with or without the help of the successful playwright portrayed by Van Heflin. Byington would be reunited with Garland six years later in one of her more nostalgic MGM musicals, *In the Good Old Summertime* (R.Z. Leonard, Buster Keaton, MGM, 1949). Here Byington played a spinster shop assistant in S.Z. "Cuddles" Sakall's music shop with sinister marital designs on her boss. Her goiter looks as if it is being so painfully pressed between her chinbone and her high, starched turn-of-the century collar, that it is a wonder she can act at all.

After *Lily Mars*, Byington still had eighteen films yet to make at MGM, but henceforward she would face stiff competition in playing what Mary Astor called "mothers for Metro." Astor herself was one competitor, as she turned film mother and character actress with *Meet Me in St. Louis* in 1944 and played mothers for Metro and elsewhere for the next twenty years. Most significantly in this connection, Astor (1906–87) nabbed the part of Marmee March in the 1949 remake of *Little Women*, starring June Allyson and Peter Lawford, with Elizabeth Taylor, Lucile Watson, Rossano Brazzi, Margaret O'Brien, C. Aubrey Smith, and Janet Leigh in supporting roles.

From the time she had taken over the role of Mickey Rooney's mother after the first film in the "Andy Hardy" series, Fay Holden (1893–1973) acted as a sort of B-movie Byington at MGM. Holden, though, would never threaten Byington's preeminence at the studio the way Fay Bainter would, starting with *Young Tom Edison* in 1940. Byington's most important rival in the middle-class mother category, and arguably a finer and more versatile actress than her, Bainter (1891–1968) had entered movies in 1934 after a prominent stage career. In 1938, she had scored major hits in *Jezebel* and *White Banners*, being nominated both for a Leading Actress and Supporting Actress Oscar the same year. She won for *Jezebel*, beating Byington, who had been nominated for the first and only time for *You Can't Take It with You*.

Starting in the mid–1940s, Byington also had to compete for MGM's maternal roles with the twenty-years-younger Selena Royle (1904–83), Rosemary DeCamp (1910–2001),[199] and to a certain extent, Agnes Moorehead (1900–74). DeCamp would emerge as the major symbol of American motherhood in the late 1940s and '50s.

This is not to suggest that Byington's acting career languished, though roles became fewer in the fifties. Never one to be easily beaten, Byington found greener pastures in television, primarily as the star of a hit comedy series called *December Bride* (1954–59). Despite all her films, she is probably best remembered in the role of Lily Ruskin, a fun-loving widow with a new lease on life and Verna Felton as her zany sidekick. Lily may be seen as a development of Byington's favorite film role as the eponymous heroine in *Louisa* (A. Hall, Universal, 1950). Louisa is Ronald Reagan's peppy, attractive, widowed mother, who is courted both by her son's boss, Charles Coburn, and the corner grocer,

Spring Byington may have been a "December Bride," but she retained her youthfulness until her death in 1971 at age eighty-four. Her favorite part was the title role in *Louisa*, because she was "an older woman with young ideas." Louisa Norton formed the basis for Lily Ruskin in Byington's hit TV series, *December Bride*.

Edmund Gwenn. (These two veteran character actors had first been rivals for Byington's affections in *The Devil and Miss Jones* [S. Wood, 1941].) Byington was Emmy nominated for *December Bride* both in 1958 and 1959. For several seasons in the early sixties, she played a cook on *Laramie* and she continued to make guest appearances on television until 1967.

Spring Byington's last feature film role was in *Please Don't Eat the Daisies* (C. Walters, 1960), playing Suzie Robinson, a pet shop owner, Doris Day's mother and confidante, and her five-time co-star David Niven's mother-in-law. Casting her was clearly meant to capitalize on the success of *December Bride*, which had ended the previous year. The film marked Byington's twenty-fifth anniversary at MGM. She had aged gently and remained to the last a petite, five-foot-three-inch, blond, blue-grey-eyed charmer with a characteristic pug-nose that one might in charity call "retroussé."

Byington spent the years of her retirement in her modest home on a hill at 2946 Beachwood Drive. She died of cancer on September 7, 1971. This elegant, well read, strong-minded woman—so different from the flibbertigibbets and scatterbrains she played on screen—willed her body to science.

Doyenne of Dowagers
GLADYS COOPER (1888–1971)

Ivor Novello said of her: "When she enters a room all the lights seem to burn more brightly." Philip Merivale, her third husband and greatest love, said she was impossible to live with and impossible to live without. Noël Coward called her, jokingly, "the Hag." To her friends and family she was simply "G."[200]

Gladys Cooper made her Hollywood debut in the least interesting part in a most interesting film. The part was that of Laurence Olivier's sister and Joan Fontaine's sister-in-law, Beatrice Lacy, and the film, Alfred Hitchcock's *Rebecca* (Selznick Int., 1940). Separated from part of her family and her friends in England by the breadth of the Atlantic Ocean and the American continent, by World War II, and the need to earn a living, Cooper wrote home with characteristic candor shortly after the film's release: "People who've seen me in *Rebecca* say they can't understand how I was once known as a famous British beauty unless there weren't other beauties around at the time, and I must say I can't blame them ..." She added: "I really look quite terrible on the screen, a strange hunchbacked creature in an ill-fitting tweed suit out of whose mouth such a frightful grating noise comes that I thought something must have gone wrong with the soundtrack! If that's what I look like in films no wonder nobody else will hire me!"[201]

The year 1939 had been a professional low point for Gladys Cooper and the offer to do a film in Hollywood was a godsend.[202] Despite her disenchantment at her lackluster appearance, it was an auspicious beginning for a fifty-two-year-old fading British beauty and waning star of the London stage, in a brave new Californian world where it seemed no one had ever heard of her. *Rebecca*, based on the bestselling novel by Daphne du Maurier, daughter of Cooper's great friend and longtime co-star, Sir Gerald du Maurier, was also Hitchcock's Hollywood debut and would prove the only film for which he would receive an Academy Award for Best Picture. *Rebecca* was producer David O. Selznick's first film after *Gone with the Wind* and was important in the careers of all its lead actors: It was the best film Olivier had been involved in since he started in movies ten years before; it marked the breakthrough for Olivia de Havilland's little

After seeing herself on screen for the first time in middle age in *Rebecca* (United Artists, 1940), Gladys Cooper wrote home to England that neither she herself nor anybody else could believe she had once been a great beauty. With her in this shot are her four-time co-star and husband in *Rebecca*, Nigel Bruce, and the film's female star, Joan Fontaine. Both had been in Hollywood films since 1935.

sister, Joan Fontaine; it introduced movie audiences to that creator of gloriously awful, man-eating dowagers, Florence Bates; and last but not least, it was Judith Anderson's first major role and the only one for which she would receive an Oscar nomination. Thus, the film had a splendid cast that also included Cooper's best buddy in Hollywood, Nigel Bruce, in the role of her husband.

The remarkable woman who was nominated for three Oscars, two Tony awards, and who was finally made a Dame Commander of the British Empire in 1967, at the age of seventy-nine, was born Gladys Constance Cooper in Lewisham outside London on December 18, 1888. She shared this birth year with Dame Edith Evans and her birthplace with Elsa Lanchester, who with her husband, Charles Laughton, would invite Cooper to her first big Hollywood party.[203] Among other Hollywood character actresses, Cooper was born the same year as her *Rebecca* co-star, Florence Bates, and was the contemporary of fellow English beauty turned character actress, Elisabeth Risdon, as well as Blanche Yurka, Beulah Bondi, and Margaret Dumont.

There was nothing in Cooper's family and social background to indicate that she would become an actress or, for that matter, a remarkably convincing portrayer of ladies with a capital "1."[204] Though born in Lewisham, a southeastern suburb of London, her early memories of growing up with a journalist father, a homemaker mother, and two younger sisters were all of Chiswick, where the middle-class family moved in the early 1890s.[205] Cooper was a photographic model from age six. Despite her father's opposition, her mother encouraged her interest in the theater and on her seventeenth birthday, without any theatrical training, she made her stage debut in the starring role of a show called *Bluebell in Fairyland*.[206] She learned the business from the inside and, according to director George Cukor, "had the most wonderful training in the world."[207] She became a "Gaiety Girl" in 1907, got her first role in a straight play as Cecily Cardew in a summer revival of *The Importance of Being Earnest* in 1911, and the following year had her first stage success in the legitimate theater in Arnold Bennett and Edward Knoblock's play *Milestones*. Her twenty-year theatrical partnership with Du Maurier began with *Diplomacy* in 1913, and a partnership of another kind, managing the Playhouse Theatre in London with Frank Curzon, began in 1917, laying the foundation for a series of hits at that theater, of which she was the sole manager from 1925 till 1933.

In 1923 Gladys Cooper had ranked first in a magazine poll of the twenty most popular British actresses.[208] By the early 1930s, she had gone from triumph to triumph in the West End, including starring roles as the titular heroine of *The Second Mrs. Tanqueray* (1922) and *The Last of Mrs. Cheyney* (1925). Curiously enough, she had never played in the United States, nor had she ever acted in a Hollywood movie.[209] The former situation would be rectified when she starred in *The Shining Hour* on Broadway in 1934. As fate would have it, she would never reprise any of her great stage roles on film. When she finally arrived in Hollywood in September 1939, it was too late.

Writers who consider Gladys Cooper's sixty-six-year acting career, tend not to take her Hollywood years too seriously. In this they may have taken the lead from the actress herself. Apparently she never bothered to read more of her film scripts than her own scenes. She would have her friends relate the plots of her movies, as she herself didn't bother to see many of them.[210] Yet Cooper spent twenty-five years of her life in Hollywood, where she made thirty of her thirty-four sound films (she had made ten silents, 1913–23). This is not a large body of films compared to other British character actresses of her generation, such as Elisabeth Risdon or Mary Forbes or Isobel Elsom. Unlike more frequently employed actresses, though, Cooper only played credited, named roles and that mostly in A movies at major studios, such as MGM (nine films) and RKO (six films). As a result of her remarkable performance in *Now, Voyager*, she was under contract with MGM from 1943.[211] She was occasionally loaned out and made her best films at other studios, but her contract was renewed for five of the customary seven years. Louis B. Mayer's reaction on first meeting her was symptomatic of studio attitudes to the role of mature British actresses in movies as, in Sheridan Morley's words, "a sort of composite of Lady Bracknell and May Whitty."[212] Confronted with the still youthful and fair Cooper, Mayer said almost indignantly: "But Miss Cooper, we thought you were so much older."[213]

Daphne du Maurier once wrote that Gladys Cooper had "a face like Danae and eyes that will never be surpassed in our lifetime."[214] One might claim that Cooper was beautiful all her life, if we can still see beauty in an aged face that a scalpel has never touched. She claimed herself to have her good looks from her father,[215] which may account for the increasingly masculine handsomeness of her features. Her face was dominated by her blue eyes, so large and luminous that age and experience could do nothing to extinguish their brilliance. And her eyes were only the most striking feature of a face extraordinary in its serene, yet cold, beauty.

The evidence of Cooper's youthful beauty remains in the more than four hundred picture postcards taken of her between 1905 and 1920. What we see in her Hollywood films is a different face, no less striking, but one overwritten with the effects of time and the depredations of the California sunshine. On screen it was a remarkably supple and changeable face and one that could at times even look appallingly ugly. Cecil Beaton noted cavalierly that Cooper had the complexion of a walnut and private photographs bear this out.[216] Yet on film she appeared remarkably youthful and vibrant both of face and figure, when the roles allowed for it. Frequently they did not.

The name Gladys Cooper does not even begin to suggest the heights of hauteur attained by this aristocratic actress during her fifty-six-year film career. Despite getting off to a slow start in Hollywood, Cooper more or less cornered the market on distinguished, often aristocratic, older women in Hollywood films of the '40s. And the competition was stiff. She was up against compatriots such as Dame May Whitty, Flora Robson, Isobel Elsom, Mary Forbes, and Elisabeth Risdon and natives such as Florence Bates and Cora Witherspoon. One of the few who could touch her was the Canadian-born Lucile Watson, albeit it in a more homely and amply-proportioned way. Mary Forbes could sometime come up to her level in the icy stare department, as when she catches her son, James Stewart, together with Jean Arthur in *You Can't Take It with You* (1938). Yet none of the competing dowagers had Cooper's awesomely glacial presence, a combination of looks and carriage unsurpassed in its haughty disdain and understated sophistication. She was a regal iceberg you just knew someone would run afoul of sooner or later. Cooper also had an effective sideline in religious fanatics (with and without a nun's habit).

In *Kitty Foyle* (S. Wood, RKO, 1940), her second film in Hollywood, Cooper portrayed Mrs. Stafford, an upper-class Chicago matriarch and Ginger Rogers's mother-in-law from hell. Rogers won her only Oscar for her spirited opposition to Ma Stafford's attempts to bring her into line. In *That Hamilton Woman* (A. Korda, 1941), Cooper was less convincing as the austere, rigid, and long-suffering wife of Lord Nelson (Laurence Olivier), particularly wooden in the confrontation scene with Nelson's mistress, Lady Hamilton (Vivien Leigh). The scene had some interesting private resonances. In the early 1930s, Vivien Leigh had had an affair with Cooper's son, John Buckmaster.[217] She would later have a much longer relationship with Cooper's stepson, Jack Merivale, which only ended with her death in 1967.

After several unremarkable films, including *The Black Cat* (A.S. Rogell, Universal, 1941), where she polished off both Cecilia Loftus and Gale Sondergaard, Cooper got her big break with *Now, Voyager* at Warners in 1942. Lo and behold, director Irving Rapper even remembered her from her Playhouse days! She wrote home that she was thrilled about the part—which meant five weeks of steady work—even if she had to wear a wig and thought she looked like her own mother.[218] Her interpretation of the Boston Brahmin dowager, Mrs. Henry Windle Vale, was to be one of her most distinctive performances on film and gave her her first Oscar nomination for Best Supporting Actress. Inexplicably, she lost out to Teresa Wright in *Mrs. Miniver*, as did Dame May Whitty (also for *Mrs. Miniver*) and Agnes Moorehead (*The Magnificent Ambersons*). Cooper got on surprisingly well with her screen daughter, Bette Davis, despite that fact that she was worse than ever at remembering her lines.[219] Nearly thirty years later, Davis would send one of the largest bouquets at Cooper's funeral with a card that read: "She was a great Lady."[220]

Cooper played a mother who receives word that her bomber son has been killed in action the same day he was to arrive home on leave in what Simon Callow has called "the Hollywood Raj's big do," *Forever and a Day* (various directors, RKO, 1943). Even at a moment of extreme (yet controlled) emotional stress, Cooper was able to incorporate her signature raised right eyebrow. In 1943 she also played the captain of the Welfare Relief during World War II, who gets charmed by Cary Grant into using gambling to raise money at a charity ball. Her role in *Mr. Lucky* (H.C. Potter, RKO, 1943) is interesting for showing the more feminine and high-spirited side to her personality, a side that seldom shows up in her films.

Cooper's next role was a "biggie" supporting David O. Selznick's new discovery and future wife, Jennifer Jones, in *The Song of Bernadette* (H. King, Twentieth Century–Fox, 1943). Of all her film roles, the forbidding and judgmental Sister Marie Therese Vauzous was the furthest from her own character and she claimed not to have recognized herself when she saw the film.[221] Her stern-faced and unvarnished portrayal of a nun struggling with envy and religious doubt garnered her a second Oscar nomination. Never afraid to voice a strong opinion, Charles Higham and Joel Greenberg call this film "one of the ugliest and most vulgar quasi-religious pictures that has ever disgraced the screen, inexcusably inept in every department."[222]

In *The White Cliffs of Dover* (C. Brown, 1944), her first film at MGM, she was the aristocratic Lady Jean Ashwood, who loses her son in World War II and through suffering grows close to her American daughter-in-law, Irene Dunne, before her own death. Cooper's next role, a personal favorite of mine, was playing Greer Garson's world-weary, hard-drinking, pants-wearing daughter in *Mrs. Parkington* (T. Garnett, MGM, 1944). This must have made for a nice change for an actress who would never be anyone's daughter on film again. It also gave Cooper her first screen opportunity to show her intuitive gift for stylish light comedy. It was like seeing her in one of her starring roles at the Playhouse twenty years on, still "the archetypal cool Maugham lady."[223]

Cooper's interpretation of the Scottish puritan grandmother in *The Green Years* (V. Saville, MGM, 1946), sad to say, does little to abate the jaw-cracking boredom of this story of an orphaned boy and his bacchanalian grandfather (Charles Coburn). *Green Dolphin Street* (1947), also directed by Victor Saville for MGM, has withstood the test of time no better. In this period piece set on St. Pierre in the English Channel, Cooper got to be the still attractive mother of Lana Turner and Donna Reed, the wife of Edmund Gwenn, and the boyhood sweetheart of Frank Morgan.

Cooper is much better remembered, and rightly so, for her role in *The Bishop's Wife* (H. Koster, 1947), starring David Niven as the beleaguered bishop, Loretta Young as his saintly wife, and Cary Grant as the angel sent to Earth to sort things out. A Christmas classic à la *It's a Wonderful Life* (1946), here Cooper plays Mrs. Hamilton, the imperious endower of Niven's projected cathedral and the bane of his existence. A high point in the film is when she tells Niven that she would like the countenance of St. George in the stained glass window of the memorial chapel to suggest her late husband, and he responds: "Who do you see as the dragon?" Cooper's hair is done up in the pseudo–German *Mädchen* braided twist she sports several times in films of the '40s, which lends a curious air of the Third Reich even to propagandistic war films such as *The White Cliffs of Dover*.

In her first musical, Vincente Minnelli's camp extravaganza *The Pirate* (MGM, 1948), Cooper plays Judy Garland's down-on-her-luck aunt with a young, layabout

Daphne du Maurier once wrote that Gladys Cooper had "a face like Danae and eyes that will never be surpassed in our lifetime." Here we see her at fifty-seven and in costume for her role in *The Valley of Decision* (Metro-Goldwyn-Mayer, 1945), which starred Greer Garson and Gregory Peck. According to du Maurier: "[W]ith her firm chin and wide nostrils she strode through life brushing obstacles from her path, her eyes on the horizon, an intolerant and rather gallant figure."

husband to support. Aunt Inez tries to arrange an advantageous marriage for Garland with the unattractive mayor, all the while wearing the most absurdly anachronistic and fanciful costumes. Minor roles in Minnelli's *Madame Bovary* and Fred Wilcox's *The Secret Garden* (both 1949) rounded out Cooper's most active film decade and her tenure at MGM. In the latter filmatization of Frances Hodgson Burnett's children's classic, she played the unsympathetic housekeeper, Mrs. Medlock, and got to be mean to Margaret O'Brien; and in the former film, she had only one scene, in which she tries to get her son out of the clutches of the eponymous heroine and siren of Yonville, played by Jennifer Jones.

This might well have been the end of Cooper's film career, which slowed considerably in the '50s and '60s, but there was still some go in the old girl yet. By the time she triumphed in what may well be her most distinguished film role, as the insufferably judgmental, snobbish, and condescending Mrs. Railton-Bell in *Separate Tables*, she was seventy years of age. *Separate Tables* (D. Mann, 1958) has been called the "last united stand of the Hollywood English"[224] and had a distinguished cast in support of the stars Burt Lancaster, David Niven, Deborah Kerr, and Rita Hayworth. Wendy Hiller won an Oscar for Best Actress for her role as the proprietor of a small seaside hotel, one of the seven Oscars for which the film was nominated. Besides forming a friendship with Hiller that would last until her (Cooper's) death, she was reunited with Felix Aylmer, who had played in her first sound film, *The Iron Duke* (V. Saville, 1934), nearly twenty-five years before. And if that wasn't enough, in the role of Mrs. Railton-Bell's aristocratic sidekick, Lady Matheson, we find Cooper's contemporary, Cathleen Nesbitt, famous for playing Rex Harrison's mother in both the stage and musical version of *Pygmalion/My Fair Lady* till the end of her very long life.

The screen version of *My Fair Lady* (G. Cukor, Warner Bros., 1964) would, of course, feature Cooper in the role of Mrs. Higgins. It is probably the role for which she is best remembered today and got her a third and final Oscar nomination. Cecil Beaton does himself and the dear old lady proud, particularly in the final scene of the film, at Mrs. Higgins's home, where Cooper looks like the high priestess of some Ancient Greek cult. Her somewhat surprising warmth and sympathy for a Cockney flower girl who has fallen on soft times seems almost a symbolic reparation for Cooper's decades of snobbish austerity.

While she had not sung in any of her musicals to date, she went out singing in the last of them, *The Happiest Millionaire* (N. Tokar, Walt Disney, 1967). This was yet another wonderful part, as Fred MacMurray's patrician aunt, who worries about her great-niece Lesley Ann Warren's upbringing and is quite delightful in her refined imperturbability. At the high point of the film, with butler Tommy Steele looking anxiously on, Cooper sings a barbed duet with Geraldine Page about old versus new money and Philadelphia versus New York society. Not bad for seventy-nine! In this film Cooper's career came full circle. She had made her London debut in a musical comedy, *The Belle of Mayfair*, more than sixty years earlier. *The Happiest Millionaire* was Cooper's last Hollywood movie and, coincidentally, her three-time co-star Greer Garson's as well.

Gladys Cooper never retired. She might have liked to, but in her eighties she was still having to provide for her deaf sister and her mentally ill son.[225] Her theatrical career had blossomed again in the 1950s, as the number of film roles decreased, and she had a great success in the West End with Coward's *Relative Values* (1951) and on Broadway with Enid Bagnold's *The Chalk Garden* (1955–56). A revival of the latter in London was to be her last show. In the mid–1960s she even had a recurring role as the matriarch of a family of gentlemen crooks in a series on television called *The Rogues*, starring Charles Boyer and David Niven.

Cooper spent most of the last decade of her life on the banks of the Thames, as she had spent her first. In the early 1950s she bought a house, Barn Elms, at Henley, which would be her final home.[226] After several years of commuting between England and California, she finally sold the property in Pacific Palisades that she had bought with Merivale and where she had lived for most of the last thirty years. It seemed to a neighbor and friend when she moved out of 770 Napoli Drive in 1966, that the last of the British colonial settlers had gone.[227] Terminally ill with lung cancer, she died of pneumonia at her Henley home on November 17, 1971. On her last evening, she had risen from her bed with considerable effort and seated herself at the dressing-table to brush her hair and make up her celebrated face. Looking at her reflection for the last time, she said to the nurse: "If this is what virus pneumonia does to one, I really don't think I shall bother to have it again."[228]

"We can never go back to Manderley again, that much is certain." The evidence of Cooper's riveting star quality during her triumphant twenties in the West End is irrevocably lost and most of her hit plays—*My Lady's Dress, The Sign on the Door, The Letter, Cynara*—are long out of fashion and seldom revived. What we do have is her films. When considering the development of her long, long career, I'm reminded of a story told of an American star actress of the '20s, Ina Claire, which might equally apply to Gladys Cooper. When a friend introduced Claire to Sarah Bernhardt after a performance as "one of our great young actresses," Claire said self-deprecatingly: "No, no, I'm just a popular actress." Bernhardt responded: "Very well, very well. First come popular, then come great."[229]

Aunt Pittypat
LAURA HOPE CREWS (1879–1942)

For any actor associated with *Gone with the Wind*, their role in that film would eclipse everything they had done before or would do after. Thus, Laura Hope Crews lives on in our cultural memory as the perpetually bothered and bewildered Aunt Pittypat Hamilton, swathed in sashes and bows, her fat face framed by those ludicrous corkscrew curls and her smelling salts always close at hand. To theater audiences and people in show business in the late 1920s, Crews was a leading lady of the American stage, who had played Shakespeare with the late, great John Drew and Sir Herbert Beerbohm Tree and who had starred more recently in plays like Noël Coward's *Hay Fever* and Sidney Howard's *The Silver Cord*.

For Ruth Elizabeth Davis, better known as Bette Davis, her first encounter with this grand-dame of the stage had been a disconcerting experience. Crews had cast her in the role of the English ingénue Dinah in A.A. Milne's *Mr. Pim Passes By*, a play in which Crews had starred in with great success on Broadway both in the original Theatre Guild production in 1921 and in a revival in 1927. Crews "had lovely hands," Davis recalled in her autobiography, "and was famous for using them." When Davis tried to use her own hands in a similar fashion, Crews slapped her! Clearly, Crews gave Davis a more brutal induction into the Temple of Thespis than May Robson had given Joan Fontaine or Mary Boland gave Katharine Hepburn.

Fast forward to the end of Crews's life. She and Davis are reunited on the set of *The Man Who Came to Dinner* in 1942. Now the tables have turned and Crews is on Davis's turf. Yet Davis decides to let bygones be bygones and greets the older actress warmly. At the end of filming her tiny part, Crews comes to Davis's dressing room and gives her a box, which contains a beautiful, jewel-encrusted watch. It remained one of the movie star's "truly cherished possessions."[230]

By the time Crews and Davis first worked together at the Cape Playhouse in Dennis, Massachusetts in the summer of 1928, the

Aunt Pittypat: Laura Hope Crews (1879–1942)

Laura Hope Crews is looking butch but jolly as Aunt Minnie Stickney, next to her pretend butler, Edward Everett Horton, in this scene from *Her Master's Voice* (Paramount Pictures, 1936), based on a hit comedy by veteran playwright Clare Kummer. Crews was reprising her role on Broadway, as did Elizabeth Patterson (playing her beleaguered sister).

forty-eight-year-old Crews was a veteran of thirty-four shows on Broadway. She had been born in San Francisco on December 12, 1879, the second daughter and fourth child of John Thomas Crews, a carpenter, and Angelena (Lockwood), a sometime actress and member of the California Stock Company. Crews herself went on stage for the first time when she was only four and on tour when she was six. After a break to attend school and training to become a school teacher, she found it was easier to get an acting than a teaching job and her fate was sealed. In 1898 she returned to the stage professionally to play ingénue roles for the Alcazar Stock Company. When she and her mother moved to New York in 1900, Crews joined the Donnelly Stock Company at the Murray Hill Theatre. Her Broadway debut was in *Merely Mary Ann* at the Garden Theatre in 1903. In 1904 she started her long collaboration with producer Henry Miller that lasted until his death in 1926. Crews made her London debut in *The Great Divide* in 1909, a play she had also done on Broadway. She was with John Drew and his then leading lady, Mary Boland, in a revival of *Much Ado About Nothing* in 1913 and played Mistress Page in *The Merry Wives of Windsor* with Sir Herbert Tree in Boston in 1916. She'd also played Thea Elvsted to Alla Nazimova's Hedda Gabler in the latter's legendary Broadway debut in 1906 and starred in the original production of *Peter Ibbetson* with both the Barrymore brothers in 1917.[231]

It was the role of Mrs. Phelps in *The Silver Cord* that Crews would be best known for up until the Atlanta premiere of *Gone with the Wind* on December 15, 1939, three days after Crews's sixtieth birthday. The play was by Sidney Howard, who would later be chiefly responsible for the *Gone with the Wind* screenplay before his sudden death in 1939. His 1926 play dealt with a possessive, upper-class widow and her inability to let her two sons lead their own lives. Crews's interpretation of this self-centered, self-serving, and manipulative woman was riveting. Mrs. Phelps was the most prominent example of a character type to be found in several plays and films at this time; women who in Mrs. Phelps's own words have "made a profession of motherhood." Two other examples are Mrs. Piper in John Golden and Hugh Stange's *After Tomorrow* (1931), played by Josephine Hull on stage and screen, and Mrs. Hallam in Rose Franken's *Another Language* (1932–33), created by Margaret Wycherly on Broadway and played by Louise Closser Hale on film. In 1943 Philip Wylie would launch an attack on these ostensibly overprotective mothers and their weakling sons in his famous book *Generation of Vipers*.[232]

Fortunately, in 1933 RKO gave Crews a chance to reprise her landmark performance on film with the support of Irene Dunne, Joel McCrea, Frances Dee, and Eric Linden. It was her fourth film since her sound film debut in *Charming Sinners* (R. Milton, Paramount) in 1929. She had originally come to Hollywood as a speech coach, to help stars like Norma Talmadge, Gloria Swanson, and Carole Lombard make the transition to sound, but it didn't take long before she was putting theory into practice.[233] She bought a house at 730 N. Bedford Drive and would also own a home in Santa Monica, which she turned over to the U.S. military during the Second World War.[234]

During her dozen years in Hollywood, Crews specialized in playing dowagers, demimondaines, and dizzy dames, exemplified most famously by Mrs. Phelps, Prudence in *Camille*, and Aunt Pittypat. In addition to Mrs. Phelps, another important entry in the domineering dowager category was Aunt Minnie Stickney in *Her Master's Voice* (J. Santley, Paramount, 1936). Like *The Silver Cord*, this was a reprise of a role Crews had created on Broadway, in a comedy by Clare Kummer. Crews plays the wealthy sister of Elizabeth Patterson and the aunt of Peggy Conklin, who cut off all support of her niece's musical career after Conklin married Edward Everett Horton without her aunt's approval. Yes, it is hard to imagine any old biddy objecting to Edward Everett Horton and, indeed, Crews becomes quite fond of him when she comes on an unexpected visit and mistakes him for the butler.

The Blue Bird (W. Lang, 1940), an unsuccessful Technicolor filmatization of Maurice Maeterlinck's play, starred an uncustomarily unpleasant Shirley Temple; Crews was cast as a rich hostess in the "Land of Luxury," togged out like the Empress Josephine in her dotage with a bad dye job. This was her first part after Pittypat and eminently forgettable. She fared better in her final dowager role in *One Foot in Heaven* (I. Rapper, Warner Bros., 1941), a film sorely in need of comic relief. Here she is Methodist preacher Fredric March's near nemesis as a prominent parishioner and caterwauling member of the church choir, who objects vocally to being replaced by a children's choir and losing her chance to shine every Sunday.

The demimondaine was the mature, cosmopolitan, big city woman living on the fringes of society, in the shadowy underworld of prostitution, gambling, and racketeering. Crews played her fair share of these women, most famously in *Camille* (G. Cukor, MGM, 1936), as Greta Garbo's fair-weather friend Prudence Duvernoy. Officially a dressmaker, Crews is dressed to the nines, showing more shoulders and cleavage than good taste, and looking somewhat like an overstuffed, overdressed Pekinese. Frivolous and flirtatious, Prudence is anything but prudent. She smokes cigars and utters lines like: "Wine used to go to my head and make me gay. Now it goes to my legs and makes me old."

Crews had equally dubious, though less showy roles in *Angel*, *The Sisters*, and *Idiot's Delight*. In *Angel* (E. Lubitsch, Paramount, 1937), she was a Russian grand duchess, though a working girl and proprietress of a "salon" of a questionable nature. In *The Sisters* (A. Litvak, Warner Bros., 1938), her part was even smaller, as Lee Patrick's colorful mother, who takes Bette Davis into what in Patrick's description is a "boarding house for theatricals" after the

Girl from Avenue A (Twentieth Century–Fox, 1940) was the third film version of Maude Fulton's play, *The Brat*. Laura Hope Crews played Mrs. Forrester, who is giving some sage advice to Kay Aldridge in the "pre–Nyoka Gordon" phase of her film career.

San Francisco earthquake. Finally, in a showy part at the start of a film based on Robert Sherwood's hit play, *Idiot's Delight* (C. Brown, MGM, 1939), Crews was the gin-soaked half of a bogus telepathic act with her soon-to-be *Gone with the Wind* co-star Clark Gable.

Crews's versatility and her unique qualities as an actress come more sharply into focus when we compare her with other actresses who specialized in similar parts. However talented they were, it is difficult for example to imagine those doughty thirties dowagers Jessie Ralph and Lucile Watson as Mrs. Phelps. Ralph's persona was too genial and down-to-earth and Watson too levelheaded and reasonable. The actress who primarily carried on the great tradition of unpleasant aging womanhood represented by Crews was no doubt Florence Bates, another no-neck monster to be reckoned with. Bates was more butch than Crews, though, and it is hard to imagine her as Mrs. Phelps either, not to mention that silly old thing Prudence.

In the "woman with a past" category, Crews was more than equaled by Alison Skipworth, sixteen years her senior, but amazingly youthful and active in films until 1938. Skipworth was another large, galleon-shaped woman, who played aging ladies of ill repute in such classic films as *The Song of Songs* and *The Devil Is a Women* (both in support of Marlene Dietrich) and *The Princess Comes Across* (in support of Carole Lombard), but also in her own starring vehicles, such as *Madame Racketeer* and *A Lady's Profession*. Unlike all these other women, though, Crews had a uniquely pettish quality about her, like an overgrown, grotesque child who has been indulged too long. In brief, Crews was kind of cute. You would hardly call Ralph,

Watson, Bates, or Skipworth cute. Of course, there were some cute women in the dizzy dame category. Here Crews most resembled Mary Boland and Billie Burke, though she looked older than both of them. Interestingly, Burke was her only real rival for the role of Aunt Pittypat, though David. O. Selznick thought she looked too young.[235]

Crews did not entirely abandon the stage during her Hollywood years. In the mid–30s she replaced Mary Boland in her hit Broadway musical *Jubilee* and in 1938 she starred with Leo G. Carroll, Mady Christians, and Tallulah Bankhead's husband, John Emery, in a flop called *Save Me the Waltz*. In 1942 she stepped in for Josephine Hull as one of the two murderous Brewster sisters in the original Broadway production of *Arsenic and Old Lace*. She fell ill during the run of the play and died of kidney disease at LeRoy Sanitarium in New York City on November 13, 1942. Her grave in Cypress Lawn Memorial Park, Colma, California is marked simply by a small, white stone cross that says "Laura."

Earth Mother
JANE DARWELL (1879–1967)

Do you remember Almira Sessions? Does the name Nora Cecil ring a bell? What about Esther Dale? Ever seen her in a film? Or Emma Dunn? No, you say? And you consider yourself an expert on old movies? What about Jane Darwell, then? Yes, of course. You've heard of her. She was Ma Joad in *The Grapes of Wrath* and the Bird Woman in *Mary Poppins*. And wasn't she in *Gone with the Wind* too?

Yes, Jane Darwell was in *Gone with the Wind* (V. Fleming, Selznick Int., 1939). She played Mrs. Dolly Merriwether, who objects to the auctioning off of dance partners at the charity ball in Atlanta and gives Rhett advice about stopping his daughter from sucking her thumb. If you can name other of Darwell's roles than Ma Joad, the Bird Woman, and Mrs. Merriwether, though, you probably know quite a lot about old movies (or you're related to Jane Darwell). In that case, I'll bet you even know who Sessions, Cecil, Dale, and Dunn were.[236] There were so many of them, weren't there, older women in the background, in the group shots (never in close-up), going about their business, playing their tiny part in the big picture. Most of the time, you don't even notice them. If you go to answer a call of nature, you might very well miss their performance entirely.

Darwell was one of those women: the run of the mill, dime a dozen, Hollywood character actress. She had no prestigious Broadway career behind her, like Ethel Barrymore or, albeit on a less exalted plane, Mary Boland, Lucile Watson, and Laura Hope Crews. She hadn't gone to college or drama school, like Beulah Bondi or Elisabeth Risdon. She didn't have a rich or famous husband, like Margaret Dumont or Billie Burke. All she had was her salt of the earth ordinariness, her dignity or humor (as the situation required), her industriousness and sheer gumption. So she did a scene here, a line or two there. She was the first character to be cut if the film ran too long; the face you might see a dozen times and never think to inquire the name of. Then something happened. Something wonderful. Darwell got a break. After doing ninety-six films in ten years in parts mostly the size of peanuts, she got the role of a lifetime. She even won an Oscar for it! Imagine that. She beat Barbara O'Neil and Ruth Hussey and Marjorie Rambeau, and even Judith Anderson. It made it all worthwhile.

When you're a character actress playing

Earth Mother: Jane Darwell (1879-1967)

While Jane Darwell is best remembered as Ma Joad in *The Grapes of Wrath*, she also starred in *Star for a Night* (Twentieth Century–Fox, 1936) as the blind Mrs. Martha Lind, who comes to visit her three children in America thinking they are successful. Here we see her at a festive board with her family around her, including Claire Trevor to her left.

small parts, your appearance becomes very important. Not in the way it is important to the stars, of course, but important nevertheless. You may only have one or two lines in the entire film. You're on and then you're off. What the producer wants is a presence, the physical embodiment of a stereotype: "stern nurse," "sturdy frontierswoman," "devoted mother," "nosy neighbor." Everything you are must be conveyed at once. For more than thirty years, Darwell was one of the most ubiquitous character actresses in Hollywood, because her dumpy, formless body and bland visage could lend itself to all these stereotypes. She did it all: nurses, neighbors, mothers, grandmothers, aunts. Most of her performances cannot be described or analyzed. She is simply there and then she's gone. She fills a space, performs some function, and then it's on to the next role and the next film.

She is matronly, motherly, grandmotherly, rustic, or gossipy in a generic way, without individualization or quirks. Even though you recognize her at the time, in retrospect it is almost impossible to recall her performance in many of her films. Who remembers her as Mrs. McGonegal in *Child of Manhattan* (E. Buzzell, Columbia, 1933)? Mrs. Lane in *Only Yesterday* (J. M. Stahl, Universal, 1933)? Maude in *Finishing School* (G. Nichols Jr., W. Tuchock, 1934)? What part did she play in *Private Number* (R. Del Ruth, Twentieth Century–Fox, 1936)? *Craig's Wife* (D. Arzner, Columbia, 1936)? *The Rains Came* (C. Brown, Twentieth Century–Fox, 1939)? *Caged* (J. Cromwell, Warner Bros., 1950)? This is just a random selection of some of Darwell's typical roles and films. You can test yourself and find the answers below.[237]

Like many of her sister actresses, Jane

Darwell never married, devoting herself entirely to her craft. She worked relentlessly in the movies for more than thirty years. You can be sure she counted herself lucky. She'd got a late start, even for a character actress. She was born Patti Woodard in Palmyra, Missouri on October 15, 1879, the daughter of W.R. Woodard, president of the Louisville Southern Railroad.[238] Though Darwell had made a dozen or so silent films between 1913 and 1915, her real film career began with the Widow Douglas in *Tom Sawyer* (J. Cromwell, Paramount) in 1930, when she was fifty-one years old. Jackie Coogan was Tom Sawyer and Clara Blandick was Aunt Polly.[239]

Paramount was Darwell's frequent employer during the first years of the sound era, putting her into other prestige pictures, such as *Ladies of the Big House* (M. Gering, 1931), as a head matron; *Design for Living* (E. Lubitsch, 1933), as Gary Cooper's housekeeper; not to mention *The Scarlet Empress* (J. von Sternberg, 1934), in an uncredited role as a governess. Paramount was quite the studio then, in the early 1930s, with stars like Marlene Dietrich, Mae West, and Tallulah Bankhead. Alison Skipworth was the resident granddame. At this time, Darwell also worked for RKO, Universal, and Columbia. Yet her home studio from 1933 would be Fox, which in 1935 was transformed into Twentieth Century–Fox. *Bondage* (A. Santell, 1933) was the first of her fifty-five films at this studio and *Hound-Dog Man* (D. Siegel, 1959) was the last. Here she made all six of her Shirley Temple pictures, including *Curly Top* (I. Cummings, 1935) and *Little Miss Broadway* (I. Cummings, 1938); here she supported Loretta Young six times between 1934 and 1938 and Henry Fonda five times between 1939 and 1946; and last but not least, here she made her most important films, not just *The Grapes of Wrath* (1940), but equally *Star for a Night* (1936) and *The Ox-Bow Incident* (1943). Incidentally, *Star for a Night* (L. Seiler) was one of the few films in which she was given top billing.

While *Gone with the Wind* ended one highly productive decade for Darwell, *The Grapes of Wrath* began another in which she would play fewer roles, but be given more opportunities to show what she was good for. I'm thinking particularly of films like *Brigham Young* (H. Hathaway, Twentieth Century–Fox, 1940), starring Tyrone Power and Linda Darnell, where she was billed fifth as Power's mother; *The Devil and Daniel Webster* (W. Dieterle, 1941), where she was third billed as Ma Stone, a minor Ma Joad, God-fearing New Hampshire farmer's wife, and the mother of James Craig in this American capitalist version of the *Faust* story; and *Captain Tugboat Annie* (P. Rosen, Republic, 1945), in which Darwell starred in yet another attempt to revive the magic of the original from 1933, with the legendary Marie Dressler. But first and foremost, I'm thinking of my personal favorite among Darwell's films: that riveting study of group psychology and Western clannishness, *The Ox-Box Incident* (W.A. Wellman,

Jane Darwell in 1944 in a portrait for RKO. At age sixty-five, she still had two decades of her film career left and nearly forty films yet to make.

Twentieth Century–Fox, 1943). As the mannish Jenny Grier, Darwell has a rare opportunity to form a unique, idiosyncratic individual on screen and she makes the most of it. As one of the butchest members of an otherwise all-male posse, she sets out rifle in hand to revenge the murder of a rancher. She is even selected to whip up one of the horses the three men to be lynched are sitting on. For this part, Darwell created a shrill, screeching laugh to drive falsely accused Dana Andrews to distraction.

The real star of The Ox-Bow Incident was Henry Fonda. Among the many stars Darwell supported, she had a special relationship with Fonda built up through their six films together: In addition to The Grapes of Wrath and The Ox-Box Incident, these were Jesse James (H. King, Twentieth Century–Fox, 1939), Chad Hanna (H. King, Twentieth Century–Fox, 1940), The Battle of Midway (a documentary short directed by John Ford for the U.S. Navy in 1942), and My Darling Clementine (J. Ford, Twentieth Century–Fox, 1946). Darwell was to Ford what Beulah Bondi was to Jimmy Stewart. She had played his mother so often, he simply called her "Ma" and she called him "Son."[240]

Darwell is the actress in this volume most closely identified with the Western. Characterized by its paucity of women, the genre is also distinguished by its limited range of female types. Darwell actually acted in more musicals than she did in Westerns, yet the Western gave her her biggest screen opportunities, so we tend to remember her best in those films. Several of her Westerns were for the brilliant and irascible John Ford, the one among her numerous directors with whom she would be most closely associated.

Down through the years, Ford developed a special working relationship with a select number of actresses, that he would use repeatedly in his films. In addition to Darwell, these included Mae Marsh, Mary Gordon, Anna Lee, Tiny Jones, Maureen O'Hara, Mildred Natwick, and Una O'Connor. Ford cast Darwell in seven of his films between 1940 and 1958. Their most important film together was The Grapes of Wrath (Twentieth Century–Fox, 1940), which as it happens, was also their first collaboration. According to Beulah Bondi, she had been promised the plum role of Ma Joad and had even begun to prepare when word came that Darwell would be cast instead.[241] According to John Ford's biographer, Scott Eyman, Ford's main contribution to the casting process was weighing in in favor of Darwell rather than Bondi. Physically, the two women were quite different, Bondi being much leaner and, if the role required it, meaner. "Ford wanted something more expansive and more of an earth-mother,"[242] writes Eyman. Darwell was an obvious choice. She had made no less than thirty-nine films for Fox at this point and was the studio's resident old lady. Bondi, by comparison, was a freelancer and had only made a single film at Fox.

Eyman also tells that Darwell particularly dreaded doing the scene in which she was required to sing and dance. Yet she did it perfectly on the first take.[243] It is possible that on the whole Darwell's performance in this film has been overrated, but one would have to have a heart of lead not to be moved by her closing monologue to Pa Joad (Russell Simpson), which ends: "We keep a-comin.' We're the people that live. They can't wipe us out. They can't lick us. We'll go on forever, Pa, 'cause we're the people." Film historian and preservationist William K. Everson nevertheless considered Henrietta Crosman in Pilgrimage (1933) "the finest character actress performance in any Ford film, not even excepting Jane Darwell in The Grapes of Wrath."[244]

Between 1952 and 1964, Darwell made more than thirty appearances in television dramas. She retired from films in 1959, but was lured out of retirement for one last hurrah in what ironically would become one of her most familiar roles: the Bird Woman in Mary Poppins (R. Stevenson, Walt Disney). The film was released in August 1964. The last lines Jane Darwell would ever speak on film were "Feed the birds! Tuppence a bag."

Darwell died of a heart attack on August 13, 1967 at the Motion Picture Country Home and Hospital in Woodland Hills, California.[245] She was buried in the "Whispering Pines" section of Forest Lawn Cemetery in Glendale.

Not So Big Mama
MILDRED DUNNOCK (1901–1991)

Mildred Dunnock was a "superb actress who didn't find nearly the roles she deserved" and "suffered the deprivations more keenly than less sensitive artists would have." Thus Dunnock's most frequent director somberly summed up her long career. Yet, before we accept this orphic pronouncement from Elia Kazan,[246] let us not forget that Dunnock is the only actress apart from Maureen Stapleton to have created major roles in major plays by the two leading American playwrights of the twentieth century, Tennessee Williams and Arthur Miller. Unlike Stapleton, Dunnock had a long film career, more than four decades long, but it was not a prolific one, as she only made twenty-five feature films in that time. Her career on the stage was even longer, including twenty-three shows on Broadway over a period of forty-five years.

Dunnock was thirty-one when she made her debut on the "Great White Way." Her journey to her first Broadway show had been long and indirect. She came from what used to be called a "solid" family in Baltimore, Maryland, where she was born on January 25, 1901. Her father, Walter Dunnock, was president of the Dumari Textile Company. Her mother, Florence, was a Saynook. Dunnock attended public schools in Baltimore, including Western High School, went on to college at Goucher (which has since named their theater after her) and completed her MA at Columbia University. She acted throughout her college years with the Vagabond Players and the Johns Hopkins University troupe in Baltimore, but first began working as a teacher, at the Friends' School in her native city and later in New York. In New York she acted with the Morningside Players. It was their show, *Life Begins*, which ultimately brought her to Broadway when it transferred to the Selwyn Theatre on March 28, 1932.[247]

Dunnock's breakthrough role came eight years later, as Miss Ronberry in the original production of Emlyn Williams's hit play, *The Corn Is Green* (1940–42). Dunnock supported Ethel Barrymore in the crowning glory of her long stage career, as Miss Moffat, the spinster schoolteacher determined to bring the light of culture and education to the young Welsh coal miners. Dunnock was her initially reluctant assistant teacher in this daredevil venture. Her performance brought her to the attention of Hollywood. Ironically, it was she, not Barrymore, who was asked to reprise her role on film when Warner Bros. bought the rights as a vehicle for their own star, Bette Davis, in 1945, and set Irving Rapper to direct it.

While we can regret that Barrymore's performance has not been preserved, we can be all the more glad that Dunnock's was. She is delightful as the prissy, sentimental spinster, virginal yet attractive, feminine yet ethereal. The opening scene is particularly amusing. Miss Ronberry eagerly awaits the new tenant, whom she believes to be a military man, going into ecstasies over his books and his "virile" wastepaper basket, only to discover that "L.C." in the letter she received stands for "Lilly Christabel" and the new tenant is indeed a woman. Davis was no slouch in the lead role, either. Rosalind Ivan, Gwyneth Hughes, and Rhys Williams also reprised their Broadway roles. As the worm in the bud, Bessie Watty, we find a young, promising actress also making her film debut, Joan Lorring. Lorring was nominated for an Oscar for her performance. She lost to Anne Revere for *National Velvet*.

Dunnock's stage and screen careers would continue to be intimately intertwined. In 1945, she supported Tallulah Bankhead on Broadway in a new comedy by Philip Barry called *Foolish Notion* and the following year Dunnock created the role of Lavinia Hubbard in Lillian Hellman's *Another Part of the Forest* with Patricia Neal as Regina. This play was a prequel to Hellman's *The Little Foxes* (1939), detailing the rise of an

Not So Big Mama: Mildred Dunnock (1901–1991)

In *The Corn Is Green* (Warner Bros., 1945), Emlyn Williams's classic of Welsh village life, Mildred Dunnock (Miss Ronberry) went from supporting the queen of Broadway, Ethel Barrymore, in her last great stage role, to supporting the queen of Warner Bros., Bette Davis, in her last great role at that studio. Dunnock looks characteristically pensive and uncharacteristically youthful in this still from her first film. She was forty-four and Davis was seven years younger.

avaricious, conniving, and materialistic Southern family in the wake of the Civil War. Dunnock's role went to Florence Eldridge in the film version from 1948.

It was at the Morosco Theatre on February 10, 1949, that Mildred Dunnock premiered in the role for which she will always be remembered: Linda Loman in Arthur Miller's *Death of a Salesman*. With her in the original Broadway cast were Lee J. Cobb as Willy Loman and Arthur Kennedy and Cameron Mitchell as the Lomans' sons Biff and Happy. Dunnock and Mitchell went on to star in the film version directed by László Benedek in 1951, while Fredric March took over the lead role and Kevin McCarthy played Biff. Opinions have been divided about the success of this venture. The *Times*'

influential film critic, Bosley Crowther, turned thumbs up, writing of Dunnock that she was "simply superb, as she was on the stage": "Her portrayal of a woman who bears the agony of seeing her sons and husband turn out failures supports the one pretension of this drama to genuine tragedy."[248] The role brought Dunnock her first Oscar nomination. The award was won by Kim Hunter for *A Streetcar Named Desire*.

Not surprisingly, Dunnock's vast success in *Death of a Salesman* inaugurated a productive decade for her both in the theater and in film. On Broadway she starred in plays like Henrik Ibsen's *Peer Gynt* (1951), where she played the mother, Aase, to John Garfield's Peer in Lee Strasberg's short-lived production; Jane Bowles's *In the Summer House* (1953–54), with Judith

The filmatization of Arthur Miller's instant classic, *Death of a Salesman* (Columbia Pictures, 1951), was Mildred Dunnock's third film. Here we see her as Linda Loman mending her silk stockings, while her husband, Willy Loman (Fredric March), is entertaining a lady friend (Patricia Walker) in his Boston hotel room. This film has never been released on video or DVD.

Anderson and Jean Stapleton in her Broadway debut, which Tennessee Williams considered one of Dunnock's most poignant performances[249]; and Williams's own *Cat on a Hot Tin Roof* (1955–56), which won the Pulitzer Prize and where Dunnock created the role of Big Mama. Again she lost the role in the filmatization, this time to Judith Anderson, who was maybe not ideally suited to playing a Southern 1950s version of the dizzy dame. After *Child of Fortune* (1956), based on Henry James's novel *The Wings of the Dove*, Dunnock was not seen on Broadway for almost four years. It was during these years she delivered some of her best and most beloved screen performances in films like *Baby Doll*, *Peyton Place*, *The Nun's Story*, *The Story on Page One*, and *BUtterfield 8*. In the first three of these films, she played spinsters, one of her specialties; in the final two, middle-class mothers, her other film specialty.

Baby Doll (E. Kazan, 1956) was the one drama Tennessee Williams wrote directly for the screen. Sultry, sensual, and Southern in setting, as per usual, this was a subtly amusing story of erotic tension and frustration starring Carroll Baker, Karl Malden, and a superbly charismatic Eli Wallach. Dunnock's part as Aunt Rose Comfort, a spinster, unpaid domestic, and shrinking violet deluxe, was modest and fairly peripheral to the plot of the film. For what amounted almost to a caricature of Dunnock's customary roles, she was nominated for her second Academy Award. The Oscar for Best Actress in a Supporting Role in 1957 went to Dorothy Malone for *Written on the Wind*.

Dunnock's roles in *Peyton Place* (M. Robson,

Twentieth Century–Fox, 1957) and *The Nun's Story* (F. Zinnemann, Warner Bros., 1959) gave her more to work with. In the former she was luminous as the dedicated school teacher, Miss Elsie Thornton, who is passed over as principal. She tells one of her pupils: "Allison, if there is anything in life you want, go and get it. Don't wait for anyone to give it to you." She got a Golden Globe nomination for the role herself. The part of Sister Margharita, "Mistress of Postulates" in *The Nun's Story* was Dunnock's big nun role; a beautiful part in a beautiful film. She plays a "living rule," which means a shining example to the novices and other nuns. This film, starring Audrey Hepburn, was the first for Colleen Dewhurst, who played a madwoman, and was the final film for Scarlett O'Hara's mother, Barbara O'Neil, and for veteran stage actress Patricia Collinge. Peggy Ashcroft was also in the cast.

The Story on Page One (1960), written and directed by Clifford Odets, was a classic courtroom drama which gave Dunnock more screen time than most of her films. It also gave her a rare opportunity to play a "Monster Mom," rather than the devoted, long-suffering variety she usually played. As Mrs. Ellis, the mother of Gig Young, one of the defendants in a murder trial, Dunnock delivers a chilling portrayal of meaningless propriety and boundless selfishness. Equipped with the requisite pearls, gloves, hat, and handbag, Mrs. Ellis is full of pious platitudes, such as "It's one of the great lessons of life: There's no substitute for breeding." Described by one of the lawyers for the defense, Anthony Franciosa, as an "unmitigated monster" and by one reviewer as "a cruel and voracious she-wolf in deceptively virtuous sheep's clothing,"[250] Mrs. Ellis has subtly tyrannized her son from an early age. We haven't seen the like since Laura Hope Crews's Mrs. Phelps in *The Silver Cord* in the early thirties!

Dunnock's mother role in *BUtterfield 8* (D. Mann, MGM, 1960), despite her "Wandrous" name, is more run-of-the-mill, as she tries her best to help her troubled daughter, Elizabeth Taylor. Taylor would later have little good to say about this film, which she was forced to do to complete her MGM contract, but Dunnock delivers the goods as usual. All told, the sixties were less stellar for her professionally, but then you could say that for many actresses of her generation. Good roles for older women were increasingly difficult to come by; aging stars and their supporting players alike frequently had to seek refuge in horror films and thrillers. Fortunately, one might say, Dunnock made only one such venture: *Whatever Happened to Aunt Alice?* (L.H. Katzin, 1969). Here she was made to suffer at the hands of the film's star, Geraldine Page, as was Ruth Gordon, who ended up equally dead. In a grey wig, it looked like the widowed Linda Loman had gone to work as a housekeeper in the Arizona desert.

Other of Dunnock's sixties films were *Sweet Bird of Youth* and *Seven Women*. *Sweet Bird of Youth* (R. Brooks, MGM, 1962) was a filmatization of Tennessee Williams's play from 1959, where Geraldine Page reprised her role as the faded screen star, Alexandra del Lago, and Paul Newman played her ill-fated companion, the former golden boy Chance Wayne. Dunnock played the role of Aunt Nonnie, sister-in-law to Wayne's nemesis, Boss Finley (Ed Begley), and aunt to Wayne's hometown girl, Heavenly Finley (Shirley Knight). The role had been created by Martine Bartlett on Broadway. Dunnock brought to it her customary quiet authority and timorous tenderness.

Seven Women (1966) was veteran director John Ford's last film and a rather unusual one for him, as it was awash with women. These included Anne Bancroft as an idealistic doctor, Margaret Leighton as a neurotic mission chief, Betty Field as Eddie Albert's perpetually whining pregnant wife, and Flora Robson and Dunnock in the least interesting parts, as two elderly missionaries, trapped like the others by a band of Chinese bandits. That same year, Dunnock and Lee J. Cobb returned to their standout roles in a television version of *Death of a Salesman* (A. Segal, CBS, 1966). James Farentino and George Segal played their sons. Dunnock was nominated for an Emmy for this performance. She lost to Geraldine Page for a dramatization of Truman Capote's "A Christmas Memory."

Between *Whatever Happened to Aunt Alice?*

in 1969 and her final feature film in 1987, Dunnock was absent from the big screen, though she made several TV movies, including *The Patricia Neal Story* (A. Harvey, A. Page, CBS, 1981), where she played herself. She remained active as an actress by participating in numerous stage productions at the Long Wharf Theater in New Haven (where she starred in *Long Day's Journey Into Night* and added Amanda Wingfield to her many Williams roles); she had two final shows on Broadway (a new play by Marguerite Duras, *Days in the Trees*, in 1976; and an innovative, Tony-nominated revival of *Tartuffe* at the Circle in the Square Theatre the following year); and she taught at Yale Drama School and elsewhere.

Dunnock's final film was geared at a younger audience and starred Robert Downey, Jr. in his pre-drug bust days and Molly Ringwald at the height of her bratpack fame. In *The Pick-up Artist* (J. Toback, Twentieth Century–Fox, 1987), Dunnock makes the most of her three small scenes as Downey Jr.'s aged, diabetic grandmother, Nellie, who nevertheless has the energy to go on dates with men she meets in Central Park. One wonders if it isn't indeed she who is the "pick-up artist" of the title! Janet Maslin noted at the end of her *New York Times* review that Dunnock gave "a brief, lovely performance."[251] It was a modest farewell to film and to acting from an artist who had little to be modest about. Despite her long devotion to acting and her many splendid performances, Mildred Dunnock never won a major theatrical or film award.

At the end of her long life, Dunnock lived at West Tisbury, Massachusetts. She died in Martha's Vineyard Hospital in Oak Bluffs on July 5, 1991 at the age of ninety. Her surviving daughter, Linda McGuire, gave the cause of death as "old age."[252] Dunnock was also survived by her husband of nearly sixty years, Keith Urmy, an executive at Chemical Bank in Manhattan, who died in 1996.

The Star That Wasn't
GLADYS GEORGE (1900–1954)

While many a character actress made her way from Broadway to supporting roles in Hollywood films in the 1930s, no comparable migration of stage stars took place from the Great White Way to Movieland. Hollywood preferred to construct their own constellations. While a character player might be offered to reprise his or her role in the screen version of a stage play, the lead players seldom were. Thus, Gladys George was somewhat the exception to the rule when she was brought from a phenomenal success in the play *Personal Appearance* to star in the film *Valiant Is the Word for Carrie* (W. Ruggles) at Paramount in 1936.

For 501 performances between October 17, 1934 and December 1935, George had starred as Carole Arden, the movie star who goes "back to nature" when her car breaks down in bucolic surroundings while she is on a publicity tour for her latest film. *Valiant Is the Word for Carrie* was a different story. Here George set the mould for her many portrayals of women from the wrong side of the tracks. As Carrie Snyder, a former prostitute living in a small rural community, befriended only by Hattie McDaniel, Harry Carey, and a small boy whom she subsequently adopts (Jackie Moran), she struggles to escape her past in a series of ingenious plot twists that starkly reveal the double standards of middle America and Carrie's innate nobility. For what was only her second sound film role, George was nominated for an Academy Award in the category Best Actress in a Leading Role in competition with such established stars as

Luise Rainer, Norma Shearer, Carole Lombard, and Irene Dunne. This was a remarkable achievement and one which she would never repeat, despite her many fine film portrayals in the ensuing years. Rainer won the Oscar for *The Great Ziegfeld*.

Gladys Anna Clare was born into a show business family on September 13, 1900 in Patten, Maine, where her parents were on tour. Apparently, she made her stage debut at the tender age of three and toured with her parents in a vaudeville act called "The Three Clares."[253] Her Broadway debut was in Maurice Maeterlinck's *The Betrothal* when she was eighteen. A couple of Broadway shows followed, but no spectacular hits until *Personal Appearance* in 1934.

George had a handful of silent films to her credit from the early 1920s. In 1934 she had starred with Franchot Tone, May Robson, and Karen Morley in a filmatization of Dana Burnet and George Abbott's play *Four Walls*, retitled *Straight Is the Way* (P. Sloane, MGM, 1934), which was released before she opened in *Personal Appearance*. Ironically, George would not star in the film version of her biggest Broadway hit. Paramount secured the rights for their very own middle-aged blonde bombshell, Mae West, who was supported in the 1936 film version by Randolph Scott, Warren William, Alice Brady, and Elizabeth Patterson.

Despite showy lead roles at MGM in *They Gave Him a Gun* (W.S. Van Dyke, 1937),

Gladys George's own brand of fragile beauty is apparent in this double portrait from *Valiant Is the Word for Carrie* (Paramount Pictures, 1936). Photographed with her is veteran Western actor Harry Carey, who plays her friend and protector in the film. Irene Dunne had originally been slated to star, but turned down the role because she feared the Production Code would make the story, revolving around a reformed lady of easy virtue, difficult to adapt into a film. It would certainly have been a departure for the steel magnolia.

Gladys George in her finest role as Jacqueline Fleuriot in Sam Wood's 1937 version of the weeper *Madame X* (Metro-Goldwyn-Mayer). Here the Parisian wife on the run is seen costumed for her assumed identity as the governess Miss Pran. A more powerful and naturalistic performance is hard to imagine in an MGM melodrama that telescopes a woman's entire adult life into an hour and a quarter.

Madame X (S. Wood, 1937), and *Love Is a Headache* (R. Thorpe, 1938), George never attained screen stardom. Alone the paucity of her films makes it clear that the studio can have had no strong intention to build her up. According to Alex Barris, "George's natural habitat was the live theater."[254] Yet the money was better and steadier in Hollywood and, like so many "maturing" actresses before her, George buckled down to the harsh realities for a female performer who would never see thirty again, despite shaving four years off her real age. That was part of the problem. George was thirty-four when she made her first sound film and she looked it. She was an alluring woman, but not conventionally pretty nor classically beautiful. By her mid-thirties, her face had begun to take on that sharp-featured, foxy quality that in later years would be so characteristic of her and lend such credence to her character roles.

David Quinlan observes that between 1936 and 1942, George was the "wry-faced queen of Hollywood's brassy blondes with a heart of gold. They had seen better days and never got the hero—but they usually stole the picture."[255] As a whiskey-voiced "woman of experience," then, George was in a class of her own, but it is worth comparing her with some other bottled blondes of the period to bring out her particular qualities. There was square-jawed, steel-dimpled Minna Gombell (1892–1973), for example, great in any part that required crass, lower middle-class unpleasantness and maybe best remembered for playing the former wife of *The Thin Man* (1934) in the first of what became a series of Myrna Loy-William Powell comedies. Claire Trevor (1910–2000) was another not-quite star who developed into a fine character actress. She was of course more prolific than George, younger by ten years, and more conventionally beautiful. One can't imagine that even a veteran screen alcoholic like George could have done a better job as Gaye Dawn in *Key Largo* (1948) and Trevor, indeed, won an Oscar for her portrayal. Ona Munson's tragic life and erratic film career bears some resemblance to that of Gladys George. Three years her junior, Munson took her own life only a year after George was suspected of having done the same. Interestingly, they were both in the running for the part of Belle Watling in *Gone with the Wind* (1939). Finally, we must not forget Marjorie Rambeau (1889–1970) and Jo Van Fleet (1914–96). Like George, both were underused in Hollywood. Like George, both specialized in playing veteran drinkers; Rambeau most memorably in her Oscar-nominated role as Joan Crawford's mother in *Torch Song* (1953); Van Fleet in her Oscar-winning performance as James Dean's mother in her first film, *East of Eden* (1955).

Yet, could any of these talented actresses have had the quality of waiflike world-weariness, sympathetic toughness, and deep human understanding that George displayed in creating characters like Panama Smith in *The Roaring Twenties* (R. Walsh, Warner Bros., 1939), Valerie de Merode in *Christmas Holiday* (R. Siodmak, Universal, 1944), and Lute Mae Sanders in *Flamingo Road* (M. Curtiz, Warner Bros., 1949)? Could they have been quite as gloriously Déclassée as George's fast-fading singer figures in *The Hard Way* (V. Sherman, Warner Bros., 1943) and *Lullaby of Broadway* (D. Butler, Warner Bros., 1951)? And what about her Madame Du Barry? Who could imagine a more terrific combination of obnoxious self-assertion and petite bourgeoisie insecurity?

As the milliner turned mistress to Louis XV, George is delicious as she refers to Norma Shearer in the title role of *Marie Antoinette* (W.S. Van Dyke, MGM, 1938) as "a sob in a wig" and calls her liege lord "Booby," as if she was a eighteenth-century gangster's moll. Her confrontation with Shearer at the court ball is one of the best scenes in the film. The Texas Guinan–inspired figure of the speakeasy hostess Panama Smith in love with bootlegger boss Jimmy Cagney is another classic George portrayal. She speaks the epitaph over her lost love in the final scene of *The Roaring Twenties*, when a cop asks who Cagney, dead in her arms, was: "He used to be a big shot." Here, as in *Madame X*, she sings in a haunting manner that does not make comparisons with Piaf entirely unjust. Down-on-their-luck songstresses would become a byline for George. Alcoholic vaudeville "has been" Lily Emery in *The Hard Way* is a brief yet engaging acquaintance, while Jessica Howard, Doris Day's long lost mother in *Lullaby of Broadway*, is more conventional and surprisingly well dressed, considering her straitened financial circumstances.

The Maltese Falcon (J. Huston, Warner Bros., 1941) is the most available Gladys George film these days and is likely to remain so. That is a shame, because judging her acting ability on the basis of *Falcon* is like judging Jane Darwell on the basis of *Gone with the Wind* or Beulah Bondi on the basis of *Mr. Smith Goes to Washington*. George has the least interesting of the women's parts and, in fact, only appears in two scenes. In both she is covered in mourning for her murdered detective husband, who was Humphrey Bogart's partner and who gets shot by an unknown assailant early in the film. Iva Archer has been conducting an affair with Sam Spade (Bogart), so the film capitalizes on George's adulterous screen image from *Madame X*, but her function is basically to provide a minor plot complication as a suspect in her husband's demise and the jealous lover who is always being told to "run along." Not much for George to get her canines into, in other words.

In a sense, Gladys George was transformed into a character actress in the course of her greatest film: *Madame X*. There she went from the glamourous society woman with her own code of morals (the kind Norma Shearer might have played) to a down-and-out lush with all the signs of impending doom hanging over her (which the Queen of the Lot would not have played). What a transformation! What a performance! *Madame X*, which clocks in at a scant seventy-two minutes, is a triumph not just for director Sam Wood, screenwriter John Meehan, and MGM's makeup department, but primarily for George, who manages convincingly to portray the gradual physical and mental deterioration of the upper-class Frenchwoman Jacqueline Fleuriot, who is thrown out of her home when her husband, Warren William (looking like a John Barrymore who's been stretched) discovers she is having an affair. She flees the police, because she thinks they want to arrest her for her lover's murder at the hands of his jealous fiancée, when ironically, they only want to put her in touch with her repentant husband. The plot is not unlike a fanciful *Anna Karenina* with a dash of *Evelyn Prentice* and a pinch of *Dodsworth*. The French play by Alexandre Bisson was an old chestnut even by 1937. It was not the first attempt by Hollywood to bring the story to the screen, nor would it be the last, but I suspect that it may well be the best. Because of George's performance, this is one of the truly remarkable melodramas of this or any other decade. It is inconceivable that she was not Oscar-nominated for this film.

George made only two further appearances on Broadway after her move to California in the mid–1930s. In 1940 she had a moderate success starring in a new comedy called *Lady in Waiting*, while her final show, *The Distant City* (1941) was a dismal flop, closing after only two performances. In both plays George performed with her then current husband, Leonard Penn (1907–75). Penn was also a movie actor, most easily recognizable as Toulan, the handsome guardsman who helps the royal family escape from the Tuilleries in *Marie Antoinette*. Penn also had a small role in another of his wife's films, *The Way of All Flesh* (L. King, Paramount, 1940).

All told, Gladys George was married four times. Penn was her third husband and the one she stayed with the longest. They were married on Sept. 18, 1935, during the run of *Personal Appearance*, and divorced in 1944. George's first husband was also an actor, though more "minor" than Penn. George married Arthur Benjamin Erway (1892–1981) in 1922 and the marriage lasted eight years. Her second husband was Edward H. Fowler, a wealthy paper manufacturer whom she divorced after two years to marry Penn; and her fourth and final husband was Kenneth Bradley, a bellboy she was married to for four years from 1946. Like many of her characters, George was not lucky in love.

On December 8, 1954, George's landlady found her unconscious in her Los Angeles apartment. She died only hours after being admitted to the hospital. As she had been living as a recluse and the police described the circumstances of her death as "mysterious," an autopsy was conducted. It was found that rather than the barbiturate poisoning that had been suspected, Gladys George had died of a massive cerebral hemorrhage. Her funeral in Santa Monica was paid for by the Motion Picture Relief Fund and she was laid to rest in Pierce Brothers Valhalla Memorial Park in North Hollywood.[256] It was one of the saddest ends of any character actress of the studio era.

Bride of Laughton
ELSA LANCHESTER (1902–1986)

She was a hippie before the breed had a name, she was a believer in flower power and making love not war forty years before Vietnam, and she was a love child born only a year after Queen Victoria passed out of this world. She was once described as a "human exclamation mark,"[257] she had the most memorable bad hair day in movie history, and she is certainly the only character actress to be immortalized in a twelve-inch action figure. Among the clan of character actresses in Hollywood, Elsa Lanchester was decidedly different.

"She's alive! Alive!" Lanchester's most obvious claim to fame and the role that followed her all her life—to her evident delight[258]—was her incarnation of the Bride of Frankenstein in James Whale's horror classic from 1935. Knowing the extent to which moviegoers identify Lanchester with the titular role in Whale's follow-up to *Frankenstein* (1931), it is somewhat surprising to discover on watching the film that she only makes her appearance as the bride in the final fifteen minutes and does not speak an intelligible line. The stars, apart from Boris Karloff, are Colin Clive and Valerie Hobson, and even Una O'Connor has a bigger part than Lanchester. It is no surprise, then, that the totally unknown wife of Charles Laughton did not get star billing on this film. Yet with her characteristically electric, Nefertiti-inspired hairdo, her Hollywood glamour makeup with scars added courtesy of Universal makeup wizard, Jack Pierce, and her self-invented, goose-inspired hiss, Lanchester has gone down in film history as the creator of "the only iconic female monster ever to come out of the movies" in a film that has been called "the most visually accomplished Universal horror classic."[259]

The future bride of Frankenstein was born in Lewisham, England. Being born in Lewisham must have been the only thing she had in common with her aristocratic countrywoman and fellow expatriate, Gladys Cooper, apart from three Hollywood movies they made together in the 1940s. Lanchester's birth took place on October 28, 1902. Lewisham would not foster another Hollywood actor until Jude Law was born there seventy years later.

Who's Who in the Theatre for 1933 dutifully records that Lanchester was the "d. of James Sullivan and his wife, Edith (Lanchester),"[260] neatly eliding the fact that Lanchester was born out of wedlock. Her parents had decided to cohabitate without the sanction of church or state and continued to do so for the fifty years of their life together, raising two children without the benefit of matrimony. When the upper-class miss, Edith Lanchester, had told her father and brothers of her intention to move in with a near illiterate common laborer, they kidnapped her and put her in an insane asylum. She managed to escape and the "Lanchester Kidnapping Case" was big news in October 1895.[261] Her independence of mind would make Edith Lanchester a heroine of the women's movement she so actively supported. Her daughter found it "rather glamourous" to be a bastard, but considerably less thrilling to be dragged along to endless marches and demonstrations with her iconoclastic, perpetually crusading parents.[262]

Lanchester was taught at home until the local authority intervened and she was sent to a small private school of an appropriately radical stripe.[263] After being a pupil and later a teacher at Isadora Duncan's school in Paris, Lanchester returned home on the eve of the First World War to a varied career as a full-time bohemian and a sometime dance instructor, artist's model, cleaning lady, and—not least profitably—co-respondent in divorce cases (see *The Gay Divorcee* with Astaire and Rogers, if you don't know what a co-respondent is).[264] Like her friend, Talullah Bankhead, who would take her to a good abortionist when the need arose,[265] Lanchester became a cult figure in London in the 1920s. Herbert Farjeon wrote in *Vogue*: "Her hair is in the chestnut trees of London and her feet are in the mud of the Thames."[266] Simon Callow describes her as "outrageous" and "the consciously Bohemian, red-headed elfin child of almost comically radical Irish-Marxist-Suffragette parents."[267] In 1924 she started a club, The Cave of Harmony. Among the luminaries that frequented Elsa's "boîte" in Gower Street were Aldous Huxley, Evelyn Waugh, H.G. Wells (who wrote three short film scripts for her in the '20s), and last but not least, her talented tango partner, James Whale.[268] Whale would, of course, crop up again in Elsa's life in another decade and on another continent and they would remain friends until his suicide in 1957 (as recorded in the 1998 biopic *Gods and Monsters*, starring Ian McKellen as Whale and Rosalind Ayres as Lanchester).

In her late teens, Lanchester had started a children's theater in Soho and made her stage debut as a snake dancer in a music hall act at £2 a week.[269] Her West End debut was in 1922 as a shop girl in a play called *Thirty Minutes in a Street*. In the ensuing years, she acted in several good productions with the likes of Claude Rains, her childhood friend Angela Baddeley, John Gielgud, and Edith Evans, before in 1927 fate put her in an Arnold Bennett play, *Mr. Prohack*, as the title character's secretary. The rest, as the saying goes, is history.

You see, the single most decisive event in Lanchester's artistic career was not her childhood training with Isadora Duncan in Paris, nor being cast as the last Peter Pan personally approved by James Barrie,[270] nor even appearing in the title role in Whale's instant classic. No, the most decisive event of Lanchester's career was not strictly speaking a career event at all, but rather a personal event: In 1929 she married Mr. Prohack, that is to say, Charles Laughton. From that point on it is difficult to separate Lanchester's career from that of the rising star she married after living with him for nearly two years in Karl Marx's former home in Dean Street, Soho.[271]

To say that Lanchester and Laughton were

a queer couple is an understatement. According to Laughton's biographer, Simon Callow, "Neither socially, sexually, intellectually, or temperamentally did they seem to have any affinity: only mutual—but quite different—oddity seems to have brought them together."[272] Laughton was bent as a half-penny nail, yet he and Lanchester remained married for better or for worse, in sickness and in health, for richer or for poorer for more than thirty years. Their only child was aborted early on in their relationship.[273] After Lanchester discovered her husband's true bent when he was arrested on a morals charge, she decided to forgo motherhood.[274]

It is hard to say how Lanchester's career would have developed had she not married Laughton. I suspect that she would not have done anything to merit inclusion in this book at any rate. Certainly, she went to Hollywood on his coattails. When in 1935 she got her first American film role in George Cukor and David O. Selznick's classic filmatization of *David Copperfield*, it was undoubtedly because Laughton was to play Mr. Micawber. As it happened, W.C. Fields ended up playing Micawber, but Lanchester remained in the tiny role of the Micawbers' maid of all work, Clickett. She was given a courtesy contract and $150 a week at MGM when the studio signed her husband.[275] After *Copperfield* and the first Eddy-MacDonald musical, *Naughty Marietta* (R.Z. Leonard, W.S. Van

Charles Laughton and Elsa Lanchester during a pensive moment in the otherwise tumultuous film *The Beachcomber* (a.k.a. *Vessel of Wrath*; Paramount Pictures, 1938). This was the third of their eight feature films together and was released nine years into their thirty-three-year marriage. Laughton was then thirty-nine and Lanchester thirty-six. Their last film together was also arguably their best: *Witness for the Prosecution* (1957).

Dyke, 1935), MGM promptly loaned her out to Universal for *Bride*. She wouldn't make another film at Metro till 1943.

In Lanchester's assessment, MGM never knew what to do with her husband, who made nine films at the studio, including *The Barretts of Wimpole Street* (1934), *Mutiny on the Bounty* (1935), *The Canterville Ghost* (1944), and *Young Bess* (1953). It might be said in equal fairness, that MGM didn't know what to do with Lanchester either. She made seven films at Metro over a period of almost thirty years, including *Lassie Come Home* (F.M. Wilcox, 1943), *The Secret Garden* (F.M. Wilcox, 1949), and *The Glass Slipper* (C. Walters, 1955). None of them are among her best. The first and most famous Lassie film had her cast as the strict and common-sensible yet warm-hearted mother of child star Roddy McDowall and the unsentimental and moderately bossy wife of Donald Crisp. Most viewers are not likely to remember her in this uncongenial and dull role. The same goes for *The Glass Slipper*, her penultimate film at MGM, where she plays the grasping and socially ambitious Widow Sonder in this musical version of the Cinderella story starring Leslie Caron and Michael Wilding.

We find her in a typical maid role in the adaptation of Frances Hodgson Burnett's classic, *The Secret Garden*. Though her frequent maid roles were always small, it must be said in her defense that she put a stamp of originality on many of them. Thus, in *The Secret Garden* she invents a characteristic, almost hysterical laugh, much to the enjoyment of her master's ward, Mary Lennox (Margaret O'Brien), and the

Elsa Lanchester complained that she had friends who had seen *Come to the Stable* (Twentieth Century–Fox, 1949) two or three times and still could not remember her in it. At any rate, in 1950 her role as the absent-minded religious painter Amelia Potts garnered the actress her first of two Oscar nominations. With her are the stars Celeste Holm and Loretta Young, who were also Oscar-nominated. None of the three won.

annoyance of the housekeeper, Mrs. Medlock (Gladys Cooper).

Often Lanchester's maids have a thinly veiled eroticism, which lends a welcome spark of life to museum pieces such as the wartime epic, *Forever and a Day* (various directors, RKO, 1943). Flirtatious and flustered as usual, Lanchester's brief participation in this saga of a London house up until its destruction in World War II is chiefly memorable for the ludicrously large bow she wears on her head. Another of Lanchester's maid roles is Matilda in *The Bishop's Wife* (H. Koster, Samuel Goldwyn, 1947), starring David Niven, Cary Grant, and Loretta Young (remade in 1996 in a working class, African American version as *The Preacher's Wife*). Lanchester seems quite enamored of the handsome angel, Dudley (Grant), who comes to Earth to help the bishop, Henry Brougham (Niven), get his cathedral built despite the imperious demands of his benefactress, Mrs. Hamilton (Gladys Cooper). As a maid, Lanchester clearly had it...

In broad outline, Lanchester's film career began with costume dramas in the thirties, with a brief but notable detour into horror, and consisted for the next forty odd years of maids, more maids, mothers, and assorted eccentrics. During her fifty-year film career, she would work for all the major studios and make more than fifty feature films. As a general rule: The bigger the film, the smaller was Lanchester's part. One exception to this rule, and one of her luckiest breaks at "the majors," was landing the part of Amelia Potts in *Come to the Stable* (H. Koster, Twentieth Century–Fox, 1949). In what was her favorite film role,[276] Lanchester plays an absent-minded, idealistic, and impecunious painter of religious pictures in Bethlehem, Connecticut. She shelters two nuns, Celeste Holm and Loretta Young, who show up one day in her stable-studio and want to build a hospital as thanks to God for carrying their French convent safely through World War II. The film still holds up well. It was nominated for seven Academy Awards, including Best Actress in a Leading Role for Young and Best Actress in a Supporting Role for both Holm and Lanchester. They lost out to Mercedes McCambridge in *All the King's Men*, as did Ethel Barrymore and Ethel Waters in *Pinky*.

Part of the Hollywood studios' confusion about Lanchester may have been due to her appearance. Taking after her father, her face was so full of characteristic features there hardly seemed to be room for them all: the large, dark, googly eyes, the oddly blunted nose, the uneven teeth, the dimpled chin, not to mention what Arnold Bennett described in 1924 as a "wonderful shock of copper hair."[277] In her youth, the total effect was not unpleasing, for all its lack of classic lines and conventional beauty. Lanchester herself thought she looked her best as Mary Shelley in the prologue to *Bride of Frankenstein*.[278]

As the years went by, her petite five foot

In this studio portrait from 1950, we see Elsa Lanchester back at Universal for the first time since making *Bride of Frankenstein* fifteen years before. After a car accident in her youth, she bore a scar that meant she had to pencil in the end of her left eyebrow every morning.

four and a half inch frame became increasingly burdened with avoirdupois. Lanchester was little burdened with vanity, though, and seems quite happily to have let herself go. Irving Thalberg's kind-hearted attempts to make her dress better appear to have fallen on stony ground. The Thalbergs—Irving and his wife, Norma Shearer—were among the few Hollywood types Lanchester felt comfortable with during her first years in Hollywood.[279] She was restless, lonely, and dissatisfied there in the '30s and made frequent and lengthy trips home. The Second World War put an end to that. After 1940 she would reside permanently in the United States. The Laughtons became American citizens on April 29, 1950.[280]

Of the eleven films Lanchester made with her husband, four are among her best: *The Private Life of Henry VIII* (1933), *Rembrandt* (1936), *The Beachcomber* (1938), and *Witness for the Prosecution* (1957). Interestingly, none of these films were produced at a major Hollywood studio. Playing Anne of Cleves in *The Private Life of Henry VIII* (A. Korda, 1933) was Lanchester's first role in a major film and the first of the many "Laughton grabbers"[281] she played in, that is to say films in which she was promised a part to induce her husband to star. In this case, director-producer Alexander Korda wanted Laughton for the lead role of Henry VIII and, though he never cared for Lanchester, he cast her as the king's fourth wife; the only one to leave his side without losing her life. As it turned out, Lanchester delivered a wonderfully quirky impersonation of the frumpy German princess. The scene in which she plays drunk on first meeting her future husband to make him send her back home is very funny and the card-playing scene on the couple's wedding night is an intriguing commentary on the Laughton-Lanchester marriage. *Rembrandt* (1936) was also directed by Korda and again starred Laughton in the title role. Lanchester played Hendrickje Stoffels, a kitchen maid who becomes Rembrandt's model and the last love of his life. Billed third after Laughton and Gertrude Lawrence (in one of her rare film appearances), Lanchester delivered what is probably the best dramatic performance of her film career.

The Beachcomber (a.k.a. *Vessel of Wrath*; E. Pommer, 1938) was the Laughtons' third feature film collaboration, set on a Caribbean island and filmed in France. Lanchester plays a missionary and schoolteacher whose frequent upsets over the beachcomber Laughton's unconventional behavior finally exhausts his patience. In the climactic scene of their conflict, he delivers the following delightfully phrased request to get lost: "Madame, would you remove your little tea kettle to another stove." In a rather Hollywood ending to a non–Hollywood film, the missionary and the reprobate marry and go home to England to run a pub.

In *The Beachcomber*, Tyrone Guthrie, whom Lanchester would later describe as "the butterfly that stamped,"[282] played Lanchester's charmingly fey doctor-missionary brother. Guthrie was primarily a director rather than an actor and had taken charge of a production of *The Tempest* during the Laughtons' nine-month tenure at the Old Vic in 1933–34. In *The Tempest*, Lanchester did a star turn as Ariel to Laughton's Prospero. This season at the Old Vic, where she also played Miss Prism in *The Importance of Being Earnest* ("Nothing is quite so lowering as being a miscast character actress"[283]) and did Congreve's *Love for Love* and Chekhov's *The Cherry Orchard* with her friend and contemporary, Flora Robson, was Lanchester's last work on the English stage and within the classical repertoire. Apart from a ten-year stint in the forties as a founding member of the Yale Puppeteers at the Turnabout Theatre in Los Angeles, various revue sketches, night club acts, and her one-woman show in the fifties, most of her acting would be in film and television during the remaining five decades of her career.

In 1957, Lanchester and Laughton starred in what is probably their most famous collaboration, *Witness for the Prosecution*, a Billy Wilder film based on a play by Agatha Christie, which also dusted off and starred Marlene Dietrich and Tyrone Power (in what would prove his final film role). Laughton is the great defense lawyer, Sir Wilfrid Robarts, and Lanchester his exasperated nurse, Miss Plimsoll, in a role that even in 1957 must have seemed too close for comfort. The film was nominated for six Oscars, including Best Film, Best Actor in a Leading Role for Laughton, and Best Actress in a Supporting Role for Lanchester.

Lanchester would soon take a six-year break from film work. Her last film from the '50s and the last film she made before Laughton's death was *Bell, Book, and Candle* (R. Quine, Columbia, 1958), a sort of Upper East Side Manhattan precursor of *Bewitched* with Kim Novak as a working girl Samantha, Lanchester as a daffy Aunt Clara figure, and Lanchester's old friend, Hermione Gingold, aptly cast as an Endora-like rival witch. Lanchester's part was not a bad one, but a terribly boring film was made all the more so by starring a fifty-year-old James Stewart being even more of a dull old fart than he was when he was a young, dull old fart.

As it happened, Lanchester played out her filmatic life in never-never land. The most famous of her many movies for Walt Disney was *Mary Poppins* (R. Stevenson, 1964), in which she played Katie Nanna, the last of a long line of nannies to quit the Banks household before Julie Andrews is hired. Her childhood friend, Hermione Baddeley, played the maid, Ellen. This was Lanchester's first film role since Laughton's death from bone cancer on December 15, 1962. As in *Bell, Book, and Candle*, she looks fat, frumpy, and unwell. In the sixties, Lanchester also had quite a few TV guest appearances in series like *The Man from U.N.C.L.E.* (with a Bride of Frankenstein-style hairdo), *Mannix*, and *The Bill Cosby Show*. She had recurring roles on *The John Forsythe Show* (1965–66) and *Nanny and the Professor* (1971).

One of Lanchester's last films was the mystery movie parody *Murder by Death* (R. Moore, Columbia, 1976), a production with more big names than you could shake a stick at (and you might well want to do that—shake a stick, I mean—after wasting a couple of hours of your life watching it). The world's greatest detectives are invited for a murder mystery weekend at a country house hosted by Truman Capote (playing Truman Capote). In her role as Miss Jessica Marbles, a parody of Agatha Christie's Miss Jane Marple, Lanchester makes no attempt to imitate the classic '60s film portrayals by Margaret Rutherford, who had died in 1972. Why Miss Marple should have been saddled with an ancient nurse in this film is anyone's guess, but it gave Estelle Winwood a welcome opportunity for one last hurrah. The scene with the two old ladies in a double bed in nighties, robes, and nightcaps is one of the few high-points of the film. Lanchester looks like a dyspeptic hippo and Winwood, with her hooded eyes and parchment skin, looks like a benevolent iguana.

Murder by Death can only be enjoyed by the most intense devotees of its individual cast members, hence it held some interest for me as a fan of Winwood and—to some extent—Lanchester. Primarily a stage actress with too few films to rate a separate entry in this book, Winwood is almost completely forgotten today. Yet, as she was keen competition for Lanchester in the eccentric old lady category starting in the 1950s, a digression on her life and career at this point is not inappropriate. Furthermore, anyone who has been Tallulah Bankhead's best friend for nearly fifty years deserves to be discussed in a book about remarkable women.

When Winwood played her last role as Lanchester's aged nurse, Miss Withers, she was ninety-three and the oldest active member of the Screen Actors Guild. Born in 1883, Estelle (née Goodwin) was a grown woman when fellow English eccentrics Lanchester, Hermione Baddeley, and Hermione Gingold were born. Three things worth knowing about this "ageless Victorian Venus,"[284] as Noël Coward called her, are that she starred in the first play to win a Pulitzer Prize (that was way back in 1917); she lived to be 101 (longer than any actress in this book); and she had the biggest eyes of any actress in the United States, including ZaSu Pitts. Her eyes—called "bovine" by unkind tongues—seemed all the larger for being set in a very small face.

Like the two Hermiones (forgive me, Ms. Gingold, I know you hated being referred to that way), Winwood was a late bloomer in Hollywood and never a very strong growth. "Tremendously underused by Hollywood" according to one observer,[285] Winwood made only a dozen or so films there, including *The Glass*

Slipper (1955), where she played fairy godmother to Leslie Caron; *The Swan* (1956), where she was Grace Kelly's curious old aunt, Symphorosa; and *The Misfits* (1961), where she was a churchwoman trying to collect money from Marilyn Monroe and Clark Gable in what would prove the final film for both of them.

Lanchester fondly recalled her reunion with Winwood on the *Murder by Death* set. They had first acted together in *The Glass Slipper* twenty years before. "Estelle," Lanchester told an interviewer, "is one of the few people as free-spirited as me. Her façade is very prim and even somewhat gothic, but she's a merry old soul, and we always laugh together."[286] It is interesting that Winwood did not recall their collaboration on the film with the same fondness. She told one interviewer that Lanchester was "Not a friendly woman, and rather daft" and claimed that she'd ignored her during most of the filming. "She came here [to America]," Winwood sniffed, "and made a living playing English eccentrics. It wasn't talent—it's being herself, and she's got barmier with the years."[287]

In her old age Lanchester said she missed and mourned her husband more than she had on his death. Back in 1962 a feeling of newfound freedom had predominated, after more than thirty years in a highly volatile relationship with much bitterness and resentment on both sides.[288] Curiously, Lanchester claimed never to have gone to any other funeral than her husband's and never to have attended any other wedding than her own. "Acute undemonstrativeness," as she called it, was a Lanchester family trait.[289]

"La Laughton," as Louella Parsons dubbed her,[290] stayed on in the house in central Hollywood that she had bought with Laughton in 1949 and where he died. "Houses and places and flowers and trees always played a principal part in our life," she wrote in her 1983 memoirs, "Charles and I were held together by them."[291] Elsa Lanchester survived her husband by twenty-four years, dying from bronchial pneumonia at the Motion Picture Country Home and Hospital in Woodland Hills, California on December 26, 1986. Summing up her career, she reflected with her customary modesty, "You might call what I do vaudeville." "Laughter," she added, "was never very far away."[292]

Mother Hen
JESSIE ROYCE LANDIS (1904–1972)

Hollywood continued even in the late 1940s and '50s to be the saving of many an aging stage actress's career. Jessie Royce Landis had made a false start in the movies in 1930 with a film called *Derelict* for Paramount, but she had not fared well with her director, Rowland V. Lee, nor had she found Los Angeles congenial.[293] It would be nineteen years till she made another venture into film. By the late '40s her theatrical career was in decline. When she was asked to do a screen test for Twentieth Century-Fox, she jumped at the chance. The test was a disaster. She looked like Whistler's mother.

After viewing it, Landis was sure she would never work in the movies again or, for that matter, television. Fortunately for her, the powers that be were not put off by the test.[294] With *Mr. Belvedere Goes to College* (E. Nugent, 1949), starring her old friend Clifton Webb and a grown Shirley Temple, Landis embarked on a productive film career, making nineteen feature films in eleven years.

Jessie Royce Medbury was born on November 25, 1904, making her the contemporary of character actresses Anne Revere, Una Merkel, Thelma Ritter, Mildred Natwick, and Mona

Washbourne. Her father was a professional musician, her mother rented out rooms to augment the family finances, and Landis grew up in relatively modest circumstances in the Ellis Park neighborhood of Chicago. Her mother encouraged her only child's artistic aspirations, which manifested themselves at any early age. When she was fourteen, she was awarded a scholarship to the Hinshaw Dramatic School and from there she was engaged by the Evanston Stock Company two years later. Her acting career might have come to an end with her secret marriage in June 1923 to Perry Lester Landis, a scion of one of Evanston's prominent families, but the family went into a financial decline, making it possible for Landis to justify going back to work. She became the director and leading lady of the North Shore Players, before being hired to go on tour with a play called *The Highwayman* in December 1924.[295]

This was more than Mr. Landis had bargained for and he gave his wife an ultimatum: She must choose between her marriage and the stage. She chose the latter, leaving her son, Medbury Perry Landis, who had been born with Down's Syndrome in 1924, at a special school where he would stay for the remainder of his short life. Landis and "Royce," as she preferred to be called, would never live together as husband and wife again, though they were not divorced until 1935.[296] Jessie Royce Landis, as she would be known throughout her career, would marry again twice, the pressman Rex Smith (1937–44) and the major-general J.F.R. Seitz (from 1956 until her death), but have no more children.

Landis had been an actress for thirty years when she broke into the movies. Some of the highpoints of her varied if not particularly stellar stage career included playing Jo in *Little Women* with Jessie Bonstell's legendary stock company; performing with the equally legendary Laurette Taylor in *Delicate Balance* (Taylor's husband, Hartley Manners's last play); *Solid South* on Broadway with Elizabeth Patterson and Landis's lifelong friend, Bette Davis; *Merrily We Roll Along* (1934) by George Kaufman and Moss Hart, her longest run in New York; *Love's Old Sweet Song* with her favorite actor heartthrob, Walter Huston (1939–40); and *Papa Is All* (1941–42), where she played, to her own and the audience's amazement, a Mennonite grandmother. Landis herself claimed that she had made her reputation as an actress the hard way, by getting good reviews in unsuccessful plays. She regretted that she had not specialized in one type of role.[297] When she said this in 1954, she could not have known that she was soon to find her type—in the movies.

It would be an exaggeration to say that Landis had a long or illustrious film career, but she was good in some good pictures and she came to symbolize a certain type of American woman at a specific point in time. During the Eisenhower and Kennedy years, Jessie Royce Landis fairly defined middle-aged, middle-class motherhood in the movies, as Fay Bainter and Spring Byington had done in the '30s and '40s. As a screen mother, Landis had some of the most attractive children in Hollywood: Grace Kelly, Cary Grant, James Garner, and Tab Hunter.

Landis's "limp kind of beauty," as Brooks Atkinson once described it,[298] was quite a bit limper by the time she first appeared in glorious Technicolor in 1952, but Landis was a colorful lady in many ways and the medium suited her. Like another of her contemporaries, Agnes Moorehead, she was a redhead by nature and—as the years went on—by art, but where Moorehead was hard and angular, Landis was soft and rounded. Where Moorehead was tart, Landis was bland. And we can safely say that Agnes Moorehead was a more talented and versatile actress. Yet, within her fairly narrow range of society woman and mature middle-class mother roles, Jessie Royce Landis was preeminent in the second half of the fifties and the first half of the sixties.

After a modest success with *Mr. Belvedere Goes to College*, Landis made three further films in Hollywood in 1949–50, before having to decide between making her first film for MGM or starring in a play by Somerset Maugham.[299] Landis chose the play and, as fate would have it, this choice gave a new impetus both to her stage and screen careers. *Theatre*, as the play was originally called, was such a success that Landis took it to London, where it opened at the Duke of York's Theatre under a new title, *Larger than Life*, in February 1950.[300] One thing led to another and Landis would stay three years in England, three glorious years, if we are to believe the actress's account in her autobiography *You Won't Be So Pretty (But You'll Know More)*.[301]

Someone said once that one should avoid meeting in person authors or artists one admires, as one may find one doesn't like them half as much as their art. Maybe one should avoid reading their autobiographies as well. This goes for Landis, anyhow, who in 1954 published one of the most self-congratulatory, turgid volumes to date within a subgenre of books notorious for just those qualities. For all I know, Landis may have been a delightful, charming ol' gal, but the smug, self-satisfied image she projects in *You Won't Be So Pretty* makes that seem doubtful. It would appear that during her long periods as a gay divorcée, she had more "gentleman callers" than Amanda Wingfield in *The Glass Menagerie* and, like Amanda, she makes sure we never forget it. Apropos of this great role in the Tennessee Williams repertoire: It was created by Landis's friend and mentor, Laurette Taylor. In her autobiography Landis takes credit for engineering this comeback and final stage triumph for the heavy-drinking Taylor, but that's another story.[302]

Jessie Royce Landis at her worst puts one in mind of a russet brood hen clucking around the henhouse in a triple strand of Barbara Bush

In this photo from the unsuccessful 1957 remake of *My Man Godfrey* (Universal International), we find a horizontal June Allyson in the leading role of Irene Bullock; Jessie Royce Landis as her mother, Angelica: Jay Robinson as Landis's "protégé"; and David Niven as Godfrey, the vagrant turned butler. Landis ought to have sued costume designer Bill Thomas for putting her into a frock that looks like a combination of a trenchcoat and a cabbage patch.

pearls. Granted, the henhouse might well be a palace or a Park Avenue apartment, but the effect is as irritating as a repeated drop of water on the forehead. Fortunately Landis had a cooler, wittier, more modern side. She was adept at playing experienced, sophisticated, yet earthy women of the world, who aren't fazed by anything and who have few illusions about life. No one brought out this side of Landis like Alfred Hitchcock and the two films he made with her are without a doubt her most popular and memorable ones.

At age fifty-one Landis finally found her type in Hitchcock's *To Catch a Thief* (Paramount, 1955), starring Grace Kelly as her "ice princess" daughter and Cary Grant as an ex–cat burglar. Hitchcock may well have become aware of Landis through her work in the West End. At any rate there is an allusion in the film to her final stage hit in London, *And So To Bed*, a musical about so unlikely a topic as the life of Samuel Pepys. As Jessie Stevens in *To Catch a Thief*, a wealthy, worldly widow from the American West, watching the world go by on the French Riviera and cuddling up with her jewelry for want of anything better ("Nobody calls me Jessie anymore!"), Landis is in her element.

Four years later, Hitchcock paired her with Grant once again. In her signature role, Landis plays Clara Thornhill, Grant's ironical mother in *North by Northwest* (MGM, 1959). As viewers will recall, she trails around after him and by every available means—verbal and otherwise—

Jessie Royce Landis as rich expatriate American Mrs. Van der Besh instructs her new interior decorator, Paula Tessier (Ingrid Bergman), on her requirements for her Paris home in *Goodbye Again* (United Artists, 1961). Little does Landis know that her apartment is not the only thing Bergman will be doing over.

give expression to her increasing incredulity, as he makes a futile attempt to prove his innocence. The film shows to the full what Landis could do with a strong part and a strong script.

At least two of her intervening films, on the other hand, are Landis and water. *The Swan* (C. Vidor, MGM, 1956) also attempted to capitalize on the success of *To Catch a Thief* by casting her again as Grace Kelly's mother. Landis is a princess of some imaginary little kingdom this time and is trying to engineer a good match for her daughter with Alec Guinness. Naturally, Kelly falls for someone inappropriate in the enticing figure of Louis Jourdan, and Landis runs the gamut of hair-tearing and hand-wringing, her face screwed up into a perpetual frown that doesn't do much for her. Estelle Winwood as the whacky old aunt, Symphorosa, and Agnes Moorehead as the commonsensical queen add a little tanginess to this sickly sweet cotton candy of a romantic comedy.

My Man Godfrey (Universal, 1957), Henry Koster's remake of Gregory La Cava's classic screwball comedy, makes *The Swan* look like a veritable masterpiece. The ever dependable June Allyson is about fifteen years too old to play the ingénue of the piece, Irene Bullock. Carole Lombard was twenty-eight when she played the role in the original version from 1936. Eva Gabor should have sued the makeup department for dereliction of duty and Jay Robinson in the role of Landis's resident lapdog isn't a patch on Mischa Auer. But perhaps the biggest disaster is Landis herself as the mother, Angelica, one of Alice Brady's famous dizzy dame roles. Landis is about as funny as a giant zit on prom night and delivers her dizzy responses with a lardlike lack of spontaneity.

Landis also scored some hits in the 1960s. In *Goodbye Again* (A. Litvak, 1961), she was the only seemingly dizzy dame, Mrs. Van der Besh, a rich expatriate American in Paris with faith in astrology, a fondness for the bottle, and a ne'er-do-well son, played by Anthony Perkins. Perkins has an affair with mommy's decorator, Ingrid Bergman, and one hung over morning, Landis reveals: "He drinks, you know."

In *Boys' Night Out* (M. Gordon, MGM, 1962), she played dishy divorcé James Garner's live-in mother. She worries about her son, longs for grandchildren, and plays the go-between between her son's buddies and their wives, when the latter discover their hubbies have collectively been "keeping" a young woman, Kim Novak, in a sumptuous New York apartment. Landis is the calm eye of the storm in a film that must have been every middle-aged, middle-class, married Jo Schmo's fantasy come to life. The following line is typical of her character, Ethel Williams: "Have you noticed how insolent the help have gotten lately? Ever since the Kennedys got in!"

Landis's last feature film was the justly famous *Airport* (G. Seaton, H. Hathaway, Universal, 1970), released two years before her death. Landis has a small but entertaining cameo as a rich lady with the incredible moniker, Mrs. Harriet DuBarry Mossman, who gets caught trying to smuggle clothes, furs, and jewelry back from Paris, including a diamond bracelet she has hidden in her poodle's collar. This, and her penultimate role as Aunt Albertina Blythe in *Gidget Goes to Rome* (P. Wendkos, Columbia, 1963), was probably the closest Landis ever came to playing herself, something she does very convincingly. In her autobiography, she describes how smuggling has added zest to her life and makes the dubious claim that "a lot of women are smugglers at heart."[303] She also relates in vivid detail how she once almost created an international incident by arriving at Rome Airport without a valid passport.[304] This was a foreshadowing of her apparition in the third of the Gidget movies, where elaborately behatted, bewigged, and begowned she acts as an entirely inappropriate chaperone for Gidget and her gang, flirting wildly with the boys and fishing desperately for compliments. Clearly, the real life Landis was a force to be reckoned with.

Jessie Royce Landis died of cancer in Danbury, Connecticut on February 2, 1972, and was laid to rest in Branchville Cemetery, Ridgefield, Connecticut. We can be sure she arrived at the gates of Heaven immaculately dressed.

The Magnificent Mammy
HATTIE McDANIEL (1893–1952)

Hattie McDaniel was a force of nature. After acting in seventy known films in seven years, she won the role of a lifetime and went on to glory as the first African American to win an Academy Award. Ironically, though she would secure a handful of interesting roles in the wake of her Oscar win, *Gone with the Wind* marked the end of the most productive period of her film career. She made only twenty films in the 1940s. A troubled woman, who felt fully the stresses and contradictions of her fame, social position, and professional reputation, McDaniel was married four times. Starting with her false pregnancy in 1944, she went into a slow decline that would lead to a suicide attempt and ultimately death from cancer at the relatively early age of fifty-nine.[305] It takes a strong back to bear the burden of success.

From Claudette Colbert to Margaret Sullavan, as maid, mammy, or cook, Hattie McDaniel supported more than a dozen of the period's biggest stars. Just consider this list: Colbert in *Since You Went Away* (J. Cromwell, Selznick Int., 1944) and *Family Honeymoon* (C. Binyon, Universal, 1949), Joan Crawford in *The Shining Hour* (F. Borzage, MGM, 1938); Bette Davis in *The Great Lie* (E. Goulding, Warner Bros., 1941) and *In This Our Life* (J. Huston, Warner Bros., 1942); Marlene Dietrich in *Blonde Venus* (J. von Sternberg, Paramount, 1932); Irene Dunne in *Show Boat* (J. Whale, Universal, 1936); Olivia de Havilland in *They Died With Their Boots On* (R. Walsh, Warner Bros., 1941), *The Male Animal* (E. Nugent, Warner Bros., 1942), and *In This Our Life* (1942), Jean Harlow in *China Seas* (T. Garnett, MGM, 1935) and *Saratoga* (J. Conway, MGM, 1937); Katharine Hepburn in *Alice Adams* (G. Stevens, RKO, 1935); Vivien Leigh in *Gone with the Wind* (V. Fleming, Selznick Int., 1939); Merle Oberon in *Affectionately Yours* (L. Bacon, Warner Bros., 1941); Ann Sheridan in *George Washington Slept Here* (W. Keighley, Warner Bros., 1942); Barbara Stanwyck in *The Bride Walks Out* (L. Jason, RKO, 1936), *Stella Dallas* (K. Vidor, Samuel Goldwyn, 1937), and *The Mad Miss Manton* (L. Jason, RKO, 1938); and Margaret Sullavan in *The Shopworn Angel* (H.C. Potter, MGM, 1938). In truth, though, Hattie McDaniel was herself a star and had histrionic talents to match any of the white actresses she performed with. Jill Watts writes: "[I]f the measure of an artist is in the ability to provoke feelings and emotions, to challenge audiences to think and react, then perhaps Hattie McDaniel may really have been one of the most talented performers of her time."[306]

From McDaniel's film debut in 1932 till her apotheosis seven years later as the most famous black actress in America, "She emerged as the one servant of the era to speak her mind fully." "[T]he world of her eccentric characters," continues Donald Bogle, "was a helter-skelter, topsy-turvy one in which the servant became the social equal, the mammy became the literal mother figure, the put-on was carried to the forefront of the action, and the style of the servant overpowered the content of the script."[307] Yet, without Mammy in *Gone with the Wind* and her subsequent Oscar triumph, McDaniel would be no better known today than any of a dozen other prominent black actresses of the first decades of sound, such as Louise Beavers, Ethel Waters, Libby Taylor, Marietta Canty, and Lillian Yarbo. Based both on the number and quality of her roles, Louise Beavers was the most important African American actress in Hollywood in the 1930s. That all changed the night Hattie McDaniel won the Academy Award.[308]

Another point of contrast with Hattie McDaniel is her *GWTW* co-star and personal friend, Butterfly McQueen. McQueen didn't arrive in Hollywood till 1939 and first appeared in *The Women*. Unlike the myriad films of McDaniel and Beavers, she only made nine films in as many years. John Springer and Jack Hamilton observe, "Where Hattie McDaniel could be gruff and bossy, and Butterfly McQueen squeakily idiotic, the Beavers image was all big protective bosoms and benevolent smiles."[309] According to Donald Bogle:

> No two black actresses of the 1930s differed so widely as did Hattie McDaniel and Butterfly McQueen.... McDaniel was tough and resilient and could take a small incident and magnify it into a mountain. Butterfly, however, could take a big scene and condense it into the tiniest of lyrical poems. Her performance was marked by fragility, hysteria, and absurdity.[310]

McQueen was all of nineteen years younger that McDaniel and from the South.

McDaniel herself was born on June 10, 1893 in Wichita, Kansas, the youngest of ex-slave Henry McDaniel and his wife Susan Holbert's thirteen children, nearly half of whom died either at birth or shortly afterwards.[311] Hattie grew and thrived, going to an integrated school in Denver, Colorado, where her family moved in 1898.[312] She would later claim to have won an elocution contest in 1908 with her rendition of "Convict Joe," the same year we know she had her first professional engagement in a minstrel show.[313] On January 19, 1911, McDaniel married for the first time. Her husband was Howard J. Hickman, born in Kansas in 1889, "from a good family with solid standing in Denver's black community."[314] Hickman died suddenly of pneumonia in 1915. McDaniel's mother died in 1920, at the age of seventy, followed by Henry McDaniel in 1922. McDaniel had remarried sometime before her father's death. Her second husband was Nym Lankford, a native of St. Joseph, Missouri, but the marriage soon went sour.[315] By 1924, McDaniel was a headline singer on the Pantages vaudeville circuit.[316] She may have broken into radio on station KOA in Denver at about this time,[317] and she would end her career in radio with the popular serial *Beulah*.

If you see a train porter in a '30s or '40s film who looks like a male version of Hattie McDaniel, chances are it is her brother Sam, who was seven years her senior. He and Hattie's sister, Etta, preceded her to Hollywood and began to work in the movies.[318] Hattie followed in 1931.[319] Sam

In this candid from some long-forgotten Hollywood social event, Hattie McDaniel poses with a suave, unidentified escort. McDaniel wears her favorite fur cape. She enjoyed the company of gay men and was herself rumored to be bisexual.

and Hattie would appear in nine films together between 1932 and 1946. They referred to themselves as the "Dark Barrymores."[320] Sam made the last of his more than two hundred known films in 1960 and died, the last of the talented McDaniel siblings, at Woodland Hills in 1962. Etta McDaniel (1890–1946) made more than fifty films, starting as a native dancer in *King Kong* (1933) and making her last film in 1945. The sisters were in only one film together, *Stella Dallas* (1937), where Etta played Barbara Stanwyck's first maid, Agnes, who welcomes her and the baby home from the hospital, and Hattie is briefly glimpsed as her second maid, Edna.[321]

Hattie McDaniel's finest roles were those that, in addition to giving her time to develop her character, gave full play to her peerless personality. In addition to Mammy in *Gone with the Wind*, the list must include Malena Burns in *Alice Adams* (1935), Queenie in *Show Boat* (1936), Ellen in *Valiant Is the Word for Carrie* (1936), Violet in *The Great Lie* (1941), Minerva Clay in *In This Our Life* (1942), playing herself in *Thank Your Lucky Stars* (1943), Aida in *Johnny Come Lately* (1943), and Fidelia in *Since You Went Away* (1944).

McDaniel had played mostly maids in almost thirty films, including *Blonde Venus* with Dietrich and *I'm No Angel* with Mae West, before she came to portray the hired maid from hell in *Alice Adams*. In *Blonde Venus* she was tow-headed and uncustomarily unkempt, in *I'm No Angel* she was one of four maids surrounding the star, who exclaims that she had West pegged as a "one-man woman," to which remark the blond bombshell responds typically: "One man at a time." It was not until *Alice Adams* that McDaniel came into her own as the "could-not-care-less-about-these-white-folks maid"[322] Malena Burns, hired by the Adams family to impress Fred MacMurray, toney beau of the socially ambitious daughter of the house, Katharine Hepburn. From the moment McDaniel butts open the kitchen door with her behind, chewing gum in mouth, maid's white cap awry, and serves the host first, we are in the thrall of her passive-aggressive antics. Here McDaniel first begins to build the screen persona that would make her more than just a maid and culminate in the O'Hara's Mammy four years later.

She followed up with a fine portrayal of the cook Queenie in *Show Boat* (1936), a role she had also played on stage.[323] In a much larger part than in *Alice Adams*, McDaniel is beginning to metamophosize into the gravelly voiced and bellicose individual we know and love, and even sings a duet with her screen husband, Paul Robeson. Villain Donald Cook compares Queenie to an eight ball, which does not sit so well with a racially conscious, modern audience, but is somewhat justified by McDaniel's famous girth, if nothing else. She was only 5'2" inches tall, but in her prime weighed in excess of 200 lbs.[324]

Valiant Is the Word for Carrie (W. Ruggles, Paramount, 1936) is a much less well known film than *Alice Adams* or *Show Boat*, but it allowed McDaniel to appear as the friend and confidante of a white woman for whom she was not working. Granted, this was a woman of "ill repute," Carrie Snyder, played by that almost star and later doyenne of the shopworn blondes, Gladys George. McDaniel acts as a buffer between George and the village community that wants to be rid of her and as a messenger between George and the young boy she has befriended and will later raise.

The Great Lie (1941), McDaniel's second film after *GWTW*, is interesting for the screen time it gives to a depiction not just of "upstairs," but of "downstairs," the life of the African American servants working on the Maryland estate of Bette Davis (Maggie Patterson Van Allen). McDaniel is Davis's protective mammy, Violet, who tries to keep George Brent (Pete Van Allen) from breaking their collective heart again, as he did when he married concert pianist Mary Astor (Sandra Kovak). Part of the humor of the situation is that McDaniel appears to be more distraught than Davis. Several of the "downstairs" scenes are played out between McDaniel and her brother Sam, playing the butler and man-of-all-work, Jefferson Washington.

In This Our Life (1942), despite its melodramatic element, is an important, race-conscious film from the forties, unique in its willingness to tell the story also from the African American characters' point of view. In playing Minerva Clay, the cook in the once wealthy Timberlake family, McDaniel became "the first black actress to voice direct criticism of American racism on the Hollywood screen."[325] Clay's young son Parry (Ernest Anderson[326]) works first for the daughter of the family, Roy Timberlake (Olivia de Havilland), as a helper in her interior decorating business, and later in George Brent's law office, while studying for the bar. Intelligent and ambitious, the young man's future and life are threatened when dastardly Stanley Timberlake (Bette Davis) tries to pin the blame on him for her hit-and-run accident. McDaniel and de Havilland have an important scene in which the concerned mother tries to make her suspicions clear, knowing all the while that it will be her word against the word of a white woman and the daughter of a prominent family. The brief glimpse it offers of the domestic world of the African American servant and its "positive images" of African Americans as individuals with lives and troubles of their own make the film more than the story of two sisters—one good, one bad—and the dubious rewards of boundless selfishness.

Thank Your Lucky Stars (D. Butler, Warner Bros., 1943) was Warner Bros. cavalcade of stars to benefit the war effort and is maybe best remembered for Bette Davis's amusing rendition of "They're Either Too Young or Too Old." It deserves equally to be remembered for Hattie McDaniel's stunning appearance as the most glamourous and gorgeous version possible of herself. Here we can imagine what she might have been like in her glory days on the Pantages circuit, where she was known as the female Bert Williams and the "black Sophie Tucker,"[327] suggesting both her androgyny and her diva quality. Dressed to the nines, McDaniel performs an all-black number entitled "Ice Cold Katie." The Katie of the title is not herself, but rather a young woman McDaniel is trying to convince to marry a callow, unattractive soldier before he goes off to war. McDaniel is also a prominent part of the grand finale, where she sits resplendent in white satin, singing on the moon.

McDaniel's two final major roles were in *Johnny Come Lately* (W.K. Howard, 1943) and *Since You Went Away* (1944). In the former she plays Grace George's trusty cook, Aida, who helps feed the homeless and everyone else. She was billed fifth, after star James Cagney, George, Marjorie Main, and Marjorie Lord. Grace George will not be remembered by many today, but she was a Broadway star in the early decades of the last century, wife of fabled Broadway producer William A. Brady, and stepmother of Alice Brady. This was her only film role, as the owner of a local newspaper who takes the homeless Cagney under her wing. In *Since You Went Away*, McDaniel portrayed the aptly named Fidelia, Claudette Colbert's trusty housekeeper and later, when Colbert can no longer afford to retain her services, her lodger. In this role, McDaniel is a regular Mrs. Malaprop and lends welcome comic relief to David O. Selznick's overlong and rather sentimental epic of the home front, which also starred Joseph Cotten, Jennifer Jones, Agnes Moorehead, and a teenage Shirley Temple.

That leaves only *Gone with the Wind* to discuss among McDaniel's major films, coming as it did midway in her seventeen-year cinematic career. Exactly how good was she as Mammy? I'd say that she was darn good and that her performance has held up remarkably well. McDaniel took hold of the role with both hands and wrung every last drop of drama, pathos, humor, and power out of it. Everyone remembers her hanging out the window of Tara and yelling to Scarlett to "Come on in the house" and, shortly afterwards, lacing her up and admonishing her to eat, while trying to keep her décolleté to a minimum. The *New York Times* film critic wrote of this scene with the paternalism of another age (or is it irony?) that Mammy "must be personally absolved of responsibility for that most 'unfittin' scene in which she scolds Scarlett from an upstairs window." He continues: "She played even that one right, however wrong it was." [328]

Though maybe not so well remembered, McDaniel has many other fine scenes in the film. What about when she welcomes Scarlett back to war-scarred Tara and must convey both the joy at seeing her "chile" again and her grief

This still from Hattie McDaniel's first scene with Vivien Leigh in *Gone with the Wind* (Metro-Goldwyn-Mayer, 1939) conveys nothing of the energy, the animosity, and the humor of the power struggle between Mammy and Scarlett, as the former gets the latter ready for the big party at the Wilkes's Twelve Oaks plantation.

at Miss Ellen's death? What about the scene in which she tells Melanie of Rhett's grief over Bonnie's death, such a poignant contrast to the earlier moment when she shares a celebratory drink with Rhett at Bonnie's birth? According to McDaniel's biographer, Carlton Jackson, it was her long, grief-stricken monologue as she and de Havilland ascend the stairs that "clinched the Oscar for her."[329] My personal favorite McDaniel scene in *GWTW* is the long sequence played out in the streets of post-war Atlanta, where Mammy barges through the crowds of male loiterers, clearing the way for Scarlett. That delicious episode ends with a look of incredulity on Mammy's face, as Scarlett plays up to Frank Kennedy, her sister's beau. Here is the key to Mammy's unique function in the film. On the one hand, she knows Scarlett better than anyone else, she sees through her falsehoods, vanities, and intrigues. Yet she cannot but love her. Invested with the love of this goodhearted, righteous, respectable black woman, Scarlett, ethically a highly ambiguous figure, is in a sense cleared of blame and made a possible object of love and even admiration for the audience as well.

Gone with the Wind is one of the finest films ever made for many different reasons, but surely a significant one is the extent to which the actors hired to play the leading roles are all stunningly well cast. Much has been written of the nationwide search for Scarlett, but there was

The Magnificent Mammy: Hattie McDaniel (1893-1952)

competition for the role of Mammy as well. The main contenders in addition to McDaniel were Louise Beavers and Hattie Noel.[330] Madame Sul-Te-Wan and Georgette Harvey are also sometimes mentioned as candidates for the coveted role.[331] At any rate, Beavers appears to have lost her chance by being too well-dressed for her meeting with producer David O. Selznick.[332] One wonders, though, if it is not more likely that the benevolent, beaming persona she had created on screen during the past decade was not quite what the role required. McDaniel, on the other hand, was perfect in that she "personified the all-knowing, all-seeing, all-hearing, sometimes helpful, sometimes haughty mammy figure, who, when the chips were down, could usually be counted on to come to the aid of her white employers although she would often bark and grumble the whole time."[333] "[I]n her pre-1940s films," writes Bogle, "McDaniel was often enough at odds with her leading ladies and her better films are those in which she appeared with actresses who could fight back."[334] Thus, all the work she had put into seven years of playing maids, mammies, and cooks finally paid off. She was tested with Vivien Leigh on December 6, 1938, and offered a contract on January 27, 1939, to begin on February 1 and to run for renewable 15-week periods at $450 a week.[335]

Yes, Mammy *is* another mammy, but she is first and foremost an individual, a fully realized African American woman, who despite her devotion and dependence is allowed idiosyncrasies, vanities, and quirks of her own. Isn't it charming how she holds high the banner of respectability and decency, so that Scarlett cannot fail to see it? Her favorite expression, "po,' no 'count white trash," becomes almost

In *Mickey* (Eagle-Lion, 1948), McDaniel shows lead Lois Butler how to put a little vanilla essence behind her ears. McDaniel's outlandish hat has surely been designed by her personal hatmaker from 1941, Leon Bennett. The more original the hats, the better McDaniel liked them.

an incantation, signifying as it does on like-sounding white collocations about blacks, but even Mammy has something to learn about judging a book by its cover. Even nouveau riche snobs like Rhett Butler can be noble. The red petticoat she gets from Rhett symbolizes her recognition of a new standard of ethics in the post-war South. Now she too has a touch of scarlet about her. "It ain't fittin.' It just ain't fittin.'"

Bogle observes a loss of vitality in the roles available to African American actresses in the 1940s:

> Because they had carried the servant tradition to its highest point, the black characters of *Gone with the Wind* brought the tradition to a fitting close. In the 1940s, although the servants still appeared in films, the enthusiasm and creativity that distinguished figures such as Hattie McDaniel and Butterfly McQueen were gone.[336]

Though McDaniel would never appear in an uncredited role after *GWTW* and made five of her most interesting films after her triumph as Mammy, her part in a film such as *Song of the South* shows the extent to which she had developed as far as she or any other African American actress would be allowed to. After *GWTW* and *In This Our Life*, almost every role she played would be an anticlimax. As Aunt Tempy in *Song of the South*, McDaniel is nothing but beaming and benevolent to her white employers, though belligerent to white children and blacks of all ages.[337] According to one film historian, McDaniel here "displayed a newfound Christian domesticity that was the exact antithesis of her haughty grandeur in the late 1930s."[338] This brings even McDaniel's pugnacious film persona more into line with the Beavers benevolent maid and mammy tradition.

McDaniel made fewer and fewer films as the forties progressed. *The Big Wheel* (E. Ludwig, 1949) was the last of the lot. After the producers finally decided it was better to have a black woman rather than a white man play the lead role in the popular radio serial *Beulah*, McDaniel took over the part on November 24, 1947.[339] She had taped six episodes for television, before her final illness cut short both her life and career.[340] A boil under her arm turned out to be breast cancer.[341] McDaniel was the first black person to be admitted to the Motion Picture Country Home and Hospital at Woodland Hills, California and died there alone on Sunday afternoon, October 26, 1952.[342] She was buried in the Angelus Rosedale Cemetery in Los Angeles. Her first choice, Hollywood Park Cemetery, refused to allow her to be buried there.[343] On the forty-seventh anniversary of her death, though, a cenotaph was dedicated to her memory at the renamed Hollywood Forever Cemetery in recognition of the wrong that had been done all those years ago.

Butterflies Are Free
BUTTERFLY McQUEEN (1911–1995)

Butterfly McQueen had the briefest and most erratic acting career of any easily recognizable and popular Hollywood character actress. In fact, "career" is too highfalutin' a word for it. McQueen didn't have a career, she had jobs. And a mixed bag of jobs it was too. In addition to her work as an actress on stage, radio, and on both the small and large screen, McQueen was at various periods in her long life a paid companion, a tour guide, an employee in the toy department at Macy's, a cab dispatcher, the operator of a small restaurant, the manager of a little theater group, a factory worker, a waitress and dishwasher, a playground assistant, a receptionist, and a teacher of tap dancing and ballet. She also gave music lessons and had her own radio program.³⁴⁴ Almost the only typical low-paying job she is not on record as having is the one she almost always had on screen: being a maid.

All told, McQueen made only a dozen feature films; an unlucky thirteen, if you count *Gone with the Wind* producer David O. Selznick's World War II homefront epic, *Since You Went Away* (J. Cromwell, Selznick Int., 1944), where her scenes were cut.³⁴⁵ One might say that McQueen achieved the maximum of exposure out of a minimum of screen time. She is the actress in this volume with the smallest body of work and, relatively speaking, the largest proportion of unpromising maid roles. In fact, the only one of her Hollywood films in which she was *not* a maid was *Cabin in the Sky* (V. Minnelli, MGM, 1943). In this filmatization of Mark Connelly's patronizing musical comedy, McQueen plays Lily, lead actress Ethel Waters's church-going, ironical friend. Apparently, McQueen did not have happy memories of making this film: "Rochester [Eddie Anderson] teased her, Lena Horne treated her with contempt and Minnelli was nice to her face but cutting when she was not present."³⁴⁶ McQueen played Joan Crawford's erstwhile maid Lulu in *The Women* (G. Cukor, MGM, 1939), Ann Dvorak's maid Beulah in *Flame of Barbary Coast* (J. Kane, Republic, 1945), Crawford's maid again in *Mildred Pierce* (M. Curtiz, Warner Bros., 1945), and the McCanles family's maid, Vashti, in *Duel in the Sun* (K. Vidor, Selznick Int., 1946), to mention only her most high-profile maid roles (if that is not a contradiction in terms). In most cases, she gave the same basic performance: seemingly dim-witted, always helium-voiced, often ridiculously romantic. She was usually there and gone before you knew it.

So why do we remember Butterfly McQueen? Why does she live on in our cultural memory long after Marietta Canty, Lillian Yarbo, Libby Taylor, Gertrude Howard, and even Louise Beavers have been forgotten? There

The storm is about to break over Butterfly McQueen's hapless head in this shot from her classic scene with Vivien Leigh in *Gone with the Wind* (Metro-Goldwyn-Mayer, 1939), when it is revealed that Prissy "don't know nothin' 'bout birthin' babies." Though Prissy is a young girl, McQueen and Leigh were in fact the same age, both being born in 1911.

is a simple and a more complex answer to that question. The simple answer is: *Gone with the Wind*. McQueen was fortunate, though she did not always consider herself so,[347] to be cast in the second most memorable African American role in what many consider the greatest film ever made and certainly one of the most popular. So Butterfly McQueen's posterity will ever be tied to GWTW. Most would be hard pressed to come up with any other films she was in.

The more complex reason for her "memorability" is related to her unique personal qualities as an individual and a performer. McQueen, like a handful of other character actresses, was intensely watchable chiefly for looking and sounding bizarre. Maria Ouspenskaya, Hope Emerson, and Alice Pearce also spring to mind in this exclusive category. Pioneering African American film historian Donald Bogle has best analyzed her special screen charisma. He describes her physically as "Diminutive, delicate, with a distinctive high-pitched voice and the demeanor of a very sweet, well-brought-up but spacey schoolgirl"[348]: "She had a pleasant waiflike quality, too ... Tiny and delicate, Butterfly McQueen seemed to ask for protection and was a unique combination of the comic and the pathetic."[349] Writing that she "had to be handled as a surreal creature rather than as the stock comic servant,"[350] Bogle has also best described the effect of the "almost otherworldly" McQueen's brief screen appearances (if "apparitions" is not a better word):

> McQueen seldom seemed to be in her movies, instead it's almost as if she had distanced herself outside them, as if she simply were making a highly polished entrance—doing her bit—then anxiously running off to some other world or planet. Her unfailing sense of decorum was the secret of much of her screen charm and humor.[351]

McQueen once said herself: "I'd like to play just an American, they can see I'm black."[352]

It is easy to forget that Butterfly McQueen didn't make her film debut in GWTW. She made her debut in an uncredited role in that scorching all-female satire, *The Women* (1939). As Lulu, McQueen assisted Joan Crawford (Crystal Allen) both behind the perfume counter and in preparing dinner for Crawford's crucial rendevous with her married soon-to-be lover. Exactly how McQueen landed her first film role is not clear, but it is possible David O. Selznick or his East Coast talent scout, Kay Brown, noticed her in George Abbott's hit show *What a Life* (1938–39), which ran for 538 performances at the Biltmore Theatre. Director and producer Abbott, who also produced McQueen's first Broadway show, is said to have created a role especially for her in *What a Life*.[353] Prior to her Broadway debut in *Brown Sugar* in 1937, which only ran for four performances, McQueen had been part of Venezuela Jones's Negro Youth Group in Harlem and acquired her stage name while dancing in the "Butterfly" ballet of a production of *A Midsummer Night's Dream*.[354] She would later have her name legally changed from Thelma to Butterfly.[355] After the unsuccessful show *Swingin' the Dream* in late 1939, it would be thirty years till McQueen again stood on a Broadway stage.

McQueen's director in *The Women*, George Cukor, would go straight on to direct *Gone with the Wind*, though we do not know if he had a hand in casting her in the latter film. Producer Selznick had full control over the casting process, so any influence would have been indirect. We know McQueen was initially told she was too old and wrong for the part of Prissy.[356] Though twenty-nine, she would go on to portray the thirteen-year-old girl with utter conviction. As fate would have it, one of the two scenes Cukor is known to have directed before he was summarily relieved of his duties and replaced by Victor Fleming was McQueen's tour de force "I dun know nothin' 'bout birthin' babies" episode.[357] You will recall that Melanie Wilkes is about to conceive in the midst of the burning of Atlanta, when it materializes that Prissy's midwifing skills have been vastly exaggerated. Scarlett slaps her in a scene that, however justified by the stresses of the moment, is now certainly one of the less politically correct aspects of the film. Part of Prissy's humorous effect is her unexpected gentility. It turns out her mother has never allowed her to be present while children are born, she is afraid of cows, and goes into paroxysms of moral anguish when

Butterfly McQueen in quite a fancy get-up for a maid, as Annette in the Vincente Minnelli romantic comedy musical thriller *I Dood It* (Metro-Goldwyn-Mayer, 1943) starring Eleanor Powell (center) and Red Skelton. With McQueen and Powell in this photograph is the veteran character actor Thurston Hall.

she is sent to get Rhett at Belle Watling's "establishment." Apart from providing much needed comic relief, Prissy serves quite a unique function in GWTW: "Her maddening hysterics anchors the film in a ditsy kind of reality, that of genuine nightmarish fear turned comic, so it can be better handled. And the audience identifies with her fears perhaps more than it has ever wanted to admit."[358] McQueen was one of the supporting players singled out for praise by *New York Times* reviewer Frank S. Nugent, though he only had space enough to "wave an approving hand."[359]

Nine years and only eight films after GWTW, McQueen's Hollywood career was over. It is hard to say whether this was chiefly due to the reduction in the number of films being made and the opportunities for African American actresses in a post-maid era, or because of McQueen's personal idiosyncrasies.[360] She had a recurring role as the titular heroine's friend Oriole both in the radio and television versions of the hit series *Beulah* (TV, 1950–53), before disappearing entirely from both the big and small screen for more than twenty years. During these two lean decades McQueen lived in various places, including New York City and Augusta, Georgia, where she had moved with her mother as a child and been educated by the nuns at St. Benedict's Convent.

She was born Thelma McQueen in Tampa, Florida on January 7, 1911, the daughter of a stevedore on the Tampa docks and a housekeeper.[361] McQueen is known to have attended high school in Babylon, Long Island and briefly studied nursing before pursuing an acting career that would take her to Harlem, Broadway, and ultimately Hollywood.[362] She would return to Broadway in the successful revival of a comedy co-written and directed by her old mentor George Abbott, *Three Men on a Horse* (1969–70); and replaced Dody Goodman as Jennie in a revival of *The Front Page* (1970). In 1975, the same year she understudied Clarice Taylor as Addaperle in *The Wiz*, McQueen graduated with a degree in political science from the City College of New York.[363] She was sixty-four years old.

McQueen had a moderate resurgence in her acting career in the 1980s. She appeared in a few TV movies and made her final appearance on the big screen forty-seven years after her debut in *The Women*. The movie was a filmatization of Paul Theroux's *The Mosquito Coast* (P. Weir, Warner Bros., 1986), starring Harrison Ford as a mixture of Jim Jones and the father in Swiss Family Robinson and Helen Mirren as his hard-tried wife. If you blink at the wrong moment, you may miss McQueen's performance entirely. Vincent Canby observed in his negative review of *The Mosquito Coast* for the *Times*: "Appearing very briefly is the indomitable Butterfly McQueen. It says something about the film that just one shot of Miss McQueen's face immediately evokes the siege of Atlanta, though in middle of Central America."[364] As Ma Kennywick, a member of Ford's idealist community in the Central American jungle, she has one small scene, if you can even call it that, where she is upbraided by a local missionary for not attending church. McQueen must have felt a personal satisfaction in this. Not only was she back on screen, however briefly, but as a lapsed churchgoer! McQueen was an ardent atheist and willed the contents of her personal bank account to the Freedom From Religion Foundation, that had honored her with a "Freethought Heroine" award in 1989.[365] She once said: "As my ancestors are free from slavery, I am free from the slavery of religion."[366]

Butterfly McQueen lived nearly to the age of eighty-five, dying on December 22, 1995. She was critically burned when a kerosene heater caught fire in her one-bedroom cottage just outside Atlanta. She suffered burns over seventy percent of her body and died at Augusta Regional Medical Center.[367] It was an ugly and painful death and one she shared with fellow original Maria Ouspenskaya. Like Spring Byington and Elisabeth Risdon, McQueen donated her body to medical science.

One might well agree with Donald Bogle when he sums up his excellent discussion of McQueen in *Blacks in American Films and Television* (1988) with the words: "She had a rare talent that few seemed to know what to do with."[368] The question is, though, if there was much more to be done with it. That we will never know.

Ma Kettle
MARJORIE MAIN (1890–1975)

She was the star of "the most successful comedy series in cinema history." Damon Runyon called her "the first picture stealer and the greatest picture saver in Hollywood." She had a bird's nest hairdo, a voice like a file, and a stride like a section boss. Decades before the bra-burning feminists of the '70s began their struggle for women's rights, she was giving men hell and letting it all hang out. Marjorie Main called herself "one of the best battle-axes in the business."[369]

In 1947, at the age of fifty-seven and after a decade of steady work in the movies, something extraordinary happened to Marjorie

Main. She suddenly became a star. It all began when she was loaned out to Universal to support Claudette Colbert and Fred MacMurray in a comedy about a newlywed couple who decide to go "back to nature" and start a chicken farm in the boondocks. As many will recall, Main played the couple's neighbor, Ma Kettle, messy mother of thirteen and wife to ne'er-do-well Percy "Pa Kettle" Kilbride. The combination proved a stellar success. Main and Kilbride that is. The film world hadn't seen such a comic coupling since Marie Dressler and Wallace Beery teamed up in the early '30s. Besides marking the beginning of Main's decade as a star character actress, *The Egg and I* also garnered her one and only Oscar nomination. She lost out to Celeste Holm in *Gentleman's Agreement*, as did fellow nominees Ethel Barrymore, Gloria Grahame, and Anne Revere.

By the time *The Egg and I* premiered on March 21, 1947, Marjorie Main had come a long way from her native state of Indiana. She was born Mary Tomlinson on February 24, 1890 near the town of Acton, twelve miles southeast of Indianapolis. She was the second daughter of Samuel Joseph Tomlinson, a Disciples of Christ minister and the founder of the Third Christian Church in Indianapolis, and his wife, Jennie (née McGaughey). At the time of Main's birth, the family was living on a farm to which they had moved when Rev. Tomlinson's health began to fail. The Tomlinsons would move several times within the state during Main's childhood. She attended Franklin College in Franklin, Indiana (1905–06) and took a three-year course at Hamilton School of Dramatic Expression in Lexington, Kentucky (1906–09).[370]

After a year teaching drama at Bourbon College in Paris, Kentucky, where she was fired for demanding a raise, Main decided to become a bonafide actress, despite her father's opposition.[371] According to legend, her first stage role was playing Katherine in *The Taming of the Shrew*.[372] Prophetic casting, many would say. During the teens and twenties, she had several successes in vaudeville and the legitimate theater and got plenty of experience touring with stock companies all over the country. She later claimed she got her brassy, deadpan manner from fighting boarding house keepers while on tour.[373] She settled in New York City and appeared on Broadway for the first time in 1916. W.C. Fields picked her to play his wife in the vaudeville sketch, "The Family Four"; she played Mae's West's mother in *The Wicked Age* in 1927 (though West was only three years her junior); and she also supported Barbara Stanwyck and both John and Ethel Barrymore.

It was either when she first performed in her native state of Indiana or when she started in vaudeville, that Mary Tomlinson became Marjorie Main. She gave herself a new name to save her family the potential embarrassment of being connected with the less exalted forms of "theeayter" and she chose the alliterative alias Marjorie Main because she thought it would be easy to remember.[374] Damon Runyon once observed: "It's difficult to reconcile the name Marjorie with Marjorie Main's appearance and her manner.... She has bright, squinty eyes. She generally starts off looking as if she never smiled in her life, then suddenly she smiles from her eyes out."[375] Others have been equally complimentary, saying her voice resembled a crow's, her figure was like a "sack-of-taters," and her hair was a "messy nest."[376] Her distinguishing marks throughout her career were, indeed, her masculine frame (she was 5'7" and broad-shouldered), her thick, loosely top-knotted hair, and her raspy, twangy, western voice.

After marrying the twenty-six-year older former minister, lecturer, and doctor of psychology, Stanley LeFevre Krebs, on November 2, 1921, Main quit the stage to act as his secretary. When Krebs retired from the lecture circuit a few years later, Main returned to the theater. She had a stab at film work in California in the first half of the thirties, but returned to New York in the spring of 1935 to care for her husband in his illness. Though they had been living separate lives for some time, the death of Dr. Krebs from cancer on September 27, 1935, at age seventy-one, marked a turning point in Marjorie Main's life.[377] She opened in Sidney Kingsley's play, *Dead End*, at the Belasco Theatre in New York only a month after her husband's death. She played the small but significant part of a slum mother with a gangster son 460 times, before going on to a larger and juicier part in another hit, Clare Boothe Luce's *The Women*. Playing Lucy, the proprietor of a stud farm and hostelry for divorcées in Reno, would prove her final stage role. In 1937 California beckoned once again. This time she would stay for good.

Readers who know Main's film career well may already have recognized a familiar pattern in the career development of many character actresses of the period. With the coming of sound in the late 1920s, there was a great need for actors who could speak dialogue in addition to emoting. It meant a vastly expanded job market for older actresses willing to make the transition from the boards to the silver screen. While stars of the stage did not necessarily make stars on the screen—Tallulah Bankhead is a case in point—character actresses often found themselves playing the same roles on film that they had played on Broadway. Main is a good example of this phenomenon. During her first film decade, she reprised three of her stage "hits" in Hollywood: the maid, Anna, in Gloria Swanson's failed comeback, *Music in the Air* (J. May, Fox, 1934); Humphrey Bogart's mother, Mrs. Martin, in *Dead End* (W. Wyler, Samuel Goldwyn, 1937); and Lucy in *The Women* (MGM, 1939), where Main was one of only three of the women to be retained from the original cast, together with director George Cukor's pal, Phyllis Povah, and Mary Cecil.

In a film career spanning twenty-six years, in which she acted in no less than eighty-seven

Marjorie Main was often teamed with Wallace Beery in the 1940s, having taken over from Marie Dressler, who had died of cancer in 1934. This still is from the third of their seven films together, *Jackass Mail* (Metro-Goldwyn-Mayer, 1942). Their partnership was cut short by Beery's death in 1949. In real life, Main was not partnered with a man again after the death of her husband in 1935 and she lived for forty years a widow.

films, Main worked with some of Hollywood's finest directors. William Wyler was her personal favorite.[378] He directed her first film, *A House Divided* (Universal, 1931), with Walter Huston; *Dead End*, with Humphrey Bogart, Sylvia Sidney, and Claire Trevor; and joined her for a last hurrah twenty years later, in her final non–Ma Kettle role as the Widow Hudspeth in *Friendly Persuasion* (1956), starring Gary Cooper and Dorothy McGuire. Main also made three films each with George Cukor, Vincente Minnelli, and W.S. Van Dyke. Charles Lamont directed five out of the ten Kettle films.

After almost a decade of freelancing, which she felt would give her a wider choice of roles, Main decided to settle down.[379] She found a professional home at the most glamourous of the major studios and for fourteen years, from 1940 till 1954, Main was an integral part of the MGM stock company. Her second seven-year contract, starting in 1947, paid her $1,000 a week and provided her with her own dressing room trailer on the MGM lot.[380] She would make thirty-nine films at MGM, seventeen at Universal, and seven at Paramount.

Three years after Lucy in *The Women*, Main scored another comic hit as the lady blacksmith Mehitabel in *Wyoming* (R. Thorpe, MGM, 1940) and stole the show from the master scene stealer himself, Wallace Beery. From this point on, the majority of her roles would be light rather than dark. Judging from her more realistic film roles in the '30s, it is probably just as well. Had she been taken up by John Ford, she might have developed into a Beulah Bondi or a Jane Darwell. As it happened, she developed into something quite different and, many would say, vastly more entertaining.

It was an indicator of Main's toughness and professionalism that she put up with the notoriously crass and temperamental Beery in no less than seven films. *Wyoming* was their first and *Big Jack* (R. Thorpe, 1949) their last; in fact, Beery died shortly after completing his scenes in *Jack*.[381] The five films in between—*Barnacle Bill* (R. Thorpe, 1941), *The Bugle Sounds* (S.S. Simon, 1942), *Jackass Mail* (N.Z. McLeod, 1942), *Rationing* (W. Goldbeck, 1944), and *Bad Bascomb* (S.S. Simon, 1946)—are not among the high points of Main's career. In fact, it was in working with quite another type of anti-hero that things would fall into place for Main. Ironically, what MGM had not been able to achieve—creating a new Marie Dressler by teaming Main with the boorish Beery, Universal did by hitching her to the old-maidish Percy Kilbride. It was when Main wore the pants in the family, as she herself recognized, that she finally grew into full weed, if not flower.[382]

While Dressler had been an uncannily naturalistic actress when she wanted to be (viz. *Anna Christie*), Main had the subtlety of the proverbial bull in a china shop. It was a good thing, then, that she was able to specialize in "bullish" roles for so many years. Her major hit film might well have been renamed *Ham and Eggs and I*, as from this point on she grew more and more stereotypical. Even before the musicals and the B-comedies, though, Main's more serious roles do not stand up to closer scrutiny. In a film such as *Honky Tonk* (J. Conway, MGM, 1941), where she supports Clark Gable and Lana Turner as a preacher's widow turned boarding-house keeper and morality crusader, she is stagey to say the least, with the diction and facial expressions required to reach the uppermost gallery of a large theater. When reacting to other characters' lines, she looks as if she's playing charades.

In tragic roles, such as her two Mrs. Martins in *Dead End* and *Stella Dallas* (K. Vidor, Samuel Goldwyn, 1937), and even in one of her more important dramatic roles, Granny Becky in *The Shepherd of the Hills* (H. Hathaway, Paramount, 1941), Main had a tendency to give the same slow, whiney, deadpan performance, which we might in a charitable spirit call "mournful minimalism." Main's celebrated scene with Humphrey Bogart in *Dead End* is rather anticlimactic when viewed today. One suspects the powerful impression it made on the initial audience was due to the fact that the slum mother slapping her gangster son and calling him "a dirty yellow dog" awoke that half of the audience that was already fast asleep. To the still conscious moviegoer, it was no doubt a welcome spark of action in a film that gets off to a very slow start. The aptly titled *Dead End* is so freighted with social significance, it never leaves the harbor.

Though she played a variety of minor roles in the '30s, by the time she came to MGM Main had begun to specialize in big-boned, blowsy, western women, with or without a passel of children. There was some competition in this category, but Main was able to hold her own against the Darwells, Bondis, Connie Gilchrists, and Aline MacMahons. In her many portrayals of rural woman, she adopted the more or less permanent demeanor of someone with their chin jutting out and their arms and legs akimbo, ready for all comers. She said she'd taken this characterization from the aggressive country women she had known in her youth.[383] Increasingly, she came to look like a woman imitating a man imitating a woman—a kind of female-to-female drag queen. This mannish aspect was equally evident in her work in musicals, particularly *Summer Stock* (C. Walters, MGM, 1950) and *Rose Marie* (M. LeRoy, MGM, 1954). In the former, she was fairly androgynous as Judy Garland's aunt in what proved to be Garland's final MGM musical. In the latter remake of the MacDonald-Eddy classic, and Main's own final film at MGM, she played the manager of the Northern Lights Hotel in a ludicrous brunette wig, that makes her look more than ever like a not very convincing female impersonator.

Main made five musicals while under contract with MGM, including three with Judy Garland. The two in which she did herself proud was the first and most popular of them, *Meet Me in St. Louis* (Minnelli, 1944), where she played the Smith family's trusty housekeeper,

Marjorie Main, James Craig, and Donna Reed in *Gentle Annie* (Metro-Goldwyn-Mayer, 1944). For some inexplicable reason, Reed has bigger sideburns than Craig. Main's tendency to ham it up is evident.

Katie, and *The Belle of New York* (C. Walters, 1952), in which she was cast against type as Fred Astaire's well-to-do dowager aunt and a dragon of charity, assisted in her philanthropic pursuits by Vera-Ellen and the always delightful Alice Pearce. For the most part, Main's mainly non-singing participation in musicals supports George Cukor's assertion that, "A lot of people in musical comedy are like mimics or impersonators, which is not real acting."[384] She did a song and dance, though, in *The Harvey Girls* (G. Sidney, 1946), starring Judy Garland, and in *Rose Marie*, with Ann Blyth, Fernando Lamas, and Bert Lahr.

Though the Ma and Pa Kettle type of humor is not in vogue today, several of Main's comic interpretations still retain their original freshness. In *Another Thin Man* from 1939 (W.S. Van Dyke, MGM), the third of the series, she had a small role as the landlady, Mrs. Dolley, who rents out rooms for "assignations." Her conversation with William Powell, entirely at cross purposes, is still highly amusing. When in a fit of egalitarianism, Joan Crawford in *Susan and God* (G. Cukor, MGM, 1940) insists that her housekeeper, Mary Maloney, call her by her first name, it is wonderful to observe the ironic nuances Main puts into "Susan."

Main's grotesquely comic presence was the saving of at least one film, as mentioned initially. I'm thinking particularly of a dud like *Heaven Can Wait* (E. Lubitsch, Twentieth Century–Fox, 1943), where she plays Gene Tierney's mother and Don Ameche's mother-in-law, Mrs. Strabel, the nouveau riche, stern, but in essence amiable wife of a Kansas meatpacking magnet (Eugene Pallette), who displays more décolleté than good taste. Technicolor does full justice to her gloriously garish costumes in this new departure for the working-class-type actress.

Some would claim that Main's most original comic creation was Mamie Johnson in *Murder, He Says* (G. Marshall, Paramount, 1945). As the horsewhip wielding, back country mother of two addled twin sons and the harridan wife of mousy Porter Hall, she effectively starred with Fred McMurray. Charles Higham and Joel Greenberg have described this rural romp as "a neglected masterpiece and perhaps the Forties' funniest farce."[385] No faint praise from these critical gentlemen.

Main was already a familiar face at Universal, when MGM loaned her out for *The Egg and I* in 1947. She had done five films for the studio, most recently playing the title role in *The Wistful Widow of Wagon Gap* (C. Barton, 1947), with Universal's star comic duo, Abbott and Costello. Their popularity was on the wane and the unexpected spin-off success of Main and Kilbride gave the studio a new lease on life. *The Egg and I* was the biggest box-office hit at Universal to date and was said to have earned the studio $5.5 million in U.S. and Canadian rentals. Altogether the ten Kettle films brought in an estimated thirty-five million dollars.[386] Main herself saw little of this money, though she achieved a unique status at her new studio and in the industry. Stereotyping—the undoing of many a fine actor—was for Main the sweet smell of success.

As Main would impersonate Ma Kettle ten times in all, it was a good thing it was one of her two favorite roles, the other being "Gashouse Mary" McGovern in *Johnny Come Lately* with James Cagney (W.K. Howard, 1943).[387] Main once said that a chief delight of doing *The Egg and I* was the opportunity to work with Claudette Colbert.[388] Looking back on her career thus far, we see that she had never worked closely with such a class act. She had been in the movies with many of the biggest female stars of the period—Swanson, Stanwyck, Shearer (in her last film, *We Were Dancing*, 1942), Crawford three times (*The Women*, 1939; *Susan and God*, 1940; *A Woman's Face*, 1941), Loy four times (*Too Hot to Handle*, 1938; *Test Pilot*, 1938; *Lucky Night*, 1939; *Another Thin Man*, 1939) and Hepburn (*Undercurrent*, 1946), but playing a maid or a landlady or a cook didn't necessarily mean many and meaningful interchanges with Hollywood's biggest and brightest, be it on or off camera. *The Egg and I* was different. The relationship between Ma Kettle and Colbert's character, Betty MacDonald, was integral to the plot, the two women had many scenes together, and Main clearly had a soft spot for the sophisticated, Parisian-born Colbert.[389]

Main never mixed much with film folk.[390]

A widow for the last forty years of her life, she is not known to have entered into a long-term, romantic relationship with anyone during these years. She lived a quiet, retiring life, first in a rented apartment off Hollywood Boulevard, buying a bungalow in the Cheviot Hills when she signed her first contract with MGM. She also bought a car at that point, but preferred to take the bus in to work, to be able to mix with people and get ideas for her characters.[391] One of her few show biz friends was Spring Byington, in Boze Hadleigh's words, "another once-wed but non-man-oriented thespian."[392] She also kept in touch with Mae West, who shared her interest in spiritualism, and visited West at her apartment in the Ravenswood.[393] Though she respected and admired Percy Kilbride, calling him "a complete gentleman," they did not mix socially.[394]

Main didn't drink or smoke and legend has it that she had been in Los Angeles for fifteen years before going to a night club, in this case to see the female impersonator Arthur Blake imitate her at the Hollywood Trocadero.[395] Unlike her screen alter ego, Main was a stylish and immaculate dresser, who wore her thick, steely-grey hair in a considerably tidier "do" than many of the unkempt characters she played.[396] I imagine that the tidy, widowed innkeeper she portrays in *Mr. Imperium* (D. Hartman, MGM, 1951), Mrs. Cabot, who with her niece, Debbie Reynolds, is witness to Lana Turner's on-screen affair with Ezio "Mr. Imperium" Pinza, comes closest to the look of the real life Marjorie Main: a quiet, unassuming, comfortable woman, with a light in her eye and a keen sense of humor, when anyone was interested enough to discover it.

Boze Hadleigh, who interviewed her in 1974, described her as being "like Ma Kettle's older, city-bred sister, and charming."[397] She might well not have been so charming. Hadleigh, who from an early age has been on a crusade to blast open as many Hollywood closets as possible, asked her what many would consider rather personal and impertinent questions (questions of a kind that would get him thrown out of Barbara Stanwyck's house thirteen years later). Nothing could faze the eighty-four-year-old "Widder Krebs," despite the fact that she was the granddaughter of one of the founders of the Women's Christian Temperance Union, the daughter of a preacher, had refused to play Ma Kettle tipsy, and had come to believe that the

The most successful comic coupling of Marjorie Main's career was with Percy Kilbride, two years her senior. They made eight Ma and Pa Kettle films together, starting with *The Egg and I* in 1947 and ending when Kilbride bowed out after *Ma and Pa Kettle at Waikiki* in 1955, the final film of his career. Kilbride would die nine years later, after being hit by a car when crossing the street.

Moral Re-Armament Movement was "the one hope for the world."[398] When asked what she thought of lesbians who marry men, she replied, with a twinkle in her eye: "I think they're ambitious." Her reply to the question, "So how old does one have to be to be open about one's [lesbian] life and loves?" was: "Probably dead."[399]

Main's last two films were Kettle vehicles, though without Percy Kilbride, who called it quits after *Ma and Pa Kettle at Waikiki* (L. Sholem, 1955). Main had invested her earnings wisely and was able to retire comfortably in 1957 to her homes in Los Angeles and Palm Springs.[400] She felt she had worked during the best years of Hollywood and got out at the right time. In old age, she enjoyed watching late night movies. As she told one reporter, there she could see the many friends who had passed on[401]: Main's frequent co-star, Esther Dale, died after surgery in 1961; Kilbride was hit by a car when crossing the street in 1964;

and Spring Byington died of cancer in 1971. Among her generation of character actresses, only Beulah Bondi lived longer than Marjorie Main.

Her public appearances in later years were few, though she was a familiar presence in Los Angeles' annual Santa Claus Lane Parade for many years and attended MGM's Fiftieth Anniversary celebration in the spring of 1974.[402] After a lengthy battle with lung cancer, Main died at Los Angeles' St. Vincent's Hospital on April 10, 1975. She was buried next to her husband in Forest Lawn Memorial Park in the Hollywood Hills. Her simple gravestone tells us who she was: Mrs. Mary Tomlinson Krebs—Marjorie Main." The marker might also have read "Ma Kettle," for never before, nor since, has a film actress been identified so closely and successfully with a single role. For the last decade of her film career, for the last twenty-eight years of her life, she was Ma Kettle, and thus she will remain for as long as we remember her.

Lavender Lady
AGNES MOOREHEAD (1900–1974)

Agnes Robertson Moorehead was the quintessential character actress. For moviegoers of the 1940s and '50s, she became one of the most familiar female faces on the silver screen. With the hit sitcom *Bewitched* in the sixties, her name became a household word. As she said herself: "I suppose you could call me a character star."[403]

It all started in Clinton, Massachusetts on December 6, 1900,[404] though Moorehead was commonly believed to have been born in 1906. She was the eldest of the two daughters of John Henderson Moorehead, a Presbyterian minister, and Mary Mildred McCauley Moorehead.[405] Her ancestry was Irish, Scottish, English, and Welsh. Moorehead was closely tied to her family and in later years would travel the world with

her widowed mother. She kept up the 320-acre farm, Kitchen Middens, in the foothills of southeastern Ohio that had been in her family for generations.[406] Toward the end of her life, she built a new home on the property, which she visited often.[407]

Though born in New England and seeming temperamentally to belong there, like a latter-day Edna May Oliver, she and her younger sister had grown up in Reedsburg and Hamilton, Ohio, and in St. Louis, Missouri. In St. Louis, Moorehead first appeared professionally at the age of twelve, as a singer and dancer in the municipal opera.[408] Like other actresses of her generation with a similar class background—Mildred Dunnock, Mildred Natwick, and Gale Sondergaard, for example—Moorehead was highly educated. She got a B.A. from Muskingum College in New Concord, Ohio in 1923 and went on to do a graduate degree in English and Public Speaking at the University of Wisconsin in Madison.[409] In 1927 she enrolled at the American Academy of Dramatic Arts in New York and graduated two years later.[410]

Agnes Moorehead stood 5'4" tall and weighed 116 lbs. in her twenty-sixth year. She had auburn red hair, almond-shaped eyes, and high cheekbones.[411] All points and sharp angles, her face resembled a Cubist painting. A quizzical smile customarily played about her lips and her eyebrows frequently registered their wonder at the world. She remained slim and trim and red-haired—and "wonderful"—throughout her seventy-three year life.

Moorehead could be grander than Jessie Royce Landis and Mabel Albertson, a more Middle American mother than Rosemary De-Camp and Selena Royle, more spinsterish than the two Mildreds—Dunnock and Natwick, a fiercer friend than Lee Patrick and Una Merkel, more sharp-tongued than Aline MacMahon, more exotic than Gale Sondergaard, and even more proletarian than Thelma Ritter and Ellen Corby. Which is also to suggest that, at times, Moorehead could be too much.

Moorehead's career in moving pictures both began and ended with a resounding bang. Not many actresses have started out in a film of the caliber of Citizen Kane and rounded off their careers in a legendary television series like Bewitched. But the real question is: How did she use and develop her talent in the three intervening decades? What opportunities was she given? What, if anything, did she miss out on?

Moorehead was a late arrival in Hollywood. She missed the madcap, pioneering thirties entirely, spending that decade in radio and with the touring companies of Broadway shows. Except for latter-day museum pieces like Hush ... Hush, Sweet Charlotte, Moorehead also missed out on supporting nearly all of the major stars of the thirties: Joan Crawford, Mae West, Marlene Dietrich, Greta Garbo, Norma Shearer, Jeanette MacDonald, Irene Dunne, Ginger Rogers. Among the major female stars of the first decade of sound, Moorehead only acted with Claudette Colbert (Since You Went Away, 1944) and Katharine Hepburn (Dragon Seed, 1944). She would be most closely identified with four more recent stars: Greer Garson, Jane Wyman, Susan Hayward, and Debbie Reynolds.

She was forty years old before she made her first film, but she more than made up for it in the ensuing years. As she said once, there are actresses who work mostly before they're forty and others that work mostly after.[412] She acted in more than sixty feature films between 1941 and 1972. Despite the variety of her roles with respect to age, class, occupation, nationality, and even race, it is possible to organize her many characters into five main categories: 1) married women, usually rural housewives and mothers; 2) unmarried women, that is to say spinsters, maiden aunts, domestics, and nuns; 3) friends and companions (of the female lead player); 4) professional or working women; and 5) dowagers, matriarchs, aristocrats, and queens. Naturally, these categories to a certain extent overlap, but they allow us to chart Moorehead's artistic development within various types of classic character roles and across genres, studios, and decades.

Though today she is best remembered for her more outlandish or old maidish roles, Moorehead was many times mundanely married and often living in fairly humble circumstances on screen. That was the starting point for her first and most famous film, Citizen Kane (O. Welles, RKO, 1941), in which she had to give up her young son, Charles Foster Kane, in order to allow him to rise in the world. She has only one scene, at the beginning of the film, but she makes it count. Through the quest for the identity of "Rosebud," the sled she has given her boy, Mary Kane is with us in spirit throughout the film (at least the second time we watch it).

Meeting the Citizen Kane's director and star, Orson Welles, in the mid-thirties and joining his "Mercury Players" was the decisive event in Moorehead's acting career and their collaboration ultimately brought her to Hollywood. After The Magnificent Ambersons, Welles called her one of the greatest actresses he had ever seen.[413] She considered him, Charles Laughton, and the producer Paul Gregory, the three most influential men in her life.[414]

The rural mom would be a character type she would return to time and again. *Dragon Seed* (H.S. Bucquet, J. Conway), one of her three MGM films released in 1944, was a new departure, as she played a poor Chinese woman, the termagant wife of an impoverished, impractical scholar, played by Henry Travers. Dissatisfied with her husband, bitter that her son has been killed during the Japanese invasion, envious of Walter Huston, Aline MacMahon and their brood, including three sons and proto-feminist daughter-in-law, Katharine Hepburn, who all continue to thrive in adversity, Moorehead turns informer. Oddly, she fails to get her comeuppance. Maybe that scene landed on the cutting room floor.

Set entirely in China, *Dragon Seed* is notable for having only one Chinese American among the adult cast (Clarence Lung). In that respect at least *The Good Earth* (1937) was more genuine. Hepburn's performance as a Chinese Joan of Arc is one of her most embarrassing efforts. As Boze Hadleigh puts it: She is "Bryn Mawr all the way."[415] Moorehead fares better (and not only because her features lend themselves more readily to "yellowface"). She would return to Oriental drag a dozen years later in *The Conqueror*, but then on the opposite end of the social scale, as the mother of Mongolian emperor, Genghis Khan. Among the female

Based on a popular nineteenth-century thriller by Wilkie Collins, *The Woman in White* (Warner Bros., 1948) had a fine cast that included (from left) Eleanor Parker, Agnes Moorehead, Sydney Greenstreet, Alexis Smith, and John Emery. Emery, whose resemblance to John Barrymore was often remarked upon, had been married to Tallulah Bankhead in the late 1930s. Moorehead would make only five films at Warner Bros., including *Dark Passage*, *Johnny Belinda*, and *Caged*.

cast, *Dragon Seed* belongs to Aline MacMahon (1899–1991), a long-lived, though not very prolific character actress, who like Moorehead often played rural women, vinegary housewives, and embittered spinsters. MacMahon was Oscar-nominated for her role as Walter Huston's chummily devoted wife, Ling Tan. To hear her and Huston joshing each other, it is as if Myrna Loy and William Powell have been transformed into Chinese peasants.

Both *Our Vines Have Tender Grapes* (R. Rowland, MGM, 1945) and *The Stratton Story* (S. Wood, MGM, 1949) featured Moorehead as a farmer's wife closely tied to the kitchen sink and stove. In the first named, hokey saga of joys and sorrows in rural Wisconsin, she was the brusque yet devoted wife of Edward G. Robinson and mother of Margaret O'Brien (for the first and only time in both cases). The film was part of a current fascination with Scandinavian immigrants, which reached its Aryan apogee in RKO's *I Remember Mama* (1948), starring Irene Dunne. It is not easy to say which film of these two has the most appalling Norwegian American accents, but the Muppets' Swedish chef positively pales in comparison. Apparently, Moorehead "enjoyed the opportunity to display a foreign-accented vocabulary."[416] Bully for her ...

The Stratton Story was a biopic about Chicago White Sox pitcher Monty Stratton (James Stewart). Moorehead played Stewart's stalwart, skeptical, widowed mother. She houses him and wife, June Allyson, on her farm while he gets himself literally back on his feet (or foot) after a hunting accident has led to the amputation of his right leg. Talk about a film that literally shoots itself in the foot! The chief interest of the movie for Moorehead fans is that the role of Moorehead's ruggedly handsome nephew, Earnie, is played by her future husband, Robert Gist. They met on the set and married in 1953. It was her second marriage.

The 1951 remake of *Show Boat* (G. Sidney, MGM), starring Kathryn Grayson, Ava Gardner, and Howard Keel, gave Moorehead another chance to lord it over her husband as the sourpussed scold, Parthy Hawks, the role first played on film by British-born Emily Fitzroy in 1929 and sharp-featured Helen Westley in 1936. The hapless husband and captain of the show boat this time was munchkin-like Joe E. Brown and Grayson played the Hawks's daughter, Magnolia. This was the last film Moorehead made under her seven-year contract with MGM, though she had eleven films yet to make there on a freelance basis.[417]

Show Boat was the most famous of Moorehead's nine musicals. *Meet Me in Las Vegas* (R. Rowland, MGM, 1956)—with a title reminiscent of *Meet Me in St. Louis* (1944), though the plot has nothing to do with that classic—was of a lower grade. The film starred Dan Dailey and Cyd Charisse. Moorehead was billed third as Dailey's no-nonsense, chicken ranch–owning mother sporting the actress's real-life, signature red hair, but a shorter, more modern cut than she customarily wore on screen or off. Gambling cowboy Dailey is a bit of a mamma's boy. Taking potential spouse Charisse home to mother is an anxious business, but mater approves and all is well.

Far different, but hardly more interesting, is *Raintree County* (E. Dmytryk, MGM, 1957), one of the many poor *Gone with the Wind* imitations (despite a fine cast including Elizabeth Taylor, Montgomery Clift, Eva Marie Saint, Rod Taylor, and Lee Marvin). This is a film that makes one grateful for the invention of the fast-forward button. Moorehead plays the wife of a minister, Walter Abel, and the mother of troubled young Montgomery Clift. The only reason to watch this film in real time is the direct comparison it affords of Clift's face before and after the near-fatal car accident he was involved in during filming, which required extensive facial plastic surgery.

Considering the number of mediocre and downright bad films Moorehead played in, it is somewhat surprising that her reputation remains as sterling as it does. This is not to suggest that she herself was necessarily bad even if the film as whole was poor, but it is difficult for a character actress to rise above the material she is given and the level of her fellow players. We see it happening in *The Magnificent Ambersons*, but most of the time Moorehead is a hostage to the mediocrity of her artistic surroundings, particularly at MGM.

Agnes Moorehead's patrician profile appears to advantage in this photo from *Jeanne Eagels* (Columbia Pictures, 1957), where she played Eagels's mentor, the caustic Madame Neilson. Kim Novak played Eagels and Jeff Chandler (left) her lover and manager, Sal Satori. In her 1999 autobiography, Esther Williams claimed that hunky, 6' 3" Chandler enjoyed wearing women's clothing.

The last of Moorehead's rural mother roles was in her only major Western, *How the West Was Won* (various directors, MGM, 1962). Predictably, given the period and the setting, this was yet another bonnet-and-sprigged-muslin role for Moorehead and her Rebecca Prescott is really not that easy to distinguish in memory from her other naturalistic, costume drama matrons: Mary Kane, Mrs. Edmonds in *Those Redheads from Seattle* (L.R. Foster, Paramount, 1953), Ellen Shawnessy in *Raintree County*, and Mrs. Samuel in *The True Story of Jesse James* (N. Ray, Twentieth Century–Fox, 1957). Hubby in *How the West Was Won* was Karl Malden and the kids, Carroll Baker and Debbie Reynolds (in the first of her four collaborations with Moorehead). Incidentally, this was the only film Moorehead did with Thelma Ritter, though they had no scenes together.

In the 1950s and '60s, Thelma Ritter was the only one who could touch her in popular appeal and recognition. To say that Ritter and Moorehead were the leading character actresses of their generation is somewhat like saying Adlai Stevenson and Hubert Humphrey were the leading non-elected presidents of theirs. Yet Moorehead's career shows how rewarding it could be *not* to be a star. A very private person, as her first biographer subtitled his book, she was able to lead a fulfilling life almost entirely out of the public eye. Only with her tenure on the cult television series *Bewitched* in the 1960s did this change.

Most of Moorehead's maternal roles were in films for MGM, making her what Mary Astor called a "mother for Metro" with the likes of Spring Byington (1884–1971), Fay Bainter

(1893–1968), Selena Royle (1904–83), Astor herself (1906–87), and Rosemary DeCamp (1910–2001). We can also conclude from this survey of some of Moorehead's major wife-and-mother roles that they hold little intrinsic interest and left the actress scant room for character development. As such the category of *unmarried* women holds more interest, including as it does several of Moorehead's celebrated portrayals of maiden aunts, maiden domestics, and—a staple of most character actresses' repertoires—nuns.

A prime example of this second type of role and one of Moorehead's signature performances was Fanny Minafer, the frustrated, neurotic spinster in *The Magnificent Ambersons* (O. Welles, RKO, 1942). This "mangled masterpiece"[418] was only Moorehead's second film and her first substantial role and it garnered her an Oscar nomination for her sharply drawn, almost caricatured, yet deeply human portrayal. This is the one of the four Oscars she definitely deserved to win, though the competition was stiff: May Whitty in *Mrs. Miniver*, Gladys Cooper in *Now, Voyager*, and the ill-fated Susan Peters in *Random Harvest*. The award went, incomprehensibly, to Teresa Wright for *Mrs. Miniver*.

In *Summer Holiday* (R. Mamoulian, MGM, 1948), Moorehead played the same role in a minor key or what may be seen as a lighthearted parody of Fanny Minafer. At a time when MGM was beginning to dig up thirties classics to travesty in musical form, *Summer Holiday* was a fairly innocuous remake of *Ah,*

Gloria de Haven, Mickey Rooney, and Agnes Moorehead after the high school graduation ceremony in Summer Holiday (Metro-Goldwyn-Mayer, 1948), where Rooney gives a quasi-radical speech as senior class valedictorian. Moorehead plays his spinster aunt, Lily, a role played by Aline MacMahon in the original filmatization of Eugene O'Neill's piece of classic Americana (Ah, Wilderness!, 1935).

Wilderness! (1935), which had had Lionel Barrymore and Spring Byington as the parents and Eric Linden, Frank Albertson, Mickey Rooney, and Bonita Granville as the children. These roles were now taken over by Walter Huston, Selena Royle, Mickey Rooney (as the middle boy this time), Michael Kirby, Jackie "Butch" Jenkins, and Shirley Johns respectively. Moorehead played Cousin Lily and Frank Morgan her grotesque, hard-drinking beau, Uncle Sid, parts originally played by Aline MacMahon and Wallace Beery. To lovers of the original, *Summer Holiday* is *Ah, Wilderness!*-and-water, but you don't want to miss Marilyn Maxwell's imitation of Mae West in *Belle of the Nineties* and the most outrageous collection of hats ever found in one film. Costume designers Walter Plunkett and Irene went all out on this one.

Moorehead's maiden aunt in Jane Wyman's breakthrough film, *Johnny Belinda* (Warner Bros., 1948), was lower on the social scale than Fanny Minafer and Lily Davis, being the hard-working, shrewish sister of an impoverished Nova Scotia farmer (played by Charles Bickford). In the first of three films for Romanian-born director Jean Negulesco (*Scandal at Scourie*, 1953; *Jessica*, 1962), the entire MacDonald family—stern father, deaf mute daughter, and acerbic aunt—was Oscar-nominated and Wyman won. This time Moorehead lost out to Claire Trevor in *Key Largo*, a most worthy opponent and a deserving winner in middling good company with Jean Simmons (for *Hamlet*) and Barbara Bel Geddes and Ellen Corby (both for *I Remember Mama*). Moorehead would support Wyman in five films (*The Blue Veil*, 1951; *Magnificent Obsession*, 1954; *All That Heaven Allows*, 1955; and *Pollyanna*, 1960), more often than any other star.

Moorehead went about as far down the social scale as she could go playing a white-skinned woman in her 1964 Oscar-nominated interpretation of the white trashy, slatternly maid Velma Cruther in the cult thriller *Hush ... Hush, Sweet Charlotte* (R. Aldrich, Twentieth Century–Fox, 1964). Moorehead's Oscar nomination for the film is surely the least deserved of her four nominations.[419] She sounds as if she's trying to play the role as Hattie McDaniel would have played it. Just close your eyes and listen ... Velma makes even Ma Kettle seem sophisticated in comparison.

In *Sweet Charlotte*, Moorehead was reunited with her frequent co-star and fellow Mercury Player, Joseph Cotten (*Citizen Kane, The Magnificent Ambersons, Journey Into Fear, Since You Went Away*) for the first time in twenty years and the last. When Joan Crawford was replaced by Olivia de Havilland in the role of Bette Davis's steel magnolia cousin, Miriam Deering, Moorehead missed her last chance to act with the former star of MGM. It was more than twenty years since Moorehead had supported de Havilland in *Government Girl* (D. Nichols, Warner Bros., 1943) and this was her first film with Bette Davis. Moorehead had only done a handful of films at Davis's and de Havilland's home studio, Warner Bros., where she supported Lauren Bacall (*Dark Passage*), Alexis Smith and Eleanor Parker (*The Woman in White*, 1948), and Eleanor Parker again (*Caged*, 1950), in addition to Wyman in *Johnny Belinda*. In *Sweet Charlotte*, Moorehead also came the closest in her career to performing with her *bête noire*, Barbara Stanwyck. Stanwyck had nabbed the starring role in *Sorry, Wrong Number* (1948), a part especially written for Moorehead that was her star turn on radio in 1943. The part offered Stanwyck, Jewel Mayhew, finally went to Mary Astor and was her last. Even if it is too camp to turn on the waterworks, *Hush ... Hush, Sweet Charlotte* certainly trots out the waxworks...

In *The Singing Nun* (H. Koster, MGM, 1966) and *What's the Matter With Helen?* (C. Harrington, 1971), Moorehead rounded off her film career with two professional spinsters, the nun, Sister Cluny, and the evangelist, Sister Alma. The former was crotchety, the latter charismatic. Moorehead had played a nun for the first time in the 1953 drama *Scandal at Scourie* (J. Negulesco, MGM), the last of eight Greer Garson-Walter Pidgeon films. *The Singing Nun* was Moorehead's twenty-third and last film for Metro. As was so often the case, MGM had offered her steady, remunerative work, but her chief artistic challenges were to be found at other studios, such as RKO and Warner Bros. In what was Greer Garson's penultimate feature film, Moorehead played her right-hand nun and a sour-pussed killjoy who is envious of Debbie Reynolds's singing success. In real life, Moorehead counted both Garson and Reynolds among her few, close show business friends.[420]

All told, Moorehead was more at an advantage playing the friend or close companion of the leading lady, than she was as a more or less sour celibate. These frequently false friends might be divorcées like Emily Hawkins in *Since You Went Away* (J. Cromwell, Selznick Int., 1944), mistresses like Aspasia Conti in *Mrs. Parkington* (T. Garnett, MGM, 1944), bachelorettes like Madge Rapf in *Dark Passage* (D. Daves, Warner Bros., 1947), or married ladies like Sara Warren in *All That Heaven Allows* (D. Sirk, Universal, 1955). They were nearly always fascinating portrayals of a woman's psyche.

The pairings of Emily Hawkins-Anne Hilton (Claudette Colbert), Madge Rapf-Irene Jansen (Lauren Bacall), and Sara Warren-Cary Scott (Jane Wyman) were all variations on the theme of the friend whose values or interests come in conflict with those of the film's heroine, leading to a parting of the ways. Emily Hawkins and Madge Rapf are most closely linked in their aggressive, rapacious, man-eating tendencies. As Bacall's character says of Madge: "Causing unhappiness is the only thing that gives her happiness." "Hell hath no fury," and all that. In portraying these women, we feel as if Moorehead's unusual, even unsettling physiognomy becomes an active and productive factor in the performance for the first time. She simply looks the part![421]

In the same category, though completely different in character, the "Baroness" Aspasia Conti is a fairy godmother rather than a villainess. Imagine a woman going out of her way to help the rival for her lover's affections! This was casting against type and Moorehead had to fight hard to get what would prove one of her favorite roles.[422] She appears in some of the film's retrospective scenes, as she teaches Garson's character, Susie Parkington, how to become the worthy wife of a man of fortune. However sophisticated, cosmopolitan, and Old World charming Moorehead is in this role, it is difficult to see that this is Oscar caliber acting.

She was nominated nevertheless, with her *Since You Went Away* co-star Jennifer Jones, her *Dragon Seed* co-star Aline MacMahon, Angela Lansbury (*Gaslight*), and Ethel Barrymore (*None But the Lonely Heart*). Barrymore won for the first and only time. Moorehead never did.

The fourth type of role for Moorehead is the professional or working woman who, whatever other function she may have, is present in the film by virtue of her position or to perform specific, job-related tasks. I'm thinking here of roles like Lt. Col. Spottiswoode in *Keep Your Powder Dry* (E. Buzzell, MGM, 1945), the attractive owner of a gold mine in *Station West* (S. Lanfield, RKO, 1948), the hard-as-nails agent Mildred Waterbury in *Main Street to Broadway* (T. Garnett, MGM, 1953),[423] the sympathetic prison warden, Ruth Benton, in *Caged* (J. Cromwell, Warner Bros., 1950), and even the steely blonde madame, Bertha Parchman, in *The Revolt of Mamie Stover* (R. Walsh, Twentieth Century–Fox, 1956). This category also accounts for some of Moorehead's more interesting or amusing cameo roles, such as Madame Marelli, the Jewish seamstress, who gives escaped concentration camp prisoner, Spencer Tracy, a new set of clothes in *The Seventh Cross* (F. Zinnemann, MGM, 1944) or the red-headed judge in *Bachelor in Paradise* (J. Arnold, MGM, 1961).

The fifth and final category is the upmarket class of characters: dowagers, matriarchs, aristocrats, and queens. Moorehead played her fair share of these—even having a crack at Queen Elizabeth I in a cameo in *The Story of Mankind* (I. Allen, Warner Bros., 1957), though women of power were on the wane in Hollywood during her tenure there. Moorehead's appearance and bearing were not a little queenly *in propria persona* and lent her a natural authority when the part required it. Like Gladys Cooper, she had a moth-butterfly quality on screen: She could look attractive, even glamourous at a stretch, but also shockingly plain or downright ugly. In one role she was even unrecognizable as a 105-year-old Venetian recluse in *The Lost Moment* (M. Gabel, 1947), a film loosely based on Henry James's short novel *The Aspern Papers*.

Mrs. Reed in *Jane Eyre* (R. Stevenson,

Twentieth Century–Fox, 1944), starring Orson Welles and Joan Fontaine, was her first crack at an upper-class matriarch and a nasty piece of business at that. This is one of my personal favorites among Moorehead's middling large roles, particularly the reunion scene when Jane Eyre returns to her old home to find her aunt bedridden after a stroke. Her next important entry in this category was *The Woman in White* (P. Godfrey, Warner Bros., 1948), in which Moorehead depicted the twisted sister, Countess Fosco, downtrodden wife of Sydney Greenstreet (whom she ends up stabbing in the back) and mother, as it turns out, of the "Woman in White" of the title, played by Eleanor Parker.

The role of Genghis Khan's mother in the "oversized Oriental western"[424] *The Conqueror* (D. Powell, RKO, 1956) is surely one of her more bizarre. It is a curious parallel to Flora Robson's role as the Dowager Empress Tzu Hsi in a later Oriental epic: *55 Days at Peking* (1963). The role cost Robson her hair, which had to be dyed rather than using a wig due to all the plasticene she had on her face. The dye made Robson's hair fall out permanently. If some sources are to be believed, the role of Hunlun cost Moorehead not only her hair, but her life. Parts of the film were shot near a nuclear test site in the Utah desert and a suspiciously large proportion of the cast, including Susan Hayward, John Wayne, Lee Van Cleef, and director Dick Powell, would die of lung cancer.[425]

Nineteen hundred fifty-six was the big year for monarchs, as in addition to Mother Khan Moorehead played Queen Maria Dominika in *The Swan* (C. Vidor, MGM) that year. Despite a star-studded cast headed by Grace Kelly, Alec Guinness, and Louis Jourdan, and including Moorehead's fellow redhead, Jessie Royce Landis, and eccentric Estelle Winwood, the film is chiefly interesting for being Grace Kelly's swan song (pardon the pun). Moorehead does little more than stand around looking regal and officious.

Another of Moorehead's six films in the bumper year 1956 was the remake of the 1939 George Cukor classic, *The Women*, based on the hit play by Clare Boothe Luce. Entitled *The Opposite Sex* (D. Miller, MGM), this musical version starred June Allyson in Norma Shearer's old role and cast Moorehead as the lovelorn and many times married countess originally played by Mary Boland. Critical opinion is largely thumbs down on the success of this venture, which replaced Moorehead's old drama school classmate, Rosalind Russell, with ex-dancer Dolores Gray, director Cukor's old pal Phyllis Povah with a suitably fat and forty Joan Blondell, rustic Marjorie Main with slapstick queen Charlotte Greenwood, made perfume counter saleswoman Joan Crawford into show dancer Joan Collins, combined Lucile Watson's role as mother and Florence Nash's as best friend into Ann Sheridan's confidante role (her last) and, not least of all, introduced men into the cast, including a debonair young Leslie Nielsen as Allyson's wayward husband and a dishy Jeff Richards as Moorehead's current paramour, Buck Winston. Moorehead is considered by many to have been miscast in this role. Suffice it to say that the worldly, feminine, expert comedienne Mary Boland was a hard act to follow.

The starring role Moorehead had dared to hope for in *Sorry, Wrong Number* (1948) finally came in 1959, though in a film of a different and lesser caliber. *The Bat* (C. Wilbur, 1959) is interesting not only as a generic thriller of the 1950s and a camp classic, but because among all the roles she played, the lady author Cornelia Van Gorder may be the one most closely to resemble Ms. Moorehead herself. I'm not thinking personality-wise, necessarily, though the imperiousness and suave self-assurance were surely aspects of Moorehead's own character, but more of the lifestyle—cook, chauffeur, gardener, secretary, country house, limousine, tailored clothing, etc.—and the general air of breeding, culture, and respectability Ms. Van Gorder exudes.

Moorehead herself had a lifestyle worthy of a star. In 1948, five years into her lucrative MGM contract that paid her $1,500 a week, she bought composer Sigmund Romberg's Mediterranean villa at 1023 North Roxbury Drive in Beverly Hills. "Villa Agnese" remained her home until her death. She had it redecorated in what she called the "Venetian" style and spent hours studying scripts, reading the Bible and listening to devotional cassettes on the terrace, which was her open-air office. Moorehead did not drink, though she was known to sip champagne on occasion. Called by one friend "an artist in living,"[426] she was a gracious hostess whose annual combined Christmas and birthday party in early December was one of the big events of the Hollywood social season. Her servants were devoted to her and stayed with her for decades. It was one of her maids who first called her "The Lavender Lady," due to her fondness for that color.[427] To keep her company, Moorehead had two French poodles, Dusa and Sara.[428] Starting in 1955, her neighbor down the street and *The Big Street* co-star, Lucille Ball, was her regular Scrabble partner and her best friend, Debbie Reynolds, would be in and out of the house after they had become friends on the set of *How the West Was Won* in 1962.[429] By that time, Moorehead was twice divorced. She would be single, if not emotionally unattached, for the remainder of her life.

Moorehead met her first husband, John Griffith Lee, while at drama school in New York. Lee was a radio and television actor with rugged good looks. They were married on June 5, 1930 and divorced twenty-two years later, during the only hiatus in Moorehead's film career.[430] After the termination of her seven-year contract with MGM and at the instigation of her co-star in *The Blue Veil* (C. Bernhardt, RKO, 1951), Charles Laughton, she took a break to go on tour with a dramatic reading of Act Three of George Bernard Shaw's play *Man and Superman*, entitled "Don Juan in Hell." Her fellow performers were veteran actors Laughton, Sir Cedric Hardwicke, and Charles Boyer. "The First Drama Quartette," as they dubbed themselves, played to standing-room-only audiences across the United States. Moorehead would return to the show in later years both as an actress and a director.

In 1950, not long after her separation from Lee, Moorehead became the foster mother of a baby boy, Sean.[431] He was later sent to a military academy and a private school in Wales, but disappeared prior to Moorehead's death and to this day no one knows what became of him.[432]

Moorehead remarried in Yuma, Arizona on Valentine's Day, February 14, 1953.[433] It is indicative of the lack of public interest in character actresses vis-à-vis stars, that the fact that her new husband, Robert Gist, was twenty-four years her junior did not cause a scandal. There had been quite a hullabaloo when Greer Garson married her son in *Mrs. Miniver*, Richard Ney, in 1943. He was "only" eleven years her junior. Moorehead and Gist soon separated and were divorced on March 12, 1958.[434] Gist went on to become a director for television. He died in 1998. In an interview with *Photoplay* in 1966, Moorehead may have hinted at the cause of the demise of one or both of her marriages: "It's terrible for a man to see his wife famous if he is a performer ... and not so well-known."[435]

It has been suggested from time to time, even by her *Bewitched* co-star, Paul Lynde, that Agnes Moorehead was a lesbian. There is no concrete evidence to support these claims, though the common refutations—that Moorehead was a highly religious woman, that she was twice married—are no more convincing.[436] The year before her death, she gave one of her most revealing interviews. The inquisitive young interviewer was the future entertainment writer Boze Hadleigh, who included the piece in his boldly named collection *Hollywood Lesbians* in 1994. There Moorehead discusses the proclivities of various fellow actors quite openly and without prejudice, yet there is an undertone of dissatisfaction with the diehard sexual divisions of the modern world and the emphasis on sex rather than love. "*Love* doesn't have a sex," she says.[437]

It becomes clear from the 1973 interview at her Beverly Hills home that Moorehead valued deep and intimate female friendships, as much as she appears to have devalued purely sexual or erotic attraction. This may suggest that she was a throwback to an earlier era of intense, yet often non-sexual, same-sex romantic friendships of the kind Emily Dickinson and many other nineteenth-century American women are known to have engaged in throughout their lives. One might say that Moorehead was not a lesbian for the simple reason that, whatever emotions she may have felt, she clearly did not *identify* as a lesbian. She said herself in what may have been her last in-depth, personal interview, "Although my career might be described or capsulized in a few paragraphs by some writers, I won't let that happen to my life."[438] She added the wise and suggestive observation that "fear of life closes off more opportunities for us than fear of death ever does."[439] She said in an interview in 1971: "My life has been very free."[440]

Let's return to our survey of Moorehead's roles. We were talking about the high and mighty lady roles in her career. A classic in this fifth and final category is the character for which Moorehead is best remembered, Elizabeth Montgomery's acid-tongued, extraterrestially gifted, and zany mother, Endora, in the long-running comedy series *Bewitched* (1964–72). I shan't set out to elucidate the whole *Bewitched* phenomenon here, but rather concentrate on the enduring popularity of Moorehead's character. In my view, Endora may be seen as a metaphysical, slightly psychedelic, sixties heir to the tradition of powerful and charismatic matriarchs in the films of the thirties and early forties. I'm thinking of the women portrayed by oldtimers like May Robson, Alison Skipworth, Jessie Ralph, Lucile Watson, and Edna May Oliver. Except for costume dramas like *The Swan*, *My Fair Lady*, and *Gigi*, these old dames, duchesses, and dowagers had all but faded from the screen by the 1960s and the few that remained—often played by Isobel Elsom (1893–1981), Natalie Schafer (1900–91), Mabel Albertson (1901–82), Jessie Royce Landis (1904–72), or Moorehead herself—were made to look increasingly ridiculous. A good example of this is Moorehead's role in *Who's Minding the Store?* (F. Tashlin, Paramount, 1963), where as the rich owner of a department store and outfitted with an uncustomarily long, bouffant hairdo, a series of lavender outfits signed Edith Head and appropriate histrionics, she plays straight woman to Jerry Lewis.[441] The persistent devaluing of older women that began in the fifties meant that for a mature woman to have any genuine authority, she had to be literally out of this world. Endora stepped into the void and conquered. Here was a fabulous, camp creature, looking like a wise old drag queen, a law unto herself, an older woman—a grandmother even, on a collision course with conformity, conventionality, and boredom. Was it strange audiences loved her?[442]

Endora will endure after most viewers have forgotten that Moorehead made more than sixty films and what films they were. This is an ironic twist of fate, considering that she didn't even want a role in a television series and only agreed to do the pilot for *Bewitched* because she was sure it would never fly.[443] Gaining greater fame from a single role on television than dozens of roles on film is a fate she shared with several other character actresses, including fellow MGM mother, Spring Byington (*December Bride*); her *Bewitched* co-star, Alice Pearce; her frequent film co-star, Ellen Corby (*The Waltons*), Mildred Natwick (*The Snoop Sisters*), Natalie Schafer (*Gilligan's Island*), and even Judith Anderson (*Santa Barbara*). We can thank the newfound fame Endora brought her for most of what we know about Moorehead's life, as without Endora there would have been no upsurge of press interest, no interviews, no fan clubs, and no websites.

Sad to say, Moorehead's last feature film was the very gory minor horror film, *Dear Dead Delilah* (J. Farris, 1972), in which she played a wheelchair-bound Southern matriarch with an assortment of oddball relatives and a head-chopper rampaging through her ramshackle plantation house. It is some consolation that fellow divas like Tallulah Bankhead, Bette Davis, and Joan Crawford played out their careers in similarly tasteless cinematic circumstances. On the bright side, Moorehead's final acting assignment was giving voice to the goose in the animated classic *Charlotte's Web* (C.A. Nichols, I. Takamoto, 1973). Debbie Reynolds "starred" as the spider, Charlotte.

In the early seventies, as the number of available and interesting roles in film continued to decline, Moorehead returned to the stage. She reprised her standout role as Doña Ana in *Don Juan in Hell* and starred in a Tony award-winning production of the Lerner and Loewe musical *Gigi*, where she played Aunt Alicia, the retired courtesan role rendered so sublimely by Isabel Jeans on film. The show opened at the

Uris Theatre on November 13, 1973. Due to the onset of her final illness, cancer, Moorehead had to be replaced by Arlene Francis before the show closed on February 19, 1974.[444] She entered the Mayo Clinic in Rochester, Minnesota for the last time on April 9 and died there on April 30, 1974.[445] In accordance with her last wishes, there was no funeral.[446] Her body was laid to rest in the Memorial Abbey Mausoleum in Dayton Memorial Park, Dayton, Ohio.

Blithe Spirit
MILDRED NATWICK (1905–1994)

In 1940, as he was about to embark on what would become yet another of his classic films, *The Long Voyage Home*, director John Ford mentioned to a friend that he needed an actress to play a prostitute in a central scene where the sailor hero on shore leave is drugged and shanghaied in a dark, desolate dockside tavern. He needed, he said, a young Una O'Connor. O'Connor, best remembered today for her deliciously histrionic portrayals in two horror classics by James Whale, *The Invisible Man* (1933) and *Bride of Frankenstein* (1935), had played in Ford's mid-thirties, Irish dramas, *The Informer* and *The Plough and the Stars*. At this point, O'Connor was sixty; too old to portray the lady of easy virtue who gets friendly with John Wayne. Ford's friend suggested he take a look at a dark-haired, warm-eyed, sharp-featured, thirty-five-year-old actress, who for the past eight years had been building a reputation on Broadway.[447] Thus Mildred Natwick came to Hollywood and added yet another string to her bow. Thus an actress best remembered for her portrayals of spinsters, widows, and dowagers in films such as *The Quiet Man*, *The Trouble with Harry*, *Barefoot in the Park*, and *Dangerous Liaisons* made her film debut with the unladylike line: "'Ello mates, ship ahoy!" Natwick would make films regularly, but rarely, for nearly half a century.

While Una O'Connor was all Irish, Mildred Natwick was very WASP, born into an affluent family in Baltimore, Maryland on June 19, 1905. Her father, Joseph Natwick, was in the lumber business and she grew up on Greenbury Road in Mount Washington with her mother, Mildred, and her sister Mary Meredith. Millie, as she was known to her family and friends, was given a first-rate education, which she completed at Bryn Mawr College. At age seventeen, she had been an original member of the National Junior Theater in Washington, DC, and during the summer of 1930 she joined the University Players at Silver Beach on Cape Cod. There she acted with Henry Fonda, James Stewart, Margaret Sullavan, and Joshua Logan. Logan directed her Broadway debut in 1932, in a melodrama called *Carrie Nation*. The plays *The Wind and the Rain* (1934) and *Missouri Legend* (1938) were among Natwick's stage successes by the time she came to Ford's attention.[448]

Had it not been for her unexpectedly positive first film experience with a notoriously difficult director, she might not have acted in many more films.[449] It would appear that she made movies out of interest rather than necessity. The stage would always be her greatest love.[450] In 1941 she created the role of Madame Arcati in Noël Coward's *Blithe Spirit* on Broadway (she got an Emmy nomination for the television version in 1957). This was followed by notable successes in *Candida* with Katharine Cornell in 1942, *The Playboy of the Western World* in 1946, *Waltz of the Toreadors* in 1957 (Tony nomination), *Barefoot in the Park* with Elizabeth Ashley and Robert Redford in 1963, and a revival of *Our Town* with Henry Fonda and Margaret Hamilton in 1969. Harold Pinter's *Landscape* (1970) and the musical *70, Girls, 70* (1971) were her final Broadway hits. In the latter

Mildred Natwick only worked twelve days out of the six summer weeks she spent in Ireland with director John Ford and the rest of the company filming The Quiet Man (Republic, 1952). This was the last of the four Ford films Natwick lent her talents to over a dozen years.

production she made her debut in a singing role at age sixty-six and received a Tony nomination for her portrayal of the leader of a gang of senior citizens who try to regain their dignity by stealing furs.

All told Natwick appeared in nearly thirty productions on Broadway. She also did extensive work in television between her debut in Sorry, Wrong Number in 1946 and her final television role in a movie called Deadly Deception in 1987. She and Helen Hayes enjoyed great success in the mid-seventies as a pair of mystery writers turned detective in a series called The Snoop Sisters. In 1974 both actresses were nominated for an Emmy for their roles in this series and Natwick won.

New York Times critic Brooks Atkinson once described Natwick as "protean."[451] There is a sense in which her presence, both on stage and screen, was so multifarious that any broad statement one makes about her is all too easily contradicted. Natwick's film persona was often spinsterish, but never prudish. She was physically unattractive, yet sensual and charismatic. Her face was far from conventionally beautiful, yet she grew handsomer with age. She seemed the typical old maid, yet one of her best film roles was playing a mother and she started out portraying a prostitute.

Thirty-five when she began in the movie business, Natwick belonged to the younger generation of character actresses during Hollywood's studio era. While her twenty-four feature films were not always of the first order, she endowed every role with her considerable authority and vast and varied talent. Natwick simply could not give a one-dimensional performance even in the most caricatured of roles. Here she differed from her grotesquely funny, yet more limited predecessor, Una O'Connor. A more telling comparison is to be made with her fellow Baltimorean and namesake, Mildred Dunnock. Dunnock, four years Natwick's senior, was also primarily a stage actress. Both were highly successful on Broadway during the middle decades of the last century. If Dunnock had a slight edge on Natwick in the theater, it was because she worked with better dramatists, creating both the role of Linda Loman in Arthur Miller's Death of a Salesman and Big Mama in Tennessee Williams's Cat on a Hot Tin Roof. Natwick, on the other hand, triumphed in both comic and dramatic roles and might be said to have had a more varied film career. We cannot imagine, for example, that little sparrow of a woman, Mildred Dunnock, playing the exuberant Aunt Amarilla in Yolanda and the Thief, a role in which the blackbird Natwick finally got to play a hummingbird. The prodigious talents of these two ladies were united only once on film, in Alfred Hitchcock's The Trouble With Harry (Paramount, 1955), where Dunnock played a mannish storekeeper and Natwick a spinster who is courted by retired sea captain, Edmund Gwenn.

Mildred Natwick was fifty-one and Ginger Rogers forty-five when they played neighboring suburban moms with teenage children in *Teenage Rebel* (Twentieth Century–Fox, 1956). This was one of Rogers's last starring roles. She would make her last feature film in 1965, Natwick in 1988.

Natwick's fruitful collaboration with John Ford continued throughout the forties and into the early fifties. Eight years after *The Long Voyage Home*, Ford used her in another of his male-dominated dramas starring John Wayne, *3 Godfathers* (MGM, 1948). Here Natwick had only one scene, though an important one, as a dying mother who entrusts her newborn baby to the outlaw Wayne and his two equally disreputable sidekicks. The following year she was given a more substantial role in Ford's frontier Western *She Wore a Yellow Ribbon* (RKO, 1949). The woman wearing the ribbon was Joanne Dru; Natwick played Abby Allshard, Dru's aunt and the wife of a fort commander facing a Native American uprising in the 1870s. Again Natwick invested the role with all her natural authority and made it completely believable that she could bring the drunken sergeant played by Victor McLaglen more effectively into line than any of his fellow soldiers.

Ford may have felt that this pairing of Natwick and McLaglen was so successful as to merit a repeat performance three years later. Natwick was among the merry band who spent twelve weeks in Ireland during the summer of 1951 filming *The Quiet Man* (Republic). In the role of the wealthy Widow Tillane, she played the object of the affections of Maureen O'Hara's hard-drinking, rubicund, belligerent, and avaricious father, played by McLaglen. This would be the last of Natwick's four films with Ford, whose career suffered a decline in the latter 1950s. Natwick had been among his favorite character actresses and his biographer, Scott Eyman, notes that he always treated her with the greatest respect.[452]

Many character actresses were born old. Mildred Natwick is a good example of this phenomenon. Ingénue roles on stage or screen were never within her reach. With her plain, irregular features and air of maturity, she started playing crones and spinsters when she was in her thirties. One of the advantages of being a character actress from the start was that you never had to experience the agony of the fall from stardom and the inevitability of more secondary roles, or no roles at all, as the years went by. Some stars—Greta Garbo and Norma Shearer are two prime examples—retired rather than make the transition from star to character actress, while others—such as Myrna Loy and Mary Astor—took the bull by the horns and started playing mothers sooner then they strictly speaking had to.

Natwick had to wait more than twenty-five years to find herself the romantic interest of a matinee idol, yet she did not wait in vain. The star in question was Charles Boyer, the film *Barefoot in the Park* (G. Saks, Paramount, 1967). Boyer had starred with Dietrich in *The Garden of Allah* and *I Loved a Soldier* (both 1936), with Garbo in *Conquest* (1937), with Claudette Colbert in four films in the 1930s, and with Bette Davis in *All This, and Heaven Too* (1940). By 1967, these stars had faded considerably and most were no longer making movies. None of them could have given the performance Natwick gave in what is probably her most famous film role, as Jane Fonda's bemused, bothered, and bewildered mother. Natwick had created the role of Ethel Banks, a fifty-two-year-old, widowed, middle-class housewife from New Jersey, in Neil Simon's classic comedy on Broadway in 1963. On film the role garnered her an Oscar nomination.

Not often cast as a mother, Natwick was most anybody's idea of a fun-filled, mischievous, favorite aunt.[453] After seeing her in the stage version of *Barefoot in the Park*, critic Walter Kerr called her "the most hilarious woman in the Western hemisphere."[454] Her comic exuberance comes gloriously to the fore in one of MGM's campiest musicals, Vincente Minnelli's *Yolanda and the Thief* (1945), starring Fred Astaire and Lucille Bremer. In only her third film role, Natwick pulled out all the stops and showed her glamourous side as Bremer's quixotic Aunt Amarilla, the ruling princess of an equally fabulous South American state. With perfect poise she appears in one outrageously kitsch costume after another, takes command of every scene she is in, and delivers deathless lines, such as "Conchita, do my nails immediately and bring them to my room!" and "A girl on the verge of being a bride is a frightened thing. I know, I've been on the verge constantly."

If Natwick herself was ever "on the verge" is not known. Certainly, she never married and lived till the end of her days a "bachelor girl," as one publication described her.[455] She was a devout Christian Scientist and resided in singular style in a duplex on Park Avenue and later at Sutton Place South.[456] Another of Natwick's eccentric, spinster aunt roles was in *Tammy and the Bachelor* (J. Pevney, Universal, 1957) as Leslie Nielsen's painter and would-be bohemian Aunt Renie, who dreams of moving to the French quarter of New Orleans. She makes her first appearance in a smock spattered with paint and wearing a cat around her neck, as she welcomes long-term guest and heroine Tammy (Debbie Reynolds) to her Southern estate. In *Cheaper by the Dozen* (W. Lang, Twentieth Century–Fox, 1950), her screen spinsterhood even extended to playing the leader of a birth control society, who calls on Myrna Loy to enlist her help in starting a local chapter. When she finds out that Loy is the mother of twelve, she exclaims: "And within eighteen miles of headquarters!"

There was a period feeling about Natwick that made her perfectly suited to costume dramas, though she didn't do many of them and only late in her film career. Peter Bogdanovich's *Daisy Miller* (1974) is one example. There is a magical scene in this largely unsuccessful filmatization of Henry James's classic novella from 1878, in which Natwick takes tea with her nephew, played by Barry Brown. They are both standing in a swimming pool, while the tea tray floats serenely on the water. Even in this potentially ludicrous position, Natwick loses none of her period poise and her elaborate hairstyle—very John Singer Sargent—remains intact. Even in so forbidding a role as that of the snobbish Mrs. Costello, who refuses to "know" the young, nouveau riche Daisy Miller (Cybill Shepherd), Natwick was able to reveal some inner warmth and human frailty.

At the age of eight-three Mildred Natwick, a true survivor, created her final film role in Stephen Frears's spectacular costume drama *Dangerous Liaisons* (1988), starring John Malkovich, Glenn Close, and Michelle Pfeiffer. Natwick's role as Malkovich's aged aunt, Madame de Rosemonde, was largely a decorous and decorative part of the stunning *mise-en-scène*. Fortunately for us, the veteran actress was given one fine scene in which her friend and houseguest, the pious young wife played by Pfeiffer, admits that she has fallen in love with the notorious seducer portrayed by Malkovich. Pfeiffer wasn't even born when more than forty years earlier, Natwick had started out supporting young female stars such as Dorothy McGuire and Lucille Bremer. In her final performance, Natwick's wise and kindly eyes continue to twinkle and her voice remains the same: rich and sonorous, and all Baltimore.

Natwick died of cancer on October 25, 1994. She was laid to rest in Baltimore's Lorraine Park Cemetery. In her autobiography published the year after Natwick's death, Maureen Stapleton recalled a conversation she once had with "the great character actress Mildred Natwick" about when and how you know you're a good actress. Natwick had said: "Face it, Maureen, till the day you die you'll never know whether you're a good actress or not."[457]

A Real Scream
Una O'Connor (1880–1959)

Charles Laughton once gave some unforgettable advice to his friend and fellow actor, Dame Flora Robson. He once told her, when she was despondent about her lack of conventional beauty, to remember that the plain man or woman wasn't threatened by time the way one with beauty was. "It's true—being handsome or beautiful is like being born rich," he said, "but growing unavoidably poorer every day of one's life."[458] He might well have said this to his even more plain-faced co-star in five films, Una O'Connor. O'Connor was graced with what might be described as an ageless ugliness, yet she began her American screen career at age fifty-three and made her last of her more than three score films when she was seventy-seven.

By comparison, Diana Wynyard, who came to Los Angeles about the same time as O'Connor and starred in O'Connor's first American film, *Cavalcade*, saw her Hollywood career come to a standstill after only seven films in 1934. Irene Dunne, who starred in *Stingaree* (W.A. Wellman, RKO, 1934) with O'Connor as yet another maid, managed to hang on longer than most, but her film career was over when she was fifty-four. Norma Shearer, who played O'Connor's ethereal mistress Elizabeth Barrett Browning in the first (1934) biopic about the Barretts, quit making movies when she was forty rather than face the inevitable demotion to supporting player. Jeanette MacDonald, the star of *Rose-Marie* (W.S. Van Dyke, MGM, 1936), one of O'Connor's relatively few musicals, made her last film when she was forty-six. Dolores Costello, who played little Lord Fauntleroy's devoted mother in the filmatization of Frances Hodgson Burnett's children's classic (J. Cromwell, Selznick Int., 1936), with O'Connor as her equally devoted maid, bowed out before she was forty, her skin destroyed by the heavy screen makeup. Jean Harlow died young, so it is rather hard to say how her career would have developed. If the two of Harlow's final films are anything to go by, she was in a decline. O'Connor was Harlow's landlady in *Suzy* (G. Fitzmaurice, MGM, 1936) and her beleaguered maid Clara in the last film completed before Harlow's death in 1937, *Personal Property* (W.S. Van Dyke, MGM). Ann Sheridan (*It All Came True*, L. Seiler, Warner Bros., 1940) made her last film when she was forty-two. Loretta Young (*He Stayed for Breakfast*, A. Hall, Columbia, 1940) was finished as a movie star at forty. Only Joan Crawford (*Chained*, C. Brown, MGM, 1934), Barbara Stanwyck (*The Plough and the Stars*, RKO, 1936; *Christmas in Connecticut*, P. Godfrey, Warner Bros., 1945), and Greer Garson (*Random Harvest*, MGM, 1942), among the many, many female stars O'Connor supported, showed the same staying power as her.

O'Connor's career demonstrates better than most that for someone who had neither the looks nor the desire to be a star, the career of a Hollywood character actress could be at least as rewarding as the more precarious and publicized existence of a lead player. O'Connor was born Agnes Teresa McGlade in Belfast, Ireland on October 23, 1880. Thus she belonged to the highly talented generation of actresses that included Mary Boland (with her in *Stingaree*, 1934), Lucile Watson (*Ivy*, 1947), Ethel Barrymore, Jane Darwell (*Government Girl*, 1943), Laura Hope Crews, and her legendary fellow Irishwoman, Sara Allgood, who was part of O'Connor's first American tour with the Irish Players and made four films with her in the forties. McGlade's adoption of a stage name may have been motivated by her family's disapproval of her choice of career, as it had been had been for Marjorie Main (Mary Tomlinson). At any rate, McGlade appears to have been known as Una O'Connor from her debut at the Abbey Theatre in Dublin in 1911, playing Jessie in a revival of *The Shewing Up of Blanco Posnet*. She was thirty-one. If she was a slow starter, she would more than make up for it in the ensuing four and a half decades, which were filled with a continuous stream of theater engagements and, starting in 1929, film roles as well.

O'Connor's long and productive career may be divided into three distinct phases: First, her early theatrical career in the West End of London and on Broadway in the teens and twenties, culminating in her star turn in Noël Coward's dual family saga, *Cavalcade*, which led to her first American film role; second, her heyday in Hollywood from 1933 till 1948, when she made sixty films in fifteen years, including more than half a dozen classics; third, her final decade, when she moved to New York, devoted herself to stage work and guest spots in television drama, and glided gracefully into semi-retirement.

O'Connor specialized in maids (Irish and otherwise), ladies in waiting, innkeepers, landladies, and gossips. In her first Hollywood film, *Cavalcade* (F. Lloyd, Fox, 1933), many of the hallmarks of her characteristic acting style were already in place, including her twittery voice, her little cough (what that woman could do with a cough!), her disapproving sniff, her darting eyes and "basilisk stare,"[459] and a barrage of other mock genteel mannerisms. In a film where the acting for the most part is as stiff as the stiff upper lip of the British upper classes, O'Connor delivers a polished performance as Ellen Bridges, a maid on the rise, and carries the day and the film. With only four films in England under her belt before she came to Hollywood (including Alfred Hitchcock's *Murder!* from 1930), she must either have been a natural or a very quick study. As a whole, *Cavalcade* was a mixed success. Sheridan Morley has pointed out that "no other English subject was to be similarly Oscared" until *Mrs. Miniver* almost a decade later, but the film did badly at the box office.[460]

In all the glitz and glamour of Hollywood films of the first decade of sound, O'Connor became a representative of the common lot, the average man and woman. Whatever the circumstances of her birth and upbringing, on screen she became a woman of the people. She was one of those incomparable actresses who are all the more real for being entirely unreal. In truth, this pinch-faced, purse-lipped, Irish gnome— only five foot two inches tall—was a flesh and blood cartoon character, a living, breathing caricature. Yet how memorable an impression did she manage to convey even in the tiniest part. I venture the assertion that, however unpromising the starting point, as an actress Una O'Connor simply could not be bad.

In *The Barretts of Wimpole Street* (S. Franklin, MGM, 1934), for example, she played Norma Shearer's trusted maid and confidante, Wilson, with hardly a word to say for herself. Yet who can forget that special gliding gait she invented for the part, as if she was moving around on roller skates (maybe she was, her hooped skirts hide her feet). Years later she was given a tiny but pivotal role in the classic romance *Random Harvest* (M. LeRoy, MGM, 1942), starring Greer Garson and Ronald Colman. The plot turns on an escaped mental patient and amnesiac (Colman) returning to O'Connor's little tobacco shop and regaining his memory on seeing her, including the realization of his past life with Garson. If Colman could not forget O'Connor as a slatternly, evil-minded little tobacconist, neither can we. It takes a special kind of acting genius to make so much of so little. In yet another film from the forties, *Cluny Brown* (1946), she plays Richard Haydn's snooty, disapproving mother. Without speaking a single word, there is never any question of who she is and what she is thinking. Like other curios in the Hollywood cabinet—Elsa Lanchester, Hope Emerson, Margaret Hamilton, Alice Pearce—O'Connor's range was perhaps limited, but a single string of pearls can be as beautiful as a whole diamond and emerald choker.

O'Connor was the mother of all eccentric, emaciated, exasperated maids. After her standout performance in *We Are Not Alone* (E. Goulding, Warner Bros., 1939), she also became the symbolic leader of the clan of cackling screen gossips that would include the equally sharp-featured actresses Eily Malyon, Nora Cecil, Almira Sessions, and Minerva Urecal. O'Connor has also gained a reputation as a legendary screamer, which is somewhat disproportionate to the limited number of horror movies she made. Yet, if you have had the privilege of putting your personal stamp on two Universal horror classics by James Whale, you have to expect people to remember you for it. If they also remember you for the films you made with the equally legendary director John Ford, then you have every reason to be satisfied. Not many character actresses can claim to have been a favorite of two such distinctive and disparate film directors as Whale and Ford.[461]

O'Connor's first five years in Hollywood were remarkably productive and arguably the best years of her film career. During this brief period she was seen in more than half a dozen 1930s classics: *The Invisible Man*, *The Barretts of Wimpole Street*, *David Copperfield*, *Bride of Frankenstein*, *The Informer*, *The Plough and the Stars*, and *The Adventures of Robin Hood*.

The Invisible Man (Universal, 1933) was James Whale's follow-up hit to *Frankenstein* (1931). O'Connor had a baptism of fire in this soon-to-be horror classic, as the wife of an innkeeper who gets the unenviable task of sheltering the invisible man himself, Jack Griffin. Claude Rains starred in the title role, in what must be the most thankless Hollywood debut any actor ever had. O'Connor was delightfully dowdy as the mock-sophisticated, overly inquisitive Mrs. Jenny Hall.

Like most of the parts in George Cukor's expansive and textually authentic *David Copperfield* (MGM, 1935), O'Connor's role as the "lone and lorn" Mrs. Gummidge was a small one. That same year she made another hit in a James Whale classic, *Bride of Frankenstein* (Universal, 1935) as Minnie, a nosy domestic at Frankenstein Castle. Much has been made of Elsa Lanchester's dual role in the film, playing Mary Shelley in the prologue and the Bride in the film proper, but no one seems to have noticed that O'Connor also does double service. Her stiff-necked posture is unmistakable in the opening scene, as she glides across the drawing room behind a passel of afghan hounds.

If that wasn't enough, in 1935 O'Connor also played in John Ford's *The Informer* (RKO). In one of her most important roles, she played Mrs. McPhillip, the mother of an IRA soldier (Wallace Ford), who is killed by the "tans" after his friend (Victor McLaglen) informs on him. In the celebrated ending to the film, McLaglen stumbles into a church mortally wounded and finds O'Connor praying. She forgives him, as

A Real Scream: Una O'Connor (1880-1959)

The Invisible Man (Universal Pictures, 1933) was the last of Una O'Connor four films to be released in 1933, her first year in Hollywood. As the innkeeper's wife, Jenny Hall, she was wed to Forrester Harvey (center), and scared witless by "The Invisible Man" Claude Rains (left) in his ethereal American screen debut.

he expires on the floor before her. In the final shot of the film, her face upraised in prayer and framed by a black shawl, O'Connor attains a rare moment of transcendent beauty as a timeless image of sorrowing humanity. In *The Plough and the Stars* (RKO, 1936) Ford cast her again, this time as the drunken and possibly unmarried mother of two, Maggie Gogan. Apparently she was to make an appearance in Ford's *How Green Was My Valley* (Twentieth Century–Fox, 1941) as well, but her scenes were deleted. By then O'Connor had passed on the crown in Ford's films to the multi-talented and twenty-five-years-younger Mildred Natwick.

The *Adventures of Robin Hood* was the first of three costume drama adventure films starring Errol Flynn in which O'Connor played handmaiden and lady in waiting to Flynn's romantic interest. In *Robin Hood*, the fair lady was Olivia de Havilland as Maid Marian.[462] The second film was *The Sea Hawk* (M. Curtiz, Warner Bros., 1940) with Brenda Marshall playing the Spanish ambassador's niece and O'Connor her timorous duenna. The third film was *Adventures of Don Juan* (V. Sherman, Warner Bros., 1948) with Viveca Lindfors in the guise of Queen Margaret of Spain and O'Connor her lady in waiting. *Robin Hood* is easily the best of the three, as O'Connor is given a storyline and a romantic interest of her own in the shape of her butler husband from *Cavalcade*, Herbert Mundin, here togged out as Much-the-Miller's-Son. As the five-times-married Bess, she is consulted by de Havilland as an expert of affairs of the heart. The film is also well worth seeing for the sake of the costumes (courtesy of Milo

Una O'Connor in costume for her most famous screamer role as Minnie the maid at Frankenstein Castle in *Bride of Frankenstein* (Universal Pictures, 1935). Fifty-five when this photo was taken, O'Connor would remain characteristically gaunt and google-eyed throughout her long life.

both Mrs. Emma Lory in *This Land Is Mine* and Mrs. Wilson in *Cluny Brown* are the live-in mothers of old bachelor sons, school teacher Charles Laughton and chemist Richard Haydn respectively. In the former film, set in a French village under Nazi control, O'Connor is all too audible with her "Albert, don't leave me!" and informs on a resistance fighter to get her son out of jail. In the latter, she is entirely silent, communicating a wealth of subtle nuances through guttural sounds in what is an even more remarkable performance. In *The Bells of St. Mary's*, a follow-up to Bing Crosby's successful *Going My Way* (1944), O'Connor plays Crosby's housekeeper when he arrives as the new pastor of a parochial school. Her opening scene is particularly good, as she utters prophetically: "I can see you don't know what it means to be up to your neck in nuns."

O'Connor retired from the movie business after *Don Juan* and left Hollywood for New York City to revitalize her stage career. Nearly a decade later, though, she was lured back to the silver screen to repeat a role she had originated on Broadway in Agatha Christie's 1954 hit play *Witness for the Prosecution* (B. Wilder, United Artists, 1957). The cast was very fine, with veteran actors Charles Laughton, his wife Elsa Lanchester, Marlene Dietrich, Tyrone Power, and Norma Varden in the leading roles. O'Connor played Varden's devoted housekeeper, Janet McKenzie, who gives evidence at the trial after Varden is murdered. At age seventy-seven, smaller, thinner, and more birdlike than ever, O'Connor is still every inch the comic genius. Few actresses were fortunate enough both to begin and to end their film careers on such a high note.

Una O'Connor died of a heart ailment on February 4, 1959, at the Mary Manning Walsh

Anderson): just imagine *Star Trek* coming to Sherwood Forest! In one scene, O'Connor wears something resembling a flying saucer on her head; in another, a fuchsia bucket turned upside down. *The Sea Hawk* and *Don Juan* are rendered not a little ludicrous by Flynn sporting a "do" that makes him look like he's in drag as Garbo's Queen Christina, who, come to think of it, was also in drag... You figure it out.

Three of O'Connor's standout roles of the 1940s were in *This Land Is Mine* (J. Renoir, RKO, 1943), *The Bells of St. Mary's* (L. McCarey, RKO, 1945), and *Cluny Brown* (E. Lubitsch, Twentieth Century–Fox, 1946). Her parts in the first and the last named films had some similarities, as

Home at 420 East 59th St. in New York, where she had been a resident for the last two years.[463] In 1944, the year she made *The Canterville Ghost* (J. Dassin, MGM) based on a tale by Oscar Wilde, she had been named the outstanding Irish film actress of the year by the Catholic Film and Radio Guide.[464] It was the only award she ever got. As Simon Callow once wrote of Elsa Lanchester: "It was a tiny kingdom of which she was queen, but it was all her own."[465]

A Real Nutter
EDNA MAY OLIVER (1883–1942)

Words like inimitable, redoubtable, "one of a kind" quickly come to mind in attempting to describe Edna May Oliver. When Katharine Hepburn was asked to play Aunt March in the 1994 remake of *Little Women*, starring Wynona Ryder and Gabriel Byrne, she responded: "Please tell them, I would never even think of competing with Edna May Oliver."[466] Hepburn had played Jo in the original 1933 film version of Louisa May Alcott's classic, in which Oliver played the part of Aunt March.

Myrna Loy, Oliver's co-star in the ill-fated Irish Nationalist biopic *Parnell* (J.M. Stahl, MGM, 1937), remembered Oliver in her 1988 autobiography as someone who "wasn't English but might as well have been": "She was a terrific lady, very amusing, a staunch Yankee spinster living in a little house out in Westwood."[467] Joan Crawford recalled in her ghost-written autobiography *A Portrait of Joan* (1962) that Oliver had stolen the show in the only film they did together: "*No More Ladies* [E.H. Griffith, MGM, 1935] wasn't my picture. It went strictly to Edna May Oliver as a highball-drinking grandmother, a grandma who wore trains and said 'Scram.'"[468]

Though one often reads that Oliver was born in Malden, Massachusetts, the birth of Edna May Nutter in fact took place on Charlotte Avenue in Boston on November 9, 1883. Her parents were Charles Edward Nutter, a plumber and descendant of President John Quincy Adams, and Ida May, née Cox.[469] Edna May's formal education ended when she was fourteen. Her father died and she went to work in a milliner's shop. She had a good singing voice, though, and found more congenial work in the chorus in summer opera and touring with an all-female orchestra until she at the turn of the last century joined Lindsay Morrison's Boston Stock Company at $25 a week. Her first role was playing Miss Hazy in *Mrs. Wiggs of the Cabbage Patch*.[470]

Oliver would tour for fifteen years until she finally got a stab at the big time in a Broadway show called *Oh, Boy!* with music by Jerome Kern and lyrics by Guy Bolton and P.G. Wodehouse. *Oh, Boy!* was a hit musical, racking up no less than 463 performances between February 1917 and March 1918. Oliver's landmark dramatic role was playing a tragic, gawky spinster in Owen Davis's Pulitzer Prize–winning play *Icebound* in 1923. Oliver scored a hit of a different kind in the racy comedy *Cradle Snatchers* (1925–26). There she played Ethel Drake, one of three bourgeois ladies wanting to pay their husbands back for their real and imagined infidelities by indulging themselves with three younger men, including Humphrey Bogart as the Spanish lover Jose Vallejo. Oliver's Broadway career culminated with her participation in the long-running, original production of Kern and Hammerstein's smash musical *Showboat* (1927–29). Oliver played Parthy Ann Hawks for 572 performances and went on to play the same part on a national tour and in the 1932 revival. It proved her final stage role and brought her to the attention of Hollywood.[471]

During the second month of *Showboat*'s long original run at the Ziegfeld Theatre, the 44-year-old Oliver took the unexpected step of getting married. The groom was a Virginia-born, New Jersey resident stockbroker, David Welford Pratt. The ceremony took place at New York City's municipal building, and the wedding dinner at Oliver's home at the Hotel Warwick. Apparently the couple continued to live separately.[472] They divorced in 1933 and Oliver returned to the state of spinsterhood that seemed to suit her so well. In *Who's Who in the Theatre* for 1933 she listed her "recreations" as "swimming and music."[473] She made her home in Beverly Hills, which included a housekeeper, and had a small circle of close friends, which included fellow actors Virginia Hammond and Franklin Pangborn.[474] In an interview with Boze Hadleigh in 1974, Marjorie Main stated that Oliver "preferred the ladies" and "had a good lady friend." Main also remembered her as "a wonderful actress. Very funny. But lots of dignity."[475]

Like Alice Brady, Oliver abandoned Broadway and the live theater for good in the early 1930s when she moved to California and embarked on a film career in earnest. She had ten silent films under her belt, including the film version of her Broadway hit *Icebound* (W.C. de Mille, 1924), when she made her first sound film, *The Saturday Night Kid* (A.E. Sutherland, 1929), starring Clara Bow, Jean Arthur, and James Hall. In the course of the next dozen years, she would make a total of thirty-eight films, not a great number, but including such prestige projects as *Cimarron* (1931), *Little Women* (1933), *Alice in Wonderland* (1933), *David Copperfield* (1935), *A Tale of Two Cities* (1935), *Romeo and Juliet* (1936), and *Pride and Prejudice* (1940). Oliver simply looked like something out of a storybook, particularly the nineteenth-century literary classics favored by leading producers like Irving Thalberg and David O. Selznick. Her most frequent director was George Cukor, whose directing skills were frequently put to work in the thirties translating literary classics from the page to the screen.

By the time of her third sound film, the epic of the westward settlement *Cimarron* (W. Ruggles, RKO, 1931), most of Oliver's trademark mannerisms were in place. The most famous of these was what Parish and Leonard call her "constant, exemplary sniff": "accomplished

Joan Crawford would recall years later that Edna May Oliver stole the show as her grandmother, Fanny Townsend, in *No More Ladies* (Metro-Goldwyn-Mayer, 1935). Here we see her with a canine companion and decked out in Adrian's idea of an appropriate costume for an eccentric old lady.

A Real Nutter: Edna May Oliver (1883–1942)

by twitching her nose to the left, lifting the left side of her lips, and sniffing audibly." Apparently this sniff was an accident. Oliver had been doing a scene with the RKO comedy duo Bert Wheeler and Robert Woolsey when, thinking the scene over, she sniffed her opinion of the clowns' antics. The sniff was captured on film and the rest is history.[476] In *Cimarron*, starring her co-star on the touring company of *Showboat*, Irene Dunne, and Richard Dix, Oliver plays Mrs. Tracy Wyatt, a style- and status-conscious D.A.R. from Illinois, who does her darndest to stir up the intellectual life of Osage, Oklahoma.

In Cukor's *Little Women* (RKO, 1933), Oliver was the overdressed, overstuffed, and overbearing rich relation, who takes Jo March under her well-feathered wing. In the long march of Aunt Marches, which in later film versions include Lucile Watson and Mary Wickes, Oliver stands out. The same year as *Little Women*, Oliver joined a top-rank cast in the ultimately unsuccessful attempt to bring *Alice in Wonderland* (N.Z. McLeod, Paramount) to the screen with sound for the first time. More readily recognizable than many of her fellow players, who were decked out in a variety of outrageous costumes and ditto disguising makeup, she is best remembered in this film for telling Alice that "Life is a chess board."

David Copperfield (G. Cukor, MGM, 1935) and *A Tale of Two Cities* (J. Conway, MGM, 1935) provided Oliver with two of her best remembered and most popular portrayals. In the former, she played the hero's matchless spinster aunt and protector, Betsy Trotwood, who makes short work of the villain of the piece, Mr. Murdstone (Basil Rathbone). In the latter, she is again a tower of strength and civic virtue as Miss Pross, who engages in a to-the-death tussle with Madame Defarge (Blanche Yurka) that is at least as memorable as the more famous catfights between Paulette Goddard and Rosalind Russell in *The Women* (1939) and Marlene Dietrich and Una Merkel in *Destry Rides Again* (1939). In Oliver's obituary, the fight was described as "an all-over-the-room ladies brawl that was worthy of

The redoubtable Edna May Oliver in the early 1930s, presumably as herself. We know she favored turbans, furs, and other signs of success and sophistication. Oliver was shocked the first time a critic compared her with a horse, but got used to being "hoss-faced Oliver" as the years went by.

the toughest male scrappers in the 'Westerns.'"[477] Blanche Yurka recalled that the fight scene had taken two days to shoot, adding: "When it was all over both Miss Oliver and I took to our beds for several days to recuperate and she swore she would never do another such scene."[478]

Oliver received high praise from the *New York Times* critic for her interpretation of the nurse in the prestigious MGM production of *Romeo and Juliet* (MGM, 1936), starring Norma Shearer and Leslie Howard. According to Frank S. Nugent, Oliver was "the very Nurse of the Bard's imagining; droll, wise, impish in her humor, and such a practical romanticist at that."[479] Director George Cukor had not wanted her in the role.[480] All things considered, though, I wonder if Oliver's Lady Catherine de Bourgh (in *Pride and Prejudice*) wasn't her finest "classic" role. With her *Cradle Snatchers* co-star and contemporary, Mary Boland, as the dithery Mrs. Bennet, Oliver was the saving of a rather dull filmatization of Jane Austen's masterpiece of English landed gentry life. Her incredibly elongated face was balanced in Adrian's costume design by huge hats creating a contrasting horizontal axis.

In addition to these many upscale films, Oliver starred in several less stellar but often amusing comedies during the thirties, particularly during her years under contract to RKO in the first half of the decade. The studio first cast her as straight woman to Wheeler and Woolsey in three films: *Half Shot at Sunrise* (P. Sloane, 1930), *Cracked Nuts* (E.F. Cline, 1931), and *Hold 'Em Jail* (N. Taurog, 1932). In *Laugh and Get Rich* (G. La Cava, 1931), they hoped to create a comic synergy between her and Hugh Herbert, but the result did not rival Dressler and Beery, as had been hoped. The pairing with Edward Everett Horton in *The Poor Rich* (E. Sedgwick, 1934) was no more successful. The studio finally found the right comic chemistry when they combined the talents of Oliver and James Gleason in what became a series of filmatizations of murder mysteries by Stuart Palmer with Oliver as the amateur detective Miss Hildegarde Withers.[481]

Oliver left RKO in 1935 and signed on with MGM for three years, before being let go due to what Parish and Leonard describe as an "economy wave."[482] She was hyped at the "Studio of the Stars" as the new Marie Dressler,[483] though two comediennes more unlike in their physical appearance, comic style, and screen persona it is hard to imagine. Oliver was never reconciled to the epithet "horsey" that clung to her. Yet she realized that, despite its lack of conventional beauty, she could live on her face at least as well as a starlet or a model.[484]

RKO's *The Story of Irene and Vernon Castle* (H.C. Potter, 1939) was the final collaboration of Fred Astaire and Ginger Rogers. Third-billed Oliver played Maggie Sutton, the famous dancing couple of the title's worldly manager with aristocratic connections and the hints of "a past" and with lines like "I find the country quiet very disturbing." *Second Fiddle* (S. Lanfield, Twentieth Century–Fox, 1939) is a fairly forgettable comedy for anyone but diehard fans of Oliver, Sonja Henie, or Tyrone Power with a storyline resembling the search for Scarlett O'Hara. While ice princess Henie has a Norwegian accent you can cut with a knife, her Aunt Phoebe (Oliver) sounds like she's straight off the *Mayflower*. Here Oliver chums around with Power Jr. sixteen years after she had made her film debut as the beleaguered wife of Tyrone Power, Sr. in a silent film called *Wife in Name Only* (G. Terwilliger, 1923). It wasn't often Oliver got to play any kind of wife. One rare exception was her role in John Ford's classic of colonial Western Americana, *Drums Along the Mohawk* (Twentieth Century–Fox, 1939). Oliver plays a formidable widow, Mrs. McKlennar, who gives stars Henry Fonda and Claudette Colbert a roof over their heads, resists an Indian attack by refusing to get out of bed, and finally expires with a kiss from hunky Ward Bond on her lips and the promise of a hasty reunion with her late husband, Barney.

Lydia (J. Duvivier, United Artists, 1941) would prove Oliver's final film. In yet another top-billed role, she plays Merle Oberon's imperious, nautically inclined, hypochondriac, former fishwife grandmother. As loud, bossy, and incorrigible as ever, Sarah MacMillan dies suddenly at the film's close from a liver complaint. The film was prophetic in the sense that within a month and a half of its release, Oliver herself was no more. She died peacefully in her sleep on her fifty-ninth birthday at Cedars of Lebanon Hospital in Los Angeles, after being hospitalized with an intestinal disorder since early October. With her during her final moments was her close friend, the ten-years-younger Virginia Hammond, whom she had befriended more than a decade before during the filming of *Newly Rich* (N. Taurog, Paramount, 1931). Her closest surviving relative was a maternal aunt living in Malden, Massachusetts. At the private funeral service held on November 12, 1942 at Forest Lawn Memorial Park in Glendale, Oliver's friend, playwright Lynn Starling, read from Kahlil Gibran's *The Prophet*: "And let today embrace the past with remembrance and the future with longing."[485] Oliver's estate at her death was valued at $156,000.[486]

Russian Gargoyle
MARIA OUSPENSKAYA (1876–1949)

No odder-looking creature has ever had a thriving career as a first-rank character actress in American film than Maria Ouspenskaya. Like Una O'Connor, she is chiefly remembered today as one of the "grandes dames" of the horror film; in Ouspenskaya's case for her portrayal of the old gypsy woman in *The Wolf Man* (1941). During her most active years in Hollywood, the late 1930s and early '40s, Ouspenskaya cornered the market on thickly accented, continental European matriarchs and "madames" of an artistic bent. With her background in the Moscow Art Theatre of Konstantin Stanislavsky, she herself was always spoken of with deference as "Madame Ouspenskaya."

"Officially" Maria Ouspenskaya had been born in 1887, as her tombstone records. In fact, she was born eleven years earlier, in Tula near Moscow on July 29, 1876, the daughter of a not too affluent lawyer. Growing up, she wanted to be an opera singer and she pursued this dream at the Warsaw Conservatory. When money ran out, she had to give up her plans for a career as a coloratura soprano. She started studying acting at Adasheff's School of Drama in Moscow instead. Then she paid her dues in touring companies all over Russia.[487]

In 1911, at the age of thirty-five, she auditioned for the great Stanislavsky and was invited to join his company.[488] Stanislavsky and his company would play the same vital role in the development of Ouspenskaya's career in the teens, as Orson Welles and his Mercury Players in the career of Agnes Moorehead in the thirties. It was when touring with the Moscow Art Theatre in America in 1923–24, that Ouspenskaya decided to defect from the now Communist Russia, as did her twenty-five-year-old fellow actor, Akim Tamiroff.[489] Tamiroff would also have a thriving career as a character actor in Hollywood, mostly in shady or villainous parts, starting in 1932 and lasting nearly until his death forty years later (e.g. *Anthony Adverse*, *Tortilla Flat*, *For Whom the Bell Tolls*, *The Bridge of San Luis Rey*, *Dragon Seed*, *Anastasia*, *Touch of Evil*). Another Russian émigré, the future film director Richard Boleslawski (*Rasputin and the Empress*, *Les Misérables*, *The Garden of Allah*), found employment for both Ouspenskaya and Tamiroff at his theater school in New York. Ouspenskaya soon found roles on Broadway—Brooks Atkinson said of her in *Daughters of Atreus* (1936) that she had "the voice and command of style that gives the classics a purpose on stage"[490]—and started her own theater school. It was to help finance the latter, that she accepted her first American film role.[491]

A resident of Los Angeles during the last thirteen years of her life, Ouspenskaya had come a long way from her early days in stock in the provinces of the far flung Russian empire. While many of the big Hollywood stars of the period came from continental Europe and Scandinavia, not many foreign women from outside the English-speaking world had successful careers in character parts. Even those foreign-born actresses who worked regularly and over a number of years, like Odette Myrtil from France or Rafaela Ottiano from Italy, never attained the position of some of their British or Irish or Australian colleagues. Ouspenskaya was an exception to the rule.

In films that called for a continental European dowager or aristocrat, she really only had one competitor: her countrywoman Alla Nazimova. Known throughout her stellar stage and silent movie career simply as "Nazimova," she had been born Mariam Leventon in Yalta in 1879, making her three years Ouspenskaya's junior. After working with Stanislavsky in her native country, Nazimova immigrated to the United States in 1905, nearly twenty years before Ouspenskaya, and became a star on Broadway with her fabled interpretations of Ibsen and Chekhov. Fame in silent movies followed, but Nazimova returned to the stage in

This portrait of Maria Ouspenskaya by the famous photographer Alfredo Valente (1899–1973) is from the stage version of *Dodsworth* (1934), where she played the Baroness Von Obersdorf. Apparently, Ouspenskaya only took the film role to help finance her acting school, but the Stanislavsky-trained Russian actress would go on to make several more films in Hollywood in the late 1930s and early '40s.

1925. Financial necessity brought her back to Hollywood and the screen after a fifteen-year absence, but she would only make a handful of films before her death in 1945. Nazimova wanted Ouspenskaya's role in *The Rains Came* (1939).[492] She would not make her film comeback until the following year's *Escape*, playing the mother of Robert Taylor, who has to enlist the help of a German countess (Norma Shearer) to save her from a concentration camp. Her two other notable character parts are the scheming, vindictive Marquesa in *The Bridge of San Luis Rey* (1944) and the haughty, aristocratic mother of Paul Henreid, heartily disapproving of his chosen wife, Ida Lupino, in *In Our Time* (1944). The latter was certainly a role Ouspenskaya might have interpreted, as it closely resembled the baroness she played in her first Hollywood movie.

Ouspenskaya burst onto the American film scene in 1936 with *Dodsworth* (W. Wyler, Samuel Goldwyn), though maybe "burst" isn't quite the word for what was more of a stately glide into the overstuffed parlor of Ruth Chatterton's rented Viennese villa. The Baroness Von Obersdorf was a role she had originated on Broadway two years before as "one of the high points of the Broadway season."[493] The film version was met with equal approval. For her small but memorable role as the forbidding, little black crow of a mother of Chatterton's young lover (played by Gregory Gaye in the film version), Ouspenskaya was nominated for an Academy Award for Best Actress in a Supporting Role the first year there was such a category. Not bad for what can't be more than ten minutes playing time! No more unprepossessing mother ever had such an attractive son. The film acquaints us with Ouspenskaya's characteristically sour expression, as if she has just sucked on a large slice of lemon. She may have had use for that look when she lost the Oscar to another film debutante and villainess, Gale Sondergaard.

During the remaining years of the thirties and into the early forties, Ouspenskaya could do no wrong, as she lent her quirky talents to a series of prestige pictures and hit movies. One of my personal favorites is her small but delightfully eccentric part in her second film *Conquest* (C. Brown, MGM, 1937). Greta Garbo's third to last film, wedged in between the more acclaimed *Camille* (1936) and *Ninotchka* (1939), it tells the story of the love affair between Napoleon (Charles Boyer) and a Polish countess, Marie Walewska, played by Garbo. Nazimova, it turns

As the completely dotty Countess Pelagia Walewska, Maria Ouspenskaya shakes her stick at Napoleon (Charles Boyer), while Greta Garbo looks anxiously on as Boyer's lover and Ouspenskaya's sister-in-law, Marie Walewska. This scene provides welcome comic relief in Clarence Brown's less than riveting biopic Conquest (Metro-Goldwyn-Mayer, 1937).

out, had turned down the role of Garbo's mad-as-a-hatter sister-in-law, Countess Pelagia Walewska,[494] a sort of mixture of Miss Havisham in Dickens's Great Expectations and "Hush ... Hush, Sweet Charlotte" Hollis, though apparently without their history of failed romance. The role went to Ouspenskaya, who was decked out in the faded trappings of "l'ancien régime," including a ringletted wig that makes her look more ludicrous than ever. She consummately brings to life a shriveled little old lady who doesn't remember anything that has happened for the last forty years. She has a terrifically funny scene playing cards with Boyer, where they accuse each other of cheating. The little old lady, who has no idea Boyer is Napoleon, who in fact doesn't even know who Napoleon is, is quite taken aback by his lack of deference and delivers deadpan lines like: "This house is getting to be an insane asylum." This scene is the companion to a later meeting in the film: Garbo's first encounter with Napoleon's formidable mother, Laetitia Bonaparte, played by the Munchkin-faced little British "Dame," May Whitty. Both venerable ladies lend some welcome comic relief to a rather long-winded, static film.

Possibly due to their sparkling interaction in Conquest, RKO reteamed Ouspenskaya with Boyer two years later, when she was cast as his grandmother in Love Affair (L. McCarey, 1939). Unfortunately her Grandmother Janou in this film was about as nauseatingly sweet as her nutty noblewoman was amusingly offbeat.

Watching the stern and impassive tartar Ouspenskaya trying to be sympathetic and benevolent in this and other conventional mother or grandmother roles is not a pleasant experience. *Love Affair*, apparently based on the real-life friendship of Ruth Chatterton and Jessie Royce Landis's pressman husband, Rex Smith,[495] starred serene Irene Dunne as a woman playboy-athlete Boyer falls in love with on a transatlantic crossing. The ship conveniently stops at Madeira, allowing Boyer to call on his aged grandmother, a former pianist and the widow of a French diplomat, who has remained at their last posting. Implausibly Boyer has his most recent romantic conquest in tow. Unlike *Dodsworth*, Ouspenskaya's frail granny figure approves of her boy's choice in a routine performance she could have given in her sleep. Incredibly, she got yet another Oscar nomination for her single scene in the film, where her parting lines to the couple give some idea of the general mood of syrupy sentimentality: "This is as far as I can go. This is the boundary of my small world." This time Ouspenskaya lost out to Hattie McDaniel, as did fellow nominees Olivia de Havilland (*GWTW*), Geraldine Fitzgerald (*Wuthering Heights*), and Edna May Oliver (*Drums Along the Mohawk*). Katharine Hepburn would play Ouspenskaya's part in the 1994 remake of *Love Affair* with Warren Beatty and Annette Bening. When she was asked to play the part, she responded: "My God. Have I become Maria Ouspenskaya now?"[496] It was Hepburn's last feature film role.

Fortunately, Ouspenskaya's part and her world were not so limited in her next and arguably her best picture, *The Rains Came* (T. Brown, Twentieth Century–Fox, 1939). Ouspenskaya plays a childless maharani, widowed during the course of the film, who looks to the western-educated doctor and officer played by Tyrone Power to take the lead in bringing her state of Ranchipur into the modern age. Ouspenskaya looks surprisingly plausible as an Indian potentate and is every one of her five foot two inches a queen. As always, she cuts quite a figure; this time with a cigarette holder clamped in her mouth, a diamond stud in her nose, and a mean hand at gin. The sterling cast includes Laura Hope Crews in a tiny role as a dowdy dowager; Marjorie Rambeau as a socially ambitious American missionary's wife; Jane Darwell as the more homespun variety; and last but not least, Mary Nash (1885–1976; *Heidi*, *The Philadelphia Story*) in one of her finest film roles as Tyrone Power's devoted, Scottish head nurse, Miss McDaid, intensely jealous of the hero's love interest, Myrna Loy. After being a good girl in goodness knows how many films, Loy finally gets to be unsympathetic and not a little naughty as the blasé, adulterous Lady Edwina Esketh. She catches the customarily virginal and guileless Power in her net and then conveniently dies, leaving him free to assume his proper position in society. Shades of *Anna Karenina* in India. Loy remembered Ouspenskaya in 1988 as "a tiny little thing, just a bag of bones but just beautiful." Loy once had to carry her onto the set, because Ouspenskaya was barefoot.[497]

During her American years, Ouspenskaya was beloved not just as an actress but as a pedagogue and one of the early teachers of Stanislavsky's "Method" acting in the United States. She was a stern task master and, as the story goes, would begin each class by smilelessly intoning, "Make for me friendly atmosphere please."[498] In her own words again, her task was not to teach talent, but to "educate it and direct it and help it to develop itself and show its own beauty and force."[499] While teaching, Madame Ouspenskaya customarily sported a monocle, chain smoked through a long holder, and brought with her a pitcher of what looked like water, but was rumored to be vodka.[500] She would lecture on "emotional truth" and might ask you, as she once did John Garfield, to "become a cup of steaming tea."[501] On screen she played several variations of the teacher (e.g. *Dance, Girl, Dance*, 1940; *I've Always Loved You*, 1946), most notably as Madame Olga Kirova, the authoritarian leader of a dancing troupe in *Waterloo Bridge* (M. LeRoy, MGM, 1940). This justly famous remake of a James Whale picture from 1931, headlines Vivien Leigh and Robert Taylor as star-crossed lovers in war-torn London. Leigh is a dancer in Ouspenskaya's company and is fired for tardiness and insubordination, setting off her downward slide into penury and prostitution. In her wizened ugliness Ouspenskaya makes a striking contrast to Leigh as "loves young dream" and her rejection of Leigh is not a little tinged with jealousy and suppressed desires. Like Nazimova, Ouspenskaya appears to have had strong same-sex interests.[502] Unlike Nazimova, she never married.

Like so many of her Anglo-American dowager peers—May Robson, Jessie Ralph, Edna May Oliver, May Whitty, Gladys Cooper—Ouspenskaya was always better when she was being downright unpleasant or, at least, vinegary. Thus her portrayal of James Stewart's devoted, Alpine farmer's widow mother, Hilda Breitner, in *The Mortal Storm* (F. Borzage, MGM, 1940) is among the mortal aspects of the film that the title suggests. The picture has not won universal approval; Charles Higham and Joel Greenberg called it "grossly contrived and sentimental, and about as German as blueberry pie" in their book *Hollywood in the Forties*.[503] Nevertheless, the movie does, I think, manage to portray the painful process through which a leading citizen, Frank Morgan's Professor Viktor Roth, and his family, become parasites in their own community, the hard choices they confront, and the very real dangers. Once again Ouspenskaya's warm approval of her potential daughter-in-law—ever intense and breathless Margaret Sullavan in this case—is less entertaining than when she is staunchly opposed to the hero or heroine's marital plans. Yet Ouspenskaya is always a riveting presence on film for her gnomelike physiognomy, if nothing else.

During these very busy years for Ouspenskaya, making as many as six films a year, she also found time to appear in an "Andy Hardy" installment, *Judge Hardy and Son* (G.B. Seitz, MGM, 1939), the eighth in the series. She played Mrs. Judith Volduzzi, one half of an aged Italian immigrant couple about to lose their home, who appeals to Judge Hardy for help.

In the forties, Ouspenskaya's parts became increasingly exotic and bizarre. Her first film in 1941 was the soon-to-be horror classic, *The Wolf Man* (G. Waggner), released only five days after Pearl Harbor and America's entry into World War II. Considered the best Universal horror film of the 1940s, the cast of *The Wolf Man* included Claude Rains as Sir John Talbot; Lon Chaney, Jr. in the title role as Rains's vulpine son, Larry; Evelyn Ankers as Larry's romantic interest; Bela Lugosi as Bela, the gypsy werewolf who bites Larry and then bites the dust; and Ouspenskaya as Bela's mother, Maleva. One of Ouspenskaya's most genuinely moving scenes on film has her mourning her dead son: "The way you walked was thorny through no fault of your own, but as the rain enters the soil, the river enters the sea, so tears run to a predestined end. Your suffering is over, Bela my son. Now you will find peace." Ouspenskaya played the role with the same seriousness and conviction that she would all her parts in Hollywood, however unreal. She returned to play Maleva again in the 1943 sequel, *Frankenstein Meets the Wolf Man* (R.W. Neill, Universal), with Bela Lugosi as Frankenstein's Monster this time and Lon Chaney reprising his role as the Wolf Man.

The Wolf Man was followed by another film with a cult following, Josef von Sternberg's *The Shanghai Gesture* (1941), "a tale of murder and mayhem" in a Chinese gambling den. The Chinese amah of the piece was Ouspenskaya's only non-speaking role. Rumor has it that her lines were cut after preview audiences found the idea of a Chinese servant speaking with a thick, Eastern European accent uproariously funny. The film features ill-fated Ona Munson in her most important role after playing Belle Watling in *Gone with the Wind*. Ouspenskaya makes a late entrance two steps behind Munson in the big dinner party scene, looking like a dwarf Martian. *The Shanghai Gesture* turned out to be a career turning-point for Gene Tierney and Victor Mature, though the film as a whole was poorly received.

Ouspenskaya had quite a large part as Robert Cummings's beloved grandmother, Madame von Eln, in the powerful melodrama, *Kings Row* (S. Wood, Warner Bros., 1942). If *The Shanghai Gesture* has "enough kinks to fill several chapters of Kraft-Ebbing"[504] (according to Frank Miller), *Kings Row* is not far behind in its depiction of malpractice, madness, and mayhem in small town U.S.A. at the turn of the last century. The cast includes Claude Rains and Betty Field as an incestuous father-daughter couple,

Charles Coburn as an inept doctor and Judith Anderson as his manically devoted wife, and last but not least, Ronald Reagan and Ann Sheridan in what many consider their best roles, as Drake McHugh (Cummings's best friend and the victim of Coburn's incompetence and sadism) and Randy Monaghan (Reagan's devoted girlfriend from the wrong side of the tracks). The film was nominated for Best Picture, Best Director, and Best Black and White Cinematography, but lost out to *Mrs. Miniver* on all counts.

After *Kings Row*, things began to slow down for Ouspenskaya. Her gallery of grotesques and eccentrics was augmented in 1945 by the role of Amazon Queen in *Tarzan and the Amazons* (K. Neumann, RKO), Johnny Weissmuller's ninth Tarzan film out of twelve before his transformation into "Jungle Jim" in 1948. I can only imagine what the diminutive, 90-pound Ouspenskaya looked like in this role. She must, at any rate, be the shortest Amazon on record. Was Hope Emerson unavailable? Today it would be like casting Linda Hunt.

Ever willing to try something new, Ouspenskaya even acted in a Western, *Wyoming* (J. Kane, 1947), which starred Republic's answer to Sonja Henie, Vera Hruba Ralston. *A Kiss in the Dark* (Warner Bros., 1949), a Delmer Daves comedy starring Jane Wyman and David Niven, would prove Ouspenskaya's last film. It was one of only three comedies among her twenty Hollywood films.

The harshness of her early years in Russia had made Maria Ouspenskaya nearly impervious to disease and infirmity. In 1943 she played five performances of a Broadway play with lobar pneumonia and a temperature of 104.[505] She might have lived to a vaster age than her seventy-two years had she not set fire to herself while smoking in bed in the early hours of Thursday, December 1, 1949.[506] She suffered a stroke from the shock. That and her burns finished her off two days later at the Motion Picture Country Home and Hospital in Woodland Hills, California. She was laid to rest in Forest Lawn Memorial Park in Glendale, where Nazimova had been lying for four and a half years. Ouspenskaya's small gravestone reads "Our Beloved Madam."

What a Pal
LEE PATRICK (1901–1982)

Lee Patrick is best remembered today as Humphrey Bogart's wisecracking secretary Effie Perine in one of the big films of the forties, *The Maltese Falcon*. Effie was Patrick's signature role and her favorite role; so much so that she came out of retirement to reprise it in a 1975 spoof called *The Black Bird*. Few character actresses have had the experience of returning to replay a part more than thirty years after creating it. In the sequel, set in San Francisco in 1975, private investigator Sam Spade Jr. (George Segal) has inherited his father's old secretary. His pet names for her—"Godzilla" and "Moby Dick"—suggest both the nature of their relationship and the current state of the seventy-four-year-old Patrick's physique. Spade Jr. and Effie are at daggers drawn, but despite her added avoirdupois, she has lost none of her verbal dexterity as she charges around jowly as a bulldog, platinum blonde as ever, in a capacious Hawaiian housedress.

The Black Bird was Lee Patrick's last acting job. Watching the movie today is poignant when we consider the changes that time had wrought in the surviving cast members (Elisha Cook, Jr. also reprised his Maltese Falcon role) and the many who had passed away by the mid-seventies: Gladys George and Sydney Greenstreet died in 1954, Bogart in 1957, Ward Bond in 1960, Peter Lorre in 1964, and Barton MacLane in 1969. Today the entire cast of *The Maltese Falcon* is gone. Mary Astor lived longest among the female players, dying in 1987; Elisha Cook among the men. He died in 1995 at the vast age of ninety-one.

The beginnings of Lee Patrick's life and acting career are fairly obscure. We know she was born in New York City on November 22, 1901 and grew up in Chicago. Studio bios claimed throughout her career that she was born in 1911.[507] She entered the acting profession on the death of her father and at the suggestion of veteran actor George Arliss. She learned her trade with various stock companies and made her stage debut in *Punch and Judy*. She later appeared on Broadway with Spencer Tracy, George M. Cohan, Pat O'Brien, and George S. Kaufman. She starred in a film for Pathé in 1929, a murder-mystery called *Strange Cargo*, but her movie career did not begin in earnest until she left the stage and moved to the West Coast in 1937, the year she married.[508] She later regretted not having spent more time in the theater, as she had found a camaraderie, professionalism, and generosity on Broadway that she seldom found in films.[509]

Patrick appears to have come to Hollywood under contract with RKO, as she made her first ten films at this most minor of the majors. For a couple of years, then, she was one of the lesser "RKO girls" at a studio that had Katharine Hepburn as the "Queen of the Lot," and Ginger Rogers and Irene Dunne as its biggest female stars in the 1930s. Patrick didn't appear with any of them. Her films were mostly B movies, though she supported the up-and-coming star Joan Fontaine in three of her earliest films (*You Can't Beat Love*, *Music for Madame*, and *Maid's Night Out*). None of these films have remained in our cultural memory and Patrick's name is found far down on their credit lists.

Her first real break came in 1938, when she got the chance to support Bette Davis in *The Sisters* (A. Litvak) at Warner Bros. The part was not a large one, but it foreshadowed her major type on film: the streetwise, loud, middle-aged woman of questionable morality, but generous spirit, or, as a less politically correct age would have put it: the whore with a heart of gold. In *The Sisters* she gives a totally over-the-top performance as Flora Gibbon, Davis's outgoing, dubiously employed neighbor in turn-of-the century San Francisco, who tries to cheer her up in her loneliness while hubby Errol Flynn is out on a spree. Patrick's even more dubious mother was played by Laura Hope Crews. The sisters of the title were Davis, Anita Louise, and Jane Bryan; their devoted parents played by Beulah Bondi and Henry Travers. Davis was the impetuous romantic of the sisters, marrying for love in a film that was clearly meant to capitalize on the success of MGM's *San Francisco* (1936), including as it did a cataclysmic 1906 earthquake sequence.[510] In retrospect, this family saga is a minor chord in the major movement of Davis's late-thirties career from *Jezebel* (1938) via *Dark Victory* (1939) to *The Old Maid* (1939) and *The Private Lives of Elizabeth and Essex* (1939). Patrick made more films with director Anatole Litvak than any other (*City for Conquest*, *The Snake Pit*, *Goodbye Again*).

Though she would work for all the majors and most of the minor studios in Hollywood, Warner Bros. would be Lee Patrick's spiritual and artistic home for the next twenty years. She made twenty-three films for Warners, eighteen of them during the period from 1940 till 1945 which was her cinematic heyday. Like other character actresses of her generation—Mildred Dunnock, Connie Gilchrist, Gladys George, Agnes Moorehead, Louise Beavers—Lee Patrick grew up with the century. In the 1940s, which were also her forties, she came into her own. Some of the many high points of these years were *The Maltese Falcon* (1941), *In This Our Life* (1942), *Somewhere I'll Find You* (1942), *Now, Voyager* (1942), *Mrs. Parkington* (1944), and *Mildred Pierce* (1945).

Though she performed a variety of roles, Patrick specialized in playing the heroine's best friend or romantic rival. According to David Quinlan, she was "hard on the heels of Veda Ann Borg and Gladys George in the shop-soiled blonde stakes."[511] Borg (1915–73) made sixteen films for Warners during Patrick's RKO years,

1937–38, but a near fatal car accident in 1939, which required the total reconstruction of her face, sidelined her career there and Patrick was able to fill in. Patrick's *Maltese Falcon* co-star, Gladys George (1900–54), belonged with Claire Trevor, Glenda Farrell, and Ona Munson in the almost-star class. She was much less prolific than Patrick and died early, in 1954. Other major entries in the tough blonde and/or fast-talking best friend category at this time were Minna Gombell, Ruth Donnelly, Patsy Kelly, Una Merkel, and Iris Adrian. Gombell (1892–1973; *The Thin Man, Make Way for Tomorrow, The Best Years of Our Lives*) worked mostly for Fox in the thirties and freelanced in the forties. Ruth Donnelly (1896–1982; *Mr. Deeds Goes to Town, Mr. Smith Goes to Washington, The Bells of St. Mary's*) had done a lot of films at Warner Bros. in the thirties, but by the time Patrick arrived there she had moved on. Arguably the funniest of the lot, Patsy Kelly (1910–81; *The Girl from Missouri, Pigskin Parade, Merrily We Live*) was kept busy wisecracking at Hal Roach Studios and Twentieth Century–Fox in the 1930s, but the major part of her film career was over by 1943. Merkel (1903–86) had her heyday at MGM in the thirties, where she made a record-breaking sixty films in ten years and most famously supported Jean Harlow in *Red-Headed Woman, Bombshell, Riffraff,* and *Saratoga.* By the early forties, this pixyish blond was freelance and in a kind of career limbo, working mostly for Universal and Paramount. Iris Adrian (1912–94; *Roxie Hart, Action in the North Atlantic,*

It is hard to tell if Humphrey Bogart is actually smiling in this uncharacteristically upbeat photo from *The Maltese Falcon* (Warner Bros., 1941). The newspaper-wrapped package between them is what they think is the Falcon. Two years previously, Lee Patrick had played Bogart's girlfriend in the crime drama *Invisible Stripes*. That film starred veteran screen gangster George Raft, who would turn down *The Maltese Falcon*, giving Bogart his big chance.

Flamingo Road) also spent most of the early forties at Universal.

Coincidentally, Una Merkel had played Effie in the original version of *The Maltese Falcon* from 1931. In the 1936 remake, *Satan Met a Lady*, starring Bette Davis and Warren William, the secretary's name was changed to Miss Murgatroyd and she was portrayed as a dumb blond by classic air-head Marie Wilson. There was also a whiff of romance between the secretary and her boss that Patrick's and Bogart's rough camaraderie doesn't leave any room for. It is John Huston's 1941 version that has fixed itself in our memory. At the heart of the film and Sam Spade's front office, sits Lee Patrick's Effie, efficient, quick-witted, and just plain cool.

Patrick played a more substantial part in Bette Davis's onscreen life in their second of three film collaborations, *In This Our Life* (Warner Bros., 1942), again helmed by Huston in what was only his second film as director. In this little known good gal–bad gal yarn, Olivia de Havilland (Roy Timberlake) is the good girl and Davis (Stanley Timberlake) the bad girl, who steals her sister's beau, Peter Morgan, even though he is ill-suited to a party girl like her. Patrick plays Betty Wismoth, a loud, worldly woman of a certain age, who becomes Davis's confidante and drinking companion, and who ends up having to nurse her after Davis goes into a "decline." This film is chiefly notable for the sparkling dramatic interaction of Davis and "dirty old man" Charles Coburn. Hattie McDaniel is given one of her more substantial parts after *Gone with the Wind* as the Timberlakes' housekeeper, whose son is falsely accused of a hit-and-run accident that Davis herself has been involved in.

Clearly the powers that be at Warners found the Davis-Patrick pairing so successful that they cast Patrick in a very similar role in a much better film, *Now, Voyager* (I. Rapper), that same year. Here Davis's character, Charlotte Vale, is famously transformed from frumpy spinster to elegant social butterfly through the magic healing powers of psychiatrist Claude Rains. On this spiritual and literal journey, Davis takes up with Patrick ("Deb" McIntyre) and her equally hearty, easy-going husband, James Rennie. The McIntyres show Miss Vale a good time on ship and shore, as she travels for rest and recreation and to find her true self.

Between the two Davis vehicles, Patrick had found time to play a part in a low-key Lana Turner-Clark Gable film at Metro, *Somewhere I'll Find You* (W. Ruggles, 1942). This was the second of three movies Turner and Gable starred in together. Gable's wife, Carole Lombard, died in an airplane crash during filming and the production was halted for more than a month. The plot has two war correspondent brothers (Gable and Robert Sterling) vie for the same doll (Turner). Patrick is Eve Manning, foot-and-leg model for her commercial artist husband (Roland Young) and Gable's former, chummy landlady, who in his absence has lodged Turner in his old room. Patrick sports her classic look in this film. There is something faintly Rubensesque about her ample forms and pleasant features. Her cheeks are dimpled, her eyes large and expressive, and her blond hair is swept up into a characteristic froth of curls on the top of her head.

The second of Patrick's four films at MGM was the Greer Garson classic *Mrs. Parkington*. One of the major woman's films of the forties and a prominent example of the "old lady looks back" subgenre, the storyline follows Garson from youth to ruminative, sentimental old age, as she retraces her personal history for the benefit of her largely unappreciative descendants. Following in the wake of Alexander Korda's *Lydia* (1941), starring Korda's wife Merle Oberon, and released five months after Warner Bros.' *Mr. Skeffington* (1944), starring Bette Davis, *Mrs. Parkington* benefited from an even better supporting cast than its epic predecessors. Garson and frequent leading man, Walter Pidgeon, were supported by Agnes Moorehead (Oscar-nominated for her role), Gladys Cooper, Edward Arnold, Selena Royle and Lee Patrick. Patrick's role was to a certain extent a new departure, at least on the social scale. She played Garson's many-times-married granddaughter, Madeleine Parkington Swann, who brings her latest husband, a younger, strapping Texan played by Rod Cameron, to the family reunion, to the evident amusement of her pickled aunt and Garson's daughter, Gladys Cooper. This was the one and only time Cooper got to play anyone's daughter on film. *Lydia* was nominated for one Oscar, *Mr. Skeffington* for two, and *Mrs. Parkington* for two. None were won.

All this was leading up to what is probably Patrick's second most familiar role: Mrs. Maggie Biederhof in *Mildred Pierce* (M. Curtiz, Warner Bros., 1945). As we have seen, Patrick was not even an "also ran" in the race for screen stardom, but she had that in common with Claire Trevor, Glenda Farrell, Ona Munson, Gladys George, and Gale Sondergaard—all those rebellious, beautiful, charismatic women who never quite made it to stardom—that she was often cast as the "other woman." Crawford had made her famous move from MGM to Warners after the silly thriller *Above Suspicion* with Fred MacMurray (1943). *Mildred Pierce* was her first film under her new contract and would prove the biggest triumph of her later career, some would say of her entire career. As the pleasantly plump, platinum blond, womanly woman, Mrs. Biederhof, Patrick was the perfect foil to Crawford's masculine energy and angular, androgynous handsomeness. The good woman/bad woman, light woman/dark woman dichotomies were inverted, as Patrick was strictly speaking Crawford's husband's mistress. This inversion is highly symbolic of the moral and social upheaval of the postwar years, which the film sets out to explore.

Then, in 1945, after *Mildred Pierce*, and for reasons unknown, Patrick's close ties to Warners were suddenly sundered. She made three more films at the studio in later years, but worked at Columbia and Twentieth Century–Fox for the remainder of the forties. Things slowed down considerably in the fifties, as they did for so many character actresses at this time. Yet Patrick's nine films from this decade included such cult classics as *Caged, Vertigo, Auntie Mame,* and *Pillow Talk*.

Caged (J. Cromwell, Warner Bros., 1950) was a pathbreaking depiction of a woman's prison with Eleanor Parker as an impressionable young woman cast into a—dare I say it?—bitch-eat-bitch world. One tagline for the film was "You don't know women until you know them without men!" This was truer than the advertisers may have envisaged, as *Caged* is one of the first films from a major Hollywood studio to allude to lesbianism, however obliquely. The large and talented cast included Agnes Moorehead as the sympathetic yet resigned prison warden, Hope Emerson in an Oscar-nominated, standout performance as a sadistic prison matron, veteran character actress Jane Darwell as a matron in the isolation ward, and Ellen Corby as a whining fellow inmate. As an exploration of the effect of a corrective institution on the development of a young woman, the film followed in the footsteps of Fox's *The Snake Pit* (A. Litvak, 1948), where Olivia de Havilland was committed to an insane asylum. Patrick was the only actress featured in both films. In *The Snake Pit*, she had a tiny part as a ranting and raving patient trying to prove her innocence of some imagined or real crime. In *Caged* her part was more substantial as Elvira Powell, a silky, sinister vice queen.

Patrick also played a part, albeit a modest one, in another cult film of the fifties, Hitchcock's celebrated *Vertigo* (1958). If you go to the bathroom, you may miss her brief scene when hero Jimmy Stewart mistakes her for Kim Novak, because Patrick has the same hairdo and drives the same car. It turns out the inquisitive lady has bought the car from Novak's husband.

Her roles in *Auntie Mame* (M. DaCosta, Warner Bros., 1958) and *Pillow Talk* (M. Gordon, Universal, 1959) were more substantial and showed her still fully capable of developing her talent in her third decade in film. In the movie based on Jerome Lawrence's hit play and Patrick Dennis's bestselling novel, Rosalind Russell reprised her starring stage role as Mame Dennis. Patrick played Mame's nephew's girlfriend's suburban mother, Doris Upson. Doris and her hubby, played by Willard Waterman, live at—wait for it—"Upson Downs." The Oscar-nominated set of their home is one of the most delicious visual satires on mid-century, upper-middle class, suburban taste (or rather the lack of it) ever designed, though in other places the film (which supposedly begins in

1929) is stylistically all over the place. Orry-Kelly's outrageously camp costumes are a whole show to themselves. The film is also notable for Peggy Cass's Oscar-nominated performance as the gawky secretary, Agnes Gooch. Coral Browne does a rather poor imitation of Tallulah Bankhead in her role as the fast fading and chronically inebriated stage star, Vera Charles. Had they only gotten the original!

The last of Patrick's films of the fifties worth mentioning is the cult comedy *Pillow Talk*, starring Doris Day and Rock Hudson. Day is a bachelor girl and interior decorator and Patrick one of her upper-class, suburban clubwoman clients. Mrs. Walters imagines both that she has good taste and that her randy son (Nick Adams) would be a suitable beau for Day. She is mistaken on both counts. In a somewhat similar vein was Patrick's starring role in the short-lived fifties television series *Topper*, based on three popular thirties comedies. Patrick played Billie Burke's classic dizzy dame role of Henrietta Topper, with Leo G. Carroll as her husband Cosmo Topper (Roland Young's old role).

Patrick fared better than most aging actresses in the sixties, making seven films in all before retiring in 1964, including *Summer and Smoke* (P. Glenville, 1961) and *7 Faces of Dr. Lao* (G. Pal, MGM, 1964). She was given plum roles in both films. In the first-named film and the smaller part, she played the hard-playing, hard-drinking, thoroughly disreputable mother of Laurence Harvey's girlfriend and future wife, Pamela Tiffin. The other female players in this film of mothers and daughters based on a Tennessee Williams play, were Geraldine Page as the repressed reverend's daughter, Alma Winemiller; Rita Moreno as the earthy, erotic Rosa Zacharias; and Una Merkel. For the first time Patrick and Merkel were in the same film, though they didn't have any scenes together.

Summer and Smoke was one of the last of Merkel's ninety-five films and she delivers an Oscar-nominated, bravura performance as Page's mentally disturbed mother, convincing us fully of the truth of Emily Dickinson's line that "much madness is divinest sense." As mentioned, Merkel had been the chief resident wisecracking best friend at MGM in the thirties, as Patrick would be at Warners in the forties. Merkel graduated to spinster, secretary, and lady companion roles in the fifties, while Patrick gravitated towards dowdy suburban housewives and widows. In the latter category was Patrick's amusing role in the fantasy film *7 Faces of Dr. Lao*. Patrick played Mrs. Howard Cassin, a flirtatious, vain, painted and powdered small-town widow, who is shown the emptiness of her life and the hopelessness of her future in a devastating scene with the fortune-telling Tony Randall.

After a small role in a hospital drama at Columbia with her future *Black Bird* co-star George Segal, Patrick decided to shut up shop at the relatively early age of sixty-three. Better to quit while you're ahead, she may have

Almost thirty-five years after *The Maltese Falcon*, Lee Patrick came out of an eleven-year retirement to reprise her role as Sam Spade's old secretary, Effie, in the parody *The Black Bird* (Columbia Pictures, 1975). It would prove her final role. She died of a heart seizure seven years later.

thought. We know she was tired of acting and wanted more time to paint and to travel. With her newsman-writer husband, Tom Wood (author of *The Bright Side of Billy Wilder*), she made annual trips to New York and London to visit friends and to see all the new shows. She was surprised at herself for going back to work in 1975 after eleven years in retirement, but it proved a one off thing.[512]

Lee Patrick died of a heart seizure on November 21, 1982, in Laguna Hills, California, the day before she would have turned eighty-one.

The Eternal Aunt
ELIZABETH PATTERSON (1875–1966)

When Elizabeth Patterson died in her ninetieth year, the *New York Times* observed that she "Was Said to Have 'Played Mother of About Every Star in Hollywood.'"[513] Despite these maternal screen propensities, Patterson will best be remembered as the quintessential spinster, be it in the guise of the mild-mannered maiden aunt or the more or less eccentric landlady. "Patty," as she was known in the business, lent her manifold acting talents to more than one hundred films, always in named, credited roles, and over the years she built up a loyal following based on her unique combination of homely looks and doughty humor. After a quarter of a century in the movies, she gained a new audience in the 1950s with her recurring role as Mrs. Mathilda Trumbull, the Ricardos' neighbor and sometimes babysitter on *I Love Lucy*.

Like most of her breed and generation, though, Patterson had long been a stage actress before she transferred her allegiance to moving pictures. From the eve of the First World War and for the next twenty years, she was a fixture on Broadway, where she made her debut in a short-lived revival of a play called *Everyman* on March 10, 1913. Also in the cast were Leo G. Carroll and the famous Shakespearean actor Ben Greet in his last Broadway play. After studying drama in Chicago, Patterson had begun her career as an actress with the Ben Greet Players, before joining Stuart Walker's Indianapolis Repertory Company.[514] Her choice of career met with the stern disapproval of her father, E.D. Patterson, who was a judge and had fought for the Confederacy in Company D of the 9th Alabama Infantry. Yet Patterson persevered in her choice of career and would continue to pursue it till she was eighty-five.

During the First World War, the Roaring Twenties, and the Great Depression, Patterson acted in a number of now long-forgotten plays on Broadway, on tour, and in summer stock. In 1917–18, she was in one of Eugene O'Neill's early one-act plays, *In the Zone*, produced by the Washington Square Players at the Comedy Theatre, while in 1921 she was personally chosen by author Booth Tarkington for the role of Aunt Ellen in his new play *The Intimate Strangers*. The star of the show, Billie Burke, remembered her as a "most gifted actress."[515] Indeed, Patterson's Broadway career gathered momentum in the 1920s and she was almost continuously employed there, though most of her plays did not run. In the fall of 1930, she starred with Jessie Royce Landis and a young actress named Bette Davis in Lawton Campbell's *Solid South* at the Lyceum Theatre. Both Landis and Davis recalled this production in their memoirs, not least of all because of some unspecified problem with aging star Richard Bennett. In Landis's words, they "went through a lot of hell together in that play."[516]

After twenty years on Broadway and a string of flops, Patterson finally scored a hit in a comedy by veteran playwright Clare Kummer called *Her Master's Voice* (1933–34). The play

In the long-forgotten film *Chasing Yesterday* (RKO, 1935), based on a novel by Anatole France, Elizabeth Patterson lent support to the young star Anne Shirley. It was Patterson's fortieth film in nine years. She would continue to play aunts, spinsters, professional women, and landladies for twenty-five more years and in sixty films. Anne Shirley, who began her film career as Dawn O'Day when she was four, would retire in 1944, age twenty-six.

ran for 224 performances at the Plymouth Theatre. In addition to Patterson, it featured Laura Hope Crews and Roland Young in leading roles. In the 1936 film version, directed by Joseph Santley at Paramount, Patterson would reprise her role as Mrs. Ellie Martin, Peggy Conklin's widowed mother and Edward Everett Horton's live-in mother-in-law, who disapproves of her daughter's marriage, worries constantly about the state of their finances, and wishes her daughter had pursued the singing career her Aunt Minnie Stickney (Crews) had planned for her. Patterson gets an all too rare love interest of her own in this film in the form of Grant Mitchell. When Horton goes off as a manservant to Crews, he gets Patterson a job as a housekeeper at the home of his former employer, Mitchell. Mitchell soon obligingly proposes to Patterson, who says no though she means yes.

By the time Patterson made *Her Master's Voice*, she was the veteran of nearly fifty films. In 1932 alone she made fifteen films, including *A Bill of Divorcement* (G. Cukor, RKO, 1932), one of her most memorable.[517] Her first films, including two silents in 1926, were shot on the East Coast, but after a short run in the Broadway play *Spring Freshet* (1934), Patterson staked her future on the new medium of sound movies and moved herself permanently to Hollywood. As with many character actresses of her generation, the 1930s would be her most productive decade. During these ten years, she made sixty of her one-hundred-and-some-odd films. From 1928 to 1949, she was most closely associated with Paramount, making thirty-six of her films at this studio. In addition to *Her Master's Voice*, these included films like *Tarnished Lady* (G. Cukor, 1932), where she was Tallulah Bankhead's genteelly poor mother, anxious for her daughter to make an advantageous match; the delightful Rouben Mamoulian musical *Love Me Tonight* (1932), where with Ethel Griffies and Blanche Friderici, she played one of Jeanette MacDonald's three spinster aunts; *The Story of Temple Drake* (S. Roberts, 1933), as yet another aunt; *The Cat and the Canary* (E. Nugent, 1939), where she got to be mean to Paulette Goddard and was well matched with piercing screamer and dizzy dame, Nydia Westman, as two heirs who spend a terrifying time on a Southern Gothic plantation under the evil eye of housekeeper Gale Sondergaard; and in three films of the "Bulldog Drummond" series (1938–39), where she had a recurring role as Aunt Blanche Clavering. Patterson's best role while at Paramount was probably in *Remember the Night* (M. Leisen, 1940), where she plays Fred MacMurray's sympathetic spinster aunt, who lives with his mother, Beulah Bondi, on a farm in Indiana. When MacMurray brings his "friend" Barbara Stanwyck to the farm for Christmas, Patterson is the first to pick up on their budding romance. In a classic spinster moment, she unearths her unused wedding dress and lends it to Stanwyck to wear to a barn dance.

Of her seventeen films at Fox and Twentieth Century–Fox between 1926 and 1959, *Tobacco Road* gave her one of the biggest if not most interesting roles of her film career, while she was also recognizable if less evident in *The Story of Alexander Graham Bell*, *Belle Starr*, *Colonel Effingham's Raid*, and *The Shocking Miss Pilgrim*. Set in rural Georgia, *Tobacco Road* (1941) was a filmatization of the sensational hit play that had been running continuously on Broadway since December 1933. In this John Ford–directed seriocomic, hillbilly mock-epic, Patterson has one of her most poignant roles as Ada Lester, the snuff-loving, dirt poor mother of seventeen or eighteen children and the wife of the egregious Jeeter Lester (Charley Grapewin). Margaret Wycherly and Leora Thatcher had played Ada Lester on Broadway, but after thirteen pictures at Fox and fifteen years in films, Patterson was a shoo-in for this plum part.

In *The Story of Alexander Graham Bell* (I. Cummings, 1939), she has a hilarious scene as the landlady of the inventor (Don Ameche), who finally throws him out with all his contraptions, including vocal chords in a bottle. Her role in *Belle Starr* (I. Cummings, 1941) may have proven her suitability for *Tobacco Road*, as in this Gene Tierney vehicle she plays the rustic wife of Belle Starr's fellow

Elizabeth Patterson's last film of the 1930s was a remake of the classic farcical thriller *The Cat and the Canary* (Paramount Pictures, 1939). As Aunt Susan, Patterson got to dress up more than was usual for her in films. In real life, she was known for her elegance and verve.

gang member and renegade, "Blue Duck" (Chill Wills), wearing a coal shovel bonnet and pants. She leads the mock revival march that is instrumental in helping Starr abscond from prison and says to her ruefully on the way to save her husband: "Ain't no man ever lived worth risking your neck for." In *Colonel Effingham's Raid* (I. Pichel, 1946), she played bumptious ex-military man Charles Coburn's live-in relative and housekeeper, who worries about the family's reputation. Finally, she had yet another landlady part in *The Shocking Miss Pilgrim* (G. Seaton, 1947), though this time a more interesting one, as an eccentric anti–Bostonian, who makes a home for artists and other Bohemians provided they are from out of town. She takes star Betty Grable under her wing.

Between 1926 and 1952, Patterson made nearly as many films at MGM as at Fox, totalling fourteen. Among the most significant were *Dinner at Eight* (G. Cukor, 1933), where as Lionel Barrymore's office factotum she gets her head bitten off by dilapidated diva, Marie Dressler, when she makes the mistake of saying she once saw Dressler on stage as a child ("We must have a nice talk about the Civil War sometime, just you and I"); *Her Cardboard Lover* (G. Cukor, 1942), where in a dark wig, she plays Norma Shearer's Spanish-inflected maid and companion, Eva, in what was to prove the queen of MGM's final film; *Little Women* (M. LeRoy, 1949), as the March family's trusty maid, Hannah (a part played by Mabel Colcord in the original sound version); and the film which gave her the role that was to Elizabeth Patterson what Ma Joad would be to Jane Darwell and Auntie Em to Clara Blandick: Miss Eunice Habersham in William Faulkner's *Intruder in the Dust* (C. Brown, 1949).

Though one of the better filmatizations of Faulkner's works, the movie is marred by a certain preachiness of tone, particularly in David Brian's uninspired, wooden performance as the idealistic lawyer, John Stevens, and his sermonizing to his young nephew, Chick (Claude Jarman, Jr.). Patterson draws on all the resources of her background and experience to deliver a standout performance as Miss Habersham, the old woman who is willing and able to rout a mob with murder on their minds. This was home ground for her, as she had been born in Savannah, Tennessee on November 22, 1875. The film's central scene takes place at the sheriff's office, where Patterson is helping to keep safe the chief murder suspect, the black man Lucas Beauchamp (Juano Hernandez), by positioning herself in a rocking chair, knitting in hand, to guard the entrance. When one of the hoodlums (who it turns out is the true murderer) pours gasoline at her feet and lights a match, she says simply: "Please step out of the light, so I can thread my needle." This is the best line in the film. Later Patterson steps out on the porch and addresses the crowd: "Go home, every one of you. Go home, you ought to be ashamed." As David Brian says, she is "the only lady anywhere who held a jail with a twenty gauge spool of thread." Bosley Crowther of the *New York Times* wrote that Patterson was "a moving symbol of Southern delicacy and strength as the elderly, insignificant lady who coolly defies a lynch mob."[518]

Patterson also worked for Universal, Warner Bros., RKO, Columbia, and Republic during her thirty-four-year film career, though none of these studios gave her opportunities to rival those she had at Paramount, Twentieth Century–Fox, and MGM. My personal favorite among Patterson's many films is *Go West Young Man* (H. Hathaway, 1936), in which she demonstrates to the full her comic capabilities. Based on a play Gladys George triumphed in on Broadway entitled *Personal Appearance*, in Hollywood it was transformed into yet another vehicle for the manifold, expansive talents of Mae West. The situation is this: Movie star Mavis Arden (West) is stranded in the boondocks of rural Pennsylvania when her chauffeur-driven car breaks down on the way to Hattiesburg (look for West's real-life driver and lover, John Indrisano, as the chauffeur). She is forced to seek refuge at a local inn run by down-on-her-luck gentlewoman, Alice Brady, with the help of her aunt (Patterson), her daughter (Margaret Perry), and starstruck maid of all work (Isabel Jewell). Patterson gets all the good lines, as the ironical, skeptical, crotchety, yet genial spinster aunt and is even able to take some wind out of

West's capacious sails. On the bombshell's arrival, Patterson mutters: "In my time, women who had hair like that didn't come outside in the daylight." Patterson advises her great-niece, who is in love with a local hunk-mechanic (Randolph Scott) and fears West will seduce him, "You've got to work for love." It turns out Patterson had been too proud to fight for her guy once and lost him. As a whole, the film is fairly trite and predictable and rests on the usual premise that all men are irresistibly drawn to West (except, as it turns out, Randolph Scott). In one of the best scenes, Patterson succeeds in routing the amorous West one night by remaining in her rocking chair and threatening to share her recipe for spinach. In her final shot, Patterson even does an imitation of West's signature sashaying walk. What a dame!

After a twenty-year absence, Patterson returned to Broadway in early 1954 in *His and Hers*, a comedy by Fay and Michael Kanin, starring Celeste Holm and Robert Preston. She made upward of forty separate appearances in television dramas and series in the 1950s, the most well-remembered being her aforementioned role on *I Love Lucy*, where she appeared in ten episodes between 1952 and 1956. She retired from acting after playing a tiny part in *Tall Story* (J. Logan, Warner Bros., 1960), a college basketball comedy starring Anthony Perkins and Jane Fonda, and a guest appearance on an episode of *The Barbara Stanwyck Show* in 1961.

Elizabeth Patterson remained unmarried, as she had so often on screen. David Ragan describes her in real life as a "genteel urban sophisticate (no rose-covered cottage for her), given to dressmaker-original fashions, keeping her hair an attractive red, a swank apartment in one of the best hotels on Hollywood Boulevard, and a limousine ever ready to whisk her off to the latest play or art gallery."[519] She died of pneumonia at Good Samaritan Hospital in Los Angeles on January 31, 1966.

Chinless Wonder
ALICE PEARCE (1917–1966)

"Ab—ner!" This brief exclamation alone is enough to conjure up the image of Alice Pearce's most well-remembered comic creation, the quintessential nosy neighbor and nagging wife, Gladys Kravitz, in the sixties comedy series, *Bewitched*, starring Elizabeth Montgomery and Dick York. Pearce had a more than twenty years of stage comedy behind her, and had been making films for fifteen years, when she moved in across the street from Darrin and Samantha Stephens, with Samantha's mother, Endora (Agnes Moorehead), and Aunt Clara (Marion Lorne) liable to drop in at any moment. The running gag in *Bewitched* was, as you will no doubt recall, that Mrs. Kravitz was a solitary, terrified, and disbelieving witness to the supernatural antics of the women next door, while her beleaguered husband, portrayed throughout the series' run by George Tobias, was an equally disbelieving party to the hysterics generated by his wife's clandestine observations.

Alice Pearce was born in New York City on October 16, 1917, making her the youngest actress in this volume and one of the few that might have still been living today. Pearce came from an upper-middle class background. Her father, Robert E. Pearce, was a National City Bank vice president and Pearce received a cosmopolitan education at schools in Belgium, France, and Italy. She studied drama at Sarah Lawrence College, graduating in 1940. Her acting career began in summer stock in Maine, she became increasingly successful on the night club circuit, and by 1942 she was one of the stars of the revue *New Faces of 1943* on Broadway with John and Marie Lund. This success led in turn to a hit night club act with Mark Lawrence at the Blue Angel in New York. From there, she went on to portray Lucy Schmeeler in the hit musical *On the Town* (1944). It was *On the Town* that would take her to Hollywood five years later. Even after she broke into film, and into television with her own short-lived series in 1949, Pearce continued to do stage work. Her last play was Noël Coward's *Sail Away* in 1961.[520]

Alice Pearce's screen and television success cannot be measured or explained by the number or extent of her film and television roles, which were limited. She made only fourteen feature films and had small parts in most of them. To understand what made her so memorable, we must seek out the most deep-seated myths and fears our culture holds about women and examine Pearce's ability to milk them for all they were worth. Pearce's characters personified every conceivable unattractive female quality, yet she made them irresistible. In the course of her eighteen-year film and television career, she created archetypal representations of the unattractive girl, the gossip, the nagging wife, and the invalid. She said herself: "playing strange, sweet oddballs is exactly my cup of tea."[521]

Part of her enduring comic appeal no doubt also stemmed from her unlikely combination of facial features: her beak of a nose and toothy grin balancing precariously over a practically non-existent chin.[522] In addition to these extreme endowments, Pearce had been given a voice fit to split even a husband's eardrums and a little slip of a body that looked wasted even before her final, fatal illness set in. One fan aptly described her as a "slight, chinless, parrot-faced, squeaky-voiced bundle of (kill) joy" and claimed that she had "made a career out of post-nasal drip."[523]

Pearce's first role in the movies was recreating her stage performance in the film version of the hit Broadway musical, *On the Town* (G. Kelly, S. Donen, MGM, 1949). Lucy Shmeeler is the unattractive roommate of a woman cab driver, who encounters a trio of sailors on shore leave in New York. Gene Kelly is hot on the trail of starlet Vera-Ellen, but when she disappears from the scene, he gets stuck with Lucy on a date with Frank Sinatra and Betty Garrett, Lucy's roommate. Lucy is the classic (under)-dog—the last girl to be picked for the team, the female nerd, the one who never gets a date, the most unattractive girl in class, with the wrong clothes or glasses or braces or acne or greasy hair or all of the above. Whether we have been her, persecuted her, or tolerated her, no one has gone through their teenage years without encountering her. In the form of Lucy Shmeeler, Pearce brings her back to us, with her disgusting nasal congestion, her hopeless, romantic dreams, her touching neediness, and her exasperating intrusiveness. That co-director and star Kelly had a real-life admiration for Pearce is clear from her being the only person asked to transfer her role from stage to screen.

Her next film was *The Belle of New York* (C. Walters, 1952), another MGM musical starring Vera-Ellen, though an inferior one. This time the blond sweetheart of America played a Salvation Army lass under the protective wing of the formidable society lady, Mrs. Phineas Hill (Marjorie Main). Pearce plays Elsie Wilkins, Vera-Ellen's gawky sidekick and admiring witness to her budding romance with Main's ne'er-do-well nephew, Fred Astaire. The film was a rare period piece for Pearce.

In 1956, Pearce was offered the small but significant role of the gossipy manicurist Olga in *The Opposite Sex* (D. Miller). This was MGM's remake of the quintessential woman's film by the fabled "woman's director," George Cukor, based on Clare Boothe Luce's mid-thirties stage hit, *The Women*. June Allyson, who recreates Norma Shearer's role as the picture perfect wife, gets more than her nails varnished when she stops by the beauty parlor. Without realizing who she is talking to, Pearce reveals that Allyson's husband (Leslie Nielsen) is having an affair with Joan Collins (playing Joan Crawford's classic role as Crystal Allen). Dennie Moore had played Olga delightfully in the original version from 1939.

In *Tammy and the Doctor* (H. Keller, Universal, 1963), the third in the gag-inducingly sweet "Tammy" series, Pearce plays a sympathetic nurse, who tries to show Tammy Tyree

Alice Pearce's parrot profile is in plain view in this photo from Tammy and the Doctor (Universal International, 1963). At left is the film's star, Sandra Dee, who had taken over from the original Tammy, Debbie Reynolds. Pearce died of ovarian cancer in 1966. Dee died of kidney disease in 2005.

(Sandra Dee) the ropes at the hospital where Tammy has taken her sick adopted grandmother, Annie Call (Beulah Bondi). This is a fairly straight role for Pearce and not among her most memorable, though the day-to-day trials and tribulations of the plain-faced, middle-aged matron are aptly characterized. As Nurse Millie, Pearce reveals a certain similarity to that other classic, chinless portrayer of nurses, Mary Wickes. At 5'10" Wickes was an Amazon compared to petite Pearce. Though her contemporary, Wickes had been playing nurses since the early 1940s in wonderful Warner Bros. films such as Now, Voyager and The Man Who Came to Dinner (both starring Bette Davis). Wickes would still be cutting capers, as Sister Mary Lazarus in Sister Act, more than twenty-five years after Pearce was dead.

Pearce's eight remaining film roles were small, but with Pearce it was always quality over quantity anyhow. Among the most memorable moments from her films of the sixties is the short scene in The Thrill of It All (N. Jewison, Universal, 1963), when the husband of fifty-six year-old yet pregnant Arlene Francis, Edward Andrews, encounters Pearce and her husband, Herbie Faye, in a traffic jam. Francis is about to give birth and Andrews buys a much-needed shoelace and later a newspaper off Faye, while Pearce with her classic nagging wife voice and characteristic facial expressions makes her low opinion of her husband's business acumen painfully clear.

Fans of Jerry Lewis and his 1964 film, The Disorderly Orderly (F. Tashlin, Paramount), will no doubt remember Pearce in her classic role as Mrs. Fuzzibee. In addition to verbal diarrhea, the aptly named Mrs. Fuzzibee suffers from a catalogue of ills that she is willing to describe at the drop of a hat. Pearce drives male nurse Lewis (and us) to distraction with an excruciatingly detailed account of her ailments, starting with her perforated gallbladder (her incantation of "drip, drip, drip" is like Chinese water torture), by way of her fractured shinbone, on to her weak kidneys. Only falling in love can cure Lewis of the urge to throttle the verbose hypochondriac on the spot.

Pearce's last film role was in The Glass Bottom Boat (F. Tashlin, MGM, 1966), starring Doris Day and Rod Taylor. Her role as Day's inquisitive neighbor, Mrs. Fenimore, was no doubt meant to capitalize on the success of Bewitched. To underscore the similarity with Gladys Kravitz, her husband in the film was played by George Tobias. Pearce's last action on film was to knock a Russian spy who invades her bedroom over the head with a table lamp and promptly faint from her exertions. By the time the film was released, she had been dead for more than three months.

Throughout her two-year stint as Gladys Kravitz in *Bewitched*, Pearce knew she was seriously ill. She died of ovarian cancer in Hollywood on March 3, 1966, at the age of forty-eight, having worked on *Bewitched* almost up till the day she died.⁵²⁴ Pearce's spiritual daughter, the thirty-years-younger Gilda Radner, would suffer the same fate in 1989. For her portrayal of Gladys Kravitz, apparently her favorite role,⁵²⁵ Pearce was awarded a posthumous Emmy. The prize was accepted by her second husband, director Paul Davis, whom she had wed in 1964, her first husband, composer John Rox, having died in 1957. Curiously enough, Marion Lorne, Pearce's *Bewitched* co-star, was awarded a posthumous Emmy in the same category in 1968. Alice Pearce was cremated and her ashes scattered at sea.

Pearce's performances were all gems. Granted, they were fairly small gems and they didn't have many facets, but they sparkled nevertheless. Wherever her spirit is now to be found, someone is laughing.

Duchesses and Domestics
JESSIE RALPH (1864–1944)

No matter what may have been the case in the real world, in the Hollywood movies of the 1930s women often ruled the roost. At no time before or since have women, particularly elderly women, wielded so much power over their men and their children. It was a glorious time to be weather-beaten, dignified, and imperious on screen. A handful of seasoned stage actresses rose to the challenge of the new medium as if they'd been born to it. One of these was Jessie Ralph. Not so familiar a face or a name today as her contemporary granddames May Robson, May Whitty, and Marie Dressler, Ralph was nevertheless a force to be reckoned with. Robson might be more aristocratic, Whitty more eccentric, and Dressler more bohemian, yet none of them combined onscreen folksiness and high station quite like Ralph. John Springer and Jack Hamilton observe that "Ralph ran the gamut from charwoman to charter members of the Four Hundred, all hearty old girls."⁵²⁶ She put the fear of God into the likes of Frank Morgan, W.C. Fields, and William Powell, yet ironically she is remembered today as "a generous dollop of twinkly-eyed benevolence" who provided stars young and old with a shoulder to cry on.⁵²⁷

Jessie Ralph Chambers was born on November 5, 1864, the thirteenth child of Captain James C. Chambers of Gloucester, Massachusetts. She made her acting debut in 1880, aged sixteen, with a stock company in Providence, Rhode Island. She played the nurse to Jane Cowl's Juliet on Broadway in 1923. In 1927–29, she supported Cowl there again (and in Paris) in a hit play entitled *The Road to Rome*, which also starred Gladys Cooper's future husband, Philip Merivale. Ralph played in many of George M. Cohan's productions. One of her earliest sound films, *Elmer the Great* (M. LeRoy, Warner Bros., 1933), was based on a Cohan play. Ralph was married to a fellow actor named William Patton from St. Louis, but was widowed long before she came to Hollywood in 1933. The couple had no children.⁵²⁸

Ralph's talents were varied. Her characterizations traversed the social scale from duchesses to domestics (including duchesses that had been domestics). Though her more benign and humane qualities were given most play in the movies, she had a more sinister side to her onscreen persona. Her quotidian look of sympathy and understanding might be seen to hide a barely suppressed malevolence or at least a mischievous twinkle to her porcine eyes. Her broad, ingratiating, dentured smile, might at any moment be transformed in a vulpine leer— or was it just gas?

Regrettably, Ralph was seldom given a chance to display this darker side. When she did, the result was memorable. Much has been said about Paul Muni's and Luise Rainer's performances in The Good Earth (S. Franklin, 1937). The next time you view this MGM classic of Chinese drag, it is well worth looking out for Ralph as the evil housekeeper Cuckoo in the early scenes at the mansion where Rainer is kept as a slave before her marriage. The original Broadway production of The Good Earth in late 1932 was Ralph's last show in New York. There she played Wang Lung's aunt, rather than Cuckoo.

Several of Ralph's early films were for Columbia. Ralph made her sound film debut as Aunt Minnie in Child of Manhattan (E. Buzzell, Columbia, 1933), starring Nancy Carroll and John Boles. In this typical Pygmalion story, Ralph is "aunt" to the girls at Loveland dance hall, where Nancy Carroll works. She is characterized by her fondness for the bottle and her thickly German-accented English, which is frequently funny, as when she says to Carroll: "When they told me you had a baby you could have knocked me down with a fender." Springer and Hamilton claim that Ralph was reprising a stage role in Child of Manhattan.[529]

Ralph's most important early role was playing Mrs. Helene Smith (a.k.a. Elsie Singer) in Paramount's camp backstage classic Murder at the Vanities (M. Leisen, Paramount, 1934). In a film with more convolutions than a drunk with delirium tremens, Ralph plays a seamstress at the "Vanities" and the secret mother of leading man Carl Brisson (incidentally, Rosalind Russell's Danish father-in-law). Brisson looks like a mixture of Liberace and Johnny Weissmuller in his tropical jungle number. Leading lady, Kitty Carlisle, is wooden to say the least and still has her baby fat intact at twenty-four. This was her film debut. Gertrude Michael plays "Rio Rita" Ross, a rival for Brisson's affections and the blackmailing villainess of the piece. She finally gets put out of her misery by Dorothy Stickney in one of her rare film roles, as a put-upon, dowdily delightful avenging angel of a theatrical maid. Murder at the Vanities was one of Paramount's last pre–Code films.

Starting in 1934, Ralph would be most closely affiliated with MGM, making a total of nineteen films there. Her first was Evelyn Prentice (W.K. Howard, 1934), starring Myrna Loy and William Powell in a collaboration designed to capitalize on the runaway success of the first "Thin Man" film. Ralph only had one scene in which she played an observant, garrulous old woman coming to testify about what she saw the day Loy's would-be lover was shot dead in his apartment. Ralph would reappear with the famously "modern" onscreen couple in 1936 in After the Thin Man (W.S. Van Dyke, MGM) and the following year in Double Wedding (R. Thorpe, MGM). In the former film, she played one of her more autocratic dowagers and Loy's aunt, Katherine Forrest.

At MGM in the mid–'30s Ralph played two of her classic faithful domestic roles in two of her most high-profile films. The first was George Cukor's celebrated adaptation of David Copperfield (1935) with more classic character actresses than you can shake a stick at, including Edna May Oliver, Elsa Lanchester, Una O'Connor, Violet Kemble Cooper, and Jean Cadell. Ralph had a large part, relatively speaking, as young Copperfield's devoted nurse, Peggotty. The following year, David O. Selznick, who had produced David Copperfield for MGM, gave Ralph a small part as the young hero's friend, the applewoman Mrs. McGillicuddy, in Little Lord Fauntleroy (J. Cromwell, Selznick Int., 1936). In both Copperfield and Fauntleroy, the boy hero was played by Freddie Bartholomew, who was then at the height of his infant fame.

David Copperfield and Little Lord Fauntleroy were followed by another classic in 1937, of French origin this time. Camille (G. Cukor, MGM) is still the most famous film version of Alexandre Dumas' novel, La dame aux camelias, and stars Greta Garbo as the courtesan, Marguerite Gaultier, and Robert Taylor as her young lover, Armand Duval. Ralph is Garbo's devoted maid, Nanine, ever at her side in palmy days as in stormy ones. Ralph's frequent co-star,

Jessie Ralph was seventy-one when this photograph was taken and had been in the movies since 1933. She is in costume for one of her major roles as the trusty nanny Peggotty in *David Copperfield* (Metro-Goldwyn-Mayer, 1935). The daughter of a New England sea captain, Ralph excelled both as duchesses and domestics and as warm- and cold-hearted older women.

Laura Hope Crews (*Girl from Avenue A*, *The Blue Bird*), has a more splashly role as a fast and fast-fading dressmaker. It is indicative of Ralph's standing at MGM by this time that she was billed ahead of Crews, even though Crews had the larger part. This was Ralph's tenth film for Metro and only Crews's fourth.

In *I Live My Life* (W.S. Van Dyke, MGM, 1935), Ralph had one of her first majorly unsympathetic roles as Joan Crawford's indomitable grandmother and the family matriarch, Mrs. O.H.B. Gage. The build-up to her first appearance is impressive and Ralph does not disappoint as one of the most autocratic, belligerent matriarchs in American film history (the only comparable performance I can think of is May Robson as Mrs. Leona Wicks in *The Perfect Specimen* [1937] with Errol Flynn as her overprotected grandson). From her canopied bed, Ralph rules the family and the family business with an iron hand (she also plays chess there). Her verdict on this vast clan, which includes Frank Morgan as her hapless son-in-law, is telling: "Eighty-three descendants and all of them women, except some of them wear pants."

During her eight years in Hollywood, Ralph was seen in fifty films. In her peak year, 1935, she took part in no less than eleven productions (including *Mark of the Vampire*, the only film in which her scenes were deleted). She worked for all the major studios and most often with directors like Richard Boleslawski, W.S. Van Dyke, Dorothy Arzner, Mervyn LeRoy, Richard Thorpe, and George Cukor. In 1939, she had the opportunity to work with a director known more as a man's man, but who nevertheless managed to wheedle fine performances out of veteran character actresses Una O'Connor, Henrietta Crosman, Sara Allgood, Jane Darwell, and later Mildred Natwick. This was John Ford and the film was the Technicolor classic of Revolutionary Era Americana, *Drums Along the Mohawk* (Twentieth Century–Fox, 1939). Here Ralph played Mrs. Weaver, one of the frontier women who help deliver Claudette Colbert's baby and add local color in myriad ways.

The Blue Bird (W. Lang, 1940) was the second most celebrated of the six films Ralph made at Fox and one of her two films in Technicolor. (Actually it was only partially in color, as had been its MGM counterpart from the previous year, *The Wizard of Oz*.) As the fairy Berylune in a script based on a play by Maurice Maeterlinck, Ralph was hard to recognize in spectacles and a hooded, patchwork quilted cloak. Her job was to send Shirley Temple on her quest to find the blue bird and happiness.

The Bank Dick (E.F. Cline, 1940) was one of three films Ralph made at Universal towards the end of her days in Hollywood. Sporting the most incredibly moniker of her film career, Mrs.

Hermisillo Brunch, she played W.C. Fields's intensely disapproving, live-in mother-in-law, with Cora Witherspoon as her subservient daughter and Fields's nagging wife. The film is slapstick comedy at its slappiest and stickiest; a series of vaudeville sketches built around Fields's inept detective figure, Egbert Sousé. Poor Fields can do no right in the eyes of his family's female members until the day he strikes it rich. In a transformation symbolic of many of Ralph's best roles, by the end of the film she has been elevated from an unkempt hag into a stately dowager.

As I suggested initially, Ralph was unbeatable when she could play an upper-class dowager or noblewoman who had risen from humble beginnings. In this category her role as Mrs. Maisie Burley in *San Francisco* (W.S. Van Dyke, MGM, 1936), starring Jeanette MacDonald, Clark Gable, Spencer Tracy, and Jack Holt, is preeminent. Holt played the guy who didn't get the girl and Ralph was his outwardly formidable mother, who reveals a softer side when her potential daughter-in-law MacDonald comes to call. By the cataclysmic end of the movie, Ralph has lost both her son and her home. The last we see of her, she is being led away from the ruins of her Nob Hill mansion. Ralph played similar roles in *The Last of Mrs. Cheyney* (R. Boleslawski, MGM, 1937) and in her final film, *They Met in Bombay* (C. Brown, MGM, 1941).

In *The Last of Mrs. Cheyney*, Ralph was the Duchess of Ebley, a part Dame May Whitty had originated on stage in London. Joan Crawford took up Gladys Cooper's celebrated role as the lady thief and gang leader of the title, who tries to steal Ralph's pearls while staying as a guest at her country estate. In this film, Ralph tells Crawford that she started life in a charity ward in a Dublin hospital and pronounces with

As the Nob Hill matriarch Mrs. Maisie Burley in *San Francisco* (Metro-Goldwyn-Mayer, 1936), Jessie Ralph came up against Jeanette MacDonald (left) and the big earthquake of 1906. She survived both, but lost her son and her home.

characteristic candor that "I'd rather have this cup of chocolate than the best male ever created." She had supported Crawford before. *The Last of Mrs. Cheyney* reunited the winning combination of Crawford, Ralph, and veteran Irish American actor, Frank Morgan, which originated in *I Live My Life*. Ralph and Morgan acted in five films together, making him one of her most frequent male co-stars.

As for the original duchess, May Whitty, she narrowly missed being able to play the role herself. She settled in Hollywood in the fall of 1937 and began her film career by reprising her stage role in *Night Must Fall*. During Ralph's remaining years in Hollywood, Whitty would be competition in filling aristocratic dowager roles at MGM, as May Robson had been up until the mid-'30s.

In *They Met In Bombay*, released in June 1941, Ralph portrayed a down-to-earth duchess for the last time in a storyline not unlike *Mrs. Cheyney*, though set in India. As yet another "old battleship," the Duchess of Beltravers, the hard-drinking, plainspoken owner of a celebrated diamond necklace coveted both by Clark Gable and Rosalind Russell, Ralph appears only in one extended scene at the beginning of the film. With a face only a mother could love and an air of wise old womanhood, we might say of her in her seventy-seventh year and her final role what Cecil Beaton once said of Gertrude Stein: "Age had not withered her ugliness." Ralph is visibly older and thinner here, her hair uncustomarily dyed, but the mischievous light in her eye is undimmed as she reassures Russell that while she carried her children like a lady, she carries her liquor like a gentleman.

The amputation of one of her legs forced Ralph to retire in 1941.[530] She died three years later, on May 30, 1944, after a short illness, in her birthplace Gloucester, Massachusetts. She was in her eightieth year.

Mother Courage
ANNE REVERE (1903–1990)

To be Oscar-nominated for three out of forty film roles is not a bad average. Anne Revere won the Academy Award for Best Supporting Actress in 1946 for her performance as Elizabeth Taylor's stalwart, sympathetic mother in *National Velvet*. If not her finest film role, it is among the two or three for which she is best remembered.

Revere specialized in upright, idealistic, careworn, working-class wives and mothers. She was herself a woman of character, who was willing to pay the price for her principles. With Gale Sondergaard, Marsha Hunt, Ruth Nelson, and Karen Morley, she was among the most prominent actresses in Hollywood to be blacklisted and effectively banned from the movie industry for her political convictions during the McCarthy era. Marsha Hunt described her as "a really dedicated liberal." As the treasurer of the Screen Actors Guild until she resigned voluntarily from the board in 1951, she belonged to what Karen Morley has called "the progressive side" with Dorothy Tree and Revere's screen son, John Garfield.[531]

Anne Revere was born on the island of Manhattan on June 25, 1903.[532] Her father, Clinton Revere, was a stockbroker and Anne grew up on the Upper West Side and in Westfield, New Jersey. She received her B.A. from Wellesley in 1926 and went on to study at the American Laboratory School in New York, which was under the direction of two talented expatriate Russians who would both go on to careers in the Hollywood movie industry: Maria Ouspenskaya and Richard Boleslawski. After paying her dues in stock and regional companies, Revere made her Broadway debut in a play called *The Great Barrington*, which opened at the Avon Theatre on February 19, 1931, but only ran for sixteen performances. Otto Kruger and Natalie Schafer were also in the cast. Revere's next Broadway play was called *The Lady with the Lamp* (1931). Eminent English actress Edith Evans led the cast as Florence Nightingale and Revere had a small part as a nurse. Alas, this play closed after twelve performances.

Revere's Broadway breakthrough and first resounding hit came on November 20, 1934, when Lillian Hellman's first hit play *The Children's Hour* opened at Maxine Elliot's Theatre on West 39th Street. Revere was cast as Martha Dobie, one of two young, idealistic women who start a school for girls. The play would be filmed as *These Three* in 1936 in a version that played down the lesbian element. Martha Dobie was played by Miriam Hopkins, an actress about as different from Revere as can be imagined. When the play was filmed again in 1961 under its original title and in a version closer to the original, Shirley MacLaine played Martha Dobie.

In 1935, during the long run of *The Children's Hour*, Revere married the actor-director-writer Samuel Rosen. They remained married for nearly half a century until Rosen's death in 1984. In 1937, Rosen directed his wife in a short-lived revival of Shakespeare's *As You Like It* at the Ritz Theatre, where she played Celia. He wrote the acting version two years later of a new production of Chekhov's *Three Sisters*, where Revere played the eldest, Masha. That show closed after only nine performances.

These failures on Broadway may have been conducive to the Rosens' move to California at the end of the 1930s. Revere had made a false start in movies in 1934, when she reprised her role in a Broadway play called *Double Door* (1933–34) in the film version directed by Charles Vidor at Paramount. Though she would work for all the major studios and many of the minor ones during her ten plus years in Hollywood, Revere would be most closely associated with Twentieth Century–Fox from *Remember the Day* (H. King, 1941) to *You're My Everything* (W. Lang, 1949). Some of the major films of her tenure at Fox were *The Song of Bernadette*, *The Keys of the Kingdom*, *Dragonwyck*, *The Shocking Miss Pilgrim*, *Gentleman's Agreement*, and *Forever Amber*. At Paramount she made eight films and at MGM five, including *National Velvet* and *The Thin Man Goes Home*. She also worked for Columbia, Warner Bros., RKO, Universal, and Republic.

The Song of Bernadette (H. King, 1943) set a standard and created a screen image for Revere in Hollywood films of the 1940s. You may recall that this well-cast ensemble film centers around a young girl called Bernadette Soubirous (Jennifer Jones), who has a mystical vision. Revere plays her long-suffering, washerwoman mother, using her sensitive, equine face and mournful eyes to good effect. Four of the leading actors, including Revere, were nominated for Academy Awards and Jennifer Jones won for Best Actress. Katina Paxinou won that year in the Best Supporting Actress category for her performance in *For Whom the Bell Tolls*.

This portrait is from *The Devil Commands* (Columbia Pictures, 1941), an early Anne Revere film where she plays the accomplice and assistant of the classic mad scientist played by Boris Karloff, who is obsessed with trying to communicate with his dead wife. This was her only horror film.

In *The Keys of the Kingdom* (J.M. Stahl, 1944), Revere had a modest role as an American missionary's wife, who with her husband befriends Gregory Peck in what is an "old-man-looks-back" film very similar in structure to MGM's hit *Good-bye, Mr. Chips* (1939). *Dragonwyck* (J.L. Mankiewicz, 1946) saw her in a period costume drama as a nineteenth-century Greenwich, Connecticut farmwife and mother of Gene Tierney, who worries about her daughter's fate as the mistress of the haunted estate Dragonwyck. This none too spellbinding film nevertheless had a strong cast, that included Walter Huston as Revere's religious husband, Spring Byington as an eerie housekeeper, and Jessica Tandy as Tierney's devoted, crippled Irish maid. As a variation on what Peter B. Flint has called "her salt-of-the-earth motif"—"straight hair carefully combed into a practical bun"[533]—Revere here bears a modified Princess Leia hairdo.

Revere's part in *The Shocking Miss Pilgrim* (G. Seaton, 1947) was a very Edna May Oliver, Boston Brahmin kind of role. She plays Alice Pritchard, a brisk bluestocking and women's suffrage leader, and the officious, meddlesome owner of the shipping company where her nephew, played by Dick Haymes, and the film's female star, Betty Grable, are both employed and fall in love. The plot is not dissimilar to Henry James's *The Bostonians*. Fox teamed Revere with Gregory Peck again in the socially conscious *Gentleman's Agreement* (1947). Directed by Elia Kazan, the film featured Peck as a journalist who pretends to be Jewish to uncover anti–Semitic attitudes. Revere was his always dependable and politically correct mother. For this performance, she garnered her third and last Oscar nomination, but lost to her co-star Celeste Holm. In retrospect, director Kazan, a left-winger who nevertheless would collaborate with the House Committee on Un-American Activities, said he liked John Garfield best in the film, as Peck's Jewish friend. He added: "The other performance I can recall is that of Anne Revere; she had bite and was at the same time caustic and affectionate."[534] Film historians Charles Higham and Joel Greenberg were not impressed, writing that Revere's Mrs. Green was "irritatingly played in her most sub–Brechtian manner."[535] In one of her last films for Fox, *Forever Amber* (O. Preminger, 1947), Revere played Mother Red Cap, the leader of a gang of thieves that heroine Linda Darnell gets involved with when she is down on her luck.

Revere won her Oscar in a generic ever toiling, ever worrying, working-class mother role. There were several other actresses one might imagine playing the fittingly named Mrs. Brown in *National Velvet* (C. Brown, MGM, 1944), including MGM's own contract player Agnes Moorehead, who arrived in Hollywood about the same time as Revere; and another contemporary, Ruth Nelson, who is the character actress most closely to resemble her and who also had her film career destroyed by the Red Scare. Nelson, like Revere, played the mother of the ultimate 1940s proletarian hero, John Garfield. In *Humoresque* (1946) with Nelson, he was a talented and ambitious violinist who worries his mother by getting entangled with wealthy socialite Joan Crawford. In *Body and Soul* (R. Rossen, 1947) with Revere, he was an unusually sensitive and intelligent boxer, whose widowed Jewish mother wants him to improve himself.

It would be wrong, though, to suggest that Revere only played run-of-the-mill proletarian moms. In another of her films for MGM, *The Thin Man Goes Home* (R. Thorpe, 1944), she played Crazy Mary, a mannish recluse who turns out to be intimately related to the film's murder victim and one of the town's leading citizens. She was a chic journalist who interviews the writer-celebrity played by Miriam Hopkins in *Old Acquaintance* (V. Sherman, Warner Bros., 1943) and a fake spiritualist medium who becomes mad professor Boris Karloff's accomplice in *The Devil Commands* (E. Dmytryk, 1941), one of her three films for Columbia.

Revere's final film in Hollywood was also destined to be her best remembered one: *A Place in the Sun* (G. Stevens, Paramount, 1951). By the time the film was released in August, 1951, she was among the more than 300 names on the infamous Hollywood blacklist, which meant that she had no future in the movie

Anne Revere is looking at Anne Baxter who is looking at Shari Robinson who is looking at Dan Dailey, who is looking right back at her in this photo from *You're My Everything* (Twentieth Century–Fox, 1949). Revere plays posh, mink-clad Aunt Jane in one of her few comedy musicals, about a society girl who marries an entertainer and goes on the road with him.

industry. She had been called before the House Committee on Un-American Activities (HUAC), but refused to testify, taking the Fifth Amendment. Her part as Montgomery Clift's mother, Hannah Eastman, was reduced to a bare minimum.[536] In what little remains, she gives yet another performance as a "Mother Courage"–type character. A devout Christian, she runs the Bethel Independent Mission in Kansas City and tries unsuccessfully to save her son's life by appealing to the governor for clemency.

The fifties were lean years for the Rosens. They operated a drama school in Los Angeles for a time, before returning to their native New York. Revere tried to find stage work and acted in three short-run plays on Broadway. The ice finally broke on February 25, 1960, when she opened in Lillian Hellman's *Toys in the Attic* at the Hudson Theatre. It was more than twenty-five years since her first hit on Broadway (that too in a Hellman play) and her final appearance there would lead to a Tony for Best Featured Actress in a Play. For Revere, her triumph as one of two frustrated spinster sisters in a play that ran for 556 performances must have tasted particularly sweet.

Yet acting jobs were still slow in coming and it was not until the late 1960s and early 1970s that she found regular work in television. She was not asked to reprise her role when *Toys in the Attic* was filmed in 1963. Her part went to veteran British actress Wendy Hiller. It would be nearly twenty years from *A Place in the Sun* till she again appeared on the big screen in *Tell Me That You Love Me, Junie Moon*

(Paramount, 1970). The director, Otto Preminger, who had worked with Revere in *Fallen Angel* (Twentieth Century–Fox, 1945) and *Forever Amber*, no doubt had a hand in her belated return to feature films. Revere's final film appearance was in *Birch Interval* (D. Mann, 1977), an independent Canadian production starring veteran character actor Eddie Albert, Rip Torn, and Ann Wedgeworth. Revere played an addled old farmwoman, who befriends a young boy on a neighboring farm and loses her home in a fire.

Anne Revere died of pneumonia at her home in Locust Valley, New York in December 1990. Befitting a direct descendant of Paul Revere, she was buried in historic Mount Auburn Cemetery in Cambridge, Massachusetts. The Rosens had no children, but Revere was survived by a sister, Winn Revere Smith, of Cross River, Long Island.

The Forgotten Woman
ELISABETH RISDON (1887–1958)

Elisabeth Risdon is not the character actress with the greatest recognition value in this book, but she has earned her place through the sheer number and variety of her roles in Hollywood movies between 1935 and 1952. From her first sound film, *Guard That Girl* (L. Hillyer, Columbia), till her last, *Scaramouche* (G. Sidney, MGM), Risdon always made the best of whatever part was given her, however small (and most of them were small), almost as if she'd made "There are no small roles, only small actors" her motto. This might be said of literally dozens of character actresses, but few of them were as productive as Risdon and as real on the big screen. In the course of only seventeen years, Elisabeth Risdon lent her calm, reassuring, and increasingly familiar presence to no less than 101 films. In addition, she had a singularly solid background from the silent era as well, being one of the stars of the pioneering period of British silent films between 1913 and 1917, when she made more than forty films. Looking a bit like a pretty Sara Allgood, if such a thing may be imagined, she was gifted with an unusually fine voice and distinguished diction. David Quinlan describes her as "delicately pretty, doe-eyed, light-haired..., with the appearance of a startled fawn."[537]

As already indicated, Elisabeth Risdon was English, born in the Wandsworth area of London on April 26, 1887 to John Jenkins Risdon and his wife, Martha (born Harrop).[538] Risdon had the benefit of studying acting at what is now the Royal Academy of Dramatic Arts, like Flora Robson, before making her stage debut in Nelson, Lancashire in 1910. The following year she made her London stage debut, and the year after that she went to New York and opened on Broadway in the title role in *Fanny's First Play* (1912–13) by George Bernard Shaw. The play was a hit and ran for 256 performances. In the cast was Maurice Elvey, who would direct no less than thirty-three of Risdon's silent films upon her return to London in 1913. Four years later, this period of her career ended when she moved with her husband and sometime director, George Loane Tucker, back to his native United States. Tucker, who had been born in Chicago in 1872 and who directed sixty silent films between 1911 and his premature death in 1921, was also an actor and had two hits on Broadway: *The Fortune Hunter* (1909–10) with John Barrymore and *Alma, Where Do You Live?* (1910–11).

For the eighteen years from 1917 onward, Risdon worked steadily on the Broadway stages. One of the highpoints of her American theatrical career was creating the role of Ellie Dunn in the Theatre Guild's original production of Shaw's *Heartbreak House* (1920–21), which also starred those future fellow film actresses Lucile Watson and Helen Westley. Risdon was in *The Enchanted April* (1925) with veteran British actress and, again, future film sensation, Alison Skipworth and in the following year shared a dismal flop with Florence Eldridge and Margaret Wycherly called *A Proud Woman* (1926). She had a hit, though, as a career woman with a mother-in-law from hell in Laura Hope Crews's biggest stage hit, *The Silver Cord* (1926–27). Irene Dunne, who was eleven years Risdon's junior, played the role of Christina in the film version from 1933. Risdon was with Jean Adair, Fay Bainter, and Leo G. Carroll in Somerset Maugham's *For Services Rendered* (1933) and with Bainter again in a revival of that old chestnut *Uncle Tom's Cabin* (1933). And get this: Risdon played the escaped slave, Eliza, and Bainter played Topsy!

Risdon would star in a total of twenty-seven Broadway plays before she quit the stage to devote herself to film work in 1935 and moved permanently to Hollywood. By that time, her first husband was long dead and she was married to another actor, Brandon Evans, who was born on the same day as her first husband, June 12, but was six years his junior. The couple had acted together in two Broadway flops in the 1920s.

Unfortunately, unlike other productive, dedicated and unassuming actresses like Elizabeth Patterson, Jane Darwell, and Clara Blandick, Elisabeth Risdon was never given that golden opportunity, that long-awaited, once-in-a-lifetime signature role that would justify the many missed opportunities, the scenes that landed on the cutting room floor, and the years of acting in bits and pieces here and there. The closest she came was quite early in her career, when she was given the role of Raskolnikov's mother in Josef von Sternberg's *Crime and Punishment* (Columbia, 1935), Aunt Mary in *Theodora Goes Wild* (R. Boleslawski, Columbia, 1936), and Cora Payne in *Make Way for Tomorrow* (L. McCarey, Paramount, 1937). These three are quintessential Elisabeth Risdon roles. Mrs. Raskolnikov is Risdon in her concerned mother guise. This time her child is Peter Lorre as Dostoyevsky's eminent anti-hero, Raskolnikov. In *Theodora Goes Wild*, Aunt Mary is revealed as a shell of snobbish hauteur over a soft, mushy interior, as she follows the transformation of her plain, spinsterish niece, Irene Dunne, into a sophisticated, devil-may-care, bestselling author. Cora Payne is the generic weary, working-class woman, who in this case has to make room for her aging father (Victor Moore) in her already cramped home. Though much less well known than *The Awful Truth* (1937) and *Love Affair* (1939) and yet to be released on video or DVD, *Make Way for Tomorrow* is arguably director Leo McCarey's masterpiece. Risdon was fortunate to be part of its extraordinarily fine ensemble cast, which included Beulah Bondi, Thomas Mitchell, Fay Bainter, and Minna Gombell.

Risdon's somewhat similar part in *Mannequin* (F. Borzage, MGM, 1937) was smaller, but she had one very fine scene over the kitchen sink with her daughter, Joan Crawford, whom

Elisabeth Risdon uses her doe eyes to good effect in this portrait, probably taken in connection with the minor political drama **The Forgotten Woman** (Universal Pictures, 1939). Risdon had a moon-shaped face and a determined chin, making her look like a pretty, blue-eyed, light-haired version of Sara Allgood.

she advises to grab all the happiness and the opportunities she possibly can before it's too late. Then there was *The Adventures of Huckleberry Finn* (R. Thorpe, MGM, 1939). Risdon was ideally suited to playing the well-intentioned Widow Douglas, who tries to "sivilize" the hero of the piece, here interpreted famously by Mickey Rooney.

All these were films from the second half of the 1930s. By comparison, the opportunities given her in her remaining dozen years in Hollywood were often even slimmer. At RKO, which was the closest thing to a home studio for Risdon between 1937 and 1950, she was given roles that were little more than walk-ons in films like *Higher and Higher* (T. Whelan, 1943) and the prestigious *Mourning Becomes Electra* (D. Nichols, 1947). Seven of the twenty-three films she made at RKO were part of the "Mexican Spitfire" series starring Lupe Velez. Risdon had a recurring role as Aunt Della Lindsay in these films from the early 1940s.

The many other studios that regularly made use of her services during these years made no greater demands on her time or talents. At Universal, the only one of her sixteen films with any recognition value today is *The Egg and I* (C. Erskine, 1947), starring Claudette Colbert and Fred MacMurray. Risdon plays Colbert's elegant, upper-class mother, who encourages her to make up with her somewhat eccentric husband. She would be teamed with Colbert again in *The Secret Fury* (M. Ferrer, 1950), where she had a relatively substantial part as a psychiatrist at a state mental hospital where Colbert is brought for treatment after

Elisabeth Risdon is having a bad hat day in this photo from the murder mystery thriller *The Unseen* (Paramount Pictures, 1945), which starred Joel McCrea and Gail Russell. Russell was being groomed for stardom at Paramount at this time. She died tragically of an alcohol-induced heart attack in 1961 at the age of thirty-six.

her breakdown. At Columbia, Risdon made the previously mentioned *Crime and Punishment* and *Theodora Goes Wild* during her first years in Hollywood, but her parts in the twelve films that followed were not of the same caliber. In *Craig's Wife* (D. Arzner, 1936), she only has one scene as Rosalind Russell's dying sister, who leaves her daughter in Russell's care. In *The Howards of Virginia* (F. Lloyd, 1940), a very poor imitation of *Drums Along the Mohawk* (1939), Risdon plays Martha Scott's class-conscious aunt, who is appalled at Scott's marriage with proletarian farmer and surveyor, Cary Grant. Finally, in the Marlene Dietrich film *The Lady Is Willing* (M. Leisen, 1942), Risdon makes a brief appearance as a ghoulish representative of the Child Welfare Department.

At MGM she also played small parts, often consisting of only one or two scenes. In *Random Harvest* (M. LeRoy, 1942), she plays a woman who comes to a sanitarium to see if Ronald Colman is her son (he is not); in *Journey for Margaret* (W.S. Van Dyke, 1942), she has a small but significant role as a wealthy British lady who changes her mind about helping Robert Young bring a child to safety in America rather than 40 lbs. of luggage; in *The Canterville Ghost* (J. Dassin, 1944), she is Margaret O'Brien's aristocratic, invalid aunt; in *High Wall* (C. Bernhardt, 1947), she plays Robert Taylor's mother; and in her final film, *Scaramouche* (1952), she is Isabelle de Valmorin, the mother of hero Stewart Granger's bosom buddy, Richard Anderson, whom Granger swears to avenge after he is killed by Mel Ferrer. Risdon also worked for Warner Bros., Paramount, Republic, Twentieth Century–Fox, and for Samuel Goldwyn's independent production company in films such as *Dead End* (W. Wyler, Samuel Goldwyn, 1937), *The Roaring Twenties* (R. Walsh, Warner Bros., 1939), *High Sierra* (R. Walsh, Warner Bros., 1941), *Reap the Wild Wind* (C.B. DeMille, Paramount, 1942), *The Shocking Miss Pilgrim* (G. Seaton, Twentieth Century–Fox, 1947), and *Life with Father* (M. Curtiz, Warner Bros., 1947).

Risdon officially retired in 1956. During her final active years she taught drama to the patients at a Veterans Administration hospital near her Brentwood home. Her second husband, Brandon Evans, passed away on April 3, 1958 and Risdon soon followed him, dying of a cerebral hemorrhage in St. John's Hospital in Santa Monica, California on December 20, 1958. Elisabeth Risdon donated her body to the UCLA Medical School and hence has no grave.

The Last Character Actress
THELMA RITTER (1905–1969)

Had Thelma Ritter chosen to remain at home in Forest Hills, New York with her two children, the world would have lost the film performances of one of the most familiar and beloved female faces in the Hollywood films of the 1950s and '60s. Ritter had quit acting in 1937, when her son was born, and became a full-time homemaker while her husband enjoyed increasing success as an advertising executive. In one of those curious twists of fate that influence not just individual lives and careers, but in this case film history, Ritter had once lived next door to and befriended director George Seaton's wife Phyllis.[539] Fast forward to 1946, when Seaton is set to direct *Miracle on 34th Street* at Twentieth Century–Fox and needs a suitably anonymous "salt-of-the-earth" type actress to play a weary Christmas shopper at Macy's with her child in tow. The rest, as they say, is history. Ritter's modest scene was noticed by Fox boss Darryl F. Zanuck, who asked that the actress be sent for and her part expanded.[540]

The Last Character Actress: Thelma Ritter (1905-1969)

In the wake of *Miracle on 34th Street*, Ritter found she had a new acting career at the age of forty-one. She would not make many films during the ensuing two decades, averaging only a little over a film a year between 1947 and her retirement in 1968, but several of the films she made would be among the most popular and critically acclaimed movies of the studio era's sunset years. She would hold the record for most Oscar nominations in the same category, six in her case, but would never win the prize. Yet she did win the prestigious Tony. In addition, she was nominated for an Emmy, three Golden Globes, and five Golden Laurel awards. Paddy Chayefsky wrote in his *New York Times* tribute on her death: "she was never properly publicly recognized as an actress."[541] Most actresses would have considered themselves fortunate to be similarly neglected!

Thelma Ritter was born on Valentine's Day, 1905 on Hart Street in South Brooklyn.[542] Her parents were the Dutch immigrant and shoe company office manager, Charles Ritter, and his Scottish wife, Lucy Hale.[543] Money was tight in the Ritter family and Thelma learned early to fend for herself. Her dream was to attend the prestigious American Academy of Dramatic Arts (AADA). To that end, she started working and saving, finally being accepted into the class of 1922.[544] Ritter did not graduate with her class, she had to go back to work, but forty years later she would be the first recipient of the AADA Alumni Award.

Ritter spent most of the 1920s and the years of the Great Depression toiling in stock and repertory companies. During her nearly fifty years as a stage actress, she only had four shows on Broadway. The first was *The Shelf* (1926), a short-run show with three fellow players destined to make their mark in American films long before Ritter herself: veteran character actress Jessie Ralph; feisty bottle blonde Lee Patrick; and the aptly named Donald Meek. *In Times Square* (1931) didn't run much longer than *The Shelf*. Ritter did not return to the Great White Way till 1957. Then she came to stay. *New Girl in Town*, a hit musical based on Eugene O'Neill's play *Anna Christie*, ran for 431 performances at the 46th Street Theatre.

Unfortunately, Thelma Ritter did not always look this attractive on screen. She is best remembered for her dog-tired, world-weary, "Everywoman" quality, "her face like a crumpled newspaper." Yet, as this picture reveals, she had beautiful eyes and fine lips set in a symmetrical face. Who would a thunk it?

Ritter won a Tony for her portrayal of that old waterfront soak, Marthy, and Gwen Verdon won for Anna. This was the first time in Tony history that two actresses from the same show had won.[545] Ritter's last Broadway play was the disastrous *UTBU* (1966), where Margaret Hamilton and Tony Randall also went down with the ship.

From the time of her marriage to a fellow actor, Joseph Moran, in 1927, she and her husband toiled together, she somewhat more successfully.[546] Harsh economic realities and his way with words led Moran to advertising, where by the late 1930s he was more than successful enough to provide for a family as a vice president of Young and Rubicam.[547] The Morans had two children: a son, Joseph Anthony, born in 1937, and a daughter, Monica Ann, born in 1940.[548] Ritter looked set for the life of a suburban housewife in the home at 65 Greenway Terrace in Forest Hills, New York, that they had bought in 1937.[549] Fate would have it otherwise.

Ritter would make nearly half and many of her best films for Twentieth Century–Fox. She signed a contract for three films a year after her success in A Letter to Three Wives (1949) and spent on average eighteen weeks out of the year in Hollywood during the six years of her Fox contract.[550] Her thirteen films at the studio, headed throughout her time there by legendary Darryl Zanuck, include such classics as All About Eve (1950), The Model and the Marriage Broker (1951), With a Song in My Heart (1952), Titanic (1953), and Pickup on South Street (1953). Ritter also made two fine films for Paramount—The Mating Season (1951) and Rear Window (1954)—and scored a major hit with Pillow Talk (1959) for Universal. Generally, her films of the 1960s were not of the caliber of her '50s films. The exception is The Misfits (1961), which ends the major period of her film career that started with A Letter to Three Wives in 1949 and All About Eve in 1950.

As a screen actress, Thelma Ritter had a desiccated, undernourished, Puckish quality and a mug only a mother could love. David Thomson once said that she had a face "like a used newspaper."[551] Nevertheless, she had been considered comely in her youth.[552] (Incidentally, she had also played Puck early on in a semi-professional production of A Midsummer Night's Dream.[553]) Her obvious forte was the working woman, the working-class mother, or a combination of the two: the working, working-class mother. Paradoxically, it was in her "Everywoman" quality that Ritter was unique. On screen Ritter projected a wonderfully sanguine and calm acceptance of human frailty and need. It is this quality, combined with her rueful humor and notorious wisecracks, that give depth to her finest performances. I'm thinking primarily of films such as The Model and the Marriage Broker, Pickup on South Street, and The Misfits, but also of Rear Window, Pillow Talk, and How the West Was Won.

Though she played a few middle- or upper-class women towards the end of her career, Ritter was obviously best suited to playing women on the lower echelons of the social ladder. In these roles, as James Robert Parish has noted, "one was never sure if she was playacting or being herself."[554] This ingrained proletarian quality was one she shared with her A Letter to Three Wives co-star, Connie Gilchrist. Though Ritter was one of a kind indeed, Gilchrist is maybe the character actress of Ritter's generation most to resemble her. Even so, the similarity is fairly superficial. Gilchrist most predominantly symbolized immigrant Irish bravado and gumption; she was a different physical type from Ritter, being built on a much larger scale; and she had an aggressive, bellicose quality, that was a far cry from Ritter's laidback, "live and let live" attitude. Gilchrist had a less high-profile film career, of course, though she made almost three times as many films. Some of the high points beyond all her genial neighbor and belligerent landlady roles were playing John Garfield's sex-starved, widowed neighbor, Mrs. Torelli, in Tortilla Flat (1942); her cleaning lady in Presenting Lily Mars (1943), who sings "Every Little Movement Has a Meaning of Its Own" to Judy Garland to convince her to pursue her dreams; Rosalind Russell's Irish maid in Auntie Mame (1958); and Linda Darnell's down-to-earth mother and Ritter's card-playing friend, Mrs. Rubey Finney, in A Letter to Three Wives (1949).

Like several other well-worn character actresses who had attained a certain level of recognition and who excelled at proletarian roles, including May Robson, Marjorie Main, and Jane Darwell, Thelma Ritter was frequently compared to the late, great Marie Dressler.[555] Twenty years before Ritter made a big splash in a tiny role through her friendship with director George Seaton, Dressler had similarly got a start in the movies with a little help from her friends. The first years of the 1920s had been the low point of Dressler's life and career, making her comeback all the more spectacular. Between 1927 and her much lamented death from cancer in 1934, Dressler made twenty-two films, nearly all at MGM. Some of the high points were Anna Christie (1930), Min and Bill (1930), Emma (1932), and Dinner at Eight (1933). As was the case with Ritter, "troubled people out there in the comforting dark always recognized her as one of themselves."[556]

The Last Character Actress: Thelma Ritter (1905-1969)

At her best, Marie Dressler was a stunningly powerful actress. Great character acting—as opposed to great *caricature* acting—is usually a case of such a close fit between actor and role that not the teeniest drop of histrionics can squeeze through. No better example need be sought than Dressler as Marthy in *Anna Christie*, the film in which "Garbo Talks." We can practically smell the alcoholic fumes about her, as she sits drinking in the saloon. A hundred small, subtle movements animate her haggard face and body, as she lives from gulp to gulp, from drink to drink. A lot of the time, though, Dressler was up to her old vaudeville tricks and engaged in what can only be described as "broad" characterizations. Ritter would never have tried or gotten away with some of the unreconstructed mugging that Dressler put over.[557] In fact, Ritter only reprised two of Dressler's roles and that was in other media than film: Marthy in *Anna Christie* in the musical version of *Anna Christie*, *New Girl in Town*, and Abby in *Christopher Bean* on television. In addition to Marthy, the Dressler role one can most readily imagine Ritter playing is the faithful family retainer who lends her name to the film *Emma*. On the other hand, it is impossible to imagine Ritter pulling off the dilapidated diva Carlotta Vance in *Dinner at Eight*.

Thus, as is usually the case when two unique actors are compared, the validity of the comparison between Dressler and Ritter only goes so far. Marie Dressler was a major star, even if as one of her biographers has written, she was "the unlikeliest star."[558] She was Hollywood's most popular performer in 1932 and 1933 in the annual exhibitors' poll, ahead of both Garbo and John Barrymore.[559] She was the first

In this scene from Alfred Hitchcock's *Rear Window* (Paramount Pictures, 1954), James Stewart as an immobilized photographer and Thelma Ritter as his nurse are discovering the joys of bird-watching. As you can see, Stewart has got a considerably bigger one than Ritter. Ritter had been with Stewart in *Call Northside 777* six years earlier, but her entire part ended up on the cutting room floor.

female movie actress ever to appear on the cover of *Time*.[560] Furthermore, Dressler was different physically from Ritter, standing five foot seven inches tall and weighing in at 200 lbs. Part of the Dressler magic was her successful comic pairings, first with Polly Moran and later with Wallace Beery. Ritter would never be involved in any recurring comic duos of this kind. Dressler was twice Oscar-nominated for Best Actress in a Leading Role and won for *Min and Bill* in 1931. Ritter was only ever nominated in the Best Supporting Actress category, albeit six times. She never won the coveted prize.

Naturally, the movie industry had changed during the dozen years since Dressler's death and would change radically during Ritter's twenty years in the business. By the early 1950s, it would be well nigh impossible to imagine an older woman gaining the position in the industry that Dressler held in the early 1930s. Yet, Ritter was singularly fortunate in being cast in several plum parts in fine films at a time when good roles for older women were becoming fewer and fewer, when the number of films being made was sharply reduced, and when the kinds of films being made were also qualitatively different from the first two decades of the sound era. Like Dressler, May Robson, Jane Darwell, and Alison Skipworth in the 1930s, Ritter sometimes received top billing. Unlike these veteran character actresses of the early sound era, though, Ritter was not infrequently given her own love interest. Unlike similarly circumstanced and plain-faced, older actresses in the 1930s, who could only look forward to playing sexless widows, resolute spinsters, or safely married old biddies, Ritter wasn't put out to pasture. The fullness of several of her female characters, despite their being "over the hill" and physically unattractive, marks in a symbolic sense the demise of the traditional character actress. The Clara Blandicks, Beulah Bondis, Elizabeth Pattersons, Jane Darwells, and Elisabeth Risdons lived almost exclusively for others. In the 1930s, a well-preserved former stage star turned character actress like Billie Burke or Alice Brady might be allowed a beau of her own, but the run-of-the-mill character actress was sexually *hors de combat*.

In contrast, Ritter was allowed to live a lot for herself, to portray a fully formed individual with her own needs and desires. We see this most clearly in *The Mating Season*, *The Model and the Marriage Broker*, and *A New Kind of Love*, but also in *Titanic*, *The Farmer Takes a Wife*, and *The Misfits*. In *The Mating Season* (M. Leisen, Paramount, 1951), a very class-conscious satire on the corporate culture of the early 1950s, Ritter manages to marry the not unhandsome big boss of her son's company, Mr. Kalinger, played with suave sophistication by Larry Keating. Kalinger, a widower, succumbs to the charm of Mrs. McNulty's alcohol rubs, accompanied by a rueful reckoning of her dead husband Sam's very limited attractions. In *The Model and the Marriage Broker* (G. Cukor, Twentieth Century–Fox, 1951), Ritter is hoist by her own petard, as matchmaker Mae Swasey, and ends up paired with Mr. Doberman (Michael O'Shea). The film is noticeable for being a romantic comedy that doesn't just focus on "sweet young things" Jeanne Crain and Scott Brady, but has a wonderful supporting cast of lovelorn misfits, including Zero Mostel, Dennie Moore, and Nancy Kulp. Finally, in yet another "Americans in Paris" film, *A New Kind of Love* (M. Shavelson, Paramount, 1963), starring Paul Newman and Joanne Woodward, Ritter's Leena, a buyer at Bergner's Department Store with a yen for her boss (George Tobias), is finally rewarded for her long service. Maybe it is her perfume, which is called "My Sin."

Frank Capra called her "the best of all character actresses."[561] In Paddy Chayefsky's words: "She was a character actress, which means only that they don't write many starring parts for middle-aged women."[562] Her *Pillow Talk* co-star, Rock Hudson, noted, "She was a doll, *the* character actress, I think."[563] Personally, I can't think of any films in which Thelma Ritter was downright bad, though I can think of some bad films she was in. The first that comes to mind is the terminally dull *As Young as You Feel* (H. Jones, Twentieth Century–Fox, 1951). The mere idea of patrician Monty Woolley playing a factory worker, however obstreperous, is about as ludicrous as having Ritter play an upper-class dowager. As Della Hodges, an ex-singer from Brooklyn who "sacrificed" her career to marry Woolley's son (Allyn Joslyn), Ritter is given little to do and the film "garnered her some of her few negative reviews."[564]

Despite the near unanimous approval of critics and fans alike, in a comparative perspective with several other character actresses in this book Ritter must take a secondary position. Compared to old timers like Beulah Bondi, Jane Darwell, and Elizabeth Patterson, her range was a limited one and her number of films as well. Even when compared with some of her contemporaries, Ritter did not have the acting range and versatility of an Agnes Moorehead, Mildred Dunnock, or Mildred Natwick. Ritter could have carried off some of Moorehead's more lackluster working-class mother roles and Parthy in Show Boat (1951) as well, though she was not all that well suited to period costume dramas, but what about Cornelia Van Gorder in The Bat (1959) or any number of Moorehead's other granddame roles? Ritter as Endora? Don't even think about it! It would have been interesting to see what she might have done with Mildred Dunnock's most famous role, Linda Loman in Death of a Salesman (stage, 1949–50; screen, 1951), but it is harder to imagine Ritter as the hard-as-nails Southern gentlewoman in The Story on Page One (1960) or in any of Dunnock's shrinking violet spinster parts from Tennessee Williams. As for the twinkly-eyed Mildred Natwick, who began her film career as a waterfront whore in John Ford's The Long Voyage Home (1940) and ended it forty-eight years later as Madame de Rosemonde in Dangerous Liaisons (1988), can we imagine Ritter as Aunt Amarilla in Yolanda and the Thief (1945), Griselda in The Court Jester (1956), or Mrs. Costello in Daisy Miller (1974)? Even Mrs. Banks in Barefoot in the Park (stage, 1963; screen, 1967) is a bit of a stretch. Ritter would play the part in stock in what may have been her last acting assignment. On the other hand, can we imagine Moorehead playing Ellen McNulty or Mae Swasey? What do you think Dunnock would have done with Birdie Coonan or Sadie Dugan in A Letter to Three Wives? Even as versatile and talented an actress as Natwick could not have done a better job with Stella in Rear Window or Alma in Pillow Talk.

To say that Ritter had a relatively limited range is to make an obvious observation rather than a harsh criticism. It is difficult, for example, to imagine her in any role that required her to be unsympathetic, underhanded, or imperious. This means that the whole negative range of older women stereotypes from dowdy dowagers to termagant wives and sour-pussed spinsters was off limits to her. Ritter played very few unsympathetic roles. It is maybe no coincidence that the few times she played more negative roles, the critical response was noticeably cool. This was the case with As Young as You Feel (1951), and even more clearly with The Birdman of Alcatraz (J. Frankenheimer, 1962). The critic for the New York Times, for example, found her Elizabeth Stroud in the latter film "merely a weak and somewhat lachrymose character."[565] Yet Ritter was Oscar-nominated for the final time for her performance as "Birdman" Burt Lancaster's overly devoted mother. She lost to Patty Duke for The Miracle Worker.

According to film historian James Robert Parish writing in 1974: "The Hollywood studios then, as the television industry of today, insisted that no major financial investment should be placed in a female contractee who could not handle sympathetic assignments."[566] In Ritter's case, that is basically all she got. As one of the most prominent second leads in the industry, she nearly always played the good helper even if, as in Pillow Talk and The Mating Season, it was a pretty helpless or hapless helper.

Ritter's first major confidante role was Birdie Coonan in All About Eve (J. Mankiewicz, Twentieth Century–Fox, 1950). After her comic excellence in Joseph Mankiewicz's A Letter to Three Wives (1949) in an Oscar-nominated maid role very much inspired by Hattie McDaniel in Alice Adams (1935), Ritter was the director's first choice to play Birdie; he even claimed he had written the part with her in mind.[567] Everyone knows how "ass" had to be replaced with "rear end" in the famously sardonic line "Everything but the bloodhounds snapping at her rear end." Film sensor Joseph Breen found the original version "vulgar."[568] It is less well known that

Ritter and star Bette Davis got on well and that Ritter was paid $1,750 a week for six weeks' work.[569] Ritter fans have noted that Birdie is mysteriously absent from the *post festum* part of the film; "summarily lopped off," as veteran *Times* critic Bosley Crowther put it.[570] This is one of the few criticisms one might level at this masterpiece.

Due to *All About Eve*'s cult status, Birdie has become Ritter's signature role. It is not her greatest performance, though the film as a whole is probably the most consummate one she lent her talents to and deservedly famous. Thus I cannot agree with Sam Staggs when he claims that Ritter's seventh film was the climax of her career and Birdie "her best role."[571] Arguably, her best and most substantial roles were Ellen McNulty in *The Mating Season* and Mae Swasey in *The Model and the Marriage Broker*, though these films are much less familiar to contemporary audiences.[572]

The Mating Season (1951) is an ingeniously plotted situation comedy with a parallel plot in which Gene Tierney employs her own mother-in-law (Ritter) as a live-in cook without realizing who she is. The fine ensemble cast includes Tierney and John Lund as a young married couple, Ritter as Lund's former hamburger flipper mother, Miriam Hopkins as Tierney's former ambassadoress mamma (and friend of Mussolini), and veteran character actress Cora Witherspoon in her best role as a witheringly snooty corporate executive's wife. Ritter goes head to head with both Hopkins and Witherspoon in some of the film's most enjoyable scenes. Among her many fine lines, we find the following in reference to her having bought an $18 hat to impress her new daughter-in-law: "If you're a chicken, you can fool people about your feathers, but when you start laying eggs all over the place, they know you're a chicken." Tierney, on the other hand, gets to say things like: "Every time I look at you, I'm glad I'm a woman." Being a character player had its compensations.

The Model and the Marriage Broker is the film in which Thelma Ritter finally receives above-the-title, star billing, along with Jeanne Crain and Scott Brady. In this film, Ritter is both literally and symbolically a helper, as she tries to find suitable mates for an oddly assorted group of clients in New York. Outfitted in an appalling fox-fur stole, she launches a frontal attack on the attractive young doctor, Matt Hornbeck (Brady), on behalf of winsome model Kitty Bennett (Crain). She will brook no opposition, responding with characteristic conviction to Brady's protestation that he is not in a position to get married: "Anybody with four pints of blood that can stand on their two feet long enough to say 'I do' is in a position to get married." One high point is the scene when Crain first comes to visit Ritter at her home. George Cukor films the two actresses in two-shot throughout, making them seem almost like mother and daughter despite their physical dissimilarities. Had Ritter not been nominated for an Oscar for *The Mating Season* that year, she should have been nominated for this one. At any rate, the Academy Award for Best Supporting Actress in 1952 went to Kim Hunter for *A Streetcar Named Desire*.

Ritter's remaining helper roles were more or less successful variations on her by now familiar folksy, feisty screen persona. *With a Song in My Heart* (W. Lang, Twentieth Century–Fox, 1952) is probably her most overrated film and garnered her her third Oscar nomination. (Gloria Grahame won deservedly in a lackluster year for the Supporting Actress category.) Ritter plays the crusty "Flatbush Florence Nightingale," Clancy, who cares for singer Jane Froman (Susan Hayward) in a Lisbon hospital after she has been in a plane crash and becomes her companion in what is a sickeningly coy film with awfully "cute" dialogue. In *The Farmer Takes a Wife* (H. Levin, Twentieth Century–Fox, 1953), which also scores high on the sick-making barometer, Ritter is billed third after stars Betty Grable and Dale Robertson, as Lucy Cashdollar, Grable's five-times married friend, who is angling for a sixth husband in Fortune Friendly (Eddie Foy, Jr.). This nauseous Erie Canal musical set in Rome, New York in 1850 ends with the double wedding of Grable and Robertson and Ritter and Foy. It is indeed a thing to be thankful for that Ritter was not often saddled with hoopskirts, bonnets, and flounces. In *Pillow Talk* (M. Gordon, Universal, 1959), she plays

This two-shot of Thelma Ritter and Jeanne Crain is from one of the best scenes in *The Model and the Marriage Broker* (Twentieth Century–Fox, 1951). Though Ritter is best remembered today for *All About Eve* and *Rear Window*, this film and *The Mating Season* allowed her to give fullest play to her comic and dramatic talents.

the maid Alma, who famously nurses a chronic hangover while listening in on her employer Doris Day's affairs.[573] In *The Misfits* (J. Huston, 1961), she chaperones Marilyn Monroe around "divorce central," Reno, Nevada, as rooming-house keeper Isabelle Steers, and in another of her Westerns, *How the West Was Won* (various directors, MGM, 1962), she is Debbie Reynolds' rustic camerado (as she had also been in *The Second Time Around*; V. Sherman, 1961). Finally, in one of her rare well-bred lady roles, as James Garner's permed and pearled mother and Doris Day's mother-in-law in *Move Over, Darling* (M. Gordon, Twentieth Century–Fox, 1963), she has to cope with a dead daughter-in-law coming back to life after her son has found love anew in the form of Polly Bergen.

As the female star's confidante and helper, providing a humorous running commentary on the action, Ritter resembled in plot function, if not in outward appearance, other major comic seconds such as Patsy Kelly and Eve Arden.[574] It is not hard to imagine a younger Ritter as Jean Harlow's sidekick in *The Girl from Missouri* (1934) and Billie Burke's comic servant in *Merrily We Live* (1938) and *Topper Returns* (1941), or as Ida Corwin in *Mildred Pierce* (1945) and Woody in *Goodbye, My Fancy* (1951). Kelly's Hollywood stint ended in 1947, just as Ritter's began. Like Kelly, Ritter had a patchy acting career. Both triumphed on Broadway late in life and won a Tony, Ritter for *New Girl In Town* (1958) and Kelly for *No, No, Nanette* (1971). Unlike Kelly and Arden, though, Ritter seldom supported any of the major stars of the 1930s, stars who were on the wane by the time she arrived in Hollywood in 1946. Bette Davis (*All About Eve*), Ginger Rogers (*Perfect Strangers*; B.

Windust, Warner Bros., 1950), and Barbara Stanwyck (*Titanic*; J. Negulesco, Twentieth Century–Fox, 1953) were the exceptions. Ritter would appear mainly with the new generation of female stars: Maureen O'Hara, Doris Day, Marilyn Monroe, Jeanne Crain, Susan Hayward, Debbie Reynolds, Jane Wyman, Deborah Kerr, Grace Kelly, Betty Grable, Gene Tierney, and Leslie Caron.

Ritter made several significant appearances on the small screen between 1953 and 1962. Especially worth mentioning are her Mrs. Fisher in *The Show-Off*, Agnes Hurley in *The Catered Affair*, and Abby in *Christopher Bean*, all in 1955. Clara Blandick (twice) and Marjorie Main had played the role of Mrs. Fisher in the 1930, 1934, and 1946 film versions of George Kelly's hit play. The film version of Paddy Chayefsky's *The Catered Affair* starring Bette Davis as Agnes Hurley would be released a year *after* Ritter played the role on television and was nominated for an Emmy. The role of Abby in *Christopher Bean* had been created by Pauline Lord on Broadway and interpreted on screen by Marie Dressler in her final film.

Nineteen fifty-five was the last year of Ritter's six-year contract with Twentieth Century–Fox and *Daddy Long Legs* (J. Negulesco) her last film under that contract,[575] though she would return for aptly named *The Second Time Around* in 1961. When explaining why her contract had not been renewed, Ritter joked that "I don't look so good in a toga,"[576] alluding to Fox's predilection at the time for CinemaScope epics of the ancient world. In fact, Ritter's film *Titanic* (1953) was the last major feature Fox produced before regearing production to CinemaScope.[577]

Coming full circle, Ritter made her last big screen appearance in a small role in George Seaton's *What's So Bad About Feeling Good?* (Universal, 1968). In February 1968, she co-starred with Tab Hunter and her own actress daughter, Monica, in a stock production of Neil Simon's *Barefoot in the Park* at the Papermill Playhouse in New Jersey, before retiring. She did not long enjoy her retirement. Thelma Ritter, Mrs. Joseph Moran, died of a heart attack at Queens Hospital ten days before her sixty-fourth birthday.[578] She has no known grave.

La Belle Laide
FLORA ROBSON (1902–1984)

Quite a few British character actresses got their start in American movies thanks to the classics of English literature. Though the studio moguls no doubt felt they could recreate any English story and locale on film, and even make an improvement on the original, clearly it would not hurt to throw in a few "locals" for the sake of authenticity. Thus MGM gave Elsa Lanchester and Jean Cadell their first American movie roles in the 1935 filmatization of *David Copperfield*. In 1936 one of Constance Collier's first American films was *Little Lord Fauntleroy*. Producer David O. Selznick brought Gladys Cooper and Judith Anderson to Hollywood in 1939 to support Joan Fontaine in the modern classic *Rebecca*. Angela Lansbury's mother, Moyna MacGill, got a start playing a dowager in *Jane Eyre* (1944) and a duchess in *The Picture of Dorian Gray* (1945) and Martita Hunt likewise playing the Duchess of Berwick in a filmatization of Wilde's *Lady Windemere's Fan* (called *The Fan*; 1949).

Flora Robson, then, was not the first nor would she be the last British actress to come to Hollywood to lend her talents to the resurrection of a literary classic when in the fall of 1938 Sam Goldwyn offered her the part of Ellen Dean in his production of *Wuthering Heights*

(1939). This was Laurence Olivier's first film in Hollywood and Merle Oberon's second. The film also introduced Irish Geraldine Fitzgerald to American movie audiences. The director was William Wyler, who had scored a hit with Bette Davis in *Jezebel* (1938) and who would go on to further glory with the same star in *The Letter* (1940) and *The Little Foxes* (1941). Initially, Wyler did not score a hit with Robson, whom he criticized for underplaying her role. A shrewd woman and a bit of an amateur psychologist, Robson managed to get into his good graces by making subtle suggestions here and there as to how certain scenes might be played. By the end of filming, Robson was the acknowledged oracle of the set, whom the director and the assistant screenwriter, John Huston, frequently consulted.

While the part of Ellen Dean had been reduced from the original to give more time to Merle Oberon, Robson recouped her losses when, as the Earnshaws' trusted nurse and housekeeper, she was made the narrator of the film. She was billed fourth, after Oberon (Cathy Earnshaw Linton), Olivier (Heathcliff), and David Niven (Edgar Linton) and ahead of veteran character actors Donald Crisp and Leo G. Carroll. For most actresses starting in Hollywood this would have been a most auspicious beginning. Robson thought not. Not only was she a star of the British stage, she was also a star in British film with several leading roles to her credit and a cult following after her performance as Elizabeth I in *Fire Over England* (1937). Before she came to Hollywood, there had been talk of her playing Elizabeth in *Mary of Scotland* (1936) with Katharine Hepburn in the title role or starring with Paul Muni in *The Good Earth* (1937). As we know, Florence Eldridge and Luise Rainer landed those plum parts. Robson had to make do with an old nanny. Maybe she should have been more grateful for the part, though, as Alexander Korda had just discontinued her four-year contract with his production company, London Film.[579]

Arguably, *Wuthering Heights*, the first film Flora Robson made in Hollywood, is also the best film she made during her American years. Her low-key performance in what is in every sense a supporting role remains forceful and convincing. Robson's biographer, Kenneth Barrow, has suggested that the key to Robson's naturalistic acting style in this film and elsewhere was the simple and subtle technique of "giving and receiving" she had learned early on in her career.[580] When this interaction with the other players did not take place, as in *Saratoga Trunk*, the end result was much less satisfactory.

Robson returned home after the end of filming *Wuthering Heights*, but stayed only a few weeks as there were no good offers of work in London.[581] At this time she made one of the worst mistakes of her film career by turning down the role of Mrs. Danvers in Alfred Hitchcock's *Rebecca* (1940). Because she had just finished playing Nelly Dean, she didn't want to get typecast as a housekeeper.[582] Even so, it is surprising Robson didn't recognize that Mrs. Danvers was much more than a menial and just the kind of borderline hysterical role that was her forté. Much to her regret, Hitchcock never asked for her again.[583]

Instead of joining in Sam Goldwyn's next prestige project, then, Robson signed a two-picture deal with Warner Bros. for *We Are Not Alone* and *The Sea Hawk*. *We Are Not Alone* (E. Goulding, 1939) starred Robson and Paul Muni as a kindly village doctor and his cold, shrewish wife locked in a loveless marriage. Robson would later say that Paul Muni was her favorite co-star on film (as Robert Donat had been on stage).[584] The film was not a hit at the box office, but Jack Warner nevertheless offered Robson a seven-year contract, which she promptly turned down.[585] With the gathering war clouds in Europe, *The Sea Hawk* was cancelled. To fulfill her contract, Robson was cast in a gangster film, *Invisible Stripes* (L. Bacon, 1939), where she played the mother of George Raft (seven years her senior) and William Holden. By the time she had finished the film, it was impossible to get back home because of the war. Robson found herself stranded at the Garden of Allah hotel with her good friends Elsa Lanchester and Charles Laughton.[586]

Though Robson's forte both on stage and screen would be emotionally overwrought, marginalized, even sociopathic women, she had a

Wuthering Heights (United Artists, 1939) was English stage star Flora Robson's first American film. She played Ellen, Merle Oberon's nanny and the film's narrator in a more modest debut role than she had hoped for. Oberon played the tempestuous heroine Cathy and David Niven her straight-laced husband, Edgar Linton.

productive and profitable sideline in queens and empresses. Depicting Queen Elizabeth I, the Virgin Queen, would become Robson's specialty (one she shared with Bette Davis) starting with her vastly popular portrayal in the 1937 Alexander Korda film *Fire Over England*. In her first major film role, she had played the Russian Empress Elisabeth in Korda's and director Paul Czinner's *Catherine the Great* (1934), starring Elisabeth Bergner and Douglas Fairbanks, Jr. (not to be confused with von Sternberg's camp classic *The Scarlet Empress* from the same year with Louise Dresser in the role of Elisabeth and Marlene Dietrich as Catherine). Robson was cast as the Empress Livia in the epic that never was, *I, Claudius* (J. von Sternberg, 1937), which was cancelled when producer Alexander Korda's protégée, Merle Oberon (Messalina), was involved in a car crash. In later life, Robson would be called upon to portray the Dowager Empress Tzu-Hsi in *55 Days at Peking* (N. Ray, 1963), when Garbo changed her mind about making a long awaited comeback.[587]

Next to *Wuthering Heights*, Robson's most familiar American film is most likely *The Sea Hawk* (M. Curtiz, Warner Bros., 1940). Production on this film was taken up again on a somewhat reduced scale in late 1939, when it was decided to shoot it in black and white rather than color.[588] Many fans of Robson have found *The Sea Hawk* inferior to *Fire Over England*. Maybe this is because what is perceived as a sequel or a spin-off starts at a disadvantage. Certainly, in *The Sea Hawk* Robson is relegated to a lesser role to make room for Warners' star swashbuckler, Errol Flynn, and his love interest, Brenda

Marshall, but the production is lavish and the supporting cast solid, including Claude Rains in the role of the villainous Spanish ambassador and Una O'Connor in one of her classic duenna roles. Rains had been in the London production of the play *Will Shakespeare* that had been Robson's stage debut twenty years earlier.[589] While Robson had tested in Bette Davis's costumes from *The Private Lives of Elizabeth and Essex* (1939), elaborate new ones were made for the film. Her interpretation is still strong and is characterized by her sonorous, authoritative voice, her right hand planted squarely on her crinolined hip, her charmingly dimpled smile and—as one a critic once wrote of her in another role—her face "lovely with intelligent emotion."[590]

Robson exerted a positive influence on the set. Highly professional, she was known as "one take Flora" and had become famous on the set of *Fire Over England* for completing a scene that was slated to take a week in a day and a half.[591] Some of Robson's professionalism even rubbed off on the notoriously lazy Errol Flynn. Robson cajoled him into learning his lines so the film would be finished on time and she could get away for rehearsals for her Broadway debut in a play written especially for her by Reginald Denham.[592] *Ladies in Retirement* premiered March 26, 1940 and ran for five months at the Henry Miller Theater in New York, followed by a seven-month tour. When the play was filmed in 1941, Robson was bitterly disappointed to be replaced in the leading role by Ida Lupino. Among the lead players, only Isobel Elsom reprised her role in this story of a woman who murders her employer so that her mentally deranged sisters won't lose the roof over their heads. Among Robson's other professional disappointments in Hollywood were her failure to land a part in a Bette Davis film—any Bette Davis film—or in two prestige projects with strong British links: *The White Cliffs of Dover* and *Jane Eyre* (both 1944).[593] There was really no obvious part for her in either film, though, unless she imagined herself playing Irene Dunne's aristocratic mother-in-law in *White Cliffs* or Mrs. Reed, Jane Eyre's evil aunt. Those parts went to Gladys Cooper and Agnes Moorehead, who had both arrived in Hollywood shortly after Robson and, unlike her, would have long and productive careers there.

Robson returned to the West Coast to do her first film in Technicolor, Paramount's *Bahama Passage* (E.H. Griffith, 1941), which was a box-office disaster. This tropical romance in which she played Sterling Hayden's neurotic mother was followed by a return to Warner Bros. and a third-billed role in Sam Wood's *Saratoga Trunk* (1945). This was yet another *Gone with the Wind* replica with Ingrid Bergman as the socially ambitious Creole, Clio Dulaine, and—believe it or not—Robson in the role of Bergman's stern but devoted mammy, Angelique Buiton. This must be just about the queerest bit of casting in a career with quite a few "exotic" parts.[594] The fact that two "mulatto" roles were played by a Swede and Englishwoman speaks volumes about racial politics in Hollywood at the time. Director Sam Wood was apparently not overly fond of African Americans and treated Robson badly the minute she got her "blackface" makeup on. The only direction she got from him was "Look at Miss Bergman, honey, look at Miss Bergman."[595]

Robson's last role in Hollywood for twenty-three years gave her nothing to do but look narrow-eyed and malevolent. If it was true, as Michael Redgrave has suggested, that Robson "made worry into an art form,"[596] then this film does not give much evidence of it. It must have seemed a bad joke to her that the part that garnered her an Oscar nomination was one of her most flat and uninteresting ones. At any rate, Robson lost out to Anne Baxter in *The Razor's Edge*, as did Ethel Barrymore, Lillian Gish, and Gale Sondergaard. After the five months of filming were over, Robson finally got a berth on a ship bound for England. Clutching the only tangible evidence of her material rewards in Hollywood, a mink coat, Robson headed for home in the late summer of 1943. On her way out, she declined yet another offer of a long-term contract, from MGM this time, which would have started with Robson playing Elizabeth Taylor's mother in *National Velvet* (1944).[597] The part went to an actress with whom Robson had often been confused, Anne Revere.[598]

It is not impossible to imagine that Flora Robson is thinking "How the hell did I get into this?" as she poses with stars Gary Cooper and Ingrid Bergman in this scene from *Saratoga Trunk* (Warner Bros., 1945). To borrow Dorothy Parker's famous line about Katharine Hepburn in *The Lake*: In this film, Robson runs the gamut of emotions from A to B.

Had Flora Robson deliberately set out to scotch her Hollywood career, she couldn't have done a more thorough job of it. Few actresses have turned down two offers of long-term contracts with major studios and two roles that would lead to Oscar nominations and all in such a short space of time. The explanation for Robson's erratic behavior is complex. The stage would always be her greatest love and many of her decisions were motivated by her desire to get back to the theater. In addition, she was closely tied to her parents and siblings in England, more so than actresses who had partners and children of their own. Finally, she sensed that she would never be happy in the artificial world of Hollywood, even with the full support of the large British colony.

Robson was born in South Shields, County Durham, Northumberland on March 28, 1902, but she grew up in Palmers Green north of London. Her family supported her in her desire to become an actress from the start. While we often see that a performer's mother plays a pivotal role in propelling a would-be thespian onto the stage, in Robson's case it was her father, the Scottish engineer David Mather Robson, who went to all her concerts and readings, who paid for her voice lessons with the best teachers, and who financed her two years at Beerbohm Tree's Academy of Dramatic Arts, where she graduated with a Bronze medal in 1921. Her mother, Eliza McKenzie Robson, was frequently ill and when she was not, her time was taken up with Robson's six siblings.[599] It was Robson's father who pronounced after a school concert in 1908, when his daughter was nearly six: "You are going to be an actress. Our next Ellen Terry."[600]

Based on what we know of Robson's popularity and support within her family, in the English theater community, and with the English public, her first meeting with the self-satisfied and self-involved world of Hollywood must have been a rude shock. Here all the West End triumphs in the world counted for nothing. No one had even heard of her breakthrough performance as the prostitute Mary Paterson in James Bridie's *The Anatomist* (1931), no one had seen her definitive performances in London productions of Eugene O'Neill's *Desire Under the Elms* (1931), *All God's Chillun Got Wings* (with Paul Robeson, 1933), and *Anna Christie* (1937), nor her recent hit play *Autumn*. Some had seen *Fire Over England*—after all, that's why she got an offer in the first place—but from a Hollywood point of view the stars of that film were Laurence Olivier and Vivien Leigh (who in December 1939 would skyrocket to superstardom in *Gone with the Wind*). Queen Elizabeth was a character part and character parts only were what Robson would be offered during her time in Tinseltown. There was never any question of her becoming an American movie star. An old maid of thirty-seven with a face as long as Edna May Oliver, a mouth as wide as the Mississippi, and the unsettling periwinkle blue eyes of a wolf simply did not become a star in Hollywood. In England, maybe, but not here.

Never one to dress the part of a star, Robson had trouble adapting to a world where Oscar Wilde's dictum from *The Picture of Dorian Gray*, "It is only shallow people who do not judge by appearances," was the rule rather than the exception. She would never forget being refused entry on first arriving at the main gate of the United Artists studio where *Wuthering Heights* was being shot, because she had arrived on foot and no one knew who she was.[601] It was the realization that Hollywood would never see her as anything but hired help that contributed substantially to Robson's decision to return home for good, that and homesickness. Her tenure in Hollywood had lasted four years and resulted in six films. For the remaining four decades of her film career, she would prefer projects closer to home.

Starting in 1947, Robson signed a ten-year contract with the Rank Film Organization.[602] *Black Narcissus* (M. Powell, E. Pressburger, 1947) and *Saraband for Dead Lovers* (B. Dearden, 1948) are among the best known of the near dozen films she made for this British production company. The former is chiefly known for making a star of Deborah Kerr, but we find Robson in an interesting supporting role as a nun who loses touch with her faith in the haunted atmosphere of a Himalayan palace. *Saraband for Dead Lovers* was a sort of seventeenth-century German *Dangerous Liaisons* based on the true story of the future George I of England's wife, Sophia Dorothea (Joan Greenwood). Robson gives one of the finest performances of her film career as the middle-aged mistress of the Elector of Hanover, who falls in love with a Swedish mercenary, Königsmark (Stewart Granger), only to be spurned by him when he in turn falls in love with Sophia. Robson always felt her best in period costumes with flowing lines. In the role of Countess Platen, a part Dietrich had turned down when she discovered she was wanted to play the older and not the younger woman,[603] Robson gave full rein to a sensuality that she was seldom allowed to reveal on screen. In both *Black Narcissus* and *Saraband*, she was given "above the title," star billing.

Robson fared no better and no worse than most aging character actresses in the 1960s and '70s. She did her share of horror flicks, made for TV movies, and international, blockbuster co-productions. *55 Days at Peking* (1963) was her first film for an American production company in twenty years. In the '60s she would work for Twentieth Century–Fox, MGM, and Columbia. By then the big studio era was a thing of the past and most films were shot at suitable and affordable locations around the world. *55 Days*, for example, set in imperial Peking, was filmed in Spain.[604] MGM's *The Eye of the Devil* (J.L. Thompson, 1967) was both set in and filmed at a chateau in France and Columbia's *Fragment of Fear* (R.C. Sarafian, 1970) was partially set and filmed in Italy.

Robson only returned once to work in

Hollywood after leaving in 1943. *Seven Women* (1966) was filmed on MGM's historic lot in Culver City.⁶⁰⁵ The film marked the end of an era, as it was veteran director John Ford's last feature film before his death from stomach cancer in 1973. Robson had been slated to work with him in the biopic *Young Cassidy* (MGM, 1965), starring Rod Taylor as the Irish playwright, John Cassidy (Sean O'Casey), but Ford fell ill and had to withdraw after directing only twenty minutes of the film.⁶⁰⁶ In *Seven Women*, Robson portrayed a missionary leader in China that seeks refuge at a neighboring mission after bandits, under the leadership of the fearsome Tunga Khan (Mike Mazurki), burn her mission to the ground. Among the many talented women in the cast, including Anne Bancroft, Margaret Leighton, Mildred Dunnock, and Betty Field, Robson makes the best job of it in what in most every way is an embarrassingly stagey ending to Ford's directing career. Robson thought it must have been his least seen film.⁶⁰⁷

Dame Flora Robson's last film appearance was a tiny role as one of three Stygian witches in the mythological extravaganza *Clash of the Titans* (D. Davis, MGM, 1981). She died of cancer on July 7, 1984 and was buried in Brighton where she had lived with two of her sisters since 1976.⁶⁰⁸ She once said of herself: "I've known very little personal love, but the public has always shown me great affection."⁶⁰⁹

Star for a Day, Grandmother for a Decade
MAY ROBSON (1858–1942)

May Robson was the earliest born actress to have a major career in Hollywood films. She was born in 1858, the same year as Theodore Roosevelt, and the year Minnesota became a state. She was also the earliest born actress to receive an Oscar nomination. That happened in 1934, when she was seventy-six. When you watch tiny, feisty, 5'2" May Robson at work on the screen, you are seeing an actress who made her acting debut in 1883. You are seeing more than half a century of American theater history encapsulated in a solitary figure. The *New York Times* noted on her death that her fifty-eight-year acting career had taken her from the "gaslit days of old Bowery theatres to the modern day of talking color films."⁶¹⁰

How fascinating it is to consider that actresses like May Robson, who were born before the Civil War, when women did not yet have the right to vote or own personal property, and when the telephone and the motion-picture camera had not yet been invented, would live long enough to act on the big screen. Though Robson was the most prominent among them, there were other actresses born in antebellum America who would also strut their stuff in sound films. Among the oldest American actresses to be preserved on celluloid are Gertrude Norman (1848–1943), Effie Ellsler (1855–1942), Emily Fitzroy (1860–1954), Charlotte Granville (1860–1942), Henrietta Crosman (1861–1944), and Adeline De Walt Reynolds (1862–1961).

Gertrude Norman had a solid pedigree in silent films when she made her sound film debut at age eighty-one. In 1932, she played a resident in the old age home where May Robson wreaks havoc in *If I Had a Million* (various directors, Paramount, 1932). Effie Ellsler had a huge hit on Broadway in *The Bat* in 1920, as the original Cornelia Van Gorder, a role Agnes Moorehead brought to the screen almost forty years later. In 1931, Ellsler played Mrs. Grant in the original film version of *The Front Page* and five years later Grandma Duval in the Garbo *Camille*. Emily Fitzroy was one of the most important character actresses in silent films. She made her sound film debut in the original 1929 film version of *Show Boat*, playing Parthy Ann

Hawks, a role that would played by Helen Westley in the 1936 version and Moorehead in the 1951 version. Fitzroy's last film was *The White Cliffs of Dover* (1944), in which she played a spinster in a boarding house. Charlotte Granville was an important Broadway character actress who played Lady Bracknell in a revival of *The Importance of Being Earnest* in 1921, played nurse to Ethel Barrymore's Juliet in *Romeo and Juliet* in 1922–23, and created the role of Mrs. Boucicault in Rachel Crothers's 1929 hit play *Let Us Be Gay* (the film role went to Marie Dressler). She had half a dozen credited roles in sound films in the first half of the 1930s.

Henrietta Crosman, the veteran of twenty-six plays on Broadway including revivals of *As You Like It* (1902), *The Merry Wives of Windsor* (1916), *The School for Scandal* (1925), *Trelawny of the Wells* (1927), and *The Beaux Stratagem* (1928), played several important roles in Hollywood films of the thirties, including Fanny Cavendish in *The Royal Family of Broadway* (1930), Mrs. Hannah Jessup in John Ford's *Pilgrimage* (1933), and Margaret Sullavan's "antediluvian tyrant" grandmother in *The Moon's Our Home* (1936). Finally, Adeline De Walt Reynolds is a particularly fascinating case, because she started acting in films in 1940, when she was seventy-eight, and with no previous acting experience. Her parts were never very large—a scene or two with a line or two in most cases—but she was always memorable with her spunkiness and incredibly lined, crabapple face. In *Shadow of the Thin Man* (1941), she has a great scene as a murder-mystery obsessed landlady replete with mob slang, who carries her radio around so as not to miss her favorite serials; in *The Human Comedy* (1943), she was a strict librarian; in *Going My Way* (1944), she was Barry Fitzgerald's long lost Irish mother; and in *The Corn Is Green* (1945), she played an ancient Welshwoman, who learns to read from Bette Davis's Miss Moffat. She acted in her final film, *The Ten Commandments* (1956), when she was ninety-four, which must be some kind of record. She lived to be ninety-eight, making her with Estelle Winwood and Ethel Griffies the longest lived of character actresses.

Strictly speaking, though, none of these older actresses were in Robson's league. The only "actress of a certain age" who could top her in the 1930s was Marie Dressler, the Canadian-born ex-vaudevillian who made one of the most spectacular comebacks in entertainment history and became one of MGM's biggest stars before her premature death from cancer in 1934 at the age of sixty-five. It might be tempting to call Robson the poor man's Marie Dressler, if it weren't for the fact that Marie Dressler *was* the poor man's Marie Dressler. Robson had at least one thing, though, that Dressler didn't: a profile. After Dressler's death she reigned supreme, according to her *New York Times* obituary, as "dowager queen of the American screen and stage."[611]

There was a lot of living and acting to be done, though, before May Robson found herself in Hollywood in 1926 or thereabouts. Her long life's journey began in Melbourne, Australia on April 19, 1858, where she was born Mary Jeannette Robison, the youngest of the four children of Captain Henry Robison of the Royal Navy, who had retired to Australia for his health, and his wife, Julia. After the captain's death when his youngest daughter was seven, Mrs. Robison took her brood to London, where Mary was educated at the Sacred Heart Convent in Highgate and later in Brussels and Paris. When only sixteen, she eloped with Charles Livingstone Gore and the couple tried their hand at cattle ranching in Fort Worth, Texas, before moving to New York City. There Gore died in the early 1880s, leaving his wife with three children to support. She provided for her family by giving painting lessons and doing embroidery work, until one day she went into a theatrical agency on impulse, thinking that stage work might be more remunerative.[612]

She made her stage debut at the Brooklyn Grand Opera House on September 17, 1883, and never looked back. It was then her name was misprinted and she decided to keep "Robson" for good luck. During her first fifteen years on stage, she was closely associated with the producer brothers Daniel and Charles Frohman. Despite being a handsome woman throughout her long life, she preferred character parts from the beginning, especially comic and eccentric roles that gave her costumes and makeup to hide behind. She said herself she couldn't act unless she looked a fright.[613]

In 1901, she finally left the Frohmans to move on in her career. She would have her first hit on Broadway in 1907 in a new play called *The Rejuvenation of Mary* and in 1910 she made her first appearance on the London stage in the same play. The following year, she wrote and starred in her own play, *The Three Lights*, co-written with Charles T. Dazey, which flopped at the Bijou Theatre. Broadway saw her no more after that, with the exception of a short run in *The Two Orphans* in 1926, her final bow on the "Great White Way." About this time, she made her home permanently in Hollywood and intensified the film work that had begun with a couple of silents in 1915 and resumed at MGM in 1926. Her last stage show was very likely the West Coast production of Edward Chodorov's psychological thriller *Kind Lady* (1935), where she played Mary Herries, a patrician philanthropist who gets swindled; a part Aline MacMahon and Ethel Barrymore would interpret in the 1935 and 1951 film versions. Joan Fontaine made her stage debut in Robson's production and had fond memories of the venerable "Miss Robson" showing her the ropes both on and off the stage.[614]

During her decade and a half in Hollywood, Robson would be most intimately associated with two studios. After Dressler's death in 1934, she became the "grand old lady" at MGM, until she transferred her allegiance in 1936 to the less glamourous but more gutsy and volatile Warner Bros. She made twenty films at MGM between 1926 and 1936, including *Red-Headed Woman* (J. Conway, 1932), where she drives a car as Chester Morris's youthful Aunt Jane; *Strange Interlude* (R.Z. Leonard, 1932), where she is Norma Shearer's mother-in-law, who divulges the Evans family's deep, dark secret; *Dinner at Eight* (G. Cukor, 1933), where as a cook with a toothache, she drops the aspic for Billie Burke's big dinner party; *Dancing Lady* (R.Z. Leonard, 1933), where she is Franchot Tone's toney, hard-of-hearing grandmother; *Anna Karenina* (C. Brown, 1935), where outfitted with ridiculous ringlets, she plays Basil Rathbone's fussy mother and Garbo's mother-in-law; and *Wife vs. Secretary* (C. Brown, 1936), where she is Clark Gable's piss-elegant mother, Mimi Stanhope, and Myrna Loy's concerned mother-in-law.

The best of her MGM films were *Letty Lynton* and *Reckless*. In *Letty Lynton* (C. Brown, 1932), Robson was given an important early role as Joan Crawford's cold mother, who is embittered by her husband's unfaithfulness and her daughter's immoral life. She speaks the prophetic words to Crawford: "I'd hate to be the man who depended on you." Yet, in the decisive hearing with district attorney Lewis Stone, she comes through for her daughter by corroborating Robert Montgomery's fictitious story and giving Crawford an alibi, making it appear that Nils Asther's murder was indeed a suicide. Mother and daughter are reconciled and the film has a happy ending that would be inconceivable after the Code. Yet, the film was withdrawn and destroyed, because it followed too closely a celebrated murder case.

Reckless (V. Fleming, 1935) was the best of Robson's four films with doomed platinum blonde bombshell, Jean Harlow. She plays Harlow's feisty grandmother and her chief support in life, love, and her singing career. Robson's Granny Leslie is torn between her liking for ne'er-do-well William Powell and her desire that her granddaughter make an advantageous marriage. At age seventy-seven Robson has great rapport with Powell, because she's still hip. The naturalistic action and acting give the film a serious undertone. Harlow almost refused to act in it, because the plot—involving the suicide of Harlow's screen husband, Franchot Tone—might be seen to try to capitalize on the recent suicide death of Harlow's real life husband, Paul Bern.

Robson made eleven films at Warner Bros., including *The Perfect Specimen* (M. Curtiz, 1937), where Errol Flynn was the perfect specimen of the title and Robson his incredibly bossy grandmother; *They Made Me a Criminal* (B. Berkeley, 1939), where Robson cares for boxer John Garfield on her date farm in addition to a bunch of Dead End Kids; and the trilogy *Four Daughters* (M. Curtiz, 1938), *Four Wives* (M. Curtiz, 1939), and *Four Mothers* (W. Keighley, 1941).

Star for a Day, Grandmother for a Decade: May Robson (1858-1942)

Granny Get Your Gun (Warner Bros., 1940) was May Robson's first film of the forties and her first starring vehicle since *Lady for a Day*, for which she was Oscar-nominated. In the publicity releases it was claimed that Robson did not use a double for the car chase. When we consider the strength and resilience that had carried Robson from her native Australia all the way to California by way of London, Texas, and New York, this seems entirely possible. With her in this photograph is the beloved character actor Harry Davenport.

Warner Bros. also gave her her own starring vehicle in *Granny Get Your Gun* (G. Amy, 1940).

At Columbia seven years earlier, she had been given her most important starring role in a film called *Lady for a Day* (1933), when Louis B. Mayer was unwilling to loan out Marie Dressler. Robson portrays the alcoholic streetseller Apple Annie. She is transformed into the social register dowager Mrs. E. Worthington Manville with a little help from her friends when her long lost daughter suddenly appears and wants her aristocratic Spanish fiancé to meet her family. Based on a short story by Damon Runyon, and nicknamed "The Senile Cinderella" by Whitney Stine,[615] the film was an early success for Frank Capra, who wrote at length about May Robson in his 1971 memoir *The Name Above the Title*. Among the forty individuals to whom the book is dedicated, there are only two women: Robson and Jean Harlow. As Capra remembered it, Mayer wouldn't loan out Dressler "if you made him ambassador to Turkey." In his recollection, Robson "was as humble and excited" by the opportunity to audition "as an understudy subbing for the star."[616] To hear Capra tell it, it seems as if Robson had never acted in films before, though she was indeed the veteran of more than twenty films at this point.

Capra is probably right, though, in suggesting that Robson would sometimes give a performance more geared towards the stage than the screen. One of the best, or rather, the worst examples of this is her performance in *It Happened in New Orleans* (a.k.a. *Rainbow on the River*; K. Neumann, 1936), which is completely over the top. When in the role of the rich, spoilt New York granddame, Mrs. Harriet Ainsworth, she comes out with all barrels blasting, all you can do is sit back and wait for the verbal barrage to end. Certainly, she gives a whole new meaning to the word "scold" in this film. The film was a variation on the *Little Lord Fauntleroy* story and was meant to rival RKO's filmatization of Frances Hodgson Burnett's children's classic. Yet for other directors, Robson delivered low-key, naturalistic performances both in comedy and drama, particularly in some of her early sound films at MGM: *Letty Lynton*, *Strange Interlude*, *Reckless*, and *Wife vs. Secretary*. It is indeed unfortunate that her best remembered and most available film these days is *Bringing Up Baby* (H. Hawks, RKO, 1938), in which her blustery performance as Katharine Hepburn's Aunt Elizabeth and Cary Grant's nemesis is among her more histrionic and less interesting.

May Robson was a survivor, who worked at her chosen profession her entire adult life. Even after she was nearly blinded by cataracts, "Muzzey," as she was known in the business, continued to work in films. Her final film, *Joan of Paris* (R. Stevenson, RKO, 1942), was released exactly nine months before her death from cancer on October 20, 1942, at her home at 610

May Robson was a handsome woman her entire, long life. Here we see her at age seventy-seven in the arms of her son in *Wife vs. Secretary* (Metro-Goldwyn-Mayer, 1936), Clark Gable. On her left is the wife of the title, Myrna Loy, and on her right, the secretary, Jean Harlow. As Loy's patrician mother-in-law, Mimi Stanhope, Robson plants the seeds of doubt in Loy's mind about the true nature of the relationship between Gable and Harlow. The 1930s was the heyday of meddling mothers-in-law!

North Bedford Drive in Beverly Hills. At her bedside were her surviving son, Edward, her daughter-in-law, and her longtime secretary-companion, Lillian Harmer.[617] Two of Robson's three children died from diphtheria and scarlet fever shortly after her first husband. She remarried in 1889, a police surgeon named Augustus Homer Brown, two years her junior, who died in 1922.[618] Twenty years later May Robson was laid to rest beside him in the Brown family plot in Flushing Cemetery, Queens, New York.

The Duchess
ALISON SKIPWORTH (1863–1952)

Alison Skipworth was the most significant British character actress in Hollywood films in the first half of the 1930s. That is no mean feat, especially if we consider that the '30s were the heyday of British character actresses and if we agree that no single group of thespians made a more substantial contribution to the films of Hollywood's Golden Age than them. Elsewhere in this book you can read about Flora Robson and Elsa Lanchester, Gladys Cooper and May Whitty. Here we will look more closely at another of the greats, but before we do that, let us briefly remind ourselves of some of the other English character actresses who not only brought their manifold talents from stageland to movieland, but from the old world to the new. Do you remember Zeffie Tilbury, Constance Collier, Ethel Griffies, Margaret Wycherly, Mary Forbes? Would you recognize Emily Fitzroy, Elspeth Dudgeon, Eily Malyon, Connie Leon, Mary Gordon, Tempe Pigott? Yes? No? Maybe? I'll try to jog your memory.

Zeffie Tilbury (1863–1950) is best remembered for playing Grandma Joad in *The Grapes of Wrath* (1940). She dies on the way to California in a touching scene where Ma Joad (Jane Darwell) must keep her death hidden, so that they will not be stopped by the authorities. The following year Tilbury was the equally decrepit Grandma Lester in *Tobacco Road*, but she only had one scene before she inexplicably disappears from the rest of the film. Tilbury played Alison Skipworth's mother in *The Gorgeous Hussy* (1936), though they were born the same year.

Constance Collier (1878–1955) was fifteen years younger than Skipworth and Tilbury, like them a veteran of Broadway, where she created the role of Carlotta Vance in *Dinner at Eight* before moving to Hollywood. She is best remembered today for one of her last film roles, Mrs. Atwater in Hitchcock's *Rope* (1948); and for both being and playing Katharine Hepburn's acting coach (*Stage Door*, 1937). Collier has a Star on the Walk of Fame.

At the time of her death in 1975, Ethel Griffies was the oldest working actress in the English theater. Born in 1878, like Constance Collier, she performed in nineteen shows on Broadway between 1924 and 1967 and in ninety American films, the last in 1965, when she was eighty-seven. She is best remembered for Hitchcock's *The Birds* (1963), where she played Mrs. Bundy, an elderly ornithologist; for the role of the Evans's forbidding housekeeper, Mrs. Nicholas, in *How Green Was My Valley* (1941), whom Angharad Morgan (Maureen O'Hara) must contend with; and for playing Grace Poole in both the 1934 and the 1944 versions of *Jane Eyre*.

Margaret Wycherly (1881–1956) was a distinguished stage actress and a veteran of forty-three shows on Broadway before she started in films in 1929 by reprising her standout role as Madame Rosalie La Grange in her husband, Bayard Veiller's murder mystery *The Thirteenth*

Chair. She was nominated for an Oscar in 1942 for playing Gary Cooper's backwoods mother in what was only her fourth film, *Sergeant York*, but lost to Mary Astor in *The Great Lie*. Wycherly only played named, credited roles, such as Katharine Hepburn's elderly, disturbed mother-in-law, Mrs. Forrest, in *Keeper of the Flame* (1942); Ma Forrester in *The Yearling* (1946); and James Cagney's gangster mother in *White Heat* (1949), the addressee of his famous parting words: "Made it, Ma. Top of the world!"

Finally, mention must be made of a regal presence in the Gladys Cooper-Isobel Elsom, gracefully aging "English Rose" category. Mary Forbes (1883–1974), like Margaret Wycherly, made her sound film debut in *The Thirteenth Chair*, as the high-toned hostess of the séance. As Mrs. Anthony P. Kirby, she froze Jean Arthur with one of the most icy stares in film history when she discovered her kissing her son, James Stewart, in Frank Capra's *You Can't Take It with You* (1938). In real life she was the mother of the dashing leading man, Ralph Forbes, and both mother and son are to be seen in the play within the play in *Stage Door* (1937), as Ralph Forbes's *Christopher Strong* co-star, Katharine Hepburn, enters speaking the famous line from her real-life Broadway disaster, *The Lake*: "The calla lilies are in bloom again."

The second list of names above contains what we might call minor figures; prolific, ubiquitous, but seldom in showy parts. Emily Fitzroy (1860–1954) was a pioneering characters actress from the silent film era who played Parthy Hawks in the first, partial-sound version of *Show Boat* in 1929 and went on to play small roles in films such as *The Flame of New Orleans*, *The White Cliffs of Dover*, and *Two-Faced Woman*, where she danced the rhumba at age eighty-one. Elspeth Dudgeon (1871–1955) is best known for having played a man and being billed as a man ("John Dudgeon") in James Whale's *The Old Dark House* (1932), though you may also have seen her briefly in such classics as *Bride of Frankenstein*, *Becky Sharp*, *Pride and Prejudice*, *Now, Voyager*, or *The Secret Garden*. Eily Malyon's (1879–1961) emaciated face and figure were a shoo-in to personify want and need or doom and gloom in eighty films ranging from *Rasputin and the Empress* and *Great Expectations*, via *A Tale of Two Cities*, *Little Lord Fauntleroy*, and *Camille* to *Shadow of a Doubt*, *Jane Eyre*, and *The Seventh Cross*. Connie Leon (1880–1955) can be spotted as Irene Dunne's sari-clad, Indian maidservant Beebe in *Anna and the King of Siam*; Paul Muni's inebriated Cockney patient in *We Are Not Alone*, who weeps at the trial after he is found guilty of murder; and as an old woman who sells violets to Peter Lorre in *Three Strangers*, among her many roles. Mary Gordon's (1882–1963) characteristically round face and even rounder form make her fairly easy to recognize, though if you blink you may miss her in one of her incredible 278 films (1925–50), including her recurring role as Mrs. Hudson in the Sherlock Holmes series with fellow Britishers Basil Rathbone and Nigel Bruce. Finally, Tempe Pigott (1884–1962) in one of her few named, credited roles played Tuerta in *The Devil Is a Woman*, the one-eyed owner of the theater where Marlene Dietrich performs. Here I've only mentioned names from the two first generations or so of British character actresses in Hollywood. In their wake followed marvelous talents like Hermione Baddeley, Binnie Barnes, Isobel Elsom, Hermione Gingold, Martita Hunt, Angela Lansbury, Joan Lorring, Cathleen Nesbitt, Elisabeth Risdon, Margaret Rutherford, Norma Varden, and Mona Washbourne.

Despite their many virtues and talents, Alison Skipworth had a quality none of these other actresses had. There was something grand yet democratic, authoritarian yet vastly understanding about her screen persona, as if no matter what you said or did, she had seen and heard it before. Her film acting was subtle at a time when subtlety was at a premium. While May Robson bellowed her way through numerous films in the 1930s, Skipworth rarely raised her voice. While Marie Dressler grimaced, Skipworth had only the tiniest of twinkles in her eyes or the most minimalist of frowns on her lips. She was equipped with a rich, mellow voice and a characteristically measured way of delivering her lines. James Robert Parish and William T. Leonard give an apt description of her: "the portly, well-trained actress of regal bearing could create striking portrayals of middle-aged demimondaines flushed with the lust for larceny, surveying an unsuspecting world with twinkling, beady eyes, and provoking laughter in pursuit of willing victims and her own tarnished, if undaunted, dignity." They add that in real life she was "freewheeling and candid in conversation."[619]

Skipworth had a long life behind her by the time she found herself on the opposite side of the world from where it all started in 1863. She was born in North Audley Street in London on July 25 and given no less than four names—Alison Mary Elliott Margaret—by her parents, Richard Ebenezer and Elizabeth Rodgers Groom.[620] If that were not enough, she would later answer to the nickname "Skippy."[621] Like her contemporary, the Yankee Jessie Ralph, and the somewhat younger but cancer-ridden Canadian, Marie Dressler, Skipworth was gloriously dilapidated by the time she got to Hollywood. Unlike her fellow granddames of the early sound era, though, she had been a beauty in her youth.[622] She had often been a model for her artist husband, Frank Markham Skipworth (1854–1929), whom she married in 1882, when she was only nineteen and he was twenty-eight.[623] It was after his death in 1929 that Skipworth went to California to try her hand at the movies. By then she had a belly to rival W.C. Fields and Wallace Beery, but her "embonpoint" at least had the effect of rendering her preternaturally smooth-skinned.

Skipworth's years in Hollywood were temporally limited, but rich in results. She lent her considerable weight and talents to forty-eight films in eight years, mostly in named, credited roles and even some starring ones. Nineteen of these films were for Paramount, who had her under contract from about 1932 till 1934,[624] but Skipworth worked for every major studio and most of the minor ones. When we take into account that she was born at the time of the Civil War and didn't take up a film career until she was sixty-seven years old, her energy and youthfulness seem all the more extraordinary. She had made a handful of silent films,[625] but her film career began in earnest in 1930 when she played the gloriously comic, vulgar wreck Lady Catherine Champion-Cheney in *Strictly Unconventional* (D. Burton, MGM), based on W. Somerset Maugham's play *The Circle* (1921). This was followed by the role of Lady Kitty Melrose in *Raffles* (G. Fitzmaurice, Samuel Goldwyn, 1930) and Mrs. Cliveden-Banks in *Outward Bound* (R. Milton, Warner Bros., 1930), two other plum parts for an actress of a certain age. On Broadway, these three roles had been created by Mrs. Leslie Carter, Hattie Russell, and Charlotte Granville respectively.

Skipworth had made her stage debut relatively late, in London in 1894, in a play called *A Gaiety Girl*. Apparently she went on the stage to keep the wolf from the door and help support herself and her "starving artist" husband.[626] A play fittingly entitled *The Artist's Model* brought her to the United States for the first time in 1895 and, after a brief return to England, she and her husband moved there permanently in 1896.[627] Skipworth soon became a fixture of the New York stage, working steadily on Broadway for the first two decades of the twentieth century.

For aficionados of twenties plays and thirties films, there is one role above all others with which Alison Skipworth will always be identified both on stage and screen: Mrs. J. Duro Pampinelli in George Kelly's first hit play, *The Torch Bearers*. Kelly (1887–1974) "one of the finest portrayers of women in twentieth-century American theater,"[628] was a former actor and the uncle of Grace Kelly. He wrote a string of hit plays in the 1920s that included *The Show-Off* (1924), filmed in a silent and two sound versions, and *Craig's Wife* (1925). The latter was filmed in a silent version in 1928; with Rosalind Russell in the lead in 1936; and with Joan Crawford as *Harriet Craig* in 1950.

The Torch Bearers was a satire on the Little Theatre movement with Skipworth in the leading role as "the amateur from hell,"[629] a self-important, self-satisfied coryphée of culture and the self-appointed artistic director of a small-town dramatic society. In the film version of *The Torch Bearers*, produced by Fox Film Corp. in 1935 and directed by David Butler, the title was changed to *Doubting Thomas*. Skipworth was the only member of the cast to reprise her role from the original 1922 Broadway production at

From 1931 to 1934, Alison Skipworth was the reigning grand dame at Paramount. *Night Angel* (Paramount Pictures, 1931), which starred Nancy Carroll (right) and Fredric March, was the first of Skipworth's nineteen films for the studio, where she supported luminaries such as Mae West, Carole Lombard, Marlene Dietrich, W.C. Fields, and Claudette Colbert, and starred in a couple of films herself. *Night Angel* has been called Fredric March's worst film by those in the know.

William A. Brady's 48th Street Theatre. As the well-to-do housewife, dizzy dame, and wannabe leading lady Paula Ritter (Paula Brown in the film), Skipworth's friend Mary Boland was replaced by another veteran comedienne, Billie Burke. Will Rogers, Burke's personal friend and support during her husband, Flo Ziegfeld's final illness and death in 1932, played her bewildered husband and the "Doubting Thomas" of the title. The comedy inheres in the encounter between Mrs. Pampinelli's highfalutin artistic values and the sausage manufacturer Mr. Brown's more materialistic and practical ones. The battle is waged over the fate of Paula Brown: Will she sacrifice everything to go on the stage ("The masses need you, dear") or return chastened and grateful to her rightful place in the home?

Ultimately, she chooses the latter alternative, but Mrs. Pampinelli remains unvanquished: "There will be actresses when husbands are a thing of the past." Of the play, Skipworth said: "It is written across my heart in letters of flame."[630]

Skipworth was not like a potato—she didn't go with everything—but we get some idea of her range, when we realize that the three stars she supported most often were as different as George Raft, W.C. Fields, and Bette Davis. Raft, if not responsible for bringing Skipworth to Hollywood (as he had Mae West), was at least partially responsible for keeping her there. He and Skipworth acted in four films together at Paramount in the early 1930s. The third and arguably the best was *Night After Night* (1932), an atmospheric, high-toned gangster flick directed by Archie Mayo, starring Raft as a suave nightclub operator and Constance Cummings as a social butterfly haunted by a family tragedy. As the tweedy Miss Mabel Jellyman, Skipworth was to play Dr. Doolittle to Raft's Eliza, teaching him how to speak and behave correctly to make him a better match for Cummings. *Night After Night* is chiefly remembered today for being Mae West's debut film. For once Skipworth had some female competition in the comedy department and, apparently, the two dames did not get on. When Skipworth felt she was not being treated with the requisite respect, she intoned: "I'll have you know I'm an actress." The twenty-years-younger Mae West is to have responded: "It's all right, dearie. I'll keep your secret."[631]

In W.C. Fields, Skipworth also met her match, but it was a more congenial one. According to Fields's biographer, James Curtis, they had an instant rapport. Skipworth's Broadway co-star, Constance Binney, was sure "she drank drink for drink with him." It was hoped they would become a comedy team to rival Marie Dressler and Wallace Beery at MGM.[632] Fields and Skipworth were paired in *Six of a Kind* (L. McCarey, Paramount, 1934), they were the stars of *Tillie and Gus* (F. Martin, Paramount, 1933), and they were both in *Alice in Wonderland* (N.Z. McLeod, Paramount, 1933). Their biggest comic success, though, was scored in *If I Had a Million* (various directors, Paramount, 1932) in an unforgettable segment known as the "Road Hog" sketch. As the co-owner with Fields of "Emily's Tea Shoppe," Skipworth, given $1,000,000 by a millionaire who wants to spite his heirs, goes on a rampage against road hogs in revenge for one of them ruining the car she had saved all her life to buy. Both from a technical and a comedic standpoint, this segment is impressive, as Skipworth and her elaborately courteous beau Fields wreak, if not death, then destruction in what must be one of the earliest car crash sequences shot almost entirely on location.

While Skipworth supported a whole constellation of '30s stars, she appeared with no female lead player more often than Bette Davis.

Their most significant collaboration was in *Dangerous* (A.E. Green, Warner Bros., 1935), which garnered Davis her first Academy Award. In what was an unusual role for Skipworth, she here plays a domestic, more precisely toney Franchot Tone's housekeeper at his home in the country and an increasingly worried witness to his developing affair with the dissipated ex-actress played by Davis. In the kind of down-to-earth role Marie Dressler specialized in, Skipworth is costumed in a series of drab housedresses. Both she and the female star are having the longest bad hair day of their lives, which makes it all the more extraordinary that Whitney Stine credits this film (and Perc Westmore) with giving Davis her characteristic pageboy look.[633]

Skipworth's film roles can be divided into two basic types and a hybrid, which merges the two. The first typical Skipworth character is the con woman or some other creature of the criminal underworld; the second type is the aristocratic or upper-class British dowager; and the combination of the two is the lady companion (titled or not) to the female star, and (as often as not) her partner in crime. In the first category, we find brilliant Skipworth creations like Martha Hicks (aka Countess von Claudwig) in her starring vehicle, *Madame Racketeer*; Beulah Bonnell in *A Lady's Profession*; Mrs. Rasmussen in *The Song of Songs*; the innkeeper Mrs. Rumford in *Six of a Kind*; and last but not least, Madame Barabbas in *Satan Met a Lady*.

In *Madame Racketeer* (H.W. Gribble, A. Hall, Paramount, 1932), Skipworth was teamed with George Raft for the first time; apparently he was peeved at her ability to steal the limelight.[634] She also starred in *A Lady's Profession* (N.Z. McLeod, Paramount, 1933), this time with Roland Young at her side. Young was also with her in *Six of a Kind*, where she played a sticky-fingered innkeeper and also had some byplay with her old comedy partner, W.C. Fields, the latter as a none too bright local marshal. In *Satan Met a Lady* (W. Dieterle, Warner Bros., 1936), Skipworth played the same role Sydney Greenstreet was later to play in the definitive 1941 version of Dashiell Hammett's classic *The Maltese Falcon*.

These kinds of shady roles were Skipworth's

In this photo from A *Lady's Profession* (Paramount Pictures, 1933), a perfectly groomed Alison Skipworth and her suave nephew, Roland Young, have just received word that the family fortune has been lost. They go across the water to seek a new start in America, much as Skipworth herself had done with her artist husband in 1896. Skipworth thought it ironic that she had only found financial security at the end of her life. "What I might have been on the screen at 22!" she exclaimed. When Skipworth was twenty-two, though, there was no screen to be on, as she was born in 1863.

forte and she is uniformly excellent in all these films. There is no disrespect to her memory, though, in saying that, taken as a whole, *Satan Met a Lady* is not one of her best. Her scene of first meeting detective Warren William is delightful (and forms an interesting parallel to the scene between Greenstreet and Humphrey Bogart), but most of the rest of this comedy version of *The Maltese Falcon* is an absolute shambles. The critic for the *New York Times* observed: "So disconnected and lunatic are the picture's ingredients, so irrelevant and monstrous its people that one lives through it in a constant expectation of seeing a group of uniformed individuals appear suddenly from behind the furniture and take the entire cast into protective custody."[635] *The Song of Songs* (R. Mamoulian, Paramount, 1933), on the other hand, must rank high in the Skipworth canon. Her portrayal of Marlene Dietrich's in every way shabby aunt, with her fondness for spiking her tea with brandy and all her old lady fussiness, tartness, and hypocrisy, is brilliantly realized.

The Skipworth dowager is exemplified by Mrs. Wey-Smith in an early film, *The Road to Singapore* (A.E. Green, Warner Bros., 1931), in which she has a small part as a British colonial who loves to tango and shanghais both Louis Calhern and hero, William Powell, onto the dance floor. After she has stepped all over the latter's toes, she coos with glee: "Dr. March says I'm like a feather, I'm so light on my feet."

The Duchess: Alison Skipworth (1863–1952)

Rouben Mamoulian's *The Song of Songs* (Paramount Pictures, 1933) was the first of two films in which Alison Skipworth supported Marlene Dietrich. "Supported" is maybe not quite the right word, as in this film she in effect sells her niece and throws her out of the house when she fails to live up to the bargain.

Marchesa Bianca San Giovanni in Gloria Swanson's sound film debut, *Tonight or Never* (M. LeRoy, Samuel Goldwyn, 1931), is a much grander figure, a former beauty and a great prima donna beloved of the crowned heads of Europe. The film this time entices us with the possibility that Skipworth is enjoying the "services" of hero Melvyn Douglas, but anticlimactically he turns out to be her nephew. Miss Vanderdoe in *Coming-Out Party* (J.G. Blystone, Fox, 1934) is a relatively small part, but characteristic, as Skipworth portrays a mover-and-shaker in New York society who charges commissions for helping organize debutante balls. Maybe the funniest of these "straight" dowager roles is Miss Crawley in *Becky Sharp* (R. Mamoulian, 1935), which featured Miriam Hopkins in the title role. Skipworth only has one scene as Thackeray's bumptious, earthy old dame, but she makes the most of it, giving May Beatty hell as her maid: "Am I to be murdered with inattention?"

Finally, we have the many roles as lady companion, relative, and/or partner in crime to the female star. I'm thinking, for example, of her screen appearances as lady-in-waiting to Kitty Carlisle in *Here Is My Heart* (F. Tuttle, Paramount, 1934); as companion and accomplice to con artist, Gertrude Michael, in *The Notorious Sophie Lang* (R. Murphy, Paramount, 1934) and Carole Lombard in *The Princess Comes Across* (W.K. Howard, Paramount, 1936); as mother to and sponger on Marlene Dietrich in *The Devil Is a Woman* (J. von Sternberg, Paramount, 1935); and as aunt to Loretta Young in *Shanghai* (J. Flood, 1935). Again, Skipworth manages to makes her presence felt in all these films, though the plots seldom revolve around her and her on-screen time is limited. In *Here Is My Heart* Skipworth reprised her Broadway role in *The Grand Duchess and the Waiter* (1925) as Countess Rostova, chaperone to the impoverished Russian princess played by Kitty Carlisle in one of her rare film roles. Skipworth is here in a blonde finger-wave phase, which reminds me of West's promise in *Night After Night*: "Stick with me, dearie, and I'll make you a platinum blonde."

The best of this lot is probably the ingeniously plotted comedy-thriller *The Notorious Sophie Lang*. Gertrude Michael and Skipworth are well matched as "Lady Raffles" and her willing accomplice, the latter fond of a tipple as always and toting around her pet goldfish in a bowl. This film was released on July 20, 1934 and thus was one of the last pre–Code films. Michael went on to make two further "Sophie Lang" films, but without her Aunt Nellie.

In 1938, Skipworth's film career came to an end. The attempt to team her up with Polly Moran in *Two Wise Maids* (P. Rosen, Republic, 1937) and *Ladies in Distress* (G. Meins, Republic, 1938) and recreate some of that old Dressler-Moran magic had not been a success. Worthwhile roles were increasingly harder to come by. Her eyes were giving her trouble after all the time she'd spent under the Klieg lamps. Skipworth accepted defeat and returned to "the only place in the world for decent living": "between 40th and 50th St. on the isle of Manhattan."[636] She acted in a handful of Broadway shows on her return, but none of them ran for very long and she retired from the stage in 1942. She died in her apartment at 202 Riverside Drive ten years later, the month she was to have turned eighty-nine.[637] Her *New York Times* obituary noted that "Virtually without exception her film performances were commended."[638]

Cat Woman
GALE SONDERGAARD (1899–1985)

The little known and long forgotten film *Echoes* (1983) holds a special charm for lovers of old movies and older Hollywood actresses, for here we have for the final time veteran sorceress Gale Sondergaard working her own kind of screen magic. Stick thin, but as jet-black-haired, honey-voiced, and handsome as ever, Sondergaard makes her final screen appearance as a psychic, Mrs. Edmunds, who tries to interpret the artist-hero's recurring dream about a seventeenth-century painter. Sondergaard was eighty-three at the time and seems remarkably youthful, though she would die only two years later. By that time, her film debut was half a century and her Hollywood heyday more than thirty years behind her. Yet for any lover of classics such as *The Mark of Zorro* (1940), *The Letter* (1940), *The Spider Woman* (1944), and *Anna and the King of Siam* (1946), Gale Sondergaard will not soon be forgotten. She was something rare in Hollywood: an attractive, powerful, and dangerous woman on screen; an independent-minded, idealistic, and radical woman in real life. Larry Swindell has called her "perhaps the most serene villainess in film history."[639]

From the most unlikely of starting points, Gale Sondergaard built a career as an exotic and oriental screen siren. Unlikely because she bore the Danish birth name Edith Holm Sondergaard, befitting her Scandinavian ancestry. She was born in the Scandinavian-American heartland, in Litchfield, Minnesota on February 15, 1899.[640] Sondergaard was one of the several Hollywood character actresses, like Beulah Bondi and Agnes Moorehead, with a solid college education. She attended the Minneapolis School of Dramatic Art and the University of Minnesota, where she participated in student drama and where her father was a professor, before going the usual route of apprentice actors via stock companies until she finally found herself on the Great White Way in 1928.[641]

Unlike most young actresses, though, Sondergaard was signed by the prestigious Theatre Guild and would do five plays with them on Broadway. The first, and her Broadway debut, was Goethe's *Faust*, which opened at the Guild Theatre on October 8, 1928. Prophetically with regard to her future screen persona, Sondergaard played the Queen of the Witches in the Walpurgisnacht scene. Alvah Bessie remembered her as "gorgeous."[642] Also in the large cast of this production was a certain Herbert J. Biberman, a Jewish actor from Philadelphia one year Sondergaard's junior also making his Broadway debut. Biberman would become Sondergaard's husband in 1930, after she had divorced fellow actor Neill O'Malley, her husband of eight years, in what would prove the most fateful decision of Sondergaard's life. The Bibermans would remain married for more than forty years and have two children: a son, Daniel, and a daughter, Joan.

From *Faust*, Sondergaard went on to a Guild revival of Shaw's *Major Barbara* (1928–29), with the veteran character actress Helen Westley as her mother; followed by a new play called *Karl and Anna* (1929) with Alice Brady, Claude Rains, Otto Kruger, and Biberman. *Red Rust* (1929–30) was Sondergaard's fourth production for the Guild. With her in the cast, directed this time by her husband, were such familiar names as Ruth Nelson, Lee Strasberg, and George Tobias. *American Dream* (1933) was her last play for the Guild, before she went on to star in *Doctor Monica* (1933) with Beatrice De Nergaard and Alla Nazimova. Rufus King's *Invitation to Murder* (1934) with Humphrey Bogart was her final play on Broadway before following her husband to the West Coast.

Sondergaard's film career would be influenced by her friend Mervyn LeRoy more than any other director. He helmed her first and final films in Hollywood. Sondergaard had moved to Los Angeles because Biberman was set to direct a film for Columbia. Once there, she was discovered by LeRoy, who wisely cast her in his film *Anthony Adverse* (1936) at Warner Bros. It starred Fredric March in the title role and the young Olivia de Havilland. The film was a historical adventure tale set in eighteenth-century Italy in which Sondergaard was cast as the comically named Faith Paleologus, housekeeper to the hero's helper, Edmund Gwenn, and mistress and later wife of the villain of the piece, her old Broadway co-star Claude Rains. Sondergaard comes into her own in the second half of the film. The performance was not really Oscar-caliber despite her nomination. She became the first performer to win in the new category of Best Actress in a Supporting Role, beating Maria Ouspenskaya, Beulah Bondi, Alice Brady, and Bonita Granville.

This was a most auspicious beginning. By the time she started in the movies, Sondergaard was too old to become a star, but she would carve out her own unique niche as the leading attractive villainess in Hollywood, a niche in which she would have precious little competition. Judith Anderson and Agnes Moorehead did not arrive on the scene until 1940 and, arguably, couldn't compare with Sondergaard in the looks department, though Moorehead had something of the same angular face.

You can say one thing for Sondergaard: Once she had found her signature look, she stuck to it. Legend would have it that her particular brand of raven-haired, slant-eyed, sinister beauty was the inspiration for the Wicked Queen in Disney's classic cartoon version of *Snow White and the Seven Dwarfs* (1937).[643] Mervyn LeRoy had originally wanted her as a glamourous Wicked Witch of the West in *The Wizard of Oz* (1939). When this idea was voted down, Sondergaard withdrew from the project and Margaret Hamilton got the part.[644]

By the end of the 1930s, Sondergaard had acted in eleven films, including *Maid of Salem*, *The Life of Emile Zola*, *Juarez*, and *The Cat and the Canary*, but her major films lay ahead of her. The 1940s would be both her most productive and the final decade of her relatively brief Hollywood career. In *Maid of Salem* (F. Lloyd, Paramount, 1937), her second film, she plays the evil-minded sister of the enlightened village doctor (Harvey Stephens) in seventeenth-century

Gale Sondergaard is seen in what is for her an uncustomarily domestic setting in this still from *The Strange Death of Adolf Hitler* (Universal Pictures, 1946). Only the photo of Hitler on the wall of the children's bedroom reassures us that Sondergaard is probably up to her usual sinister shenanigans. In real life, she had a son and a daughter with her second husband, director and "Hollywood Ten" crusader Herbert Biberman. Both her husband and her children predeceased her.

Salem, who accuses Claudette Colbert of being a witch to save her brother's life. As was the case with Beulah Bondi, most of Sondergaard's part ended up on the cutting room floor.[645]

In the critically acclaimed *The Life of Emile Zola* (W. Dieterle, Warner Bros., 1937), she played the sympathetic wife of the famous victim of anti–Semitism in the French army, Capt. Alfred Dreyfus (Joseph Schildkraut, who won an Oscar for his portrayal), in a strange foreshadowing of her own fate. Frank S. Nugent of the *New York Times* thought the film "at once the finest historical film ever made and the greatest screen biography," but added that Sondergaard's role was "an illustration of a part built up from nothing and even then scarcely able to get off the ground."[646] The film was nominated for ten Academy Awards and won three. Sondergaard also had a part in another prestige biopic of the 1930s starring Paul Muni and directed by William Dieterle. In *Juarez* (Warner Bros., 1939), Muni played the Mexican peon revolutionary, Juarez; Brian Aherne, the ill-fated Emperor Maximillian; and Bette Davis his volatile and willful empress, Carlotta. Again Sondergaard was teamed with Claude Rains, as the Empress Eugénie to his Louis Napoleon III and the power behind the throne. Davis, who never looked better, has a wonderful scene when she confronts Rains and Sondergaard with abandoning her husband to his fate in Mexico, before she runs into the darkness and loses her mind.

The Cat and the Canary (E. Nugent, Paramount, 1939) was considerably lighter fare, being a low-budget screen version of a popular farcical stage thriller by John Willard. This was the first of Sondergaard's many "Cat" films and allowed her to camp it up in a classic Southern Gothic setting complete with hanging vines, creeps and creepers, secret passageways, and, of course, a black cat. Delivering orphic pronouncements, speaking with the spirits, and contributing to the general mood of doom and gloom, Sondergaard was clearly the cat of the title and Paulette Goddard the canary in this "No Exit"–type murder mystery, whose cast also included Bob Hope in the first of four films with Sondergaard, John Beal, Douglass Montgomery, Elizabeth Patterson, and Nydia Westman. Rather than eating the canary, though, Sondergaard saves her life.

Sondergaard's fifth and final film at Warner Bros., and arguably her finest, was *The Letter* (1940), based on a play by Somerset Maugham and starring Bette Davis as the adulterous murderess, Leslie Crosbie. Set in Singapore, this masterpiece by William Wyler is a powerful study of racial politics in British colonial society. Sondergaard is the Eurasian wife of Davis's murdered lover, Geoffrey Hammond, and never speaks a word of English in the film. Yet she is magnificently effective from the first moment of her appearance, "her face like a mask," in Davis's words, "those eyes like a cobra's eyes." The most powerful scene in the film is the confrontation between mistress and wife, when Davis comes to buy an incriminating letter. Standing two steps above Davis, who symbolically wears a lace mantilla, Wyler shoots the elaborately coiffed Sondergaard effectively from below. In the mid–1970s, Davis recalled that "Gale Sondergaard's performance in *The Letter* ... was breathtakingly sinister. I was *so* lucky that she was cast in this part.[647] The original play ends on the famous line "With all my heart, I still love the man I killed," but the Hays Office demanded that Davis pay for her crime and ultimately she is stabbed to death by the vengeful Mrs. Hammond.[648]

During her first five years in Hollywood, Sondergaard worked mostly for Warner Bros. and Paramount, but her signature films in the 1940s would be for Universal. These included *The Black Cat*, *The Spider Woman*, *Christmas Holiday*, and *The Spider Woman Strikes Back*. *The Black Cat* (A.S. Rogell, 1941), Sondergaard's first of fourteen for Universal, was loosely based on a story by Edgar Allan Poe. Like *The Cat and the Canary*, it was a murder mystery thriller with a strong element of greed and vengeance, as the clan gathers to await the death of the family matriarch, Henrietta Winslow. Sondergaard plays Mrs. Winslow's devoted housekeeper, who inherits the estate for her lifetime provided she continues to care for her former employer's many cats. The cast was stronger than the vehicle, including Broadway veteran Cecilia Loftus in a rare screen appearance as the elder Mrs. Winslow, Sondergaard's deliciously dastardly five-time co-star, Basil Rathbone, comedian Hugh Herbert, Universal fixture Bela Lugosi, and regal Gladys Cooper.

Gale Sondergaard had an exotic beauty that seemed far afield from her Scandinavian ethnic roots. In this portrait from the exploitation vehicle *The Spider Woman Strikes Back* (Universal Pictures, 1944), we note her characteristically dark hair, sculpted features, and cunning expression. The film has nothing in common with *The Spider Woman* but the title.

This classic image is from *The Spider Woman* (Universal Pictures, 1944), in which Gale Sondergaard starred in the title role with Basil Rathbone as Sherlock Holmes. It was her fifth of fourteen films at Universal, her home studio between 1941 and 1947. With her in the photo is her height-challenged accomplice, Angelo Rossitto, who had a long and productive career in films from 1927 till 1987.

Rathbone and Sondergaard were reunited in the more famous film, *The Spider Woman* (R.W. Neill, 1944), where she was given a rare starring role as Adrea "Spider Woman" Spedding, with Rathbone as Sherlock Holmes and Nigel Bruce as his trusty sidekick, Dr. Watson. Sondergaard plays a con woman who swindles impoverished gamblers by having them make over their insurance policy to her partner and then driving them to suicide by introducing a spider into their rooms that bites them, forcing them to kill themselves from the pain. (If you didn't get that the first time, read it again.) Sondergard ingeniously uses a pygmy to introduce the spider into her victims' rooms. This seventh film in the Sherlock Holmes series is the one in which Holmes pretends to have drowned in the river while fishing and then makes a miraculous reappearance.

Christmas Holiday (R. Siodmak, 1944) was a straight drama starring Gene Kelly as the black sheep of a once proud New Orleans family and former child star Deanna Durbin as his picture perfect wife, who goes through hell and high water for him. Sondergaard was Kelly's equally devoted mother, who hopes Durbin will be the saving of him, but ultimately accuses her daughter-in-law of abandoning him when he is charged with murder. Finally, *The Spider Woman Strikes Back* (A. Lubin, 1946) has exploitation film and B movie written all over it and nothing in common with the original other than its female star and the title. Set in the village of Domingo, Sondergaard plays a local worthy, who pretends to be blind, feeds the blood of her companion to meat-eating plants and, if that wasn't bad enough, knits.

Sondergaard's other major studio during the 1940s was Twentieth Century–Fox, where she made films such as *The Mark of Zorro*, *The Blue Bird*, and *Anna and the King of Siam*. *The Mark of Zorro* (R. Mamoulian, 1940) has become a cult classic. Here Sondergaard plays yet another smirking and conniving female of the species as Inez Quintero, J. Edward Bromberg's wife, Basil Rathbone's lover, and Linda Darnell's aunt with a yen for star hombre Tyrone Power. *The Blue Bird* (W. Lang, 1940) was not destined to become a classic of any kind, but rather a "critical and commercial failure."[649] It provided Sondergaard with yet another cat role, this time a literal one and in glorious Technicolor at that. As Tylette, Sondergaard tries to foil Shirley Temple's attempt to find the Blue Bird. Her big opportunity at Fox came in her final film for the studio, *Anna and the King of Siam* (J. Cromwell, 1946). She here portrays Lady Thiang, the first wife of King Mongkut (Rex Harrison), and enlists the governess Anna Owens (Irene Dunne) in the cause of her and the king's son. For this second major role in Southeast Asian drag, Sondergaard was nominated for an Academy Award, but saw it go to Anne Baxter for *The Razor's Edge*.

Sondergaard had a showy part in the fifth of the Bob Hope-Bing Crosby-Dorothy Lamour "Road" movies, *Road to Rio* (N.Z. McLeod, 1947). She was billed fourth in yet another evil aunt role, this time as the guardian of Lamour with a knack for hypnotizing unsuspecting victims by aid of a star sapphire. All told 1947 was a tumultuous year in Sondergaard's life and marked the end of the major phase of her acting career. The same year she was nominated for her second Oscar in twelve years, her husband became one of the hostile witnesses who refused to cooperate with the House Committee on Un-American Activities (HUAC) and were known collectively as the Hollywood Ten. These men were sentenced to jail for up to a year and fined for contempt of Congress in refusing to give a yes or no answer to the question: Are you now or have you ever been a member of the Communist Party?[650] Biberman got six months and a $500 fine, and was let off for good behavior after five months.[651]

Worse than his temporary incarceration was the fact that from 1951 on, both he and his wife were unemployable in Hollywood. Sondergaard never made another film there and would not return to the big screen until 1969. She had been subpoenaed by Congress as one of the first witnesses in the second round of hearings. On March 21, 1951, she appeared before HUAC in room 226 of Old House Office Building on Capitol Hill.[652] *The New York Times* noted that she was "Deeply tanned and wearing a black and white checked suit." According to the report, she "agreed that Congressional committees should investigate subversive activities but said 'this committee is doing incriminating work.'"[653] She then invoked the Fifth Amendment with its privilege against self-incrimination and refused to witness further, effectively ending her Hollywood film career.[654]

What would prove her final Hollywood film was MGM's *East Side, West Side* (1949). She probably would not have gotten the part of Barbara Stanwyck's sophisticated former actress mother, if it weren't for the influence of the director, her old friend Mervyn LeRoy. Sondergaard did little acting during the final three decades of her life. She did a one-woman show off Broadway in 1967 and starred in *The Visit* at the Guthrie Theater in Minneapolis.[655] She did not work in television until 1969 and then only sporadically. In 1980, forty years after her last appearance on Broadway, she made the briefest of reappearances there in a flop, *Goodbye Fidel*, with Jane Alexander and Kathy Bates (who was making her Broadway debut).

After *East Side, West Side*, it would be twenty years before Sondergaard again appeared on the screen, big or small. Fans might have wished she had waited longer, when they consider her comeback role as faded matinee idol Miriam Hopkins's secretary and dogsbody, Miss Leslie Blair. *Savage Intruder* (a.k.a. *Hollywood Horror House/The Comeback*; D. Wolfe, 1969) belongs with that group of campy horror flicks and instant cult classics from the 1960s and early '70s in which aging divas confusedly sought refuge as their film careers crumbled around them. I'm thinking primarily of *What Ever Happened to Baby Jane?* (1962) and *Hush ...*

Hush, Sweet Charlotte (1964), but also of Lady in a Cage (1964) with Olivia de Havilland, Fanatic (1965) with Tallulah Bankhead (arguably her film career had been fading for more than thirty years), Whatever Happened to Aunt Alice? with Geraldine Page (1969), and Dear Dead Delilah (1975) with Agnes Moorehead. As a sort of psychedelic sixties Sunset Blvd. shot in Norma Talmadge's former mansion, Savage Intruder serves as an ironic commentary on the entire subgenre. This was Miriam Hopkins's last film. As fate would have it, Sondergaard gets wasted by the son of her Juarez co-star and fellow left-winger John Garfield, David Garfield.

Sondergaard had a small part in Slaves (1969), her husband's first film in twenty-two years and his last. Starring Ossie Davis and Dionne Warwick, the film was nominated for a Golden Palm at Cannes. Sondergaard made only three more feature films: The Return of a Man Called Horse (I. Kershner, 1976), Pleasantville (K. Locker, V. Polon, 1976), and Echoes (a.k.a. Living Nightmare; A.A. Seidelman, 1983). In The Return of a Man Called Horse, she was given top billing with star Richard Harris (Lord John Morgan, a.k.a. Shunkawakan), as Elk Woman, an old woman of the Yellow Hand tribe who helps Harris regain his faith in life. Harris went out in a blaze of Harry Potter glory in 2002.

Herbert J. Biberman died of bone cancer on June 30, 1971. Both Sondergaard's children also predeceased her. She lived until 1985, dying on August 14 that year of cerebral vascular thrombosis at the Motion Picture Country Home and Hospital in Woodland Hills. Gale Sondergaard was cremated and her ashes scattered at sea. She never wrote her memoirs, nor does she appear to have spoken out about the persecution she had been subject to during the McCarthy era. In 2000, director and screenwriter Karl Francis told the unique love story of Herbert Biberman (Jeff Goldblum) and Gale Sondergaard (Greta Scacchi) in the film One of the Hollywood Ten.

Grand Dame
LUCILE WATSON (1879–1962)

In her time and in her generation, Lucile Watson was one of the grandest of the grand ladies in Hollywood. She had plenty of competition in this category, and it is instructive to place her in company with that bevy of aging grand dames that added their weight—literally and metaphorically—to Hollywood films of the 1930s and '40s. This superior silver screen sisterhood included, among the older generation, May Robson, Jessie Ralph, Dame May Whitty, and Alison Skipworth; among Watson's highly talented generation of the late 1870s and early '80s, Edna May Oliver, Ethel Barrymore, Laura Hope Crews, Mary Boland, and Mary Forbes; and among the younger generation, Elisabeth Risdon, Isobel Elsom, Florence Bates, Margaret Dumont, and, last but not least, Gladys Cooper. Never before or since have there been more opportunities for distinguished older women in Tinseltown and never before nor since have there been so many talented actresses to play the mothers, grandmothers, aunts, nannies, and mothers-in-law of the stars.

One might say that Watson was a more genial, dowdy, and amply proportioned Gladys Cooper. Or maybe it was the younger Cooper, and the later arrival in Hollywood, who was a thinner and more austere Lucile Watson. Both specialized in aristocratic dowagers, titled or not. We picture them in finely furnished interiors. Like her most formidable rival, Watson had a sideline in nuns (The Garden of Allah, Till

We Meet Again). Unlike Cooper, Watson could be formidable without being forbidding. Beneath her frosty exterior, it was always possible to discern a degree of warmth. The difference was in the eyes and in their physical presence. Cooper's legendary eyes were often flat and impassive, for all their beauty. Watson was more homely of aspect and her eyes could seldom hide a mischievous twinkle of delight at the vagaries and absurdities of life. Watson was an increasingly capacious woman, making Cooper look positively anorexic in comparison. All in all, Watson was a much more Rabelaisian character than her nine-years-younger rival from across the seas. They never made a movie together. It was probably a case of "this film ain't big enough for the both of us."

Like Cooper, Watson played her share of mothers and aunts. What talented sons, daughters, nieces, and nephews she had! Bette Davis, Barbara Stanwyck, Robert Montgomery, Jeanette MacDonald, James Stewart, Norma Shearer, William Powell, June Allyson, Elizabeth Taylor, and Robert Taylor, to name but a few. Her sons- and daughters-in-law included Carole Lombard, Nelson Eddy, Paul Lukas, Myrna Loy, Errol Flynn, Greer Garson, and, very nearly, Vivien Leigh.

Throughout the thirties, Watson had seen several of her starring roles on Broadway go to other actresses when the plays were made into movies. Edna May Oliver got her role in *No More Ladies* in 1935, Fay Bainter played Watson's part in *Yes, My Darling Daughter* in 1939 and Mary Boland got the plum part of Mrs. Bennet when MGM brought Jane Austen's classic *Pride and Prejudice* to the screen for the first time in 1940. Oliver and Boland were

In *Three Smart Girls* (Universal Pictures, 1936), fourteen-year-old singing sensation Deanna Durbin broke into the movies and went on to become the savior of Universal. Both Durbin and Lucile Watson were originally from Canada. Durbin hailed from Winnipeg and Watson from Québec.

veterans of the silent screen and early sound eras, unlike Watson. It took time and perseverance to establish oneself in Hollywood and all the starring stage roles in the world were like "les neiges d'antan" to the movie moguls.

It would be nine years before Watson was sufficiently established in Hollywood to allow her to reprise one of her own stage hits on the big screen: Fanny Farrelly in Lillian Hellman's 1941 Broadway hit *Watch on the Rhine*. Of the three classic filmatizations of plays by Hellman, including *The Little Foxes* (1941) and *The Children's Hour* (1961), *Watch on the Rhine* (H. Shumlin, Warner Bros., 1943) is probably the least familiar today, but that is no reflection on its quality. In her signature role, Watson portrays the imperious, wealthy widow of a judge, who must learn to confront the evil of Nazism when it is literally brought home to her at her secluded mansion on the outskirts of Washington, D.C. We get a sense of her less than subtle personality early on in the film from a stray remark to her friend, the delightfully dithery Mary Young: "You must get new upper teeth, Mellie. Nobody can understand a word you say anymore and you used to have lovely teeth when you were young." After her precocious grandson, Bodo, delivers one of his weighty pronouncements, she asks her daughter, Bette Davis, in wonderment: "Are these your children or are they dressed up midgets?"

Upon the arrival of Davis and her family from Europe after an absence of seventeen years, Watson's part is somewhat reduced and she does a lot of standing around and listening. This is out of character for such a matriarch, but a subtle and necessary part of her development. The challenge to the cosseted, comfortable dowager Watson portrays is, in her grandson's words, that "Grandma has not seen much of the world." She has to learn fast. Davis, playing a World War II "Mutter Courage" in a tyrolean hat, has married an agent in the German anti-fascist underground, played by Paul Lukas. In her own words, she has to make her mother see that "the world has changed and some of the people in it are dangerous." It was a measure of Davis's greatness (and savvy) in the early forties, that she would dare to share the limelight with talented, dynamic older women such as Watson, Billie Burke (*The Man Who Came to Dinner*, *In This Our Life*), Gladys Cooper (*Now, Voyager*), and Patricia Collinge (*The Little Foxes*). By the end of the film, Fanny Farrelly is much the wiser about the wicked ways of the world and to her son, Donald Woods, she utters what is the film's most famous line: "Well, we've been shaken out of the magnolias." For her portrayal, Watson got her one and only Oscar nomination for Best Supporting Actress. She lost out to Katina Paxinou in *For Whom the Bell Tolls*, as did fellow nominees Anne Revere and Gladys Cooper for *The Song of Bernadette*.

Watson's first substantial part in a major film had been in *The Garden of Allah* (R. Boleslawski, Selznick, 1936), playing the Mother Superior of a convent school. As Domini Enfilden, Marlene Dietrich is a former pupil, who returns to the convent in despair after her father's death to seek Watson's counsel. This was one of Dietrich's first Hollywood films without the support of her Svengali, Josef von Sternberg. Most would say that it shows. For all its splendid early Technicolor photography, there isn't much else to get excited about. Watson's role of advice-dispensing, wise, elder woman would become a staple of her film repertoire, though she usually did not require the added distinction of a nun's habit to emphasize her authority.

Watson herself had gone to a convent school in Québec, Canada, where she was born on May 27, 1879 and raised in a comfortably well-off and eminently respectable family. Her father, Thomas Charles Watson, was a major in the Royal Sherwood Foresters; her mother was Leila, née Morlet, indicating that Watson had a mixed English and French Canadian ancestry. Her family's reaction to her choice of vocation is not on record, though for a girl of her background it must have been unusual to enter on any career other than motherhood, much less becoming an actress. She enrolled in the American Academy of Dramatic Arts in New York in 1900 and Gotham would remain her home for most of the remaining six decades of her life.[656]

Watson made her professional New York debut in a new play called *Hearts Aflame* in 1902.

Early on she caught the eye of dramatist Clyde Fitch, in his play *The Girl With the Green Eyes*, and became one of producer-manager Charles Frohman's stars. Fitch wrote several plays for her—his last, *The City* (1909–10), was the most successful of them—and Frohman gave her plays lavish productions. Watson was an early supporter of the Theatre Guild and played Lady Utterword in their production of Shaw's *Heartbreak House* in 1920–21. She continued to be a leading lady of the American stage in the 1920s and '30s. She had a London season in a play called *Dancing Mothers* in 1925. Two other highpoints of her stage career took place in 1926, when she played Mrs. Alving in Ibsen's *Ghosts* and Lady Bracknell in Wilde's *The Importance of Being Earnest*.

Had Hollywood chosen to film Oscar Wilde's *The Importance of Being Earnest* during her lifetime, Watson would have made a perfect Lady Bracknell, as she had on stage; her basic earthiness still discernable under the layers of airs and graces. This was a quality she shared with character actresses such as her great fellow Canadian, Marie Dressler, and another stalwart of the "dowagers and domestics" circuit, Jessie Ralph, and with Dame Edith Evans, who gave a definitive interpretation of Lady Bracknell in the classic 1952 British film version.

In 1928, Lucile Watson was a September bride, when at age fifty she married the novelist and playwright Louis Evan Shipman, ten years her senior. It was his second marriage and Watson's as well. Apparently she had been married in the teens to fellow Canadian actor, and later silent screen idol, Rockcliffe Fellows (1883–1950). In later life, this short-lived marriage was a well-kept secret and it was not mentioned in any of her obituaries.[657] On marrying Shipman, Watson retired from the stage and in the early 1930s the couple moved to France.

Prior to her move to France, Watson had made her screen debut in a bit part in the 1930 "film à clef" about the Barrymores, *The Royal Family of Broadway* (Paramount). The film was co-directed by Watson's good friend, George Cukor, who had moved to Hollywood in early 1929 and who was no doubt at least partly responsible for her start in the movies.[658] This proved a false start, as her film career was kept on hold until 1934 by her move to France. As fate would have it, Louis Shipman died in 1933 and Watson went back to work both on stage and screen.

Watson gave many fine performances in the course of her thirty-five films and seventeen years in the movies. She worked for most of the major studios (MGM, Warner Bros., Columbia, Paramount, RKO, Twentieth Century–Fox, Universal) and for top-notch directors, such as Cukor, Mervyn LeRoy, Richard Thorpe, W.S. Van Dyke, Alfred Hitchcock, and Billy Wilder. In her own assessment, "'Lucile Watson parts' were high comedy, with feeling, with pathos, funny, gay, kind, tart, and naughty."[659] If I had to single out three of her finest roles, in addition to Fanny Farrelly in *Watch on the Rhine*, it would have to be Mrs. Moorehead in *The Women*, Lady Margaret Cronin in *Waterloo Bridge*, and Celia Fenwick in *Harriet Craig*.

The Women (MGM, 1939) was a welcome new opportunity to work with her friend and by now veteran director, George Cukor, in what would turn out to be one of his most celebrated and popular films. The film's cast is like a who's who of the best and the brightest actresses at Metro in the late 1930s: Norma Shearer, Joan Crawford, Rosalind Russell, Mary Boland, Paulette Goddard, Phyllis Povah, Joan Fontaine, and Marjorie Main. More than a hundred players did their bit. Not a man was to be seen from beginning to end of the film based on Clare Boothe Luce's equally manless hit play. Watson played ideal wife Norma Shearer's sage mother, who tries to the best of her ability to advise her daughter when the latter discovers her husband's infidelity with perfume counter girl, Joan Crawford. Looking slim and trim, Watson is the eye of the storm and delivers deathless lines like "You mustn't kid Mother, dear. I was a married woman before you were born," "A man has only one escape from his old self: to see a different self in the mirror of some woman's eyes," and "I'm an old woman, my dear, I know my sex." Curiously enough, when MGM remade the film as a musical in the mid–50s, Watson's role was subsumed by that of the heroine's novelist friend and confidante, renamed Amanda Penrose, and played in 1956 by Ann Sheridan in what would prove to be her final screen role. Hence Lucile Watson would remain the one and only Mrs. Moorehead on film.

Equally popular with audiences today is the World War II drama *Waterloo Bridge* (M. LeRoy, MGM, 1940). This was Vivien Leigh's first film in Hollywood after *Gone with the Wind*. Watson often played mothers or grandmothers trying to save their male offspring from undesirable alliances. In *Waterloo Bridge* she was able to create her most complete and engaging portrait of an aristocratic woman trying to balance her sense of duty to her family and her class with the need for basic human sympathy and understanding. In the words of Alex Barris, Watson's Lady Margaret Cronin "was a lady down to her cushy oriental rugs."660

In the bravura performance category is also a wise old woman role in one of her last films, *Harriet Craig* (Columbia, 1950). This film, directed by Vincent Sherman, was a remake of *Craig's Wife* (1936), which had starred Rosalind Russell and John Boles in the role of the martinet housewife and her beleaguered husband, now taken up by Joan Crawford and Wendell Corey. Watson played Celia Fenwick, Corey's boss's wife, who recommends him for a promotion. Wise, worldly, imperious, with a twinkle in her eye, she is an astute judge of the Craigs' marriage and foils Joan Crawford's plan to prevent her husband from going to Japan.

Watson's roles in Hollywood were evenly divided between comedy and drama. Naturally, not all her parts allowed her to make full use of her talents. Playing the elder Mrs. Charles, William Powell's mother and Myrna Loy's mother-in-law in the fifth of the "Thin Man" films, *The Thin Man Goes Home* (R. Thorpe, MGM, 1944), did not leave her much room for nuances or individualization. *Made for Each Other* (J. Cromwell, Selznick, 1939), *Mr. and Mrs. Smith* (A. Hitchcock, RKO, 1941), *Footsteps in the Dark* (L. Bacon, Warner Bros., 1941), *Never Say Goodbye* (J.V. Kern, Warner Bros., 1946), and *Julia Misbehaves* (J. Conway, MGM, 1948) were all variations on the theme of the disapproving mother-in-law, who dotes on her child and dislikes her offspring's chosen mate, whether that be Carole Lombard in the case of the first two films mentioned, Errol Flynn in the third and fourth, or Greer Garson in the fifth. They all pale in comparison with *Waterloo Bridge*, the ultimate "everything you would not want to happen on your first meeting with your potential mother-in-law" film of all time.

Though she did not sing, Watson lent her talents to five musicals and musical dramas. *Three Smart Girls* (H. Koster, Universal, 1936) was the first of them and introduced the savior of Universal, Deanna Durbin, to movie-going audiences. Watson played the three Craig sisters' stern but basically warm-hearted housekeeper and chaperone, who goes with them to New York to prevent their father from marrying Binnie Barnes. For those who don't dig Durbin, the film is chiefly memorable for the mother-daughter pairing of Alice Brady and Barnes as two deliciously devious golddiggers.

In *Sweethearts* (W.S. Van Dyke, MGM, 1938), the fifth Eddy-MacDonald musical, Watson played Jeanette MacDonald's tippling, saccharine, and sponging mother in glorious Technicolor for the first time since her appearance in the pioneering early color film, *The Garden of Allah*. In Billy Wilder's *The Emperor Waltz* (Paramount, 1948), Watson portrays yet another high-born dowager, the Princess Bitotska, "the richest woman in Austria." Watson acts as the narrator of the film, with Julia Dean as a captive audience to the tale of the unlikely love affair between the daughter of an Austrian baron (Joan Fontaine) and an American traveling salesman (Bing Crosby). The running parallel drawn in the film between the courtship of this star-crossed couple and their dogs is quite comic and not a little risqué.

In Watson's second to last film, the Fred Astaire-Betty Hutton vehicle *Let's Dance* (N.Z. MaLeod, Paramount, 1950), Watson plays the mother of Hutton's dead husband, Serena Everett. It was one of her least sympathetic roles. The film's conflict revolves around the question of who will raise the heir to the Everett family fortune, his grandmother (Watson) or mother (Hutton). When at one point Hutton

Grand Dame: Lucile Watson (1879-1962)

Lucile Watson looks benevolently down on her grandson, Bobby Driscoll, in this group shot from Walt Disney's 1946 film *Song of the South*, as (*from left*) Glenn Leedy, Anita Brown, James Baskett, and Hattie McDaniel look on. Driscoll is getting a talking to from his mother, Ruth Warrick, who had her film debut in *Citizen Kane*, but would be best known as *All My Children* matriarch Phoebe Tyler, a TV soap opera role she played from 1970 until her death in early 2005.

tries to fake shock and dismay at her son's disappearance (she has abducted him herself), Watson dismisses her histrionics with her customary authority: "Stop babbling, Catherine. Remember, I've seen Sarah Bernhardt." Though Watson didn't sing in this musical either, she got to skip the light fantastic with Astaire in one of the final scenes.

In one way or the other, Watson most often found herself telling people what to do. She was a great advocate, as one critic has pointed out, of the "silver cord."[661] The preeminent wielder of that subtle yet powerful feminine weapon was Laura Hope Crews in the role of Mrs. Phelps (*The Silver Cord*, 1933). Watson used some of the same tactics with husbands and children in films such as *Made for Each Other*, *Sweethearts*, *Waterloo Bridge*, *Harriet Craig*, *Let's Dance*, and *Watch on the Rhine*.

Her cord was more a chain or a whip in the remake of *Little Women* (M. LeRoy, MGM, 1949). That may be part of the reason why Aunt March was not one of her best personifications. Watson was the fourth in the long march of stuffy, self-righteous Aunt Marches on screen. The third, and many would say still the finest, was Edna May Oliver in George Cukor's 1933 filmatization. Possibly the role was too flat and caricatured to allow Watson to shine. Though high comedy was very much her *métier*, she was a serious, naturalistic, "legitimate" actress, with no stomach for slapstick or histrionics. It is also interesting that Watson did very few period films. In *Little Women* she appears strangely unsuited to the fancy dress and fripperies of the full-fledged Metro Technicolor costume drama. Here we may have touched on the chief cause of her continued appeal: She was a very modern actress.

After seven years in the forties devoted entirely to film work, Watson stopped making films in 1950 and returned to Broadway in plays such as *Ring Round the Moon* (1950), *The Bat* (1953), and *Late Love* (1953). When she announced her retirement after the run of the latter play, Brooks Atkinson wrote: "There are countless theatergoers who have not had enough of her crackling mind, her peppery speech, her fluffy hair, her grand manners."[662] Lucile Watson lived in quiet retirement in her tiny New York brownstone at 143 East 63rd St. until June 24, 1962, when she died of a heart attack.[663] She was buried in Mount Hope Cemetery, Hastings-on-Hudson, Westchester County, New York.

In 1950 Wolcott Gibbs called her "one of the most extraordinary comediennes in the theatre."[664] On her death, the *New York Times* wrote that she was "incorrigibly comic" and "crisp as a fresh stalk of celery, well salted."[665] Watching Watson in her best roles today, sixty years after she created them and more than forty years after her death, she still appears like someone we might expect and hope to meet tomorrow—a worldly, sophisticated friend of our mother's perhaps or, if we're lucky, our own grandmother or great-aunt. Despite being born in 1879, she is still our contemporary. Lucile Watson was a cool broad. Let's leave it at that.

A Real Dame
MAY WHITTY (1865–1948)

She was murdered by Robert Montgomery, was Ingrid Bergman's nosy neighbor, played Charles Boyer's mother in one film, and Joan Fontaine's in another, was made into a better human being by Greer Garson, and took good care of Lassie. In her most familiar film, she simply vanished. With May Robson, Alison Skipworth, and Jessie Ralph, she was one of the oldest actresses to get a new lease on artistic life with the coming of cinematic sound. For the last eleven years of her sixty-seven-year acting career, she was one of the most valuable British imports in the American film industry and a sort of Queen Victoria to the Hollywood Raj.

Mary Louisa Whitty's story begins in Liverpool, England seventy-one years before she first set foot in California. Of Irish descent, May Whitty was born the third and youngest child of newspaper editor Alfred Whitty and Mary Ashton Whitty on June 19, 1865. Her father died when he was thirty-eight and his daughter ten, without leaving adequate provision for his widow and children.[666] Whitty would not be financially secure for many years. Her decision to go on the stage at age sixteen was at least partially determined by her need to earn a living in a dog-eat-dog world she had not been raised to deal with.[667] A voracious reader from an early age, she was given no education other than what her mother could provide at the school for young ladies she tried unsuccessfully to establish.[668]

Whitty first appeared on the London stage as a merry peasant and a lady of the court in the operetta *La Mascotte* in April 1882. She spent some uneventful years with the Kendals at the St. James's Theatre, before leaving them to join a small-time stock company, hoping the opportunities would be greater there.[669] Her big break came in 1889 when leading lady Fanny Brough lost her voice and Whitty had to replace her as Margery Sylvester in the play *Our Flat*. She stayed in the part for nearly two years and by the end of her stint was voted London's favorite actress in a newspaper poll.[670]

At age twenty-seven, Whitty altered her resolution to remain a spinster and finally succumbed to the blandishments of her dashing, blue-eyed, fellow actor, Ben Webster, one year her senior. The "high and mighty" Webster family did not approve, especially Ben's two actress sisters.[671] Ben's elder sister, Annie Webster, had been a leading lady *in spe* when unprepossessing little May Whitty was starting out in the theater and having to share her dressing room with her understudy was not at all to Miss Webster's liking.[672] For the Websters were theater royalty and Ben himself was named after his famous actor grandfather, "Old Ben" Webster. He had trained to become a solicitor, but went into the family firm, so to speak, making his official debut at the St. James' Theatre in March 1887, as Lord Woodstock in *Clancarty*.[673]

During the years following her marriage to Webster, Whitty's career suffered.[674] From 1895, she and her husband were part of Henry Irving's company at the Lyceum. Whitty elected to follow her husband on several lengthy tours to the U.S., including one in 1895–96 with Irving and Ellen Terry, who became a close friend of the couple. With his good looks, "beautiful, bountiful Benny,"[675] as Terry called him, was a rising star. When Oscar Wilde wanted "someone beautiful" for the part of Cecil Graham in *Lady Windemere's Fan* (1894), Ben Webster got the part.[676] He starred with Mrs. Patrick Campbell in *The Second Mrs. Tanqueray* (1894) and would go on tour with her to America in 1907, despite vowing never to work with her again.

The Websters' first child, a son, died at birth on Christmas Day, 1903.[677] Their second child was born in New York City thirteen years into their marriage, while they were on their second American tour. Margaret Webster would follow her parents onto the stage at an early age and later become an important stage director.[678]

The early years of the twentieth century were not a good time for Whitty, who suffered from migraine headaches, depression, and other ailments of body and mind.[679] She put her recovery of health and happiness down to her discovery of Christian Science on one of her U.S. tours and she kept the faith until her death.[680] According to her daughter, she had more energy at age eighty than she herself had at half her age, and she would enjoy an active social life until her death.[681] Whitty said famously toward the end of her days: "I've got everything Betty Grable has—only I've had it longer."[682]

Playing an old lady for the first time, a turning point in any actress's career, came for Whitty when she was forty-five and the famous actor-manager Harley Granville Barker asked her somewhat timorously to consider a part in *The Madras House*.[683] She was happy for the work, as her career was in the doldrums. During the teens she channeled a lot of her newfound energy into various good causes, including women's rights, as chairwoman of the Actresses' Franchise League, charity work through the Theatrical Ladies' Guild and war relief. It was primarily for her war work she was awarded the DBE in January 1918, only the third actress to be so honored.[684]

If it is true, as Oscar Wilde suggests in *The Picture of Dorian Gray*, that good Americans go to Paris when they die, then it seems equally true that good British character actresses go to Hollywood. The story of how Dame May Whitty came to movieland is a common one in its broad outline (she was asked to repeat a stage success in the film version), but the details are, of course, unique. Starting with *The Last of Mrs. Cheyney* in 1925, starring Gladys Cooper and Whitty's longtime friend, Gerald du Maurier, Whitty's acting career had been on an upswing. In 1932, after a twenty-four-year hiatus, she found herself back on Broadway playing the maid in *There's Always Juliet* with Herbert Marshall and Edna Best.

In the spring of 1935 she was hoping for a part in a new Rodney Ackland play called *The Old Ladies* and was bitterly disappointed when the role went to someone else. With a shrug she took the lead in Emlyn Williams's soon-to-be-classic *Night Must Fall*, complaining that no one would let her play anything but "old beasts." *The Old Ladies* ran three weeks, *Night Must Fall* ran a year in London and transferred to Broadway.[685] From there the call came from Hollywood. MGM had bought the film rights for

Robert Montgomery and Rosalind Russell and wanted Whitty to reprise her tour de force performance as the spoiled, tyrannical old biddy, Mrs. Bramson. Whitty was all set to return to London and only made up her mind five minutes before the ship was due to sail.[686] She signed the contract with MGM, packed up the attic apartment at 31 Bedford St. which had been her and Ben's home base for forty-seven years, and with a bewildered husband in tow started a whole new life for herself on the other side of the world.[687] Finally it was her turn to shine.

Whitty was fortunate in the opportunities she was given in Hollywood, as the place was— in Columbia boss Harry Cohn's characteristic phrase—"lousy with old dames."[688] She had to compete with actresses of the caliber of May Robson, Jessie Ralph, Laura Hope Crews, Lucile Watson, and Edna May Oliver. Being dyed in the wool British was no doubt an advantage, as it would be for Gladys Cooper a few years later, but it is less certain that it made any difference that May Whitty had been a Dame Commander of the British Empire (DBE) since 1918. In a world where "dame" refers to something other than a title, the potential for misunderstandings was great. Many simply thought Dame was her first name. One stage door keeper threatened to knock a man down for calling May Whitty a dame.[689]

According to David Ragan, Whitty's "smallest gesture was as eloquently magnificent as her regal presence."[690] In retrospect, it is remarkable to witness how old-timers like May Robson and Marie Dressler and May Whitty, who had been trained to reach the uppermost gallery with their performances, managed to adapt so marvelously to the demands of a medium that required quite a different kind and a greater degree of realism. Whitty played mostly dramatic parts on film, but she infused many of them with a subtle humor that is still a delight to watch more than half a century after she made them. At her best when she did not need to be grandmotherly, benign, and benevolent, she scores highest points in *Night Must Fall*, *Mrs. Miniver*, *The White Cliffs of Dover*, and *Gaslight*.

In Greer Garson's big wartime hit, *Mrs. Miniver* (W. Wyler, MGM, 1942), Whitty is given a signature role as Lady Beldon, an austere, autocratic aristocrat, who is made a little more human by Garson's sterling example, but nevertheless is symbolically punished for her hubris through the death of her granddaughter, Teresa

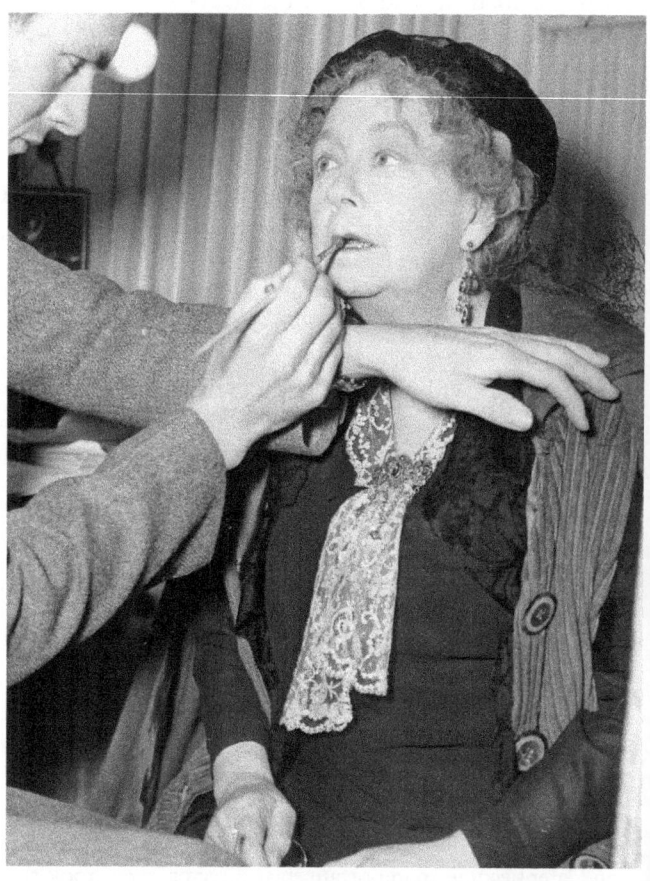

Dame May Whitty took up the role of the medium Rosalie La Grange in the 1937 remake of *The Thirteenth Chair* (Metro-Goldwyn-Mayer). The film was based on a play Bayard Veiller had originally written for his wife, Margaret Wycherly, who also played the lead in the first sound version from 1929. Here we see Whitty having her makeup adjusted between takes.

Wright, in an air raid. In *The White Cliffs of Dover* (C. Brown, MGM, 1944), Whitty shows her range by portraying a woman from the opposite end of the social scale, Gladys Cooper's faithful, temperamental old nanny, who strongly disapproves of one of her charges marrying an American (Irene Dunne), but who is gradually won over.

In her best roles, it seems, Whitty is forever being won over and shown the error of her imperious ways. In that respect, *Gaslight* (MGM, 1944) is a new departure for her. Her dumpy, doughy figure, button eyes and crab apple face, with its characteristically upturned nose, are ideally suited to playing Miss Thwaites, Ingrid Bergman's busybody neighbor in London's Thornton Square. From the moment Whitty first meets Bergman on a continental train to her final appearance at the close with the villainous husband, Charles Boyer, vanquished and Bergman in the safe arms of Joseph Cotten, Whitty is welcome comic relief in George Cukor's masterly tale of psychological terror.

By way of contrast to her classics, her role as Joan Fontaine's mother and Cedric Hardwicke's wife in *Suspicion* (RKO, 1941) holds no more interest than a stuffed armchair. That Whitty at age seventy-six is far too old to play the mother of the twenty-four year-old Fontaine, even with dyed hair, is one thing. In her second film with Hitchcock, he simply doesn't give her anything to get her teeth into. In her first collaboration with Hitchcock, *The Lady Vanishes* (1938), at least there was the expectation of finding out why Whitty had vanished. Her role as Napoleon's mother, Laetitia Bonaparte, in *Conquest* (C. Brown, MGM, 1937), her second film in Hollywood, is only a notch better than *Suspicion*. Whitty fusses about dowdily in capes and flounces, her little Munchkin face looking snooty and sympathetic at intervals. Charles Boyer is Napoleon and Garbo his Polish mistress, who wins Whitty's sympathy through her undying devotion to the little emperor.

Apart from the propagandistic *The White Cliffs of Dover* and *Mrs. Miniver*, Whitty lent her by now familiar presence to two of Hollywood's major morale boosters during World War II: *Stage Door Canteen* (F. Borzage, 1943) and the British colony's epic omelette, *Forever and a Day* (various directors, RKO, 1943), where she played C. Aubrey Smith's feisty, gun-toting wife

The Sign of the Ram (Columbia Pictures, 1948) was released only three months before May Whitty's death at nearly eighty-three years of age. Here she played a dotty neighborhood busybody, who takes tea with the wheelchair-bound villainess of the film, Susan Peters. Peters was paralyzed in real life after a shooting accident in 1945. *The Sign of the Ram* was to be her comeback film but failed at the box office.

in the earliest part of the saga. In the remake of *Raffles* (Sam Wood, Samuel Goldwyn, 1940), Whitty was third billed as a bothersome old battleaxe who invites Olivia de Havilland and her paramour, the gentleman thief and amateur cracksman, David Niven, down to the country for the weekend. Niven has designs on her jewels, while Whitty nurses her King Charles Spaniel and her gin and tonic. In *Crash Dive* (A. Mayo, Twentieth Century-Fox, 1943), she was an elderly gentlewoman enjoying a hearty camaraderie with her grandson, Tyrone Power, who even brings Anne Baxter home to meet her on their first date. Whitty also had a small part in the first Lassie film, *Lassie Come Home* (F.M. Wilcox, MGM, 1943), where she played an elderly lady living in a rural cottage, who with her husband finds Lassie, takes him in, and helps him recover his strength on his long trip home from Scotland. One of her last roles was in the fairly ridiculous costume drama, *Green Dolphin Street* (V. Saville, MGM, 1947), in which she portrayed the mother superior of a convent and the confidante of Gladys Cooper, a leading lady of the island community of St. Pierre.

Whitty did not entirely neglect the stage during her Hollywood years. She acted in two productions directed by her talented daughter, *The Trojan Women* (1941) and *Therese* (1945), and in the spring of 1940 took part, with her husband, in Laurence Olivier and Vivien Leigh's unsuccessful American tour of *Romeo and Juliet*.[691]

For her uncanny ability to delineate British upper-class eccentricity in *Mrs. Miniver* and old-womanly coquetry and quarrelsomeness in *Night Must Fall*, Whitty was nominated twice for Academy Awards for Best Actress in a Supporting Role. This was in 1938 and 1943. She had to see herself beaten by Alice Brady (for *In Old Chicago*) the first time and by her *Mrs. Miniver* co-star, Teresa Wright, the second.

"The theatre," Whitty once said, "is an opportunity for giving, not a machinery for getting."[692] She added, "So long as I can do my bit, I'll keep right on doing it."[693] That she did until May 29, 1948, when cancer claimed her. She had had to be replaced by Lucile Watson in *Julia Misbehaves* in January due to her terminal illness.[694] May Whitty's final film, *The Return of October* (J.H. Lewis, Columbia, 1948), was released four and a half months after her death.

Libeled Lady
CORA WITHERSPOON (1890–1957)

Who is the last person you'd want to be stuck with on a transatlantic crossing? Who is the last person you'd want to invite to play bridge as you await the execution of a woman you helped send to the electric chair? Who is the last person you'd want to hire as a governess for your child? All these questions have the same answer: Cora Witherspoon. Or rather: Cora Witherspoon's pesky society woman Mrs. Burns-Norvell in *Libeled Lady* (1936); her Elizabeth McGrath, the sister-in-law from hell in *Midnight* (1934); and her Mrs. Angevine, the inebriated governess in *Just for You* (1952).

If you took half a portion of Florence Bates, both in talent and physique, and added a dash of Laura Hope Crews at her most snooty, you would get Cora Witherspoon. Bates and Crews were awfully good. Witherspoon could be just plain awful. Thus, for all devotees of the camp moment in film there is always a certain frisson of anticipation when Witherspoon is on the cast list. Goodness, she could be bad. If it was possible to mess up a performance of five minutes or less, she could do it. Sometimes one is forced to ask: Is she actually under the influence or is she just acting that way?

Libeled Lady: Cora Witherspoon (1890–1957)

As it turns out, Tennessee Williams no less can provide us with at least a partial answer. Witherspoon has the dubious honor of being mentioned in his open-hearted *Memoirs* (1975). Fortunately, the subject of one of the playwright's more backhanded accolades had been dead for almost twenty years at the time of the book's publication and few would still have remembered her. Williams recalls a time in the early 1940s when he worked the night shift running an elevator at the San Jacinto Hotel on the Upper East Side of Manhattan, "a sort of retirement home for dowagers of high degree but diminished fortune":

> I remember the hotel also contained a marvelous old character actress named Cora Witherspoon. I believe it is safe for me to say that this delightful lady, now gone from us, was addicted to morphine and that the poet [a fellow worker] and I had to fill her prescriptions for her at an all-night pharmacy.
> Morphine is supposed to be a "downer" but it always gave Miss Witherspoon a "high."
> She used to rap with the poet and me till nearly daybreak in the San Jacinto lobby. Her "fix" would never wear itself out till the first cock's crow. Then the poet and I would sort of lift her into the lift, the poet would open her bedroom door and I would get her to the edge of her bed and let her drop on it.
> "What will I do without you boys?" she'd murmur, with that sweet, sad wisdom of the old who know that "all will pass."[695]

Williams makes Witherspoon out to be ancient, though she was only in her early fifties at the time he describes. He himself was about thirty.

Ruth Gordon, who starred with her in the 1925 Broadway production of *The Fall of Eve* at the Booth Theatre, recalled some advice the fabled actress Jeanne Eagels had given her. To make Witherspoon appear the "heavy," Eagles suggested that Gordon "'do it as though you're *pretty*. Not a battle-ax like Cora. Act as if you're *terribly* pretty and trying to remember what homely Cora said.'"[696] John Springer and Jack Hamilton noted in 1971 that "Cora Witherspoon was blessed with a face that might have been drawn by one of those cartoonists who specialize in dealing with the 'war between men and women.'"[697] In Alex Barris's description, she was like "a gawky tree full of birds."[698]

Little is known of the early life and career of the actress who would become a familiar, if not attractive, face on Broadway from the teens onward and in Hollywood films from the early 1930s. She was born Cora Witherspoon in New Orleans on January 5, 1890, making her the contemporary of character actresses such as Fay Bainter, Florence Bates, Beulah Bondi, Gladys Cooper, Margaret Dumont, and Marjorie Main. Apparently, Witherspoon was educated in her native city and in Paris. Her early stage training was achieved in a New Orleans stock company.[699]

In 1910 she made her Broadway debut age twenty in classic character actress fashion by playing a seventy-year-old woman. The vehicle was legendary writer-producer David Belasco's successful production of *The Concert* at his own Belasco Theatre. This was the first of more than thirty Broadway credits. For the first fifteen years of her film career, Witherspoon would continue to appear in New York productions as well. She would take her final bow on Broadway as the journalist hero's hard-done-by future mother-in-law Mrs. Grant in a 1946 revival of Ben Hecht and Charles MacArthur's pressroom drama *The Front Page*. Witherspoon supported such celebrated Broadway stars as Ruth Chatterton (*Daddy Long Legs*, 1914–15), Mary Boland (*The Matinee Hero*, 1918), Ina Claire (*The Awful Truth*, 1922; *Grounds for Divorce*, 1924–25), Ruth Gordon (*The Fall of Eve*, 1925), Ethel Barrymore (*The Constant Wife*, 1926–27), and Tallulah Bankhead (*Forsaking All Others*, 1933). In Somerset Maugham's hit play *The Constant Wife*, she created the role of the heroine's frumpy, unmarried sister, Martha Culver. In the disastrous 1932 revival of *Camille* starring Lillian Gish, she played the dubious seamstress and the heroine's fairweather friend, Prudence, a role interpreted so vividly four years later by Laura Hope Crews in MGM's film version with Garbo in the lead. Witherspoon was also Aunt Sally in the short-lived original production of Owen Davis's *Jezebel* (1933–34), which starred Miriam Hopkins after Tallulah Bankhead had to withdraw due to acute illness.

It was a stage actress of some stature, then, and vast experience who starting in 1931 would also lend her talents to the screen. Unlike many of her Broadway character actress colleagues, she didn't get a start reprising one of her stage roles, which as I've already indicated, usually went to other and more prestigious actresses. Rather, she was given a small part in *Tarnished Lady* (Paramount, 1931), Tallulah Bankhead's first sound film, which was shot in New York City. Witherspoon only appears in the film's second scene playing a frazzled department store saleslady, who has to refuse down-on-her-luck socialite Bankhead further credit. This was the first film George Cukor directed alone.[700] He may have been responsible for getting Witherspoon started in film and would be her most frequent director. Witherspoon would support Bankhead in the Broadway production of *Forsaking All Others* two years later, though the role of Aunt Paula went to Billie Burke in the film version (while Joan Crawford took over the lead).

Like her contemporaries Florence Bates and Margaret Dumont, Witherspoon would frequently be cast as an unsympathetic or downright obnoxious dowager. One of her earliest entries in this category is Elizabeth McGrath in *Midnight* (a.k.a. *Call It Murder*; C. Erskine, 1934). This filmatization of a Broadway play by Claire and Paul Sifton starred the young Humphrey Bogart in a characteristically shady role and the ill-fated Sidney Fox as his obsessive girlfriend and the daughter of O.P. Heggie. Heggie plays a principled jury foreman chiefly responsible for getting Helen Flint convicted of murder. The film details the rising tension in the Weldon family as they await the woman's execution at midnight. The irony of the situation is that by the end of the night, Heggie's own daughter has become a murderess. Witherspoon is Heggie's obnoxious, insensitive, crass, and flirtatious sister-in-law. Her telling comment when Heggie refuses to go to the governor and ask for a stay of the sentence of execution is: "Well, that's that. Oh, come on, let's play bridge."

Witherspoon rarely played domestics. One exception is *Quality Street* (G. Stevens, RKO, 1937). This is one of her better roles as the slatternly, frowsy maid Patty, working for two genteel, spinsterish sisters played by Katharine Hepburn and Fay Bainter. In one of her few period costume dramas, this one set in 1805 during the Napoleonic Wars, Witherspoon is paired off with the veteran comic actor, Eric Blore, who plays a doughty recruiting officer. Another of Witherspoon's costume dramas was MGM's eighteenth-century extravaganza *Marie Antoinette* (W.S. Van Dyke, 1938). Here she was given a named, credited role as the Countess de Noailles and billed ninth, which seems odd as her screen time is limited. Much of her role must have ended up on the cutting room floor. What there is shows her as the comically clumsy lady-in-waiting to Norma Shearer's ill-fated queen.

On the opposite end of the social scale, Witherspoon plays a dark-haired dealer in second-hand clothing in her native New Orleans in MGM's 1937 weeper *Madame X* (Sam Wood), starring the glorious Gladys George and John Barrymore look-alike Warren William. Again, Witherspoon only has one scene, in which she helps divest George of some of her French designer dresses and gets her a job as a singer at a local dive. *Dodge City* (M. Curtiz, Warner Bros., 1939), starring Errol Flynn and Olivia de Havilland, was Witherspoon's only Western. Here she plays the president of a temperance society whose all-female meeting is disrupted by jovial, hard-drinking Alan Hale and a riot that spills over from the saloon next door.

Yet films like *Libeled Lady* (J. Conway, MGM, 1936), *Personal Property* (W.S. Van Dyke, MGM, 1937), and *Dark Victory* (E. Goulding, Warner Bros., 1939) saw Witherspoon in the more typical guise of her thirties film career, as the elegant, gossipy, and alternately fawning or frowning society woman. *Dark Victory* was the most significant among these films. Witherspoon symbolizes the attitudes and responses of "good society" to the heroine's behavior, specifically the Long Island "horsey set" and heroine Judith Traherne (Bette Davis). In an early scene, Witherspoon is allowed to toy lovingly with Ronald Reagan's hair, though this intriguing suggestion is not developed and the future U.S. president is given little to do in the film apart from looking dashing and disheveled as he grows more and more drunk.

More than thirty of Witherspoon's fifty films were produced in the 1930s. She was a contract player at MGM, where she made ten films between 1936 and 1939, and was even

Cora Witherspoon in a characteristic pose, dressed to the nines, at the bar, drink in hand, observing inward-looking Bette Davis with a calculating expression in this classic photograph from *Dark Victory* (Warner Bros., 1939). In the center of the shot is Witherspoon's toyboy in the film, Ronald Reagan. She did not live to see his glory days in politics.

briefly in the running for the part of Glinda in *The Wizard of Oz* (1939).[701] As David Quinlan notes, after *The Bank Dick* (E.F. Cline, Universal, 1940) Witherspoon's film career started to peter out.[702] In the famous comedy starring W.C. Fields as the hilariously inept security guard Egbert Sousé, Witherspoon played his slatternly, bovine, termagant wife Agatha, the daughter of the live-in mother-in-law from hell, Jessie Ralph, and the mother of the ungrateful daughters Una Merkel and Evelyn Del Rio.

Though the roles were fewer in the 1940s and into the early 1950s, Witherspoon continued to hold up the banner of social respectability and traditional values in films such as *Colonel Effingham's Raid* (I. Pichel, Twentieth Century–Fox, 1946), *I've Always Loved You* (F. Borzage, Republic, 1946), and *Just for You* (E. Nugent, Paramount, 1952). Her series of dastardly dowagers was topped by what is undoubtedly her finest film performance in the masterly Mitchell Leisen comedy *The Mating Season* (Paramount, 1951). Twenty years after her film debut and back at her first studio, Witherspoon finally gets the role of her career as Mrs. Williamson, the insufferably overbearing wife of an important industrialist that John Lund wants to involve in a major project at his company. Decked out in a series of elegant suits and big, lace-trimmed picture hats, Witherspoon's deep-set, dark eyes give a whole new meaning to the word "beady." She commands every scene she's in, even giving Oscar-nominated Thelma Ritter a run for her money. One of her first lines is when she interrupts a meeting to take her husband to lunch with the remark: "We're only just keeping an

Cora Witherspoon is maybe somewhat overdressed for this all female, country breakfast served by Louise Beavers to a pensive Jane Russell and an uncustomarily thoughtful Connie Gilchrist (right). The film is *Young Widow* (United Artists, 1946) and there can be no question who is the young widow. David Ragan once wrote that Witherspoon's face "was made for gossiping." This was only Jane Russell's second film. According to the actress, recalling the film fifty years later: "The young widow should have died with her husband."

ulcer at bay." Her henpecked husband (Malcolm Keen) tries to smooth over his wife's dictatorial qualities by commenting that she "was born with rigor mortis." When her host at a luncheon inquires if there is anything he can get her, Mrs. Williamson responds: "All I want is a cool breeze blowing off the Atlantic." All in all, the film, which also stars Gene Tierney as Lund's wife and Miriam Hopkins as his histrionic mother-in-law, is a devastating satire on the rottenness of corporate America.

Witherspoon's final film role was another return to her beginnings in film. In *It Should Happen to You* (Columbia, 1954), directed by her first director, George Cukor, she was back at the sales counter just as in *Tarnished Lady*. Ironically, Witherspoon, who we've seen was never noted for her beauty, looks handsomer in her final film role than in most of her previous ones. She wears a little black dress and pearls, as she waits on Judy Holliday in the towel department of Macy's. More than forty years before the reality TV boom, this film was prophetic in its marvelous satire on ersatz celebrity. Holliday builds a career of sorts on no other talent or qualification than her desire and determination to be famous. Arguably, the scene in which Witherspoon discovers that the customer she is serving is *the* Gladys Glover is the best one in the film. No one can fawn like Cora Witherspoon and she exclaims with simpering sublimity: "It's *Gladys Glover!*"

Witherspoon retired to Las Cruces, New Mexico, where she died from a heart ailment on November 17, 1957. She was survived by her eight-years-older sister, Maude Witherspoon. Cora Witherspoon lies buried in Matairie Cemetery, New Orleans, Louisiana.

NOTES

1. John Springer and Jack Hamilton, *They Had Faces Then: Super Stars, Stars and Starlets of the 1930's* (N.p.: Castle, 1974), p. 33. As opposed to the stars and starlets, suicides among character actresses were rare. Ona Munson (1903–55) is the only other prominent example to come to mind.

2. Roy Newquist, *Conversations with Joan Crawford* (Secaucus, NJ: Citadel Press, 1980), p. 109.

3. Some film stars, like Myrna Loy and Mary Astor, chose to "mature" into character parts. They then competed with veteran character actresses for roles; in Loy's and Astor's case with Fay Bainter, Spring Byington, Selena Royle and other portrayers of middle-class motherhood at MGM and elsewhere. For stage stars, on the other hand, like Alice Brady, Billie Burke, Laura Hope Crews, and even Ethel Barrymore, Hollywood films became a way to finish their careers in the style to which they had grown accustomed.

4. See James McCourt, *Queer Street: Rise and Fall of an American Culture, 1947-1985* (New York: Norton, 2004), p. 502, 504.

5. Rosemarie Jarski, *Hollywood Wit: Classic Off-screen Quips and Quotes* (London: Prion, 2000), p. 101.

6. Ronald L. Davis, *The Glamour Factory: Inside Hollywood's Big Studio System* (Dallas: Southern Methodist University Press, 1993), p. 123.

7. Davis, *The Glamour Factory*, p. 134.

8. Jordan R. Young, *Reel Characters: Great Movie Character Actors* (Beverly Hills, CA: Moonstone Press, 1986), p. 65.

9. Lennox Robinson, *Ireland's Abbey Theatre: A History, 1899-1951* (Port Washington, NY: Kennikat Press, 1968), p. 189.

10. John Parker, *Who's Who in the Theatre: A Biographical Record of the Contemporary Stage* (7th ed.; London: Pitman, 1933), p. 187.

11. "Sara Allgood Dies: Stage, Screen Star," *New York Times* (Sept. 14, 1950), p. 31.

12. E.H. Mikhail, ed., *The Abbey Theatre: Interviews and Recollections* (Basingstoke: Macmillan, 1988), p. 81.

13. The sisters were in four films together between 1930 and 1940, the most important being *Juno and the Paycock* (1930), where O'Neill played Mrs. Madigan in her screen debut. O'Neill would work in British films until her death.

14. Parker, *Who's Who in the Theatre*, p. 187.

15. Parker, p. 187; Robinson, *Ireland's Abbey Theatre*, p. 190.

16. Parker, p. 187; Mikhail, *The Abbey Theatre*, p. 18.

17. Parker, p. 187; www.imdb.com.

18. Mikhail, *The Abbey Theatre*, p. 81.

19. Mikhail, p. xii.

20. Parker, *Who's Who in the Theatre*, p. 187; "Sara Allgood Dies," p. 31.

21. "Sara Allgood Dies," p. 31.

22. Mikhail, *The Abbey Theatre*, p. 90.

23. Allgood had a lookalike in Kate Price (1872–1943), born in Cork, Ireland and dead at Woodland Hills, just like Allgood herself. Price acted in almost two hundred silent films, starting in 1910, but only did a dozen or so sound films, including *Ladies of the Jury* and *Princess O'Rourke*. She retired three years before Allgood arrived in Hollywood.

24. Ronald L. Davis, *John Ford: Hollywood's Old Master* (Norman and London: University of Oklahoma Press, 1995), p. 161; Scott Eyman, *Print the Legend: The Life and Times of John Ford* (Baltimore: Johns Hopkins University Press, 2000), p. 38, 236, 239.

25. David Quinlan, *Quinlan's Illustrated Directory of Film Character Actors* (2nd ed.; London: B.T. Batsford, 1995), p. 16.

26. Daniel Blum, *Great Stars of the American Stage: A Pictorial Record* (New York: Greenburg, 1952), n. pag. (Profile 98).

27. Quoted in Axel Madsen, *The Sewing Circle: Sappho's Leading Ladies* (New York: Kensington Books, 2002), p. 119.

28. Faye E. Head, "Judith Anderson," *Notable Women in the American Theatre: A Biographical Dictionary*, ed. Alice M. Robinson et al. (New York: Greenwood, 1989), p. 20.

29. On the early life and career of Judith Anderson, see Blum, *Great Stars*, Profile 98; Eric Johns, *Dames of the Theatre* (London: W.H. Allen, 1974), pp. 117–18; Head, "Judith Anderson," p. 20; Eric Pace, "Dame Judith Anderson Dies at 93; An Actress of Powerful Portrayals," *New York Times* (January 4, 1992), p. 27.

30. Johns, *Dames*, p. 117.

31. Johns, p. 117; Head, "Judith Anderson," p. 21.

32. In her last show on Broadway, Anderson would play the nurse to Zoe Caldwell's Medea in the 1982 revival at the Cort Theatre. I'll be darned, if she wasn't Tony-nominated for that role too! Anderson's nurse in the 1947-48 production had been the legendary Florence Reed (1883-1967), creator of Mother Goddam in *The Shanghai Gesture* on Broadway in 1926.

33. Head, "Judith Anderson," p. 22.

34. Anderson got the role of Mrs. Danvers in competition with Alla Nazimova and Flora Robson (Rudy Behlmer, ed., *Memo from David O. Selznick* [New York: Viking, 1972], p. 257).

35. In his introduction to the 1995 Republic Pictures Home Video re-release of the film.

36. Charles Higham and Joel Greenberg, *Hollywood in the Forties* (New York: A.S. Barnes, 1968), p. 135.

37. Anderson had also run afoul of Stanwyck four years earlier in *The Strange Love of Martha Ivers* (L. Milestone, 1946). There she plays Stanwyck's evil aunt, who is struck over the head by her niece in a blackout and rolls down the stairs to her death.

38. Rosemarie Jarski, *Hollywood Wit: Classic Off-screen Quips and Quotes* (London: Prion, 2000), p. 257.

39. Boze Hadleigh, *Hollywood Lesbians* (New York: Barricade Books, 1994), p. 162, 173, 176. William J. Mann, author of *Behind the Screen: How Gays and Lesbians Shaped Hollywood, 1910-1969* (New York: Viking, 2001), reports, "None of the gay survivors interviewed recalled ever having met or heard stories about Anderson" (p. 136).

40. Hadleigh, p. 173.

41. Pace, "Dame Judith Anderson," p. 27.

42. For information on Bainter's early career, see John Parker, *Who's Who in the Theatre: A Biographical Record of the Contemporary Stage* (7th ed.; London: Pitman, 1933), pp. 224–25; Daniel Blum, *Great Stars of the American Stage: A Pictorial Record* (New York: Greenberg, 1952), n. pag. (Profile 91); "Fay Bainter, Actress, Dies at 74; Won Academy Award in 1939," *New York Times* (April 17, 1968), p. 47; James Robert Parish and Ronald L. Bowers, *The MGM Stock Company: The Golden Era* (New York: Bonanza Books, 1972), p. 46.

43. David Ragan, *Who's Who in Hollywood, 1900-1976* (New Rochelle, NY: Arlington House, 1977), p. 547.

44. James McCourt, *Queer Street: Rise and Fall of an American Culture, 1947-1985* (New York: Norton, 2004), p. 504.

45. See Parish and Bowers, *The MGM Stock Company*, p. 47, note. Repeated in James Robert Parish, *The RKO Gals* (New Rochelle, NY: Arlington House, 1974), p. 132.

46. Bette Davis, *The Lonely Life: An Autobiography* (London: Macdonald, 1963), p. 176.

47. Frank Capra, *The Name Above the Title* (New York: Vintage, 1985), p. 243.

48. Bosley Crowther, "The Screen: New *Children's Hour*: Another Film Version of Play Arrives; Shirley MacLaine and Audrey Hepburn Star," *New York Times* (March 15, 1962), p. 28.

49. John Springer and Jack Hamilton, *They Had Faces Then: Super Stars, Stars and Starlets of the 1930's* (N.p.: Castle, 1974), p. 271.

50. Ethel Barrymore, *Memories: An Autobiography by Ethel Barrymore* (London: Hulton Press, 1956), p. 204, 206.

51. Margot Peters, *The House of Barrymore* (New York: Alfred A. Knopf, 1990), p. 490.

52. Peters, p. 515.

53. William Roerick, "Remembering Ethel Barrymore and Others," *Performing Arts Resources*, ed. Barbara Naomi Cohen-Stratyner (New York: Theatre Library Ass., 1988), p. 57.

54. Daniel Blum, *Great Stars of the American Stage: A Pictorial Record* (New York: Greenburg, 1952), n. pag. (Profile 56); "Ethel Barrymore Is Dead at 79; One of Stage's 'Royal Family,'" *New York Times* (June 19, 1959), p. 25.

55. Barrymore, *Memories*, p. 120.

56. Barrymore, p. 97.

57. Peters, *The House of Barrymore*, p. 277.

58. Blum, *Great Stars of the American Stage*, n.pag.

59. Barrymore, *Memories*; Peters, *The House of Barrymore*.

60. On Barrymore's alcoholism, see Roerick, "Remembering Ethel Barrymore," p. 58; Peters, *The House of Barrymore*, passim.

61. Peters, p. 332, 429.

62. Catherine B. McGovern and Alice McDonnell Robinson, "Ethel Barrymore," *Notable Women in the American Theatre: A Biographical Dictionary*, ed. Alice M. Robinson et al. (New York: Greenwood, 1989), p. 52.

63. McGovern and Robinson, p. 52.

64. "Ethel Barrymore Is Dead," p. 25.

65. Peters, *The House of Barrymore*, p. 430.

66. Peters, p. 436.

67. Barrymore, *Memories*, p. 204.

68. This was one of only two films directed by Odets. Needless to say, the playwright of the proletariat and the Group Theatre never directed or wrote for Barrymore on Broadway.

69. Charles Higham and Roy Moseley, *Cary Grant: The Lonely Heart* (New York: Avon, 1989), p. 180.

70. Peters, *The House of Barrymore*, p. 473.

71. Not all oldtimers were willing or able to adapt their performances to the requirements of a new medium. Gavin Lambert relates, for example, that the legendary English stage star Mrs. Patrick Campbell "overacted badly on and off camera": "The famous stage actress, who openly despised the movies, refused to learn anything about screen technique ... and paid for it in the cutting room." The star of *Riptide* (1934), Norma Shearer, told him that two of Mrs. Pat's scenes ended up on the cutting room floor. (Gavin Lambert, *Norma Shearer: A Life* [New York: Alfred A. Knopf, 1990], p. 202, 303–04; see also Margot Peters, *Mrs. Pat: The Life of Mrs. Patrick Campbell* [New York: Alfred A. Knopf, 1984], p. 426.)

72. Bosley Crowther, "*The Spiral Staircase*," *New York Times* (Feb. 7, 1946), p. 35.

73. Peters, *The House of Barrymore*, p. 487.

74. Elia Kazan, *A Life* (London: Andre Deutsch, 1988), p. 375.

75. Peters, *The House of Barrymore*, p. 487.

76. Peters, p. 508.

77. Peters, p. 345.

78. www.imdb.com; Peters, p. 342.

79. Peters, p. 345.

80. Peters, p. 343.

81. Peters, p. 345.

82. James Robert Parish and Ronald L. Bowers, *The MGM Stock Company: The Golden Era* (New York: Bonanza Books, 1972), p. 57.

83. This according to John Parker, *Who's Who in the Theatre: A Biographical Record of the Contemporary Stage* (7th ed.; London: Pitman, 1933), p. 236. www.ibdb.com has no information on this production, but Margot Peters includes it in her chronology (Peters, *The House of Barrymore*, p. 535).

84. The last show at the Empire was Arthur Laurents' prize-winning play *The Time of the Cuckoo*, starring Shirley Booth (who also appears in *From Main Street to Broadway*). The play formed the basis for *Summertime* (1955) with Katharine Hepburn and Rossano Brazzi.

85. Barrymore, *Memories*, p. 211.

86. Peters, *The House of Barrymore*, p. 516.

87. "Ethel Barrymore Is Dead," p. 25.

88. "Ethel Barrymore Is Dead," p. 25.

89. Frank S. Nugent, "*Rebecca*," *New York Times* (March 29, 1940), p. 28.

90. David Quinlan, *Quinlan's Illustrated Directory of Film Character Actors* (2nd ed.; London: B.T. Batsford, 1995), p. 34.

91. DeWitt Bodeen, *More from Hollywood!* (South Brunswick and New York: A.S. Barnes, 1977), p. 268.

92. Bodeen, p. 271.

93. For information on Bates's life before she went into

the movies, see "Florence Bates, 65, Character Actress," *New York Times* (Feb. 1, 1954), p. 23; Bodeen, *More from Hollywood!*, pp. 265–74.

94. Donald Bogle, *Toms, Coons, Mulattoes, Mammies, and Bucks: An Interpretive History of Blacks in American Films* (New York: Bantam, 1974), p. 86.

95. Bogle, p. 86.

96. Rudy Behlmer, ed., *Memo from David O. Selznick* (New York: Viking, 1972), p. 181; Carlton Jackson, *Hattie: The Life of Hattie McDaniel* (Lanham, NY: Madison Books, 1990), p. 34.

97. Donald Bogle, *Blacks in American Films and Television: An Encyclopedia* (New York and London: Garland, 1988), p. 358.

98. Jill Watts, *Hattie McDaniel: Black Ambition, White Hollywood* (New York: Amistad, 2005), p. 105.

99. Bogle, *Toms, Coons, Mulattoes*, p. 81.

100. Bogle, p. 82, 86.

101. Bogle, *Blacks in American Film*, p. 114.

102. Bogle, *Toms, Coons, Mulattoes*, p. 92.

103. Bogle, *Blacks in American Film*, p. 113.

104. James Robert Parish and William T. Leonard, *Hollywood Players: The Thirties* (New Rochelle, NY: Arlington House, 1976), p. 72. Jill Watts records that the Hays Office's chief censor, Joseph Breen, also insisted that the word be excised from the film (Watts, *Hattie McDaniel*, p. 107).

105. See Bogle, *Blacks in American Film*, p. 114.

106. Bogle, *Toms, Coons, and Mulattoes*, p. 87; Parish and Leonard, *Hollywood Players*, p. 70; Watts, *Hattie McDaniel*, p. 95.

107. Thomas Cripps, *Slow Fade to Black: The Negro in American Film, 1900-1942* (New York: Oxford University Press, 1977), p. 109.

108. Cripps, p. 109.

109. "Louise Beavers, Actress, 60; Starred in *Beulah* TV Series," *New York Times* (Oct. 27, 1962), p. 25.

110. Parish and Leonard, *Hollywood Players*, p. 66, 68; Watts, *Hattie McDaniel*, p. 94.

111. Quoted in Parish and Leonard, p. 66.

112. Cripps, *Slow Fade to Black*, p. 292.

113. Parish and Leonard, *Hollywood Players*, p. 72.

114. The film was directed by Lowell Sherman, the man who plays the producer Max Carey in *What Price Hollywood?* Beavers tries to get into the movies by singing to him and he pulls her into a swimming pool. Towards the end of her life, Beavers was reunited with Mae West in the latter's Las Vegas night club act (Bogle, *Toms, Coons, Mulattoes*, p. 92).

115. Apparently Beavers was the only person at Paramount who was not afraid of Cecil B. DeMille (Parish and Leonard, *Hollywood Players*, p. 66). This was the only time he directed Beavers.

116. "Louise Beavers," p. 25.

117. Bogle, *Toms, Coons, and Mulattoes*, p. 86.

118. Parish and Leonard, *Hollywood Players*, p. 73.

119. Parish and Leonard, p. 69.

120. Parish and Leonard, p. 69; Watts, *Hattie McDaniel*, p. 303 n. 36.

121. Parish and Leonard, p. 73.

122. For information on Boland's early life and career, see "Mary Boland, 83, Actress, Is Dead," *New York Times* (June 24, 1965), p. 35; James Robert Parish and William T. Leonard, *The Funsters* (New Rochelle, NY: Arlington House, 1979), pp. 111–19; Ronald H. Wainscot, "Mary Boland," *Notable Women in the American Theatre: A Biographical Dictionary*, ed. Alice M. Robinson et al. (New York: Greenwood, 1989), pp. 74–76.

123. See Parish and Leonard, *The Funsters*, p. 115.

124. Rosalind Russell, with Chris Chase, *Life Is a Banquet* (New York: Ace Books, 1979), pp. 115–16. Russell lived in Boland's Beverly Hills house until her death in 1976.

125. Mary Astor, *Mary Astor: A Life on Film* (New York: Delacorte Press, 1971), p. 107.

126. Katharine Hepburn, *Me: Stories of My Life* (New York: Alfred A. Knopf, 1991), p. 76, 78, 417.

127. Parish and Leonard, *The Funsters*, p. 115. Parish and Leonard observe that Boland belonged to a generation of stage actresses trained to stay out of society. Boland herself said, "The height of my social gaiety is an evening at bridge." (See *The Funsters*, p. 115.)

128. Parish and Leonard, p. 114.

129. John Springer and Jack Hamilton, *They Had Faces Then: Super Stars, Stars and Starlets of the 1930's* (N.p.: Castle, 1974), p. 34.

130. Roy Newquist, *Conversations with Joan Crawford* (Secaucus, NJ: Citadel Press, 1980), p. 84.

131. Bosley Crowther, "The Screen in Review: *Pride and Prejudice*," *New York Times* (Aug. 9, 1940), p. 19.

132. Ronald H. Wainscot, "Mary Boland," p. 75; "Mary Boland," p. 35.

133. Daniel Blum, *Great Stars of the American Stage: A Pictorial Record* (New York: Greenburg, 1952), n. pag. (Profile 76).

134. "Mary Boland," p. 35.

135. Parish and Leonard, *The Funsters*, p. 119.

136. James Robert Parish, *Hollywood Character Actors* (New Rochelle, NY: Arlington House, 1978), p. 75.

137. Jordan R. Young, *Reel Characters: Great Movie Character Actors* (Beverly Hills, CA: Moonstone Press, 1986), p. 57.

138. See Young, *Reel Characters*, p. 57, the best source of information on Bondi's early years. A Valparaiso friend of the actress, Allegra Nesbit, explained in an interview that Bondi changed the final vowel of her surname, "because she thought the 'i' made it more 'stagey' and it allowed all of the letters to fit above the line on theater marquees" (see Phil Potempa, "The Beloved Mother: Beulah Bondi," in *It's a Wonderful Life: A Memory Book* by Stephen Cox [Nashville, TN: Cumberland House, 2003], pp. 62–63). I would proffer the additional explanation that Bondi might have wanted her name to look less Jewish. In retrospect, we can see that character actresses of Jewish origin were rare in Hollywood. One of the few others to have a successful career, Florence Rabe, changed her name to Florence Bates.

139. Tab Hunter with Eddie Muller, *Tab Hunter Confidential: The Making of a Movie Star* (Chapel Hill, NC: Algonquin Books of Chapel Hill, 2005), p. 98.

140. For the record, the roles were in the films *Of Human Hearts* (1938), *Vivacious Lady* (1938), *Mr. Smith Goes to Washington* (1939), and *It's a Wonderful Life* (1946), plus an episode of the short-lived *The Jimmy Stewart Show* (1971–72). Stewart was also with Bondi in *The Gorgeous Hussy* (1936), but in what must have been an egregious casting error did not play her son on that occasion.

141. See Young, *Reel Characters*, p. 63, 65. According to Young, Bondi put this casting decision down to the fact that Darwell was a contract player and would have cost less money. One might also point out, that while Bondi had only made one film at Twentieth Century–Fox, Darwell had made no less than forty. Scott Eyman explains that the director of the film, John Ford, "wanted something more expansive and more of an earth-mother" and suggested they use Darwell rather than Bondi (Scott Eyman, *Print the Legend: The Life and Times of John Ford* [Baltimore: Johns Hopkins University Press, 2000], p. 216).

142. For an extended discussion of *Make Way for Tomorrow*, including the line just quoted (from p. 191), see Eliza-

beth Kendall, *The Runaway Bride: Hollywood Romantic Comedy of the 1930s* (New York: Alfred A. Knopf, 1990), pp. 191–93.

143. See Kendall, p. 193.

144. Switzer was shot dead five years and seven films later in a conflict over money.

145. Richard Lamparski, *Whatever Became Of...? Eighth Series* (New York: Crown, 1982), p. 33.

146. Lamparski, p. 33.

147. As fate would have it, another fine character actress, Isobel Elsom, also died at Woodland Hills that day. She and Bondi never acted together on film. For information on Bondi's final years, see Jordan R. Young's interesting article in his *Reel Characters*, pp. 57–65.

148. On her near-sightedness and speech impediment, see DeWitt Bodeen, *From Hollywood* (South Brunswick and New York: A.S. Barnes, 1976), p. 190.

149. John Parker, *Who's Who in the Theatre: A Biographical Record of the Contemporary Stage* (7th ed.; London: Pitman, 1933), p. 286; "Alice Brady Dead; Stage, Film Star," *New York Times* (Oct. 30, 1939), p. 17.

150. Bodeen, *From Hollywood*, p. 188.

151. Bodeen, p. 188.

152. "Alice Brady Dead," p. 17; John Springer and Jack Hamilton, *They Had Faces Then: Super Stars, Stars and Starlets of the 1930's* (N.p.: Castle, 1974), p. 275. DeWitt Bodeen claims Brady never even read the script (Bodeen, *From Hollywood*, p. 193).

153. Arthur Hobson Quinn, *A History of the American Drama from the Civil War to the Present Day* (Rev. ed.; New York: F.S. Crofts, 1945), p. 257.

154. Bodeen, *From Hollywood*, p. 194.

155. James Kotsilibas-Davis and Myrna Loy, *Being and Becoming* (New York: Donald I. Fine/Primus, 1988), p. 82.

156. "Alice Brady Dead," p. 17; Bodeen, *From Hollywood*, p. 196.

157. Bodeen, p. 197.

158. Bodeen, p. 195.

159. Springer and Hamilton, *They Had Faces Then*, p. 275; Bodeen, p. 192.

160. Bodeen, p. 193.

161. Information on Brady's final weeks, death, and burial from "Alice Brady Dead," p. 17.

162. The one possible exception is Ethel Barrymore. The 1930 film *The Royal Family of Broadway* was based on a play by George S. Kaufman and Edna Ferber inspired by the Barrymore acting dynasty. Mrs. Fanny Cavendish (Henrietta Crosman) is based on Barrymore's maternal grandmother, Mrs. John Drew. Ina Claire plays the Ethel Barrymore character, Julie Cavendish.

163. Billie Burke with Cameron Shipp, *With a Feather On My Nose* (New York: Appleton-Century-Crofts, 1949), p. 250.

164. James Kotsilibas-Davis and Myrna Loy, *Myrna Loy: Being and Becoming* (New York: Donald I. Fine/Primus, 1987), pp. 125–26. Burke claimed herself not to have seen the film until 1960 (Billie Burke with Cameron Shipp, *With Powder On My Nose* [London: Peter Davies, 1960], p. 37).

165. Rosalind Russell with Chris Chase, *Life Is a Banquet* (New York: Ace Books, 1979), p. 61.

166. "Billie Burke Dead; Movie Comedienne," *New York Times* (May 16, 1970), p. 1 and 25.

167. Burke and Shipp, *With a Feather On My Nose*, p. 250.

168. James Robert Parish and Ronald L. Bowers, *The MGM Stock Company: The Golden Era* (New York: Bonanza Books, 1972), p. 98.

169. Burke and Shipp, *With a Feather On My Nose*, p. 17.

170. The year 1884 is given on her gravestone and in the Social Security Death Index. In *With a Feather On My Nose* (1949), Burke "admitted" to being born in 1885 (Burke and Shipp, p. 29), but by the time of writing *With Powder On My Nose* (1960), she gave her year of birth as 1886 (Burke and Shipp, p. 184).

171. Burke and Shipp, *With a Feather On My Nose*, p. 8, 16.

172. Randolph Carter, *Ziegfeld: The Time of His Life* (London: Bernard Press, 1988), p. 45.

173. Burke and Shipp, *With a Feather On My Nose*, p. 222.

174. Burke and Shipp, p. 253.

175. Burke and Shipp, *With Powder On My Nose*, p. 58.

176. Donald Spoto, "Billie Burke: The Wizard of Oz's Good Witch in Beverly Hills," *Architectural Digest* 53 (1996), p. 262.

177. Spoto, p. 264.

178. Burke and Shipp, *With Powder On My Nose*, p. 15.

179. Burke and Shipp, *With a Feather On My Nose*, p. 82.

180. Burke and Shipp, *With Powder On My Nose*, p. 258.

181. Aljean Harmetz, *The Making of The Wizard of Oz* (New York: Delta, 1989), p. 127.

182. Harmetz, p. 134.

183. Emanuel Levy, *George Cukor, Master of Elegance: Hollywood's Legendary Director and His Stars* (New York: William Morrow, 1994), p. 63.

184. Burke and Shipp, *With a Feather On My Nose*, p. 1, 118.

185. Burke and Shipp, *With Powder On My Nose*, p. 14, 15, 26, 28.

186. Burke and Shipp, p. 202.

187. Levy, *George Cukor*, p. 35, 36.

188. Mordaunt Hall, "A Bill of Divorcement," *New York Times* (Oct. 3, 1932), p. 15.

189. Patrick McGilligan, *George Cukor: A Double Life* (New York: St. Martin's Press, 1991), p. 341; Levy, *George Cukor*, p. 173.

190. Parish and Bowers, *The MGM Stock Company*, p. 99. Rosalind Russell remembered that during the filming of *Craig's Wife*, Burke used "lifts" under her hair to smooth out her forehead (Russell and Chase, *Life Is a Banquet*, p. 239).

191. Parish and Bowers, p. 99.

192. Levy, *George Cukor*, p. 329.

193. For the facts of Byington's early life, career, and marriage, see Richard Lamparski, *Whatever Became Of...? Third Series* (New York: Ace Books, 1970), pp. 78–79; John Springer and Jack Hamilton, *They Had Faces Then: Super Stars, Stars and Starlets of the 1930's* (N.p.: Castle, 1974), p. 277; James Robert Parish, *Hollywood Character Actors* (New Rochelle, NY: Arlington House, 1978), p. 94; Charles Stumpf, "Spring Byington: Eternal Spring," http://www.classicimages.com/2000/june00/byington.shtml, accessed April 28, 2003.

194. Richard Lamparski reveals that Byington was a compromise candidate between producer Merian C. Cooper and the casting director at RKO. Her old boss, Stuart Walker, had recommended her. (Lamparski, *Whatever Became*, p. 78.)

195. Gavin Lambert, *On Cukor* (London and New York: W.H. Allen, 1973), p. 77.

196. Richard Lamparski gives her birth year as 1893 in *Whatever Became*, p. 78, presumably based on information from Byington herself.

197. See James Robert Parish and Ronald L. Bowers, *The MGM Stock Company: The Golden Era* (New York: Bonanza Books, 1972), p. 102.

198. Lambert, *On Cukor*, p. 37.
199. DeCamp reveals in her autobiography *Tigers in My Lap* (Baltimore: MidMar Press, 2000), pp. 131–32, that Byington and DeCamp's father had been "childhood sweethearts" who kept in touch for forty years. In fact, she received word of her father's death from Byington.
200. Novello quoted in Sewell Stokes, *Without Veils: An Intimate Biography of Gladys Cooper* (London: Peter Davies, 1953), p. 1; Merivale and Coward from Sheridan Morley, *Gladys Cooper: A Biography* (London: Book Club Associates, 1979), p. 3, 219, 233.
201. Morley, p. 191, 193.
202. Morley, p. 181.
203. Stokes, *Without Veils*, p. 168.
204. Stokes, p. 18.
205. Gladys Cooper, *Gladys Cooper* (London: Hutchinson, 1931), p. 13; Morley, *Gladys Cooper*, pp. 3–4.
206. Morley, p. 8.
207. Gavin Lambert, *On Cukor* (London and New York: W.H. Allen, 1973), p. 164.
208. Cooper, *Gladys Cooper*, p. 219.
209. She would write in her 1931 autobiography that she regretted never having acted in America: "If I had played there I might—who knows—have got to Hollywood and the films, and that would have been a real experience, whether or not success had been my lot in the pictures" (*Gladys Cooper*, p. 277). Little did she know what fate held in store.
210. Stokes, *Without Veils*, p. 198.
211. Morley, *Gladys Cooper*, pp. 210–11.
212. Morley, p. 214.
213. Morley, p. 211.
214. Quoted in Morley, p. 113.
215. Cooper, *Gladys Cooper*, p. 18.
216. Quoted in Morley, *Gladys Cooper*, p. 266.
217. Alexander Walker, *Vivien: The Life of Vivien Leigh* (London: Weidenfeld and Nicholson, 1987), pp. 64–65, 73, 192.
218. Quoted in Morley, *Gladys Cooper*, p. 203.
219. Morley, p. 206. See also Eric Johns, *Dames of the Theatre* (London: W.H. Allen, 1974), p. 133.
220. Quoted in Morley, p. 204.
221. Stokes, *Without Veils*, p. 170.
222. Charles Higham and Joel Greenberg, *Hollywood in the Forties* (New York: A.S. Barnes, 1968), p. 112.
223. Morley, *Gladys Cooper*, p. 79.
224. Morley, p. 251.
225. Morley, pp. xviii–xix.
226. Morley, p. 228.
227. Quoted in Morley, p. 270.
228. Morley, p. 288.
229. See Lambert, *On Cukor*, p. 75.
230. Bette Davis, *The Lonely Life: An Autobiography* (London: Macdonald, 1963), pp. 68–69, 187. What Davis fails to mention is that they had played together in *The Sisters* in 1938. It is possible she is recalling their reunion in this film, rather than *The Man Who Came to Dinner*.
231. For information on Crews's early life and theater career, see John Parker, *Who's Who in the Theatre: A Biographical Record of the Contemporary Stage* (7th ed.; London: Pitman, 1933), pp. 431–32; "Laura Hope Crews, Actress, 62, Is Dead," *New York Times* (Nov. 14, 1942), p. 15; James T. Nardin, "Laura Hope Crews," *Notable American Women, 1607-1950*, Vol. I (Cambridge, MA: Belknap Press, 1971), pp. 405–06; William Lindesmith, "Laura Hope Crews," *Notable Women in the American Theatre: A Biographical Dictionary*, ed. Alice M. Robinson et al. (New York: Greenwood, 1989), pp. 176–78.
232. See John Springer and Jack Hamilton, *They Had Faces Then: Super Stars, Stars and Starlets of the 1930's* (N.p.: Castle, 1974), p. 72.
233. James Robert Parish, *Hollywood Character Actors* (New Rochelle, NY: Arlington House, 1978), p. 147.
234. John Parker, *Who's Who in the Theatre*, p. 432; "Laura Hope Crews," *New York Times* (Nov. 14, 1942), p. 15. Lana Turner later lived at 730 N. Bedford Drive. It was there on April 5, 1958 that Turner's daughter, Cheryl Crane, ostensibly stabbed and killed her mother's then boyfriend, Johnny Stompanato, though it is possible Turner may have killed him herself. What would Miss Crews have said about such goings-on in her old home?
235. Actually, Burke was only six years younger than Crews. Though she lost the part in *Gone with the Wind*, she of course won an even bigger one in *The Wizard of Oz*. In a funny coincidence, Burke and Crews ended up playing sisters in an unfunny comedy, *Remember?* (N.Z. McLeod, MGM, 1939), starring Robert Taylor, Lew Ayres, and Greer Garson, which was released the day before *Gone with the Wind*.
236. Almira Sessions (1888–1974) was a beady-eyed, beaky, spinsterish type actress in 125 films, including *Presenting Lily Mars* (1943), *The Diary of a Chambermaid* (1946), *It's a Wonderful Life* (1946), *Cass Timberlane* (1947), and *Paris Model* (1953). Nora Cecil (1878–1951) was a hatchet-faced battle-axe extraordinaire, who specialized in delivering doses of concentrated ill will, officiousness, and venom in upward of 200 films from the silent era until 1947, including *Street Scene* (1931), *Night Must Fall* (1937), *Stagecoach* (1939), *The Bank Dick* (1940), *The Thin Man Goes Home* (1944), and *Mourning Becomes Electra* (1947), her final film. Esther Dale (1885–1961) was, like Darwell, much rounder and blander than Sessions and Cecil, though she could be a menace as a rolling pin–wielding cook or a butch number in a suit and tie. Her more than one hundred films between 1934 and 1960 included *Curly Top* (1935), *The Case Against Mrs. Ames* (1936), *The Awful Truth* (1937), *Made for Each Other* (1939), *The Women* (1939), *The Mortal Storm* (1940), *Old Acquaintance* (1943), and *The Egg and I* (1947; and three more Ma and Pa Kettle films). Finally, sad-eyed Emma Dunn (1875–1966) was the essence of meek and mild as countless maids and mothers in films like *Hell's House* (1932), *The Wet Parade* (1932), *Letty Lynton* (1932), *Mr. Deeds Goes to Town* (1936), *Madame X* (1937), *The Cowboy and the Lady* (1938), *Life with Father* (1947), *The Woman in White* (1948), and the Dr. Kildare series.
237. In *Child of Manhattan*, Darwell is Nancy Carroll's stern Irish mother, who throws her daughter out of the house when she finds out what she's been getting up to with wealthy aristocrat John Boles. Darwell's role in *Only Yesterday* was not dissimilar, only to make matters worse, this time her pregnant daughter (Margaret Sullavan in her first film role) is unwed and Darwell has to pack her off to an open-minded aunt in New York City (Billie Burke). The culprit was the same: John Boles. In *Finishing School*, Darwell plays a stern nurse at the hospital where hero Bruce Cabot is an intern. In *Private Number* she is the forceful cook, Mrs. Meecham, perpetually at daggers drawn with the butler over authority. Her part in *Craig's Wife*, the second of three filmatizations of the George Kelly hit play, was somewhat more substantial. She plays Mrs. Harold, the Craigs' forthright housekeeper, who quits when Rosalind Russell begins to go ballistic and goes off on a trip around the world as Alma Kruger's companion. In *The Rains Came*, she was the crusty, hearty wife of preacher Henry Travers. Finally in the lesbian-inflected prison classic *Caged*, Darwell plays a butch matron in the isolation ward.
238. "Jane Darwell, 87, Actress, Is Dead," *New York Times*

(Aug. 15, 1967), p. 35. This source and several others, including www.imdb.com, give Darwell's original surname as Woodward, but her gravestone is inscribed Woodard and one must assume that that is correct. In fact, Darwell's *New York Times* obituary may be the original source of the mistaken spelling of her last name. Like Marjorie Main (*née* Mary Tomlinson), Darwell used a stage name so as not to bring shame on her family through her choice of career, which did not meet with her family's approval (see www.imdb.com).

239. One year younger than Darwell, Blandick was a recent arrival in Hollywood too, though she already had eight films under her belt. They would make six films together, including reprising their roles in *Huckleberry Finn* (N. Taurog, Paramount, 1931), though not necessarily sharing any scenes. Blandick retired in 1950, having made more than one hundred films.

240. "Jane Darwell," p. 39.

241. Jordan R. Young, *Reel Characters: Great Movie Character Actors* (Beverly Hills, CA: Moonstone Press, 1986), p. 63, 65.

242. Scott Eyman, *Print the Legend: The Life and Times of John Ford* (Baltimore: Johns Hopkins University Press, 2000), p. 216.

243. Eyman, p. 220.

244. Eyman, p. 141.

245. "Jane Darwell," p. 39.

246. Elia Kazan, *A Life* (London: Andre Deutsch, 1988), p. 598.

247. For information on Dunnock's early life and stage career, see Stacy A. Rozek, "Mildred Margaret Dunnock," *Notable Women in the American Theatre: A Biographical Dictionary*, ed. Alice M. Robinson et al. (New York: Greenwood, 1989), pp. 243–46.

248. Bosley Crowther, "The Screen: Four New Movies Open," *New York Times* (Dec. 21, 1951), p. 21.

249. Tennessee Williams, *Memoirs* (Garden City, NY: Anchor Press/Doubleday, 1983), p. 160.

250. Bosley Crowther, "Screen: Court Melodrama by Odets," *New York Times* (Jan. 14, 1960), p. 28.

251. Janet Maslin, "Film: *Pickup Artist*, From James Toback," *New York Times* (Sept. 18, 1987), p. C21.

252. Eric Pace, "Mildred Dunnock, 90, Acclaimed As Broadway's First Mrs. Loman," *New York Times* (July 7, 1991), p. 18.

253. Information on Gladys George's early life is scant. See "Gladys George, 50, Actress, Is Dead," *New York Times* (Dec. 9, 1954), p. 40; John Springer and Jack Hamilton, *They Had Faces Then: Super Stars, Stars and Starlets of the 1930's* (N.p.: Castle, 1974), p. 296.

254. Alex Barris, *Hollywood's Other Women* (South Brunswick and New York: A.S. Barnes, 1975), p. 122.

255. David Quinlan, *Quinlan's Illustrated Directory of Film Character Actors* (2nd ed.; London: B.T. Batsford, 1995,), p. 135.

256. Details on George's final illness, death and funeral from "Gladys George, 50, Actress, Is Dead," p. 40; "Gladys George Rites Set," *New York Times* (Dec. 10, 1954), p. 28.

257. Boze Hadleigh, *Leading Ladies* (London: Robson Books, 1992), p. 100.

258. In her autobiography from 1983, Lanchester writes that she is flattered to be still recognizable in a part she played in the 1930s (Elsa Lanchester, *Elsa Lanchester: Herself* [New York: St. Martin's, 1983], p. 137).

259. www.imdb.com.

260. John Parker, *Who's Who in the Theatre: A Biographical Record of the Contemporary Stage* (7th ed.; London: Pitman, 1933), p. 835.

261. On the unconventional relationship between Lanchester's parents, see Lanchester, *Elsa Lanchester*, p. 2, 4.

262. Lanchester, p. 14, 17.

263. Lanchester, p. 9.

264. Lanchester, p. 51, 58, 68.

265. Lanchester, p. 77, 106.

266. Lanchester, p. 79.

267. Simon Callow, *Charles Laughton: A Difficult Actor* (London: Vintage, 1995), p. 21.

268. Lanchester, *Elsa Lanchester*, p. 54, 56, 58, 133.

269. Lanchester, p. 45, 51.

270. Lanchester, p. 152.

271. Callow, *Charles Laughton*, p. 281.

272. Callow, p. 281.

273. Lanchester, *Elsa Lanchester*, p. 89.

274. Lanchester, p. 97; Callow, *Charles Laughton*, p. 158.

275. Lanchester, p. 126.

276. "Elsa Lanchester, 84, Is Dead; Actress Portrayed Eccentrics," *New York Times* (Dec. 27, 1986), p. 16.

277. Quoted in Lanchester, *Elsa Lanchester*, p. 55.

278. Hadleigh, *Leading Ladies*, p. 86.

279. Lanchester, *Elsa Lanchester*, p. 126, 127.

280. Lanchester, p. 216.

281. Lanchester, p. 145.

282. Lanchester, p. 119.

283. Lanchester, p. 118.

284. Hadleigh, *Leading Ladies*, p. 186.

285. Hadleigh, p. 185.

286. Hadleigh, p. 98.

287. Hadleigh, p. 196.

288. Lanchester, *Elsa Lanchester*, p. 278, 303.

289. Lanchester, p. 315.

290. Hadleigh, *Leading Ladies*, p. 91.

291. Lanchester, *Elsa Lanchester*, p. 271.

292. Lanchester, p. 311; Hadleigh, *Leading Ladies*, p. 100.

293. Jessie Royce Landis, *You Won't Be So Pretty (But You'll Know More)* (London: W.H. Allen, 1954), pp. 107–09.

294. Landis, pp. 218–19.

295. Biographical facts in this paragraph from Landis, pp. 39–45.

296. Landis, p. 54, 55, 57.

297. Landis, p. 117.

298. Quoted in Landis, 112.

299. Landis, p. 228.

300. The original 1941–42 Broadway production had starred Cornelia Otis Skinner. The play was filmed in 2004 with Annette Bening in Landis's role as leading lady Julia Lambert.

301. Landis, *You Won't Be So Pretty*, p. 228.

302. Landis, p. 142.

303. Landis, p. 34, 251–52.

304. Landis, pp. 244–50.

305. On McDaniel's suicide attempt in the late forties, see Carlton Jackson, *Hattie: The Life of Hattie McDaniel* (Lanham, NY: Madison Books, 1990), p. 146. McDaniel's most recent biographer, Jill Watts, does not refer to a specific suicide attempt in her thoroughgoing *Hattie McDaniel: Black Ambition, White Hollywood* (New York: Amistad, 2005), but notes that "after learning there would be no baby, Hattie McDaniel fell into deep despair; she withdrew from the public eye and even spoke of ending her life" (p. 234).

306. Watts, p. 281.

307. Donald Bogle, *Toms, Coons, Mulattoes, Mammies, and Bucks: An Interpretive History of Blacks in American Films* (New York: Bantam, 1974), p. 115.

308. McDaniel's Oscar, which she willed to Howard University, has been lost (Jackson, *Hattie*, p. 54; Watts, *Hattie McDaniel*, p. 277).

309. John Springer and Jack Hamilton, *They Had Faces Then: Super Stars, Stars and Starlets of the 1930's* (N.p.: Castle, 1974), p. 27.
310. Bogle, *Toms, Coons, Mulattoes*, p. 125.
311. Watts, *Hattie McDaniel*, p. 17. A meticulous researcher, Jill Watts revises McDaniel's commonly accepted birth year of 1895 based on the Kansas State Census of 1895.
312. Watts, p. 19.
313. Watts, p. 32.
314. Watts, p. 36.
315. Watts, p. 55. McDaniel did not divorce Lankfard until 1938 (Watts, p. 128). She was fated never to have a successful marriage, though she made two further attempts. She was married to James Lloyd Crawford between 1941 and 1945 (Watts, *Hattie McDaniel*, p. 201, 236–37). Her final wedding was to interior decorator Larry Williams and took place on June 11, 1949. Again, the marriage began to fail almost immediately. McDaniel filed for divorce in December 1950. She was fond of gay men and Williams may have been homosexual. McDaniel herself is rumored to have been bisexual. (See Jackson, *Hattie*, p. 134; William J. Mann, *Behind the Screen: How Gays and Lesbians Shaped Hollywood, 1910-1969* [New York: Viking, 2001], p. 81; Watts, *Hattie McDaniel*, pp. 259–61.)
316. Watts, p. 58.
317. Jackson, *Hattie*, p. 13; Watts, pp. 60–61.
318. Jackson, p. 19; Watts, *Hattie McDaniel*, p. 54, 61, 79–80.
319. "Hattie M'Daniel [sic], Beulah of Radio," *New York Times* (Oct. 27, 1952), p. 27; Jackson, *Hattie*, p. 19; Watts, p. 75.
320. Jackson, p. 74.
321. In fact, this glimpse is so brief, it is impossible to be certain that this is indeed McDaniel.
322. Donald Bogle, *Blacks in American Films and Television: An Encyclopedia* (New York and London: Garland, 1988), p. 416.
323. Watts, *Hattie McDaniel*, pp. 98–99.
324. Bogle, *Blacks in American Films*, p. 416.
325. Watts, *Hattie McDaniel*, p. 222.
326. Anderson was a studio service attendant at Warner Bros. and went back to being one (Jackson, *Hattie*, p. 80).
327. Jackson, p. 12, 14; Watts, *Hattie McDaniel*, p. 62. McDaniel also became known in the early 1930s as "Hi Hat Hattie" after she showed up for a radio broadcast in an elegant evening gown (Watts, p. 89).
328. Frank S. Nugent, "Gone with the Wind," *New York Times* (Dec. 20, 1939), p. 31.
329. Jackson, *Hattie*, p. xi.
330. Rudy Behlmer, ed., *Memo from David O. Selznick* (New York: Viking, 1972), p. 181; Watts, *Hattie McDaniel*, p. 151.
331. Jackson, *Hattie*, p. 35; Watts, p. 150, 151.
332. Jackson, p. 34.
333. Bogle, *Blacks in American Films*, p. 416.
334. Bogle, p. 95.
335. Jackson, *Hattie*, p. 37; Watts, *Hattie McDaniel*, p. 152.
336. Bogle, *Toms, Coons, Mulattoes*, pp. 127–28.
337. While claiming that in the role of Tempy, McDaniel "came the closest she had in years to echoing the parts she had played earlier in her film career" and "could resurrect at least some of the elements of Mammy of *Gone with the Wind*," Jill Watts also observes that "Tempy is one-dimensional and has absolutely no power" (Watts, *Hattie McDaniel*, p. 247).
338. Bogle, *Toms, Coons, Mulattoes*, p. 128.
339. Jackson, *Hattie*, p. 121; Watts, *Hattie McDaniel*, p. 253.
340. Jackson, p. 140; Watts, p. 267.
341. Jackson, p. 151.
342. Jackson, p. 152; Watts, *Hattie McDaniel*, p. 271.
343. Watts, p. 274.
344. For a description of McQueen's various non-acting jobs, see Richard Lamparski, *Whatever Became Of...?* (New York: Crown, 1968), p. 97; Lizette Alvarez, "Butterfly McQueen Dies at 84; Played Scarlett O'Hara's Maid," *New York Times* (Dec. 23, 1995), p. 28.
345. Donald Bogle, *Blacks in American Films and Television: An Encyclopedia* (New York and London: Garland, 1988), p. 420.
346. Lamparski, *Whatever Became*, pp. 96–97.
347. Alvarez, "Butterfly McQueen," p. 28.
348. Bogle, *Blacks in American Films*, p. 420.
349. Donald Bogle, *Toms, Coons, Mulattoes, Mammies, and Bucks: An Interpretive History of Blacks in American Films* (New York: Bantam, 1974), p. 127.
350. Bogle, p. 130.
351. Bogle, *Blacks in American Films*, p. 421.
352. Ken D. Jones, Arthur F. McClure, and Alfred E. Twomey, *Character People* (South Brunswick and New York: A.S. Barnes, 1976), p. 139.
353. Lamparski, *Whatever Became*, p. 96.
354. Lamparski, p. 96; John Springer and Jack Hamilton, *They Had Faces Then: Super Stars, Stars and Starlets of the 1930's* (N.p.: Castle, 1974), p. 315; Alvarez, "Butterfly McQueen," p. 28.
355. www.imdb.com.
356. Lamparski, *Whatever Became*, p. 96.
357. John Baxter, *Hollywood in the Thirties* (London: A. Zwemmer, 1968), p. 30; Gavin Lambert, *On Cukor* (London and New York: W.H. Allen, 1973), p. 89.
358. Bogle, *Blacks in American Films*, p. 95.
359. Frank S. Nugent, "Gone with the Wind," *New York Times* (Dec. 20, 1939), p. 31.
360. Bogle suggests that it may have been at least partly due to her own temperament, observing that "she was a hard cookie to cast" (*Black in American Films*, p. 421).
361. Lamparski, *Whatever Became*, p. 96; Springer and Hamilton, *They Had Faces Then*, pp. 315–16.
362. Alvarez, "Butterfly McQueen," p. 28.
363. Alvarez, p. 28.
364. Vincent Canby, "*The Mosquito Coast*," *New York Times* (Nov. 26, 1986), www.nyt.com, accessed Sept. 30, 2005. This was the most review space the *New York Times* ever devoted to Butterfly McQueen.
365. www.imdb.com.
366. www.imdb.com.
367. Information in this and the preceding sentence from Alvarez, "Butterfly McQueen," p. 28.
368. Bogle, *Blacks in American Films*, p. 421.
369. Quotes from Sylvia C. Henricks, "Marjorie Main: 'Good for a Lot of Laughs,'" www.indianahistory.org/pub/traces/mjmain.html, accessed Dec. 12, 2002; James Robert Parish, *The Slapstick Queens* (South Brunswick and New York: A.S. Barnes, 1973), p. 23; Boze Hadleigh, *Hollywood Lesbians* (New York: Barricade Books, 1994), p. 38.
370. The best source of information on Main's early life and career is Henricks, "Marjorie Main," from which the facts in this paragraph are taken.
371. James Robert Parish and William T. Leonard, *The Funsters* (New Rochelle, NY: Arlington House, 1979), p. 443.
372. Jim Hicks, "Marjorie Main," http://www.geocities.com/gimcrack.geo/MarjorieMain.html, accessed Dec. 12, 2002.

373. Hicks, "Marjorie Main."
374. Parish and Leonard, *The Funsters*, p. 444; Hicks, "Marjorie Main."
375. Parish and Leonard, *The Funsters*, p. 443.
376. Hadleigh, *Hollywood Lesbians*, p. 17.
377. On Main's marriage, see Parish and Leonard, *The Funsters*, p. 444; Hicks, "Marjorie Main"; Henricks, "Marjorie Main."
378. Parish and Leonard, p. 449.
379. Parish and Leonard, p. 445.
380. Parish, *The Slapstick Queens*, p. 30; Parish and Leonard, *The Funsters*, p. 447. According to her co-star in *Mr. Imperium*, Debbie Reynolds, this trailer was a necessity, as she had a bladder problem: "She'd be saying her lines on camera, and nature would call. Continuing on with her lines, as if it were part of the movie, she'd walk right off the set into her dressing room. You'd hear the toilet seat go up, the toilet seat go down, the flushing, and Marjorie was still saying her lines. Then she'd come right back on the set, as if we hadn't cut, and finish the scene." According to Reynolds, Main was "Off. Her. Rocker," talking to her dead husband as if he were alive at her side. (Debbie Reynolds [with David Patrick Columbia], *Debbie: My Life* [London: Sidgwick and Jackson, 1988], pp. 93–94.)
381. Parish and Leonard, *The Funsters*, p. 446.
382. See Hadleigh, *Hollywood Lesbians*, p. 23.
383. Henricks, "Marjorie Main."
384. Gavin Lambert, *On Cukor* (London and New York: W.H. Allen, 1973), p. 68.
385. Charles Higham and Joel Greenberg, *Hollywood in the Forties* (New York: A.S. Barnes, 1968), p. 164.
386. Parish and Leonard, *The Funsters*, p. 447, 448.
387. Parish, *The Slapstick Queens*, p. 27; Hicks, "Marjorie Main."
388. Hicks, "Marjorie Main."
389. This was not the first time, of course, that the classy Colbert had been hitched to a man with a hankering for the simple, rural life. In *The Egg and I*, she was only marginally less out of place than she had been back in the eighteenth-century, frontier Massachusetts of John Ford's classic colonial western, *Drums Along the Mohawk* (1939). To support her in the earlier film, Colbert had the redoubtable spinster, Edna May Oliver.
390. Parish and Leonard, *The Funsters*, p. 447.
391. Parish, *The Slapstick Queens*, p. 24; Hicks, "Marjorie Main."
392. Hadleigh, *Hollywood Lesbians*, p. 19.
393. Hadleigh, p. 28.
394. Hicks, "Marjorie Main."
395. Parish, *The Slapstick Queens*, p. 29; Parish and Leonard, *The Funsters*, p. 447; Hadleigh, *Hollywood Lesbians*, p. 19.
396. Parish and Leonard, p. 447.
397. Hadleigh, *Hollywood Lesbians*, p. 20.
398. Henricks, "Marjorie Main."
399. Hadleigh, *Hollywood Lesbians*, p. 50, 51.
400. Hadleigh, p. 19. Her home in Los Angeles was at 3066 Patricia Drive.
401. Hicks, "Marjorie Main."
402. Parish and Leonard, *The Funsters*, p. 449.
403. Quoted in Boze Hadleigh, *Hollywood Lesbians* (New York: Barricade Books, 1994), p. 177.
404. Charles Tranberg, *I Love the Illusion: The Life and Career of Agnes Moorehead* (Boalsburg, PA: BearManor Media, 2005), p. 11.
405. Tranberg, p. 11.
406. James Robert Parish, *Good Dames* (South Brunswick and New York: A.S. Barnes, 1974), p. 125.
407. Tranberg, *I Love the Illusion*, p. 7, 14.
408. Tranberg, p. 18.
409. Tranberg, p. 21.
410. Tranberg, p. 31. On Moorehead's family background and early life, see Parish, *Good Dames*, pp. 78–80; "Agnes Moorehead Dies at 67; Acclaimed in a Variety of Roles," *New York Times* (May 1, 1974), p. 48; Phyllis Scott Carlin, "Agnes Moorehead," *Notable Women in the American Theatre: A Biographical Dictionary*, ed. Alice M. Robinson et al. (New York: Greenwood, 1989), pp. 663–64; Tranberg, *I Love the Illusion*, pp. 11–22.
411. These facts are taken from Moorehead's audition report from AADA, as given in Warren Shrek, *Agnes Moorehead: A Very Private Person* (Philadelphia: Dorrance, 1976), p. 24.
412. Quoted in Hadleigh, *Hollywood Lesbians*, p. 189.
413. See James Robert Parish and Ronald L. Bowers, *The MGM Stock Company: The Golden Era* (New York: Bonanza Books, 1972), p. 506. See also David Thomson, *Rosebud: The Story of Orson Welles* (New York: Alfred A. Knopf, 1996), p. 184.
414. See Shrek, *Agnes Moorehead*, p. 3.
415. Hadleigh, *Hollywood Lesbians*, p. 187.
416. Parish, *Good Dames*, p. 92.
417. Parish, p. 98.
418. Tranberg, *I Love the Illusion*, p. 81.
419. The *New York Times*'s respected critic Bosley Crowther wrote that if Moorehead "gets an Academy Award for this performance ... the Academy should close up shop!" (qtd. in Parish, *Good Dames*, p. 122).
420. In an interview with Mike Steen in 1971, Moorehead talked about being "very good friends with Greer Garson" and having "another extremely close friendship" with Debbie Reynolds. "I can say I have an awful lot of acquaintances in the business," she added, "but very, very few close friends." (See Mike Steen, *Hollywood Speaks: An Oral History* [New York: G.P. Putnam, 1974], pp. 112–13.)
421. Sara Warren is of a slightly different order of bitchery, being more conventional and dull than her predecessors. Todd Haynes has recently directed as fascinating pastiche of *All That Heaven Allows*, entitled *Far From Heaven* (2002), with Eleanor Fine (Patricia Clarkson) as a redheaded replica of Moorehead's role. The setting is still the 1950s, but rather than being confronted with her upper middle-class friend getting involved with a white gardener, as in the original, Clarkson has to come to terms with the possibility that Julianne Moore is having an affair with an African American.
422. Steen, *Hollywood Speaks*, p. 109; Parish, *Good Dames*, p. 91; Tranberg, *I Love the Illusion*, pp. 96–97. The producer originally wanted Moorehead to play the tippling duchess portrayed by Gladys Cooper (Parish, p. 91).
423. *Main Street to Broadway* is significant for bringing together on film for the first and only time two of the biggest gay icons of the twentieth century. Among Moorehead's clients is not only the budding playwright and hero of the piece, Tony Monaco (Tom Morton), but the Broadway star, Tallulah Bankhead, fifty-one at the time and the author of a recent autobiography, which is alluded to in the film. In real life, Bankhead was in one of the frequent lulls in her acting career, after her big hit in a revival of Noël Coward's *Private Lives*. In the film, Bankhead is sick of being typecast as a "tiger woman." Moorehead wants Monaco to write an upbeat new play for Bankhead where she can shine as an exemplar of "wholesome American womanhood." Needless to say, this proves an impossible task. The puerile plot aside, *Main Street* offers a unique peek into the New York theater world of the early 1950s, with a

stellar cast of stars playing themselves, including Ethel and Lionel Barrymore, Rex Harrison, Henry Fonda, Shirley Booth, and Helen Hayes. You can also glimpse Jessie Royce Landis and Bankhead's lifelong friend, Estelle Winwood, in the first-night audience of Monaco's play, *Calico and Lust* (starring, you guessed it, Bankhead). While the film was being made, Shirley Booth was starring in Arthur Laurents' *The Time of the Cuckoo*, the last show at the legendary Empire Theatre, which was razed to make way for an office building in 1953.

424. Parish, *Good Dames*, p. 110.
425. See Herbie J. Pilato, *Bewitched Forever: The Immortal Companion to Television's Most Magical Supernatural Situation Comedy* (2nd ed.; Irving, TX: Summit, 2001), p. 245; Tranberg, *I Love the Illusion*, p. 176.
426. See Shrek, *Agnes Moorehead*, p. 17 for this quote and a description of Moorehead's lifestyle at Villa Agnese.
427. www.imdb.com.
428. Shrek, *Agnes Moorehead*, p. 95.
429. Shrek, p. 74; Steen, *Hollywood Speaks*, p. 112; Debbie Reynolds (with David Patrick Columbia), *Debbie: My Life* (London: Sidgwick and Jackson, 1988), p. 214, 241.
430. Parish, *Good Dames*, p. 80 (says June 6), 104; Tranberg, *I Love the Illusion*, p. 37, 147–48.
431. Tranberg, p. 132.
432. Tranberg, pp. 179–80, 217, 276–79.
433. Parish, *Good Dames*, p. 104; Tranberg, p. 158.
434. Parish, p. 105; Tranberg, *I Love the Illusion*, pp. 186–87.
435. See interview with Moorehead, "My Son Owes His Life to Debbie," *Photoplay* (October 1966), as reproduced at the following internet address: www.harpiesbizarre.com/agnesdebbie.htm.
436. Her most resolute biographer, Charles Tranberg, concludes: "I found no smoking gun—nothing in her papers which indicates she ever had a lesbian relationship" (Tranberg, *I Love the Illusion*, p. 320). A smoking gun is maybe not the most felicitous metaphor in this connection...
437. See Hadleigh, *Hollywood Lesbians*, p. 191. Emphasis in original.
438. Hadleigh, p. 193.
439. Hadleigh, p. 194.
440. Steen, *Hollywood Speaks*, p. 112.
441. In this capacity, she takes over from Isobel Elsom, though the latter is still very much in evidence (with her Chihuahua) in a hilarious close encounter with a vacuum cleaner in what was her fourth and final film with Lewis.
442. Apparently Moorehead could be as dramatic in real life as her character in *Bewitched*. Her co-star, Kasey Rogers, recalls how Moorehead would throw her arms into the air when talking about acting and exclaim: "I lo-o-o-ve the illusion!" (E-mail from Kasey Rogers to the author, Aug. 5, 2003).
443. Pilato, *Bewitched Forever*, p. 18.
444. Tranberg, *I Love the Illusion*, p. 312.
445. Tranberg, pp. 313–14.
446. Reynolds, *Debbie*, p. 331; Tranberg, p. 318.
447. Scott Eyman, *Print the Legend: The Life and Times of John Ford* (Baltimore: Johns Hopkins University Press, 2000), p. 228.
448. For information on Natwick's early life and career, see Alfred E. Twomey and Arthur F. McClure, *The Versatiles: Supporting Character Players in the Cinema 1930-1955* (New York: Castle Books, 1969), p. 171; Peter B. Flint, "Mildred Natwick, 89, Actress Who Excelled at Eccentricity," *New York Times* (Oct. 26, 1994), p. 13; "Affidavit of Heirship," May 6, 1993, p. 1 (New York County Surrogate's Court). There is also some information relating to Natwick's early acting career in Henry Fonda and Howard Teichmann, *Fonda: My Life, as Told to Howard Teichmann* (London: W.H. Allen, 1982), pp. 50–51, 57, 82.
449. Eyman, *Print the Legend*, p. 228.
450. Flint, "Mildred Natwick," p. 13.
451. Quoted in Flint, p. 13.
452. Eyman, *Print the Legend*, p. 228.
453. One of her few mother roles was Grace Hewitt in *Teenage Rebel* (E. Goulding, Twentieth Century–Fox, 1956), neighbor, friend, and confidante to star Ginger Rogers. Natwick is quirky despite the conventional suburban mom role as the wife of a navy man and mother of, wait for it, Dick and Jane. She hates coconut and says, "I always feel sorry for my friends."
454. Quoted in Flint, "Mildred Natwick," p. 13.
455. David Ragan, *Who's Who in Hollywood 1900-1976* (New Rochelle, NY: Arlington House, 1977), p. 320.
456. Ragan, p. 320; "Affidavit of Heirship," May 6, 1993, p. 1 (New York County Surrogate's Court). On her death, her estate was valued at over $1,000,000 (document, New York County Surrogate's Court).
457. Maureen Stapleton and Jane Scovell, *A Hell of a Life: An Autobiography* (New York, Simon and Schuster, 1995), p. 107.
458. Quoted in Boze Hadleigh, *Leading Ladies* (London: Robson Books, 1992), p. 150.
459. "Una O'Connor, 78, Actress, Is Dead," *New York Times* (Feb. 6, 1959), p. 25.
460. Sheridan Morley, *Tales From the Hollywood Raj: The British Film Colony on Screen and Off* (London: Weidenfeld and Nicolson, 1983), p. 109.
461. O'Connor was a lifelong friend of James Whale and one of the small gathering at his funeral in 1957. He left her $10,000 in his will. (Eric M. Heideman, "The Grand Dames of the Horror Film: Maria Ouspenskaya and Una O'Connor," www.monsterzine.com, accessed June 25, 2003.)
462. De Havilland starred in three other films with O'Connor: *Call It a Day* (A. Mayo, WB, 1937), *The Strawberry Blonde* (R. Walsh, WB, 1941), and *Government Girl* (D. Nichols, RKO, 1943). *Call It a Day* gave O'Connor a small but amusing role as the Hiltons' larcenous housekeeper, Mrs. Milson, who gets caught by Frieda Inescort taking some "spoiled" food home to her husband. She is a health fanatic, who is convinced cook Beryl Mercer has high blood pressure. Even if she doesn't, she will by the time this hypochondriac by proxy gets through with her! O'Connor puts Mercer quite off her food.
463. "Una O'Connor," p. 25.
464. "Una O'Connor," p. 25.
465. Simon Callow, *Charles Laughton: A Difficult Actor* (London: Vintage, 1995), p. 279.
466. A. Scott Berg, *Kate Remembered* (New York: G.P. Putnam, 2003), p. 347.
467. James Kotsilibas-Davis and Myrna Loy, *Being and Becoming* (New York: Donald I. Fine/Primus, 1988), p. 145.
468. Joan Crawford with Jane Kesner Ardmore, *A Portrait of Joan* (Garden City, NY: Doubleday, 1962), p. 108.
469. In 1931, the actress had had her last name legally changed to Oliver, which was the surname of her uncle and mentor, Freeman Adam Oliver, a member of the Boston Symphony. She explained, "No woman named 'Nutter' would ever get anywhere in the theatre." (See James Robert Parish and William T. Leonard, *The Funsters* [New Rochelle, New York: Arlington House, 1979], p. 498 note; Charles Stumpf, "Edna May Oliver: One and Only," *Films of the Golden Age* 13 [1998], p. 46.)
470. The facts of Oliver's early life are available in "Edna May Oliver Dies in Hollywood," *New York Times* (Nov. 10,

1942), p. 28; Parish and Leonard, p. 497; Stumpf, "Edna May Oliver."

471. Parish and Leonard, p. 498.

472. "Edna May Oliver Dies in Hollywood," p. 28; Parish and Leonard, p. 498; Stumpf, p. 45.

473. John Parker, *Who's Who in the Theatre: A Biographical Record of the Contemporary Stage* (7th ed.; London: Pitman, 1933), p. 1059.

474. Parish and Leonard, *The Funsters*, p. 499, 504.

475. Boze Hadleigh, *Hollywood Lesbians* (New York: Barricade Books, 1994), p. 41.

476. Parish and Leonard, *The Funsters*, p. 495 and note.

477. "Edna May Oliver Dies in Hollywood," p. 28.

478. Blanche Yurka, *Bohemian Girl: Blanche Yurka's Theatrical Life* (Athens, OH: Ohio University Press, 1970), p. 224.

479. Frank S. Nugent, "*Romeo and Juliet*," *New York Times* (Aug. 21, 1936), p. 12.

480. Gavin Lambert, *Norma Shearer: A Life* (New York: Alfred A. Knopf, 1990), p. 223.

481. The films were *Penguin Pool Murder* (G. Archainbaud, RKO, 1932), *Murder on the Blackboard* (G. Archainbaud, RKO, 1934), and *Murder on a Honeymoon* (L. Corrigan, RKO, 1935).

482. Parish and Leonard, *The Funsters*, p. 503.

483. Parish and Leonard, p. 501.

484. Parish and Leonard, p. 495.

485. Details of Oliver's final illness, death, and funeral are to be found in "Edna May Oliver Dies in Hollywood," p. 28; Parish and Leonard, p. 504; Stumpf, p. 49.

486. "Edna May Oliver Left $156,000," *New York Times* (Apr. 27, 1943), p. 18.

487. For the details of Ouspenskaya's early life and acting career, see "Mme. Ouspenskaya, Actress, 73, Is Dead," *New York Times* (Dec. 4, 1949), p. 108.

488. "Mme. Ouspenskaya," p. 108.

489. Gavin Lambert, *Nazimova: A Biography* (New York: Alfred A. Knopf, 1997), p. 265.

490. Quoted in "Mme. Ouspenskaya," p. 108.

491. www.imdb.com.

492. Lambert, *Nazimova*, p. 265.

493. "Mme. Ouspenskaya," p. 108.

494. Lambert, *Nazimova*, p. 355.

495. See Jessie Royce Landis, *You Won't Be So Pretty (But You'll Know More)* (London: W.H. Allen, 1954), p. 123.

496. A. Scott Berg, *Kate Remembered* (New York: G.P. Putnam, 2003), p. 323.

497. James Kotsilibas-Davis and Myrna Loy, *Being and Becoming* (New York: Donald I. Fine/Primus, 1988), p. 158.

498. Lambert, *Nazimova*, p. 265.

499. "Mme. Ouspenskaya," p. 108.

500. Lambert, *Nazimova*, p. 265; Jane Russell, *My Path and My Detours: An Autobiography* (New York: Franklin Watts, 1985), p. 7. Russell takes credit for originating the story about the water being vodka. She recalls Ouspenskaya more than forty-five years after her teacher's death as "a divine, tiny, seventy-five-year-old lady who could do a handstand and often proved it to the delight of her classes" (p. 7).

501. Larry Swindell, *Body and Soul: The Story of John Garfield* (New York: William Morrow, 1975), p. 35.

502. See Lambert, *Nazimova*, p. 265.

503. Charles Higham and Joel Greenberg, *Hollywood in the Forties* (New York: A.S. Barnes, 1968), p. 88.

504. Frank Miller, "The Shanghai Gesture," www.turnerclassicmovies.com, accessed July 7, 2003.

505. "Mme. Ouspenskaya," p. 108.

506. "Mme. Ouspenskaya," p. 108.

507. Until the end of her life, Patrick would give her birth year as 1911! See, for example, David Ragan, *Who's Who in Hollywood, 1900–1976* (New Rochelle, NY: Arlington House, 1977), p. 348.

508. Sources on Patrick's life and career are: Ragan, *Who's Who in Hollywood*, pp. 348–49; James Robert Parish, *Hollywood Character Actors* (New Rochelle, New York: Arlington House, 1978), p. 414; "Lee Patrick, Actress Played Secretary in *Maltese Falcon*," *New York Times* (Nov. 27, 1982), p. 33; and www.imdb.com.

509. See Ragan, *Who's Who in Hollywood*, p. 349.

510. Patrick had been offended when Bette Davis failed to mention in her 1962 autobiography, *The Lonely Life*, that she had also been in the earthquake scene in San Francisco. Thirteen years later, Davis took the opportunity to apologize in her printed commentary to Whitney Stine's book *Mother Goddam: The Story of the Career of Bette Davis* (London: W.H. Allen, 1975): "Dear Lee: You and I worked together many times. I always felt you were one of our very best actresses, and therefore felt very fortunate when you were in a film of mine. Apologies for the oversight about the earthquake scene: 'You certainly suffered through it with me!'" (p. 104).

511. David Quinlan, *Quinlan's Illustrated Directory of Film Character Actors* (2nd ed.; London: B.T. Batsford, 1995), p. 280.

512. Information in this paragraph from Ragan, *Who's Who in Hollywood*, pp. 348–49.

513. "Elizabeth Patterson Dies at 90; Well Known Character Actress," *New York Times* (Feb. 1, 1966), p. 35.

514. The biographical facts in this paragraph and the final paragraph have been taken from "Elizabeth Patterson Dies at 90," p. 35; and www.imdb.com.

515. Billie Burke with Cameron Shipp, *With a Feather On My Nose* (New York: Appleton-Century-Crofts, 1949), p. 197.

516. Jessie Royce Landis, *You Won't Be So Pretty (But You'll Know More)* (London: W.H. Allen, 1954), p. 110.

517. Katharine Hepburn relates in her memoirs that she had only learned from Patterson years later why she had been so unfriendly to her in what was Hepburn's first Hollywood film. Every time Hepburn muffed up during the breakfast scene with Patterson, they had to eat a new breakfast! (Katharine Hepburn, *Me: Stories of My Life* [New York: Alfred A. Knopf, 1991], p. 144.)

518. Bosley Crowther, "*Intruder in the Dust*," *New York Times* (Nov. 23, 1949), p. 19.

519. David Ragan, *Who's Who in Hollywood, 1900–1976* (New Rochelle, NY: Arlington House), p. 746.

520. Information on Pearce's life from Herbie J. Pilato, *Bewitched Forever: The Immortal Companion to Television's Most Magical Supernatural Situation Comedy* (2nd ed.; Irving, Texas: Summit, 2001), pp. 80–81; www.imdb.com; Fredrick Tucker (e-mail of Nov. 13, 2003).

521. Pilato, *Bewitched Forever*, p. 81.

522. Apparently her chin looked the way it did due to Pearce falling off a swing as a child. Pearce took it in stride, saying: "Look at me, I'm a chinless wonder. If I'd sustained no accident as a kid, if I had developed an ordinary chin, today I'd probably be just another starving, middle-aged actress." (Pilato, *Bewitched Forever*, p. 81.)

523. www.imdb.com.

524. Pilato, *Bewitched Forever*, p. 81.

525. Pilato, p. 254.

526. John Springer and Jack Hamilton, *They Had Faces Then: Super Stars, Stars and Starlets of the 1930's* (N.p.: Castle, 1974), p. 206.

527. David Ragan, *Who's Who in Hollywood, 1900–1976* (New Rochelle, NY: Arlington House, 1977), p. 757.

528. I have based this account on the following biographical sources: "Jessie Ralph, 79, of Stage, Screen," *New York Times* (May 31, 1944), p. 19; Springer and Hamilton, *They Had Faces Then*, p. 206, 323–34; James Robert Parish, *Hollywood Character Actors* (New Rochelle, New York: Arlington House, 1978), p. 428.

529. Springer and Hamilton, *They Had Faces Then*, pp. 323–24.

530. "Jessie Ralph," p. 19.

531. See interviews with Marsha Hunt and Karen Morley in Patrick McGilligan and Paul Buhle, *Tender Comrades: A Backstory of the Hollywood Blacklist* (New York: St. Martin's Press, 1997), p. 312, 475.

532. For the facts of Revere's life as related in this paragraph and below, see Peter B. Flint, "Anne Revere, 87, Actress, Dies; Was Movie Mother of Many Stars," *New York Times* (Dec. 19, 1990), p. D21; David Ragan, *Who's Who in Hollywood, 1900-1976* (New Rochelle, NY: Arlington House), pp. 384–85; and www.imdb.com.

533. Flint, "Anne Revere," p. D21.

534. Elia Kazan, *A Life* (London: Andre Deutsch, 1988), p. 334.

535. Charles Higham and Joel Greenberg, *Hollywood in the Forties* (New York: A.S. Barnes, 1968), p. 78.

536. Ragan, *Who's Who in Hollywood, 1900-1976*, p. 384.

537. David Quinlan, *Quinlan's Illustrated Directory of Film Character Actors* (2nd ed.; London: B.T. Batsford, 1995), p. 304.

538. Unless otherwise indicated, biographical information on Risdon in this and the final paragraph is taken from John Parker, *Who's Who in the Theatre: A Biographical Record of the Contemporary Stage* (7th ed.; London: Pitman, 1933), p. 1148; and "Elizabeth [sic] Risdon Dies," *New York Times* (Dec. 23, 1958), p. 2.

539. James Robert Parish, *Good Dames* (South Brunswick and New York: A.S. Barnes, 1974), p. 201.

540. Parish, *Good Dames*, p. 202.

541. Quoted in Parish, p. 235.

542. Parish, p. 197.

543. "Thelma Ritter, Verstile Actress With the Raspy Voice, Dies at 63," *New York Times* (Feb. 5, 1969), p. 45; Parish, *Good Dames*, p. 196.

544. Parish, *Good Dames*, p. 198.

545. Parish, p. 222.

546. Parish, pp. 199–200.

547. Parish, p. 201.

548. Parish, p. 201.

549. "Thelma Ritter," p. 45; Parish, *Good Dames*, p. 201. While Ritter went back to work as an actress, first in radio in 1944 and a couple of years later in film, the Morans remained in their Forest Hills home until Ritter's death. As the years went by, they would also be able to afford a home in Hollywood and a six-room place on Fire Island ("Thelma Ritter," p. 45; Parish, *Good Dames*, p. 201).

550. Parish, *Good Dames*, p. 203.

551. David Thomson, *The New Biographical Dictionary of Film* (London: Little, Brown, 2002), p. 740.

552. Parish, *Good Dames*, p. 198.

553. Parish, p. 196.

554. Parish, p. 196.

555. See "Thelma Ritter," p.45; Parish, *Good Dames*, p. 207, 221.

556. Betty Lee, *Marie Dressler: The Unlikeliest Star* (Lexington, Kentucky: University Press of Kentucky, 1997), p. x.

557. She had long been famous for her double takes. You'll find one of the best of them at the end of *Dinner at Eight*, when Jean Harlow remarks that she was reading a book the other day.

558. Ironically, Dressler is much less known than Ritter today, not just because her film career is more distant, but because according to writer Betty Lee, "None of Dressler's films have been reissued for general release since 1936" (*Marie Dressler*, p. 267). The exception, though, is *Dinner at Eight*, which is widely available on video and DVD.

559. Christopher Bram, "Marie Dressler: The Popular Star of *Min and Bill* on Alpine Drive," *Architectural Digest* 53 (1996): p. 186.

560. Lee, *Marie Dressler*, p. 2, 250.

561. Frank Capra, *The Name Above the Title* (New York: Vintage, 1985), p. 459.

562. Quoted in Parish, *Good Dames*, p. 235.

563. Boze Hadleigh, *Conversations with My Elders* (New York: St. Martin's, 1986), p. 203.

564. Parish, *Good Dames*, p. 210.

565. A.H. Weiler, "The Birdman of Alcatraz," *New York Times* (July 19, 1962), p. 19.

566. Parish, *Good Dames*, p. 207.

567. Sam Staggs, *All About All About Eve: The Complete Behind-the-Scenes Story of the Bitchiest Film Ever Made* (New York: St. Martin's Griffin, 2001), p. 8, 131.

568. Staggs, p. 56.

569. Staggs, pp. 132–33, 152.

570. Bosley Crowther, "All About Eve," *New York Times* (Oct. 14, 1950), p. 25.

571. Staggs, p. 12, 133.

572. Parish noted in 1974, "Many people consider her role in *The Model and the Marriage Broker* her best" (*Good Dames*, p. 211).

573. Ritter was Oscar-nominated a fifth time for this role, but saw the award go to Shelley Winters for *The Diary of Anne Frank*.

574. For a theoretical approach to the plot function and symbolic meaning of the comic secondary lead actress, see Judith Roof, *All About Thelma and Eve: Sidekicks and Third Wheels* (Urbana and Chicago: University of Illinois Press, 2002).

575. Parish, *Good Dames*, p. 216.

576. Parish, p. 217.

577. Parish, p. 213.

578. "Thelma Ritter," p. 45.

579. Kenneth Barrow, *Flora: An Appreciation of the Life and Work of Dame Flora Robson* (London: Heinemann, 1981), p. 116.

580. Barrow, p. 122.

581. Janet Dunbar, *Flora Robson* (London: George G. Harrap, 1960), p. 209.

582. Barrow, *Flora*, p. 124. See also Rudy Behlmer, ed., *Memo from David O. Selznick* (New York: Viking, 1972), p. 257.

583. Barrow, p. 125.

584. Barrow, p. 127. Donat once said to Robson: "You're as easy to act with as breathing" (Eric Johns, *Dames of the Theatre* [London: W.H. Allen, 1974], p. 108).

585. Barrow, p. 127.

586. Barrow, p. 129.

587. Barrow, p. 202.

588. Barrow, pp. 129–30.

589. Barrow, p. 131.

590. Quoted in Barrow, p. 76.

591. Dunbar, *Flora Robson*, p. 194; Barrow, p. 166.

592. Barrow, p. 131.

593. Barrow, p. 140.

594. The blatant absurdity of her casting in *Saratoga Trunk* is topped by her role in *Caesar and Cleopatra* (G. Pascal), also from 1945. We find her here in a major role as

Ftatateeta (try saying that quickly a dozen times), nurse to Cleopatra, who turns more or less against her charge when Caesar makes her a queen. In blackface again, Robson looks like an amateur drag artist doing a Diana Ross imitation. Her character is described as a "venerable grotesque," a piece of ancient Egyptian pottery, and a "tigress." She is ultimately killed by Caesar's henchman, Rufio, who sees her as a threat to his boss.

595. Barrow, p. 146, 147.
596. Boze Hadleigh, *Leading Ladies* (London: Robson Books, 1992), p. 142.
597. Barrow, p. 149.
598. Hadleigh, *Leading Ladies*, p. 140.
599. Dunbar, *Flora Robson*, p. 26.
600. Dunbar, p. 19.
601. Dunbar, p. 205; Barrow, *Flora*, p. 117, 118.
602. Barrow, p. 163.
603. Barrow, p. 165.
604. Hadleigh, *Leading Ladies*, p. 142.
605. Barrow, *Flora*, p. 206.
606. Barrow, p. 205.
607. Hadleigh, *Leading Ladies*, p. 144.
608. Marvine Howe, "Dame Flora Robson Is Dead; A Leading Actress in Britain," *New York Times* (July 8, 1984), p. 22.
609. Howe, p. 22.
610. "May Robson Dies in Beverly Hills," *New York Times* (Oct. 21, 1942), p. 21.
611. "May Robson Dies," p. 21.
612. The best source of information on May Robson's early life and stage career is H.L. Kleinfield, "May Robson," *Notable American Women: A Biographical Dictionary*, Vol. 3 (Cambridge, MA: Belknap Press of Harvard University Press, 1971), pp. 184–85. See also "May Robson Dies," p. 21; and John Springer and Jack Hamilton, *They Had Faces Then: Super Stars, Stars and Starlets of the 1930's* (N.p.: Castle, 1974), p. 325.
613. See Kleinfeld, "May Robson," p. 185.
614. Joan Fontaine, *No Bed of Roses: An Autobiography* (New York: William Morrow, 1978), pp. 65–67.
615. Whitney Stine with Bette Davis, *Mother Goddam: The Story of the Career of Bette Davis by Whitney Stine with a Running Commentary by Bette Davis* (London: W.H. Allen, 1975), p. 277.
616. Frank Capra, *The Name Above the Title* (New York: Vintage, 1985), p. 145, 149. Capra remade the film as *Pocketful of Miracles* in 1961. Shirley Booth was his first choice for the lead, but she "Announced she would never, never top May Robson—and ran off." When Helen Hayes couldn't take the part due to scheduling problems, the role of Apple Annie went to Bette Davis (Capra, p. 472, 475).
617. "May Robson Dies," p. 21.
618. Kleinfeld, "May Robson," p. 185.
619. James Robert Parish and William T. Leonard, *The Funsters* (New Rochelle, NY: Arlington House, 1979), p. 601.
620. Parish and Leonard, p. 601.
621. Parish and Leonard, p. 601.
622. John Springer and Jack Hamilton, *They Had Faces Then: Super Stars, Stars and Starlets of the 1930's* (N.p.: Castle, 1974), p. 329; Parish and Leonard, *The Funsters*, p. 601.
623. "Alison Skipworth, Actress, Dies at 88," *New York Times* (July 7, 1952), p. 21; Parish and Leonard, p. 601.
624. Parish and Leonard, p. 604.
625. One of these was a filmatization of her 1919 Broadway hit *39 East* (J.S. Robertson, 1920), a play by Rachel Crothers starring Constance Binney. Tallulah Bankhead had her first starring role on Broadway in this play when she stepped in when Binney went on holiday. Skipworth played Madame de Mailly, the stern but sympathetic proprietress of a high-toned New York boarding house.
626. Parish and Leonard, *The Funsters*, p. 601.
627. "Alison Skipworth," p. 21; Parish and Leonard, p. 603.
628. William J. Lynch, "George Kelly the Playwright," in *Three Plays by George Kelly*, ed. William J. Lynch (New York: Limelight Editions, 1999), p. 11.
629. Gerald Guttierez quoted in Wendy Wasserstein, "Foreword," in *Three Plays by George Kelly*, ed. William J. Lynch (New York: Limelight Editions, 1999), p. x.
630. See Parish and Leonard, *The Funsters*, p. 603.
631. Parish and Leonard, p. 605.
632. James Curtis, *W.C. Fields: A Biography* (New York: Alfred A. Knopf, 2003), p. 244, 246.
633. Whitney Stine with Bette Davis, *Bette Davis: Mother Goddam* (London: W.H. Allen, 1975), pp. 70–71.
634. Parish and Leonard, *The Funsters*, p. 604.
635. See Stine, *Bette Davis*, p. 79.
636. Parish and Leonard, *The Funsters*, p. 608.
637. She shares her grave in Kensico Cemetery, Westchester County, New York with the theatrical agent, Francie Hidden (1907–78). The nature of their relationship is not known, but Hidden is not mentioned in Skipworth's will of September 21, 1945 (New York County Surrogate's Court).
638. "Alison Skipworth," p. 21.
639. Larry Swindell, *Body and Soul: The Story of John Garfield* (New York: William Morrow, 1975), p. 141.
640. Biographical facts in this paragraph and the remainder of the profile are taken from Peter W. Kaplan, "Gale Sondergaard, Actress; Played Villainesses in Films," *New York Times* (Aug. 16, 1985), p. D15 unless otherwise indicated.
641. John Springer and Jack Hamilton, *They Had Faces Then: Super Stars, Stars and Starlets of the 1930's* (N.p.; Castle, 1974), p. 226.
642. See Patrick McGilligan and Paul Buhle, *Tender Comrades: A Backstory of the Hollywood Blacklist* (New York: St. Martin's Press, 1997), p. 107.
643. See www.imdb.com.
644. Aljean Harmetz, *The Making of The Wizard of Oz* (New York: Delta, 1989), pp. 122–23.
645. Springer and Hamilton, *They Had Faces Then*, p. 226.
646. Frank S. Nugent, "The Life of Emile Zola," *New York Times* (Aug. 12, 1937), p. 14.
647. Whitney Stine with Bette Davis, *Mother Goddam: The Story of the Career of Bette Davis* (London: W.H. Allen, 1975), p. 135.
648. Stine, p. 136.
649. Charles Higham and Joel Greenberg, *Hollywood in the Forties* (New York: A.S. Barnes, 1968), p. 54.
650. Victor S. Navasky, *Naming Names* (New York: The Viking Press, 1980), p. viii.
651. See McGilligan and Buhle, *Tender Comrades*, p. 109, 110.
652. Navasky, *Naming Names*, p. vii.
653. See Kaplan, "Gale Sondergaard," p. D15.
654. Navasky, *Naming Names*, p. x.
655. Kaplan, "Gale Sondergaard," p. D15.
656. For the facts of Watson's early life and career, see "Lucile Watson, Actress, Dead; Noted for Her Dowager Roles," *New York Times* (June 25, 1962), p. 29; William Lindesmith, "Lucile Watson," *Notable Women in the American Theatre: A Biographical Dictionary*, ed. Alice M. Robinson et al. (New York: Greenwood, 1989), pp. 906–08.
657. T.R. Bourgeois, "Lucile Watson: Grande Mother,"

Classic Images, www.classicimages.com/1998/october98/watsonlucile.html, accessed Jan. 23, 2003. Fellows and Watson were in one Broadway play together, *Her Sister* (1907–08).

658. One of Cukor's most prized possessions, in addition to John Singer Sargent's 1903 pencil sketch of Ethel Barrymore, was Charles Dana Gibson's portrait of Lucile Watson (Patrick McGilligan, *George Cukor: A Double Life* [New York: St. Martin's Press, 1991], p. 76).

659. Lindesmith, "Lucile Watson," p. 908.

660. Alex Barris, *Hollywood's Other Women* (South Brunswick and New York: A.S. Barnes, 1975), p. 55.

661. Bourgeois, "Lucile Watson."

662. Quoted in Lindesmith, "Lucile Watson," p. 908.

663. "Lucile Watson," p. 29.

664. Quoted in Lindesmith, "Lucile Watson," p. 908.

665. "Lucile Watson," p. 29.

666. Margaret Webster, *The Same Only Different* (London: Victor Gollancz, 1969), pp. 113–17.

667. Webster, p. 119.

668. Webster, p. 117.

669. Webster, p. 131.

670. Webster, p. 145, 146.

671. Webster, p. 129.

672. Webster, p. 124, 125.

673. Webster, p. 140.

674. Webster, p. 164.

675. Webster, p. 180.

676. Webster, p. 157.

677. Webster, p. 208.

678. May Whitty and Ben Webster would remain married for fifty-five years, until Webster's death in 1947. Greer Garson hosted a party at her home to celebrate their fiftieth wedding anniversary during the filming of *Mrs. Miniver* in 1942 (Michael Troyan, *A Rose for Mrs. Miniver: The Life of Greer Garson* [Lexington: University Press of Kentucky, 1999], p. 132).

679. Webster, *The Same Only Different*, p. 195.

680. Webster, p. 229.

681. Webster, p. 229.

682. www.imdb.com.

683. Webster, *The Same Only Different*, p. 239.

684. Webster, p. 255.

685. Webster, p. 372.

686. Webster, p. 374.

687. Webster, p. 193.

688. Frank Capra, *The Name Above the Title* (New York: Vintage, 1985), p. 149.

689. Webster, *The Same Only Different*, p. 255.

690. David Ragan, *Who's Who in Hollywood 1900-1976* (New Rochelle, NY: Arlington House, 1977), p. 831.

691. Alexander Walker, *Vivien: The Life of Vivien Leigh* (London: Weidenfeld and Nicholson, 1987), p. 144.

692. Webster, *The Same Only Different*, p. xi.

693. www.imdb.com.

694. James Robert Parish and Ronald L. Bowers, *The MGM Stock Company: The Golden Era* (New York: Bonanza Books, 1972), p. 770.

695. Tennessee Williams, *Memoirs* (Garden City, NY: Anchor Press/Doubleday, 1983), pp. 69–70. Copyright (c) 1975, renewed 2003 The University of the South. Reprinted by permission of Georges Borchardt, Inc. for the Tennessee Williams Estate.

696. Ruth Gordon, *Myself Among Others* (New York: Atheneum, 1971), p. 251.

697. John Springer and Jack Hamilton, *They Had Faces Then: Super Stars, Stars and Starlets of the 1930's* (N.p.: Castle, 1974), p. 256.

698. Alex Barris, *Hollywood's Other Women* (South Brunswick and New York: A.S. Barnes, 1975), p. 111.

699. See "Cora Witherspoon, Actress, 67, Is Dead; Performer 50 Years Made Bow at 15," *New York Times* (Nov. 19, 1957), p. 33; Springer and Hamilton, *They Had Faces Then*, p. 338.

700. Gavin Lambert, *On Cukor* (London and New York: W.H. Allen, 1973), p. 37.

701. Aljean Harmetz, *The Making of* The Wizard of Oz (New York: Delta, 1989), p. 127.

702. David Quinlan, *Quinlan's Illustrated Directory of Film Character Actors* (2nd ed.; London: B.T. Batsford, 1995), p. 376.

BIBLIOGRAPHY

Astor, Mary. *Mary Astor: A Life on Film.* New York: Delacorte Press, 1971.

Barris, Alex. *Hollywood's Other Women.* South Brunswick and New York: A.S. Barnes, 1975.

Barrow, Kenneth. *Flora: An Appreciation of the Life and Work of Dame Flora Robson.* London: Heinemann, 1981.

Barrymore, Ethel. *Memories: An Autobiography by Ethel Barrymore.* London: Hulton Press, 1956.

Baxter, John. *Hollywood in the Thirties.* London: A. Zwemmer, 1968.

Behlmer, Rudy, ed. *Memo from David O. Selznick.* New York: Viking, 1972.

Berg, A. Scott. *Kate Remembered.* New York: G.P. Putnam, 2003.

Blum, Daniel. *Great Stars of the American Stage: A Pictorial Record.* New York: Greenburg, 1952.

Bodeen, DeWitt. *From Hollywood.* South Brunswick and New York: A.S. Barnes, 1976.

_____. *More from Hollywood!* South Brunswick and New York: A.S. Barnes, 1977.

Bogle, Donald. *Blacks in American Films and Television: An Encyclopedia.* New York and London: Garland, 1988.

_____. *Toms, Coons, Mulattoes, Mammies, and Bucks: An Interpretive History of Blacks in American Films.* New York: Bantam, 1974.

Burke, Billie, with Cameron Shipp. *With a Feather On My Nose.* New York: Appleton-Century-Crofts, 1949.

_____. *With Powder On My Nose.* London: Peter Davies, 1960.

Callow, Simon. *Charles Laughton: A Difficult Actor.* London: Vintage, 1995.

Capra, Frank. *The Name Above the Title.* New York: Vintage, 1985.

Carlin, Phyllis Scott. "Agnes Moorehead," *Notable Women in the American Theatre: A Biographical Dictionary,* ed. Alice M. Robinson et al. New York: Greenwood, 1989, 663–66.

Carter, Randolph. *Ziegfeld: The Time of His Life.* London: Bernard Press, 1988.

Cooper, Gladys. *Gladys Cooper.* London: Hutchinson, 1931.

Crawford, Joan, with Jane Kesner Ardmore. *A Portrait of Joan.* Garden City, NY: Doubleday, 1962.

Cripps, Thomas. *Slow Fade to Black: The Negro in American Film, 1900-1942.* New York: Oxford University Press, 1977.

Curtis, James. *W.C. Fields: A Biography.* New York: Alfred A. Knopf, 2003.

Davis, Bette. *The Lonely Life: An Autobiography.* London: Macdonald, 1963.

Davis, Ronald L. *John Ford: Hollywood's Old Master.* Norman and London: University of Oklahoma Press, 1995.

DeCamp, Rosemary. *Tigers in My Lap.* Baltimore: MidnightMarquee Press, 2000.

Dunbar, Janet. *Flora Robson.* London: George G. Harrap, 1960.

Eyman, Scott. *Print the Legend: The Life and Times of John Ford.* Baltimore: Johns Hopkins University Press, 2000.

Fonda, Henry, and Howard Teichmann. *Fonda: My Life, as Told to Howard Teichmann.* London: W.H. Allen, 1982.

Fontaine, Joan. *No Bed of Roses: An Autobiography.* New York: William Morrow, 1978.

Gordon, Ruth. *Myself Among Others.* New York: Atheneum, 1971.

Hadleigh, Boze. *Conversations with My Elders.* New York: St. Martin's, 1986.

_____. *Hollywood Lesbians.* New York: Barricade Books, 1994.

_____. *Leading Ladies.* London: Robson Books, 1992.

Harmetz, Aljean. *The Making of The Wizard of Oz.* New York: Delta, 1989.

Hepburn, Katharine. *Me: Stories of My Life.* New York: Alfred A. Knopf, 1991.

Higham, Charles, and Joel Greenberg. *Hollywood in the Forties.* New York: A.S. Barnes, 1968.

Higham, Charles, and Roy Moseley. *Cary Grant: The Lonely Heart.* New York: Avon, 1989.

Hunter, Tab, with Eddie Muller. *Tab Hunter Confidential: The Making of a Movie Star.* Chapel Hill, NC: Algonquin Books of Chapel Hill, 2005.

Jackson, Carlton. *Hattie: The Life of Hattie McDaniel.* Lanham, NY: Madison Books, 1990.

Jarski, Rosemarie. *Hollywood Wit: Classic Off-screen Quips and Quotes.* London: Prion, 2000.

Johns, Eric. *Dames of the Theatre.* London: W.H. Allen, 1974.

Jones, Ken D., Arthur F. McClure, and Alfred E. Twomey. *Character People.* South Brunswick and New York: A.S. Barnes, 1976.

Kazan, Elia. *A Life.* London: Andre Deutsch, 1988.

Kendall, Elizabeth. *The Runaway Bride: Hollywood Romantic Comedy of the 1930s.* New York: Alfred A. Knopf, 1990.

Kleinfield, H.L. "May Robson." *Notable American Women: A Biographical Dictionary,* Vol. 3. Cambridge, MA: Belknap Press of Harvard University Press, 1971, 184–85.

Kotsilibas-Davis, James and Myrna Loy. *Being and Becoming,* New York: Primus, 1988.

Lambert, Gavin. *Nazimova: A Biography.* New York: Alfred A. Knopf, 1997.

_____. *Norma Shearer: A Life.* New York: Alfred A. Knopf, 1990.

_____. *On Cukor.* London and New York: W.H. Allen, 1973.

Lamparski, Richard. *Whatever Became Of ...?* New York: Crown, 1968.

_____. *Whatever Became Of ...? Third Series.* New York: Ace Books, 1970.

_____. *Whatever Became Of ...? Eighth Series.* New York: Crown, 1982.

Lanchester, Elsa. *Elsa Lanchester: Herself.* New York: St. Martin's, 1983.

Landis, Jessie Royce. *You Won't Be So Pretty (But You'll Know More).* London: W.H. Allen, 1954.

Lee, Betty. *Marie Dressler: The Unlikeliest Star.* Lexington, KY: University Press of Kentucky, 1997.

Levy, Emanuel. *George Cukor, Master of Elegance: Hollywood's Legendary Director and His Stars.* New York: William Morrow, 1994.

Lindesmith, William. "Laura Hope Crews." *Notable Women in the American Theatre: A Biographical Dictionary,* ed. Alice M. Robinson et al. New York: Greenwood, 1989, 176–78.

_____. "Lucile Watson." *Notable Women in the American Theatre: A Biographical Dictionary,* ed. Alice M. Robinson et al. New York: Greenwood, 1989, 906–8.

Lynch, William J. "George Kelly the Playwright." *Three Plays by George Kelly,* ed. William J. Lynch. New York: Limelight Editions, 1999, 7–12.

Madsen, Axel. *The Sewing Circle: Sappho's Leading Ladies.* New York: Kensington Books, 2002.

Mann, William J. *Behind the Screen: How Gays and Lesbians Shaped Hollywood, 1910–1969.* New York: Viking, 2001.

McCourt, James. *Queer Street: Rise and Fall of an American Culture, 1947–1985.* New York: Norton, 2004.

McGilligan, Patrick. *George Cukor: A Double Life.* New York: St. Martin's Press, 1991.

McGilligan, Patrick, and Paul Buhle. *Tender Comrades: A Backstory of the Hollywood Blacklist.* New York: St. Martin's Press, 1997.

Mikhail, E.H., ed. *The Abbey Theatre: Interviews and Recollections.* Basingstoke: Macmillan, 1988.

Morley, Sheridan. *Gladys Cooper: A Biography.* London: Book Club Associates, 1979.

_____. *Tales From The Hollywood Raj: The British Film Colony On Screen and Off.* London: Weidenfeld and Nicolson, 1983.

Nardin, James T. "Laura Hope Crews." *Notable American Women, 1607–1950,* Vol. I. Cambridge, MA: Belknap Press, 1971, 405–6.

Navasky, Victor S. *Naming Names.* New York: Viking Press, 1980.

Newquist, Roy. *Conversations with Joan Crawford.* Secaucus, NJ: Citadel Press, 1980.

Parish, James Robert. *Good Dames.* South Brunswick and New York: A.S. Barnes, 1974.

_____. *Hollywood Character Actors.* New Rochelle, NY: Arlington House, 1978.

_____. *The RKO Gals.* New Rochelle, NY: Arlington House, 1974.

_____. *The Slapstick Queens.* South Brunswick and New York: A.S. Barnes, 1973.

_____, and Ronald L. Bowers. *The MGM Stock Company: The Golden Era.* New York: Bonanza Books, 1972.

_____, and William T. Leonard. *The Funsters.* New Rochelle, NY: Arlington House, 1979.

_____, and William T. Leonard. *Hollywood Players: The Thirties.* New Rochelle, NY: Arlington House, 1976.

Parker, John. *Who's Who in the Theatre: A Biographical Record of the Contemporary Stage.* 7th ed.; London: Pitman, 1933.

Peters, Margot. *The House of Barrymore.* New York: Alfred A. Knopf, 1990.

_____. *Mrs. Pat: The Life of Mrs. Patrick Campbell.* New York: Alfred A. Knopf, 1984.

Pilato, Herbie J. *Bewitched Forever: The Immortal Companion to Television's Most Magical Supernatural Situation Comedy.* 2nd ed.; Irving, Texas: Summit, 2001.

Potempa, Phil. "The Beloved Mother: Beulah Bondi." *It's a Wonderful Life: A Memory Book* by Stephen Cox. Nashville, TN: Cumberland House, 2003, 62–67.

Quinlan, David. *Quinlan's Illustrated Directory of Film Character Actors.* 2nd ed.; London: B.T. Batsford, 1995.

Quinn, Arthur Hobson. *A History of the American Drama from the Civil War to the Present Day.* Rev. ed.; New York, F.S. Crofts, 1945.

Ragan, David. *Who's Who in Hollywood, 1900–1976.* New Rochelle, NY: Arlington House, 1977.

Reynolds, Debbie, with David Patrick Columbia. *Debbie: My Life*. London: Sidgwick and Jackson, 1988.

Robinson, Alice McDonnell, and Catherine B. McGovern. "Ethel Barrymore." *Notable Women in the American Theatre: A Biographical Dictionary*, ed. Alice M. Robinson et al. New York: Greenwood, 1989, 48–54.

Robinson, Lennox. *Ireland's Abbey Theatre: A History, 1899-1951*. Port Washington, NY: Kennikat Press, 1968.

Roerick, Wiliam. "Remembering Ethel Barrymore and Others." *Performing Arts Resources*, ed. Barbara Naomi Cohen-Stratyner. New York: Theatre Library Ass., 1988. 57–65.

Roof, Judith. *All About Thelma and Eve: Sidekicks and Third Wheels*. Urbana and Chicago: University of Illinois Press, 2002.

Rozek, Stacy A. "Mildred Margaret Dunnock." *Notable Women in the American Theatre: A Biographical Dictionary*, ed. Alice M. Robinson et al. New York: Greenwood, 1989, 243–46.

Russell, Jane. *My Path and My Detours: An Autobiography*. New York: Franklin Watts, 1985.

Russell, Rosalind, with Chris Chase. *Life is a Banquet*. New York: Ace Books, 1979.

Shrek, Warren. *Agnes Moorehead: A Very Private Person*. Philadelphia: Dorrance, 1976.

Springer, John, and Jack Hamilton. *They Had Faces Then: Super Stars, Stars and Starlets of the 1930's*. N.p.: Castle, 1974.

Staggs, Sam. *All About "All About Eve": The Complete Behind-the-Scenes Story of the Bitchiest Film Ever Made*. New York: St. Martin's Griffin, 2001.

Stapleton, Maureen, and Jane Scovell. *A Hell of a Life: An Autobiography*. New York, Simon and Schuster, 1995.

Steen, Mike. *Hollywood Speaks: An Oral History*. New York: G.P. Putnam, 1974.

Stine, Whitney, with Bette Davis. *Mother Goddam: The Story of the Career of Bette Davis by Whitney Stine with a Running Commentary by Bette Davis*. London: W.H. Allen, 1975.

Stokes, Sewell. *Without Veils: An Intimate Biography of Gladys Cooper*. London: Peter Davies, 1953.

Swindell, Larry. *Body and Soul: The Story of John Garfield*. New York: William Morrow, 1975.

Thomson, David. *The New Biographical Dictionary of Film*. London: Little, Brown, 2002.

Tranberg, Charles. *I Love the Illusion: The Life and Career of Agnes Moorehead*. Boalsburg, PA: BearManor Media, 2005.

Troyan, Michael. *A Rose for Mrs. Miniver: The Life of Greer Garson*. Lexington, KY: University Press of Kentucky, 1999.

Twomey, Alfred E., and Arthur F. McClure. *The Versatiles: Supporting Character Players in the Cinema 1930-1955*. New York: Castle Books, 1969.

Wainscot, Ronald H. "Mary Boland." *Notable Women in the American Theatre: A Biographical Dictionary*, ed. Alice M. Robinson et al. New York: Greenwood, 1989, 74–76.

Walker, Alexander. *Vivien: The Life of Vivien Leigh*. London: Weidenfeld and Nicholson, 1987.

Wasserstein, Wendy. "Foreword." *Three Plays by George Kelly*, ed. William J. Lynch. New York: Limelight Editions, 1999, ix–xii.

Watts, Jill. *Hattie McDaniel: Black Ambition, White Hollywood*. New York: Amistad, 2005.

Webster, Margaret. *The Same Only Different*. London: Victor Gollancz, 1969.

Williams, Tennessee. *Memoirs*. Garden City, NY: Anchor Press/Doubleday, 1983.

Young, Jordan R. *Reel Characters: Great Movie Character Actors*. Beverly Hills, CA: Moonstone Press, 1986.

Yurka, Blanche. *Bohemian Girl: Blanche Yurka's Theatrical Life*. Athens, OH: Ohio University Press, 1970.

INDEX

Page numbers in **_bold italic_** refer to photographs.

Abbott, George 108, 110
Abbott and Costello 115
Abel, Walter 120
Above Suspicion 150
Ackland, Rodney 209
Adair, Jean 168
Adams, Nick 151
Adrian 56, 64, 140
Adrian, Iris 148–149
Adventures of Don Juan 135, 136
The Adventures of Huckleberry Finn 169, 222n239
The Adventures of Robin Hood 9, 135
The Adventures of Tom Sawyer 62
After the Thin Man 160
After Tomorrow 74
Ah, Wilderness! 62, 123
Aherne, Brian 57, 198
Airport 99
Albert, Anna 28
Albert, Eddie 83, 167
Albertson, Frank 62, 123
Albertson, Mabel 118, 127
Alcott, Louisa May 62, 137
Aldridge, Kay **_75_**
Alexander, Jane 201
Alice Adams 102, 175
Alice in Wonderland 139, 193
All About Eve 30, 172, 175–176, 177
All God's Chillun Got Wings 183
All My Children 207
All Quiet on the Western Front 53
All That Heaven Allows 124, 224n420
All the Fine Young Cannibals 38
All the King's Men 26, 92
All This, and Heaven Too 131
Allen, Gracie 40
Allgood, George 9
Allgood, Margaret Harold 9
Allgood, Sara 6, 9–**_13_**, 22, 53, 133, 161, 167, 168
Allyson, June 65, **_97_**, 120, 125, 157

Alma, Where Do You Live? 167
Ameche, Don 63, 115, 154
American Dream 197
The Anatomist 183
And So to Bed 98
And Then There Were None 15
Anderson, Eddie "Rochester" **_58_**, 107
Anderson, Ernest 103, 223n326
Anderson, Jessie Margaret Saltmarsh 14
Anderson, Judith 5, 10, 12, 13–**_19_**, 28, 29, 32, 67, 76, 82, 127, 146, 178, 197
Anderson, Milo 135–136
Anderson, Richard 170
Anderson-Anderson, James 14
Andrews, Dana 79
Andrews, Edward 158
Andrews, Julie 94
Angel, Heather 42
Ankers, Evelyn 145
Anna and the King of Siam 190, 196, 201
Anna Christie (film) 113, 172, 173
Anna Christie (play) 171, 183
Anna Karenina 186
Another Language 74
Another Part of the Forest (film) 81
Another Part of the Forest (play) 80
Another Thin Man 115
Anthony Adverse 44, 53, 197
Arden, Eve 177
Arliss, George 147
Arms and the Girl 19
Arnold, Edward 149
Arrowsmith 44
Arsenic and Old Lace 76
Arthur, Jean **_63_**, 69, 138
The Artist's Model 191
Arzner, Dorothy 60, 161
As You Desire Me 14
As You Like It 164, 185
As Young as You Feel 174–175
Ashcroft, Peggy 83
Ashley, Elizabeth 128

Astaire, Fred 115, 140, 157, 206
Asther, Nils 186
Astor, Mary 12, 21, 23, 39, 65, 102, 121, 122, 123, 131, 147, 190, 217n3
Atkinson, Brooks 10, 96, 141, 208
Auer, Mischa 99
Auntie Mame 150–151, 172
Autumn 183
The Awakening of Helena Ritchie 23
The Awful Truth 35, 168, 213
Aylmer, Felix 71
Ayres, Lew 221n235
Ayres, Rosalind 89

Baby Doll 82
Bacall, Lauren 123, 124
Bachelor in Paradise 124
Back to Bataan 46–47
Bad Bascomb 113
Baddeley, Angela 89
Baddeley, Hermione 94, 190
Badel, Alan 16
Bahama Passage 181
Bailey, Pearl 38
Bainter, Fay 5, 6, 19–**_22_**, 35, 46, 47, 57, 63, 64, 65, 96, 121, 168, 203, 213, 214, 217n3
Baker, Carroll 82, 121
The Balkan Princess 50
Ball, Lucille 36, **_37_**, 38, 126
Bancroft, Anne 83, 184
The Bank Dick 161–162, 215
Bankhead, Tallulah 14, 28, 56, 76, 78, 80, 89, 94, 112, 119, 127, 151, 154, 202, 213, 214, 224n423, 228n625
Barefoot in the Park (film) 128, 131, 175
Barefoot in the Park (play) 128, 175
Barker, Harley Granville 209
Barnacle Bill 113
Barnes, Binnie 51, 190, 206
The Barretts of Wimpole Street 134

235

Index

Barrie, J.M. 20, 89
Barris, Alex 86, 206, 213
Barrow, Kenneth 179
Barry, Philip 80
Barrymore, Ethel 6, 23–**28**, 39, 76, 80, 81, 92, 111, 124, 133, 181, 185, 186, 202, 213, 217n3, 220n162, 225n423, 229n658
Barrymore, John 24, 39, 56, 73, 87, 111, 167, 173, 225n423
Barrymore, Lionel 19, 23, 24, **26**, 27, 28, 39, 44, 56, 62, 63, 73, 123, 155
Bartholomew, Freddie 160
Bartlett, Martine 83
Baskett, James **207**
The Bat (film) 125, 175, 184
The Bat (play) 184, 208
Bates, Florence 6, 28, 29–**33**, 42, 43, 67, 69, 75, 76, 202, 212, 213, 214, 219n138
Bates, Kathy 201
The Battle of Midway 79
Baxter, Anne 18, 25, 166, 181, 201, 212
The Beachcomber (aka *Vessel of Wrath*) **90**, 93
Beal, John 199
Beaton, Cecil 68, 71, 163
Beatty, Warren 144
The Beaux Stratagem 19, 185
Beavers, Ernestine Monroe 38
Beavers, Louise 6, 33–**38**, 47, 100, 101, 105, 106, 107, 147, **216**
Becky Sharp 59, 190, 195
Beecher, Janet 60
Beery, Wallace 40, 62, 111, **112**, 123, 140, 174, 191, 193
Beggar on Horseback 62
Begley, Ed 83
Belasco, David 213
Bel Geddes, Barbara 32, 123
Bell, Book, and Candle 94
The Belle of Mayfair 71
The Belle of New York 115, 157
Belle Starr 37, 154–155
The Bells of St. Mary's 136
Benedek, László 81
Bening, Annette 144, 222n300
Bennett, Arnold 68, 89, 92
Bennett, Constance 36, 57
Bennett, Leon 105
Bennett, Marjorie 22
Bennett, Richard 152
Bergen, Polly 177
Bergman, Ingrid 11, **31**, **98**, 99, 181, **182**, 208, 211
Bergner, Elisabeth 180
Berkeley, Busby 51
Bern, Paul 186
Bernhardt, Sarah 72
Bessie, Alvah 197
Best, Edna 209
The Betrothal 85

Beulah 106, 109
Bevans, Clem 61
The Beverly Hillbillies 32
Bewitched 94, 117, 118, 121, 126, 127, 156, 159, 225n442
Biberman, Daniel 197, 202
Biberman, Herbert J. 197, 198, 201, 202
Biberman, Joan 197, 202
Bickford, Charles 123
Big Jack 113
The Big Street 36, **37**, 126
The Big Wheel 106
The Bill Cosby Show 94
A Bill of Divorcement (1932) 44, 55, 60, 153
A Bill of Divorcement (1940) 21
Binney, Constance 193, 228n625
Biography 50
Birch Interval 167
The Birdman of Alcatraz 175
The Birds 189
The Bishop's Wife 28, 70, 92
Bisson, Alexandre 87
The Black Bird 146, **151**
The Black Cat 69
Black Narcissus 183
Blackmail 9
Blackmer, Sidney 37
Blair, Betsy 27
Blake, Arthur 116
Blandick, Clara 3–4, 5, 7, 78, 155, 168, 174, 178, 222n239
Blithe Spirit 128
Blonde Venus 102
Blondell, Joan 35, 125
Blood Money 13, 15
Blore, Eric 51, 214
The Blue Bird 63, 74, 161, 201
The Blue Veil 126
Bluebell in Fairyland 68
Blum, Daniel 43
Blyth, Ann 115
Bodeen, DeWitt 31, 50, 53
Body and Soul 165
Bogart, Humphrey 39, 43, 87, 112, 113, 137, 146, **148**, 149, 194, 197, 214
Bogle, Donald 33, 34, 38, 100, 101, 105, 106, 108, 110, 223n360
Boland, Maria Cecilia Hatton 38, 39, 140
Boland, Mary 6, 16, 38–**43**, 44, 50, 56, 59, 72, 73, 76, 125, 133, 192, 202, 203–204, 205, 213
Boland, William Augustus 38
Boles, John 60, 160, 206, 221n237
Boleslawski, Richard 141, 161, 163
Bolton, Guy 137
Bombshell 37
Bond, Ward 53, 140, 147

Bondage 78
Bondi, Beulah 6, 19, 20, 22, 35, 43–**49**, 59, 61, 67, 76, 79, 87, 113, 114, 117, 147, 154, 158, 168, 174, 175, 196, 197, 198, 213
Bondy, Abram O. 43
Bondy, Eva Suzanna Marble 43, 49
Bonstelle, Jessie 50, 96
Booth, Shirley 218n423, 228n616
Borg, Veda Ann 147–148
Bouchey, Willis 61
Bought and Paid For 50
Bow, Clara 138
Boyer, Charles 71, 126, 131, 142–**143**, 144, 208, 211
Boys' Night Out 99
Brabin, Charles 27
Bradley, Kenneth 88
Brady, Alice 16, 41, 44, 49–**53**, 57, 64, 85, 99, 103, 138, 155, 174, 197, 206, 212, 217m3
Brady, Scott 174, 176
Brady, William, Jr. 53
Brady, William A. 50, 53, 103
The Brat 75
Brazzi, Rossano 65, 218n84
Breen, Joseph 175
Bremer, Lucille 131, 132
Brennan, Walter 21
Brent, George 25, 102, 103
Brian, David 155
Brice, Fanny 58
Bride of Frankenstein 9, 88, 91, 92, 128, 134, **136**, 190
Bride of the Lamb 50
The Bride Wore Red 59
The Bridge of San Luis Ray 142
Brigham Young 78
Bringing Up Baby 188
Brisson, Carl 160
Brisson, Freddie 39
Broderick, Helen 61
Bromberg, J. Edward 201
Brontë, Charlotte 12
Brough, Fanny 208
Brown Sugar 108
Brown, Anita **207**
Brown, Augustus Homer 189
Brown, Barry 131
Brown, Clarence 143
Brown, Joe E. 120
Brown, Kay 108
Brown, Tom 57
Browne, Coral 151
Browne, Maurice 43
Bruce, Nigel 16, 64, **67**, 190, 200
Bryan, Jane 147
Buckmaster, John 69
The Bugle Sounds 113
Bullets or Ballots 35
Burke, Billie 16, 21, 22, 34, 39, 40, 41, 44, 45, 50, 54–**61**, 76,

151, 152, 174, 177, 186, 192, 204, 214, 217n3, 221n235, 221n237
Burke, Billy 55
Burke, Blanche Beatty Hodkinson 55
Burnett, Carol 32
Burnett, Frances Hodgson 132, 188
Burns, George 40
Busch, Niven 16, 17, 70
Butler, David 56, 191
Butler, Lois **105**
BUtterfield 8 83
Byington, Edwin Lee 61
Byington, Helene 61
Byington, Spring 6, 7, 12, 16, **20**, 21, 22, 23, 41, 50, 56, 61–**66**, 96, 110, 116, 117, 121, 123, 127, 165, 217n3
Byrne, Gabriel 137

Cabin in the Sky 107
Cabot, Bruce 221
Cadell, Jean 160, 178
Caesar and Cleopatra 227n594
Café Society 34
Caged 77, 119, 124, 150, 221n237
Cagney, James 87, 103, 115
Cahill, Lily 32
Caldwell, Zoe 217n32
Calhern, Louis 24, 28
Calhoun, Rory 18
Call It a Day 52, 225n462
Call Northside 777 173
Callow, Simon 69, 89, 90, 137
Cameron, Rod 149
Camille (film) 74, 142, 160–161, 184, 190
Camille (play) 213
Campbell, Mrs. Patrick 209, 218n71
Canby, Vincent 110
Candida 128
The Canterville Ghost 137, 170
Canty, Marietta 34, 100, 107
Capote, Truman 94
Capra, Frank 22, 63, 174, 187, 228n616
The Captain Is a Lady 45, 60–61
Captain Jinks of the Horse Marines 23
Captain Tugboat Annie 78
Carey, Harry 84, **85**
Carlisle, Kitty 160, 195, 196
Caron, Leslie 91, 95, 178
Carrie Nation 128
Carroll, Leo G. 76, 151, 152, 168, 179
Carroll, Madeleine 34, 46
Carroll, Nancy 160, **192**, 221n237
Carson, Jack 29
Carter, Mrs. Leslie 191
The Case Against Mrs. Ames 46

Cass, Peggy 151
The Cat and the Canary **154**, 198–199
Cat on a Hot Tin Roof (film) 16–17
Cat on a Hot Tin Roof (play) 82, 129
The Catered Affair 178
Catherine the Great 180
Cavalcade (film) 132, 133, 135
Cavalcade (play) 133
Cecil, Mary 112
Cecil, Nora 76, 134, 221n236
Chad Hanna 79
The Chalk Garden 71
Chamberlain, George Agnew 18
Chambers, James C. 159
Chandler, Jeff **121**
Chandler, Lois Irene 62
Chandler, Phyllis Helene 62
Chandler, Roy Carey 61
Chaney, Lon, Jr. 145
The Charge of the Light Brigade 64
Charisse, Cyd 120
Charlotte's Web 127
Charming Sinners 74
Chasing Yesterday **153**
Chatterton, Ruth 64, 142, 144, 213
Chayefsky, Paddy 38, 171, 174
Cheaper by the Dozen 13, 131
Chekhov, Anton 141
The Cherry Orchard 93
Child of Fortune 82
Child of Manhattan 77, 160, 221n237
The Children's Hour (film) 22, 164, 204
The Children's Hour (play) 164
The Chocolate Soldier 32
Chodorov, Edward 27, 186
Christian, Mady 76
Christie, Agatha 15, 93
Christmas Holiday 87, 200
Christopher Bean 173, 178
Christopher Strong 44, 59, 190
Cimarron 19, 138–139
The Circle 191
Citizen Kane 118, 207
The City 205
Claire, Ina 50, 72, 213, 220
Clancarty 209
Clarence (film) 41
Clarence (play) 39
Clarkson, Patricia 224n421
Clash of the Titans 184
Clift, Montgomery 120
Clive, Colin 59, 88
Close, Glenn 132
Cluny Brown 13, 134, 136
Cobb, Lee J. 81, 83
Coburn, Charles 15, 29, 45, 60, **63**, 65, 70, 146, 149, 155
Cohan, George M. 147, 159
Cohn, Harry 64, 210

Colbert, Claudette 33, 34, 103, 110, 115, 118, 124, 131, 140, 161, 169, 192, 198, 224n389
Colcord, Mabel 155
Collier, Constance 58, 178, 189
Collinge, Patricia 83, 204
Collins, Joan 125, 157
Collins, Wilkie 119
Colman, Ronald 32, 134, 170
Colonel Effingham's Raid 155, 215
Colt, Russell Griswold 23
Colt, Samuel 28
Come to the Stable **91**, 92
Coming-Out Party 195
The Concert 213
Conklin, Peggy 74, 153
Connelly, Mark 107
The Conqueror 119, 125
Conquest 131, 142–**143**, 211
The Constant Wife 23, 26, 213
Coogan, Jackie 78
Cook, Donald 102
Cook, Elisha, Jr. 146, 147
Cooper, Gary **31**, **36**, 63, 78, 113, 122, **182**, 190
Cooper, Gladys 5, 6, 10, 28, 31, 43, 60, 66–**72**, 89, 92, 124, 145, 149–150, 159, 162, 178, 181, 189, 199, 202–203, 204, 209, 210, 211, 212, 213, 224n422
Cooper, Merian C. 220n194
Cooper, Violet Kemble 160
Coquette 35
Corby, Ellen 118, 123, 127, 150
Corey, Wendell 206
The Corn Is Green (film) 80, **81**, 185
The Corn Is Green (play) 23, 24, 80
Cornell, Katharine 14, 24, 60, 128
Cossart, Ernest 13
Costello, Dolores 132
Cotten, Joseph 11, 25, 32, 103, 123, 211
The Court Jester 175
Coward, Noël 19, 66, 94, 133
Cowl, Jane 5, 159
Cracked Nuts 140
Cradle Snatchers 39, 137, 140
Craig, James 78, **114**
Craig's Wife 54, 60, 77, 170, 191, 206, 220n190, 221n237
Crain, Jeanne 25, 174, 176, **177**, 178
Crane, Cheryl 221n234
Crane, Donald 53
Crane, James Lyon 53
Crash Dive 212
Craven, Frank 60
Crawford, James Loyd 223n315
Crawford, Joan 4, 21, 32, 42, 44, 45, 56, 58, 59, 64, 86, 107, 108, 115, 123, 125, 127, 133,

137, 138, 150, 157, 162–163, 165, 168–169, 186, 191, 205, 206, 214
Crews, Angelena Lockwood 73
Crews, John Thomas 73
Crews, Laura Hope 5, 22, 29, 72–76, 83, 133, 144, 147, 153, 161, 168, 202, 207, 210, 212, 213, 217n3
Crime and Punishment 168, 170
Cripps, Thomas 34, 35
Crisp, Donald **12**, 91, 179
Cromwell, Richard 53
Crosby, Bing 28, 35, 136, 201, 206
Crosman, Henrietta 79, 161, 185, 220
Crothers, Rachel 64, 185, 228n625
Crowther, Bosley 22, 42, 81, 155, 176, 224n419
Cry "Havoc" 21
Cukor, George **26**, 42, 55, 60, 61, 62, 64, 68, 90, 108, 111, 113, 115, 125, 134, 138, 139, 157, 160, 161, 176, 205, 207, 211, 214, 216, 229n658
Cummings, Constance 193
Cummings, Robert 145
Cunningham, Cecil 45, 61
Curly Top 78
Curtis, James 193
Curzon, Frank 68
Cynara 72
The Czarina 39

Daddy Long Legs 213
Dailey, Dan 120, **166**
Daisy Miller 131, 175
Dale, Esther 76, 117, 221n236
Dance, Girl, Dance 144
Dancing Lady 186
Dancing Mothers 205
Dangerous 193
Dangerous Liaisons 128, 132, 175, 183
Dark Passage 119, 124
Dark Victory 147, 214, **215**
Dark Waters 21
Darnell, Linda 78, 165, 172, 201
Darwell, Jane 6, 9, 11, 16, 44, 45, 53, 60, 76–**79**, 87, 113, 114, 133, 144, 150, 155, 161, 168, 172, 174, 175, 189, 219n141
Daughters Courageous 21
Daughters of Atreus 141
Davenport, Harry 46, **187**
Daves, Delmer 18
David Copperfield 9, 90, 134, 139, 160, **161**, 178
Davis, Bette 5, 22, 32, 34, 46, 60, 69, 72, 74, 75, 80, **81**, 96, 102, 103, 123, 127, 131, 147, 149, 152, 158, 176, 177, 178, 179, 180, 181, 185, 192, 193, 198, 199, 204, 214, **215**, 221n230, 226n510, 228n616
Davis, Jim 32
Davis, Owen 137
Davis, Paul 159
Day, Doris 66, 151, 158, 177, 178
Days in the Trees 84
Dazey, Charles T. 186
Dead End 44, 53, 111, 112, 113, 170
Dead End Kids 186
Deadly Deception 129
Dean, James 86
Dean, Julia 206
Dear Brutus 14
Dear Dead Delilah 127, 202
Death of a Salesman 47, 81, **82**, 83, 129, 175
DeCamp, Rosemary 65, 118, 122, 221n199
December Bride 65, 66, 127
Déclassée 23
Dee, Frances 59, 74
Dee, Ruby 36
Dee, Sandra 48, **158**
de Haven, Gloria **122**
de Havilland, Olivia **47**, 52, 60, 66, 103, 104, 123, 135, 144, 149, 150, 202, 212, 214, 225n462
Delicate Balance 96
Delmar, Viña 47
Del Rio, Evelyn 215
DeMille, Cecil B. 39, 219n115
DeMille, William 39
DeNergaard, Beatrice 197
Denham, Reginald 181
Dennis, Patrick 150
Denny, Reginald 60
Derelict 95
Design for Living 78
Desire Under the Elms 183
Destry Rides Again 34, 139
The Devil and Daniel Webster 78
The Devil and Miss Jones 29, 63, 66
The Devil Commands **164**, 165
The Devil Is a Woman 75, 190, 195
Dewhurst, Colleen 83
The Diary of a Chambermaid 15, **17**, 32
Dieterle, William 16, 198
Dietrich, Marlene 32, 34, 78, 93, 102, 131, 136, 139, 170, 180, 190, 192, 194, **195**, 204
Dinner at Eight (film) 41, 54, 56, 59, 155, 172, 173, 186, 227n557
Dinner at Eight (play) 189
Diplomacy 68
The Disorderly Orderly 158
The Distant City 88
Dix, Richard 139
Dr. Jekyll and Mr. Hyde 11
Doctor Monica 197
Dodge City 214
Dodsworth (film) 64, 142, 144
Dodsworth (play) 19, **142**
A Doll's House 23
Don Juan in Hell 126, 127
Donat, Robert 179, 227n584
Donnelly, Ruth 148
Dors, Diana 48
Double Door 164
Double Wedding 160
Doubting Thomas 41, 56, 191–192
Douglas, Kirk 30, 32
Douglas, Melvyn 21, 58, 195
Downey, Robert, Jr. 84
Dragon Seed 118, 119–120
Dragonwyck 64, 165
Drake, Betsy 32
The Dream Girl 19
Dresser, Louise 180
Dressler, Marie 3, 19, 40, 49, 78, 111, 112, 113, 140, 155, 159, 172–174, 178, 185, 186, 187, 190, 191, 193, 196, 205, 210, 227n558
Drew, John 39, 54, 72, 73
Driscoll, Bobby **207**
Dru, Joanne 130
Drums Along the Mohawk 140, 161, 170, 224n389
Dudgeon, Elspeth 190
Duel in the Sun 16, 107
Duke, Patty 175
Dulcy 59
Dumas, Alexandre 160
Dumont, Margaret 12, 33, 43, 67, 76, 202, 213, 214
Duncan, Isadora 89
Dunn, Emma 6, 221n236
Dunne, Irene 19, 32, 46, 64, 70, 74, 85, 120, 132, 139, 144, 147, 168, 181, 190, 201, 211
Dunnock, Florence Saynook 80
Dunnock, Mildred 6, 17, 35, 80–**84**, 117, 118, 129, 147, 175, 184
Dunnock, Walter 80
Durbin, Deanna 51, 52, 200, 203, 206
Dvorak, Ann 107

Eagels, Jeanne 213
East Is West 19
East of Eden 86
East Side, West Side 201
Eburne, Maude **40**
Echoes (aka *Living Nightmare*) 196, 202
Eddy, Nelson 32
Edge of Darkness 15
Educating Father 62
Edwards, Sarah **31**
The Egg and I 6, 111, 115, 169, 224n389
Eldridge, Florence 81, 168, 179

Index

Ellsler, Effie 184
Elmer the Great 159
Elsom, Isobel 22, 28, 29, 50, 68, 69, 127, 181, 190, 202, 220n147, 225n441
Eltinge, Julian 27
Elvey, Maurice 167
Emerson, Hope 108, 134, 146, 150
Emery, John 76, **119**
Emma (film) 172, 173
Emma (play) 33
The Emperor Waltz 206
The Enchanted April 168
The Enchanted Cottage 64
Erway, Arthur Benjamin 88
Escape 142
Evans, Brandon 168, 170
Evans, Edith 67, 89, 164, 205
Evans, Madge 56
Evans, Maurice 13, 27–28
Evelyn Prentice 160
Everson, William K. 79
Everyman 152
The Eye of the Devil 183
Eyman, Scott 79, 131, 219n141

The Facts of Life 38
Fairbanks, Douglas, Jr. 180
The Fall of Eve 213
Fallen Angel 167
Fallen Angels 19, 20
A Family Affair 62
The Fan 178
Fanatic 202
Far from Heaven 224n421
Farentino, James 83
Farjeon, Herbert 89
The Farmer Takes a Wife 176
The Farmer's Daughter 23, **24**, 25
Farrell, Glenda 148, 150
Father of the Bride 59
Father's Little Dividend 59
Faust 197
Fay, Frank J. 10
Faye, Herbie 158
Fellows, Rockcliffe 205
Felton, Verna 65
Ferber, Edna 220n162
Ferrer, Mel 170
Field, Betty 45, 83, 145, 184
Fields, Gracie 58
Fields, W.C. 38, 40, 90, 111, 159, 162, 191, 192, 193, 215
55 Days at Peking 125, 180, 183
Finishing School 34, 45, 59, 77, 221n237
Fire Over England 11, 179, 180, 181, 183
Fiske, Minnie Maddern 19
Fitch, Clyde 205
Fitzgerald, Geraldine 11, 12, 144, 179
Fitzroy, Emily 120, 184–185, 190
Flame of Barbary Coast 107

The Flame of New Orleans 34, 190
Flamingo Road 87
Fleming, Victor 108
Flint, Helen 214
Flint, Peter B. 165
Flynn, Errol 32, 135, 147, 161, 180, 181, 186, 206, 214
Foch, Nina 18
Fonda, Henry 36, **37**, 53, 78, 79, 128, 140, 225n423
Fonda, Jane 131, 156
Fonda, Peter 48
Fontaine, Joan 12, **15**, **30**, 42, 60, 66, **67**, 72, 125, 147, 178, 186, 205, 206, 208, 211
Foolish Notion 80
Footsteps in the Dark 206
For Services Rendered 168
For Whom the Bell Tolls 164, 204
Forbes, Mary 68, 69, 190, 202
Forbes, Ralph 190
Ford, Harrison 110
Ford, John 11, 26, 79, 83, 113, 128, 129, 130–131, 134, 135, 140, 154, 161, 184, 219n141, 224n380
Ford, Wallace 134
Forever After 50
Forever Amber 165, 167
Forever and a Day 69, 92, 211–212
The Forgotten Woman 168
Forsaking All Others (film) 41, 56, 214
Forsaking All Others (play) 56, 213, 214
The Fortune Hunter 167
Four Daughters 186
Four Mothers 186
Four Walls 85
Four Wives 186
Fowler, Edward H. 88
Fox, Sidney 214
Foy, Eddie, Jr. 176
Fragment of Fear 183
Franciosa, Anthony 83
Francis, Arlene 128, 158
Francis, Karl 202
Frankenstein 88
Frankenstein Meets the Wolf Man 145
Frears, Stephen 132
Friderici, Blanche 154
Friendly Persuasion 113
Frohman, Charles 23, 28, 39, 54, 55, 185, 186, 205
Frohman, Daniel 185, 186
The Front Page (film) 184
The Front Page (play) 110, 213
Fulton, Maude 75
The Furies 14, 16, 17–18, **48**

Gable, Clark 62, 75, 95, 113, 149, 162, 163
Gabor, Eva 31, 99
A Gaiety Girl 191

Garbo, Greta 5, 74, 131, 136, 142, **143**, 160, 173, 180, 186, 211, 213
The Garden of Allah 131, 202, 204, 206
Gardner, Ava 120
Garfield, David 202
Garfield, John 81, 144, 163, 165, 172, 186, 202
Garland, Judy 7, 65, 70–71, 114, 115, 172
Garner, James 96, 99, 177
Garrett, Betty 157
Garson, Greer 11, 42, 64, 70, 71, 118, 123–124, 126, 133, 134, 149, 206, 208, 221n235, 224n420, 229n678
Gaslight (1944) 124, 211
The Gay Divorcée 41, 51–52
Gaye, Gregory 142
Gaynor, Janet 3, 5
Gentle Annie **114**
Gentleman's Agreement 25, 111, 165
George, Gladys 84–**88**, 102, 146–147, 148, 150, 155, 214
George, Grace 27, 50, 53, 103
Ghosts 205
Gibbs, Wolcott 208
Gibson, Charles Dana 229n658
Gidget Goes to Rome 99
Gielgud, John 14, 89
Gigi 127
Gilchrist, Connie 22, 53, 114, 147, 172, **216**
The Gilded Cage 50
Gillette, William 14
Gilligan's Island 127
Gingold, Hermione 94, 190
Girl from Avenue A **75**, 161
The Girl from Missouri 177
The Girl with the Green Eyes 205
Gish, Lillian 181, 213
Gist, Robert 120, 126
The Glass Bottom Boat 158
A Glass Menagerie 22, 97
The Glass Slipper 91, 94–95
Gleason, James 140
Go West Young Man 155–156
Goddard, Paulette 15, 17, 31, 32, 37, 139, 154, 199, 205
The Goddess 38
Gods and Monsters 89
Going My Way 136, 185
The Gold Diggers 35
Gold Diggers of Broadway 35
Gold Diggers of 1935 51
Goldblum, Jeff 202
Goldwyn, Samuel 43, 44, 64, 178, 179
Gombell, Minna 47, 86, 148, 168
Gone with the Wind 22, 33, 35, 66, 72, 73, 74, 75, 76, 78, 86,

87, 100, 102, 103–**106**, **107**, 108–109, 120, 145, 149, 181, 183, 206, 221n235
The Good Earth 119, 160, 179
Good Sam **36**
Goodbye Again **98**, 99
Goodbye Broadway 53
Goodbye Fidel 201
Goodbye, Mr. Chips 11, 165
Goodbye, My Fancy 177
Goodman, Dody 110
Gordon, Mary 79, 190
Gordon, Ruth 14, 43, 83, 213
Gore, Charles Livingston 185
Gore, Edward 189
The Gorgeous Hussy 44, 219n140
Government Girl 123, 133, 225n462
Grable, Betty 51, 155, 165, 176, 178, 209
Grahame, Gloria 111, 176
The Grand Duchess and the Waiter 196
Granger, Stewart 16, 170, 183
Granny Get Your Gun **187**
Grant, Cary 24, 31, 37, 46, 69, 70, 92, 96, 98, 170, 186, 188
Granville, Bonita 44, 57, 62, 123, 197
Granville, Charlotte 185, 191
The Grapes of Wrath 6, 16, 45, 76, 77, 78, 79, 189
Grapewin, Charley 154
Gray, Dolores 125
Grayson, Kathryn 27, 120
The Great Barrington 164
The Great Divide 73
Great Expectations 190
The Great Lie 12, 102, 190
The Great Sinner 26
The Great Ziegfeld 54, 85
Green Dolphin Street 70, 212
The Green Years 70
Greenberg, Joel 16, 70, 115, 145, 165
Greene, Luther 19
Greenstreet, Sydney **119**, 125, 146–147, 193, 194
Greenwood, Charlotte 125
Greenwood, Joan 183
Greet, Ben 152
Gregory, Lady 10, 11
Gregory, Paul 119
Griffies, Ethel 5, **31**, 154, 185, 189
Groom, Elizabeth Rodgers 191
Groom, Richard Ebenezer 191
Grounds for Divorce 213
Guard That Girl 167
The Guardsman 32
Guilaroff, Sydney 27, 64
Guiness, Alec 99
Guthrie, Tyrone 93
Gwenn, Edmund 42, 66, 70, 129, 197

Hadleigh, Boze 18, 116, 119, 126, 138
Hale, Alan 214
Hale, Louise Closser 49, 74
Half Shot at Sunrise 140
Hall, James 138
Hall, Mordaunt 60
Hall, Porter 47, 115
Hall, Thurston 109
Hamilton, Jack 42, 100, 159, 160, 213
Hamilton, Margaret 12, 128, 134, 171, 197
Hamlet (film) 123
Hamlet (play) 14, 23
Hammett, Dashiell 193
Hammond, Virginia 138, 140
The Happiest Millionaire 71
The Hard Way 87
Harding, Ann 50
Hardwicke, Cedric 126, 211
Harlow, Jean 33, 36–37, 133, 148, 177, 186, 187, 227n557
Harmer, Lillian 189
Harmetz, Aljean 58
Harriet Craig 191, 206, 207
Harris, Richard 17, 202
Harris, Theresa 34, 60
Harrison, Rex 71, 201, 225n423
Hart, Moss 96
Harvey, Forrester **135**
Harvey, Georgette 105
Harvey, Laurence 151
The Harvey Girls 115
Hatfield, Hurd 15
Hay Fever 72
Hayden, Sterling 181
Haydn, Richard 134, 136
Hayes, Helen 24, 39, 43, 44, 129, 225n423, 228n616
Haymes, Dick 165
Haynes, Todd 224n421
Hayward, Susan 118, 125, 176, 178
Hayworth, Rita 16, 71
Head, Edith 127
Heartbreak House 167, 205
Hearts Aflame 204
Heaven Can Wait 115
The Heavenly Body 21
Hecht, Ben 213
Hedda Gabler 73
Heflin, Van 18, 21, 65
Heggie, O.P. 214
Hellman, Lillian 46, 164, 204
Hell's Highway 35
Henie, Sonja 140, 146
Henreid, Paul 42, 142
Henson, Gerald 10
Hepburn, Audrey 83
Hepburn, Katharine 20, 39, 59, 60, 62, 72, 102, 115, 118, 119, 137, 144, 147, 179, 188, 189, 190, 214, 218n84, 226n510
Her Cardboard Lover 155

Her Master's Voice (film) **73**, 74, 153, 153
Her Master's Voice (play) 74, 152–153
Herbert, Hugh 140, 199
Here Is My Heart 195, 196
Hernandez, Juano 155
Hickman, Howard J. 101
Hidden, Francie 228n637
High Sierra 170
High Wall 170
Higham, Charles 16, 24, 70, 115, 145, 165
Higher and Higher 169
The Highwayman 96
Hiller, Wendy 71, 166
Hinds, Samuel S. 63
His and Hers 156
Hitchcock, Alfred 11, 15, 66, 98, 205, 211
Hobson, Valerie 88
Hold 'Em Jail 140
Holden, Fay 21, 62, 65
Holden, William 179
Holiday Inn 35
Holliday, Judy 216
Holm, Celeste 25, **91**, 92, 111, 156, 165
Holt, Jack 162
Honky Tonk 113
Hope, Bob 38, 199, 201
Hopkins, Miriam 22, 59, 164, 165, 176, 195, 201, 202, 213, 216
Horne, Lena 107
Horton, Edward Everett 51, **73**, 74, 140, 153
Hound-Dog Man 78
A House Divided 113
How Green Was My Valley 11–**12**, 46, 135, 189
How the West Was Won 121, 126, 172, 177
Howard, Gertrude 107
Howard, Leslie 139
Howard, Sidney 74
The Howards of Virginia 170
Hubert, René 10
Hudson, Rochelle 34
Hudson, Rock 151, 174
Hughes, Gwyneth 80
Hull, Josephine 74, 76
The Human Comedy **21**, 185
Humoresque 165
Hunt, Linda 146
Hunt, Marsha 42, 163
Hunt, Martita 190
Hunter, Kim 81, 176
Hunter, Tab 44, 48, 96
Hush ... Hush, Sweet Charlotte 118, 123, 202
Hussey, Ruth 76
Huston, John 17, 149, 179
Huston, Walter 45, 46, 64, 96, 113, 119, 120, 123

Index

Hutton, Betty 206
Huxley, Aldous 89

I, Claudius 180
I Dood It **109**
I Live My Life 161, 163
I Love Lucy 152, 156
I Loved a Soldier 131
I Remember Mama 32, 120, 123
Ibsen, Henrik 141
Icebound (film) 138
Icebound (play) 137
Idiot's Delight 75
If I Had a Million 40–41, 184, 193
I'll Be Seeing You 62
I'm No Angel 102
Imitation of Life 33–34, 35
The Importance of Being Earnest 68, 93, 185, 205
In Old Chicago 16, 53, 212
In Our Time 42, 142
In the Good Old Summertime 65
In the Summer House 81
In the Zone 152
In This Our Life 60, 102–103, 106, 149
In Times Square 171
Indrisano, John 155
Inescort, Frieda 52, 225n462
The Informer 9, 128, 134–135
The Intimate Strangers 152
Intruder in the Dust 155
The Invisible Man 9, 128, 134, **135**
Invisible Stripes 148, 179
Invitation to Murder 197
Irene 59, 123
The Iron Duke 71
Irvine, Theodora 50
Irving, Henry 209
It Should Happen to You 216
It's a Wonderful Life 43, 46, 70, 219n140
Iturbi, Amparo 27
Iturbi, José 27
Ivan, Rosalind 80
I've Always Loved You 144, 215
Ives, Burl 16–17
Ivy 133

Jackass Mail 112, 113
The Jackie Robinson Story 36
Jackson, Carlton 104
Jacoby, Will 33
James, Henry 23, 124
Jane Eyre (1934) 189
Jane Eyre (1944) 12, 64, 124–125, 178, 181, 189, 190
Jarman, Claude, Jr. 155
Jeanne Eagels **121**
Jeans, Isabel 127
Jeffers, Robinson 14
Jenkins, Jackie "Butch" 21, 123
Jesse James 79

Jewell, Isabel 155
The Jewess 19
Jezebel (film) 22, 34, 46, 57, 65, 147, 179
Jezebel (play) 213
The Jimmy Stewart Show 219n140
Joan of Paris 188
The John Forsythe Show 94
Johnny Belinda 119, 123
Johnny Come Lately 103, 115
Johnny Trouble 28
Johns, Eric 14
Johns, Shirley 123
Johnson, Van 21
Jones, Jennifer 13, 25, 69, 71, 103, 124, 164
Jones, Tiny 79
Jones, Tommy Lee 17
Jones, Venezuela 108
Joslyn, Allyn 175
Jourdan, Louis 60, 99, 125
Journey for Margaret 21, 170
Joy, Leatrice 35
Juarez 198, 202
Jubilee 76
Judge Hardy and Son 145
Julia Misbehaves 42, 206, 212
June Bride 22
Juno and the Paycock (film) 9, 217n13
Juno and the Paycock (play) 10
Just for You 28, 212, 215

Kanin, Fay 156
Kanin, Michael 156
Karl and Anna 197
Karloff, Boris 88, 164, 165
Kathleen Ni Houlihan 9
Kaufman, George S. 96, 147, 220n162
Kaye, Danny 22, 30
Kazan, Elia 26, 80, 165
Keating, Larry 174
Keel, Howard 120
Keen, Malcom 216
Keep Your Powder Dry 124
Keeper of the Flame 190
Keeping Up Appearances 41
Kellaway, Cecil 31
Kelly, Gene 157, 200
Kelly, George 39, 56, 60, 191, 221
Kelly, Grace 95, 96, 98, 125, 178, 191
Kelly, Patsy **58**, 148, 177
Kempner, Nan 49
Kennedy, Arthur 81
Kern, Jerome 137
Kerr, Deborah 64, 71, 178, 183
Kerr, Walter 131
Key Largo 86, 123
The Keys to the Kingdom 11, 165
Kibbee, Guy 46
Kilbride, Percy 111, 113, 115, 116, 117

Kind Lady (1935) 27
Kind Lady (1951) 23, 27–**28**
Kind Lady (play) 186
King Kong 102
The Kingdom of God 23
Kings Row 15, 145
Kirby, Michael 123
The Kiss Burglar 19
A Kiss in the Dark 146
Kitty Foyle 29, 69
Knight, Shirley 83
Knoblock, Edward 68
Kolb, Clarence 57
Korda, Alexander 11, 93, 179, 180
Koster, Henry 99
Krebs, Stanley LeFevre 111, 117, 224n380
Kruger, Alma 22, 221n237
Kruger, Otto 164, 197
Kulp, Nancy 174
Kummer, Clare 73, 74, 152

La Cava, Gregory 99
Ladies in Distress 196
Ladies in Retirement 181
Ladies of the Big House 78
Ladies of the Jury 217n23
Lady for a Day 3, 187
Lady in a Cage 202
Lady in Waiting 88
The Lady Is Willing 170
The Lady of the Camellias 23
Lady Scarface 14, 18
The Lady Vanishes 211
Lady Windemere's Fan 178, 209
The Lady with the Lamp 164
A Lady's Profession 75, 193, **194**
Lahr, Bert 115
The Lake 190
Lamas, Fernando 115
Lambert, Gavin 62, 218n71
Lamour, Dorothy 201
Lamparski, Richard 220n194
Lancaster, Burt 71, 175
Lanchester, Edith 89
Lanchester, Elsa 12, 35, 67, 88–**95**, 134, 136, 137, 160, 178, 179, 189
Landis, Jessie Royce 95–**99**, 118, 125, 127, 144, 152, 225n423
Landis, Medbury Perry 96
Landis, Perry Lester 96
Landscape 128
Lange, Jessica 17
Lankfard, Nym 101, 223n315
Lansbury, Angela 28, 53, 124, 190
Lanza, Mario 27
Laramie 66
Larger than Life 97
Lassie 208
Lassie Come Home 91, 212
The Last of Mrs. Cheyney (film) 162–163

The Last of Mrs. Cheyney (play) 68, 162, 209
The Late Christopher Bean 43
Late Love 208
Laugh and Get Rich 140
Laughton, Charles 16, 25, **40**, 41, 62, 67, 88, 89–90, 93–94, 95, 118, 126, 132, 136, 179
Laura 18
Laurents, Arthur 218n84
Law, Jude 89
Lawford, Peter 65
Lawrence, Barbara 31
Lawrence, Gertrude 93
Lawrence, Jerome 150
Lee, Anna 79
Lee, Betty 227
Lee, John Griffith 126
Lee, Rowland V. 95
Leedy, Glenn **207**
le Gallienne, Eva 42, 59
Lehman, Benjamin Harrison 19
Leigh, Janet 65
Leigh, Vivien **10**, 11, 69, **104**, 105, **107**, 144–145, 183, 206, 212
Leighton, Margaret 83, 184
Leon, Connie 190
Leonard, William T. 34, 40, 138, 140, 190, 219n127
LeRoy, Mervyn 161, 197, 201, 205
Let Us Be Gay 185
Let's Dance 206–207
The Letter (film) 179, 196, 199
The Letter (play) 72
Letter from an Unknown Woman 60
A Letter to Three Wives 30, 172, 175
Letty Lynton 186, 188
Lewis, Jerry 127, 158, 225n441
Lewis, Sinclair 19
Libeled Lady 212
Life Begins 80
The Life of Emile Zola 198
Life with Father 170
Linden, Eric 62, 74, 123
Lindfors, Viveca 135
Listen to the Mocking Bird 59
The Little Foxes (film) 179, 204
The Little Foxes (play) 80–81
Little Lord Fauntleroy (film) 132, 160, 178, 190
Little Lord Fauntleroy (play) 43
Little Miss Broadway 78
Little Women (1933) 62, 137, 139
Little Women (1949) 65, 155, 207–208
Little Women (1994) 137
Little Women (play) 50, 96
Litvak, Anatole 147
Llewellyn, Richard 24
Lloyd, Doris 28
Loftus, Cecilia 69, 199
Logan, Joshua 128

Lombard, Carole 35, 74, 75, 85, 99, 149, 192, 195, 206
Lone Star 48
Long Day's Journey Into Night 22, 84
The Long Voyage Home 128, 130, 175
Lord, Marjorie 103
Lord, Pauline 43, 178
Lorne, Marion 156, 159
Lorre, Peter 147, 168, 190
Lorring, Joan 80, 190
The Lost Moment 124
Louisa 65–66
Louise, Anita 147
Love Affair (1939) 35, 143–144, 168
Love Affair (1994) 144
Love Crazy 29–30
Love for Love 93
Love Is a Headache 86
Love Me Forever 63
Love Me Tonight 154
Love's Old Sweet Song 96
Loy, Myrna 13, 29, 37, 50, 52, 54, 115, 120, 131, 137, 144, 160, 186, 206, 217n3
Luce, Clare Boothe 42, 125, 157, 205
Lucky Night 115
Lugosi, Bela 145, 199
Lukas, Paul 46, 62, 204
Lullaby of Broadway 32, 87
Lund, John 157, 176, 215
Lund, Marie 157
Lung, Clarence 119
Lunt, Alfred 39
Lupino, Ida 42, 181
Lydia 11, 140, 149, 150
Lynde, Paul 126

Ma and Pa Kettle at Waikiki 117
MacArthur, Charles 213
Macbeth (play) 13
Macbeth (TV) 14
MacDonald, Jeanette 42, 132, 154, **162**, 206
MacGill, Moyna 10, 13, 178
MacLaine, Shirley 164
MacLane, Barton 147
MacMahon, Aline 27, 62, 114, 118, 119, 120, 122, 123, 124, 186
MacMurray, Fred 34, 46, 71, 102, 111, 115, 150, 154, 169
Madame Bovary 71
Madame Racketeer 75, 193
Madame X **86**, 87, 214
Made for Each Other 35, 206, 207
The Madras House 209
Maeterlinck, Maurice 74, 161
The Magnificent Ambersons 69, 118, 120, 122
Maid of Salem 197–198
Maid's Night Out 147
Main, Marjorie 6, 19, 42, 43, 44, 45, 61, 103, 110–**117**, 125, 133, 138, 157, 172, 178, 205, 213, 222n238
Main Street to Broadway 28, 124, 218n84, 224n423
Major Barbara 197
Make Way for Tomorrow 19, 20, 35, 36, 45, 47, 49, 168, 219n142
Malden, Karl 82, 121
Malkovich, John 132
Malone, Dorothy 82
The Maltese Falcon (1931) 149
The Maltese Falcon (1941) 87, 146–147, **148**, 151
Malyon, Eily 134, 190
Man and Superman 126
A Man Called Horse 17
The Man from U.N.C.L.E. 94
The Man Who Came to Dinner 42, 72, 158, 221n230
Mankiewicz, Joseph L. 30
Mannequin 169–169
Manners, Hartley 96
Mannix 94
March, Fredric 46, 74, **81**, 192, 197
Marie Antoinette 87, 88, 214
Mark of the Vampire 161
The Mark of Zorro 196, 201
Marsh, Mae 79
Marshall, Brenda 135, 181
Marshall, Herbert 21, 64, 209
Marvin, Lee 120
Mary of Scotland 179
Mary Poppins 76, 79, 94
Maryland 21
La Mascotte 208
Maslin, Janet 84
The Matinee Hero 213
The Mating Season 172, 174, 175, 176, 177, 215–216
Mature, Victor 145
Maugham, Somerset 96, 199, 213
Maxwell, Marilyn 31, 123
Mayer, Louis B. 68, 187
Mayo, Archie 193
Mazurki, Mike 184
McAllister, Lon 18
McCambridge, Mercedes 26, 92
McCarey, Leo 35, 36, 47, 168
McCarthy, Kevin 81
McCrea, Joel 74, 169
McDaniel, Etta 101–102
McDaniel, Hattie 6, 12, 33, 84, 100–**106**, 123, 144, 149, 175, **207**
McDaniel, Henry 101
McDaniel, Sam 101–102
McDaniel, Susan Holbert 101
McDowall, Roddy 12, 91
McGuire, Dorothy 25, 113, 132
McGuire, Linda 84
McKellen, Ian 89
McLaglen, Victor 130, 134

Index

McNally, Horace (Stephen) **20**
McQueen, Butterfly 12, 34, 100–101, 106–**110**
Medea 13, 14, 16, 217n32
Meehan, John 87
Meek, Donald 171
Meet John Doe 63
Meet Me in Las Vegas 120
Meet Me in St. Louis 65, 114
Menjou, Adolphe 21, 42
Mercer, Beryl 53, 225n462
Meredith, Brugess 32
Merely Mary Ann 73
Merivale, Jack 69
Merivale, Philip 66, 72, 159
Merkel, Una 58, 59, 95, 118, 139, 148, 151, 215
Merrily We Live 22, 41, **57**, 177
Merrily We Roll Along 96
The Merry Wives of Windsor 73, 185
Michael, Gertrude 160, 195, 196
Mickey **105**
Midnight (aka *Call It Murder*) 212, 214
A Midsummer Night's Dream 108, 172
Mildred Pierce 107, 150, 177
Milestones 68
Miller, Arthur 80, 82
Miller, Frank 145
Miller, Henry 73
Min and Bill 172, 174
Minnelli, Vincente 70, 107, 113
Miracle on 34th Street 6, 34, 170–171
The Miracle Worker 175
Mirren, Helen 110
The Misfits 95, 172, 177
Missouri Legend 128
Mr. and Mrs. Smith 206
Mr. Belvedere Goes to College 95, 96
Mr. Blandings Builds His Dream House 37
Mr. Imperium 116
Mr. Lucky 31, 69
Mr. Pim Passes By 72
Mr. Prohack 89
Mr. Skeffington 149, 150
Mr. Smith Goes to Washington 43, 46, 87, 219n140
Mitchell, Cameron 81
Mitchell, Grant 153
Mitchell, Margaret 33
Mitchell, Thomas 20, 35, 47, 168
Mitchum, Robert 16, 48
The Model and the Marriage Broker 172, 174, 176, **177**
Monroe, Marilyn 95, 177, 178
Montgomery, Douglas 199
Montgomery, Elizabeth 156
Montgomery, Robert 50, 186, 208, 210
The Moon's Our Home 44, 185

Moore, Dennie 157, 174
Moore, George 10
Moore, Julianne 224n421
Moore, Leroy 38
Moore, Victor 47, 168
Moorehead, Agnes 6, 7, 12, 19, 28, 43, 44, 65, 69, 96, 99, 103, 117–**128**, 141, 147, 149, 150, 156, 165, 175, 181, 184, 196, 197, 202
Moorehead, John Henderson 117
Moorehead, Mary Mildred McCauley 117
Moorehead, Sean 126
Moran, Jackie 84
Moran, Joseph 171
Moran, Joseph Anthony 171
Moran, Monica Ann 171
Moran, Polly 174, 196
Moreno, Rita 22, 151
Morgan, Frank 70, 123, 145, 159, 161, 163
Morgan, Peter 149
Morley, Karen 85, 163
Morley, Sheridan 68, 133
Morosco, Oliver 19
Morris, Chester 186
Morrison, Lindsay 137
The Mortal Storm 145
Morton, Tom 224n423
Moseley, Roy 24
The Mosquito Coast 110
Mostel, Zero 174
Mother Carey's Chickens 21, 63
Mourning Becomes Electra (film) 169
Mourning Becomes Electra (play) 13, 14, 50
Move Over, Darling 177
Mrs. Bumpstead-Leigh 19
Mrs. Miniver 69, 122, 133, 146, 210–211, 212, 229n678
Mrs. Parkington 70, 124, 149–150
Mrs. Wiggs of the Cabbage Patch 137
Much Ado About Nothing 73
Mundin, Herbert 135
Muni, Paul 18, 160, 179, 190, 198
Munson, Ona 86, 145, 148, 150, 217n1
Murder! 133
Murder at the Vanities 160
Murder by Death 94, 95
Murder, He Says 115
Music for Madame 147
Music in the Air 112
Mutiny on the Bounty 62
My Darling Clementine 79
My Dear Secretary 32
My Fair Lady (film) 71, 127
My Fair Lady (musical) 71
My Lady's Dress 72
My Man Godfrey (1936) 41, 51, 53, 57
My Man Godfrey (1957) **97**, 99
Myrtil, Odette 29, 141

Nanny and the Professor 94
Nash, Florence 125
Nash, Mary 144
National Velvet 80, 163, 165, 181
Natwick, Joseph 128
Natwick, Mary Meredith 128
Natwick, Mildred 7, 79, 95, 117, 118, 127, 128–**132**, 135, 161, 175
Naughty Marietta 90
Nazimova, Alla 42, 50, 73, 141–143, 145, 146, 197, 217n34
Neal, Frances E. 18
Neal, Patricia 80
Negulesco, Jean 123
Nelson, Ruth 163, 165, 197
Nesbit, Allegra 219
Nesbitt, Cathleen 71, 190
Never Say Goodbye 206
New Faces of 1943 157
New Girl in Town 171, 173, 177
A New Kind of Love 174
New Moon 42
Newly Rich 140
Newman, Paul 17, 61, 83, 174
Newquist, Roy 42
Ney, Richard 22, 126
Nielsen, Leslie 125, 131, 157
Night After Night 192–193, 196
Night Angel **192**
Night Must Fall (film) 53, 163, 209–210, 212
Night Must Fall (play) 163, 209
Ninotchka 142
Niven, David 66, 71, 92, 97, 125, 146, 179, **180**, 212
No More Ladies 137, **138**, 203
No, No, Nanette 177
Noble, Peter 35
Noel, Hattie 105
None But the Lonely Heart 24, 124
Norman, Gertrude 184
North by Northwest 98–99
The Notorious Sophie Lang 195, 196
Novak, Kim 94, 99, 121, 150
Novello, Ivor 66
Now, Voyager 28, 68, 69, 122, 149, 158, 190
Nugent, Frank S. 29, 109, 139, 198
The Nun's Story 83
Nutter, Charles Edward 137
Nutter, Ida May Cox 137

Oberon, Merle 11, 21, 22, 140, 149, 179, **180**
O'Brien, Margaret 65, 71, 91, 120, 170
O'Brien, Pat 147
O'Casey, Sean 11, 184
O'Connor, Una 9, 43, 79, 88, 128, 129, 132–**137**, 141, 160, 161, 181
Odets, Clifford 24, 83, 218n68

Of Human Hearts 22, 46, 219n140
Oh, Boy! 137
O'Hara, Maureen 11, 12, 21, 34, 79, 130, 178, 189
O'Keefe, Dennis 18
Old Acquaintance 165
The Old Dark House 190
The Old Ladies 209
The Old Maid 147
Oliver, Edna May 6, 11, 39, 58, 62, 117, 127, 137–**140**, 144, 145, 160, 165, 183, 202, 203–204, 207, 210, 224n389
Oliver, Freeman Adam 225n469
Olivier, Laurence 11, **30**, 42, 66, 69, 179, 183, 212
O'Malley, Neill 197
On Borrowed Time 45
On the Stairs 14
On the Town 32, 157
On Their Own 62
One Foot in Heaven 46, 74
One Hundred Men and a Girl **52**
One of the Hollywood Ten 202
O'Neil, Barbara 76, 83
O'Neil, Nance 19
O'Neill, Eugene 122, 152
O'Neill, Maire 10, 217n13
Only Yesterday 60, 77
Oppenheimer, George 22
The Opposite Sex 125, 157
Orry-Kelly 151
O'Shea, Michael 174
O'Sullivan, Maureen 42
The Other Rose 19
Ottiano, Rafaela 33, 141
Our Flat 208
Our Gang 48
Our Mrs. McChesney 23
Our Town (film) 21, 46
Our Town (play) 128
Our Vines Have Tender Grapes 120
Ouspenskaya, Maria 6, 43, 44, 108, 110, 141–**146**, 163, 197
Outward Bound 191
The Ox-Bow Incident 78–79

Page, Geraldine 71, 83, 151, 202
Pallette, Eugene 115
Palmer, Stuart 140
Pangborn, Franklin 60, 138
Papa Is All 96
The Paradine Case 25
Paris Model 30–31
Parish, James Robert 34, 40, 43, 138, 140, 172, 175, 190, 219n127
Parker, Dorothy 182
Parker, Eleanor **119**, 123, 125, 150
Parnell 137
Parsons, Louella 62, 95
The Patricia Neal Story 84
Patrick, Gail 29

Patrick, Lee 35, 74, 118, 146–**152**, 171
Patterson, E.D. 152
Patterson, Elizabeth 6, 7, 44, 60, 73, 74, 85, 96, 152–**156**, 168, 174, 175, 199
Patton, William 159
Paxinou, Katina 164, 204
Payne, John 21
Pearce, Alice 7, 108, 114, 127, 134, 156–**159**
Pearce, Robert E. 156
Peck, Gregory 11, 70, 165
Peer Gynt 81
Peg o' My Heart 10
Penn, Leonard 88
Penny Serenade 46
The Perfect Specimen 161, 186
Perkins, Anthony 99, 156
Perry, Margaret 155
Personal Appearance 84, 85, 88, 155
Personal Property 133
Peter Ibbetson 73
Peters, Margot 23, 27, 28, 218n83
Peters, Susan 122, 211
Peyton Place 82–83
Pfeiffer, Michelle 132
Piaf, Edith 87
Pickford, Mary 35
The Pick-Up Artist 84
Pickup on South Street 172
The Picture of Dorian Gray 178
Pidgeon, Walter 149
Pierce, Jack 88
Pigott, Tempe 190
Pilgrimage 79, 185
Pillow Talk 151, 172, 174, 175, 176–177
Pinky 23, 25–26, 92
Pinza, Ezio 116
The Pirate 70
Pitts, ZaSu 53, 94
A Place in the Sun 165–166
The Playboy of the Western World 9, 128
Pleasantville 202
Please Believe Me 64
Please Don't Eat the Daisies 66
The Plough and the Stars 128, 135
Plunkett, Walter 27, 123
Pocketful of Miracles 228n616
Poe, Edgar Allan 199
Portrait of Jennie 25, 32
Potter, H.C. 25
Povah, Phyllis 42, 112, 125, 205
Powell, Dick 125
Powell, Eleanor **109**
Powell, William 29, 37, 54, 115, 120, 159, 160, 186, 194, 206
Power, Tyrone, Jr. 78, 93, 136, 140, 144, 201, 212
Power, Tyrone, Sr. 140
Pratt, David Welford 138

The Preacher's Wife 92
Preminger, Otto 167
Presenting Lily Mars 21, 64, 172
The President's Lady 22
Preston, Robert 156
Price, Kate 217n23
Price, Vincent 14, 18
Pride and Prejudice 42, 139–140, 190
The Princess Comes Across 75, 195
Princess O'Rourke 217n23
The Private Life of Henry VIII 93
Private Lives 224n423
The Private Lives of Elizabeth and Essex 147, 181
Private Number 25, 77, 221n237
Professional Sweetheart 34
A Proud Woman 168
Punch and Judy 147
Pursued 16
Pygmalion 71

Quality Street 19, 20, 214
The Quiet Man 128, **129**, 130
Quinlan, David 86, 147, 167, 215
Quinn, Anthony 47
Quinn, Arthur Hobson 50

Radner, Gilda 159
Raffles 191, 212
Raft, George 148, 179, 192, 193
Ragan, David 19, 156, 210, 216
Rain 45
Rainbow on the River (aka *It Happened in New Orleans*) 33, 34, 188
Rainer, Luise 54, 85, 160, 179
Raines, Ella 13
Rains, Claude 89, 134, **135**, 145, 149, 181, 197, 198
The Rains Came 77, 142, 144, 221n237
Raintree County 120, 121
Ralph, Jessie 29, 75, 127, 145, 159–**163**, 171, 191, 202, 205, 208, 210, 215
Ralston, Vera Hruba 146
Rambeau, Marjorie 76, 86, 144
Randall, Tony 151, 171
Random Harvest 122, 134, 170
Rapper, Irving 69, 80
Rasputin and the Empress 27, 190
Rathbone, Basil 139, 186, 190, 199, 200, 201
Rationing 113
The Razor's Edge 25, 181, 201
Read, Barbara 35
Reagan, Ronald 65, 146, 214, **215**
Reap the Wild Wind 37, 170
Rear Window 172, **173**, 175, 177
Rebecca 15–**16**, 29, **30**, 32, 42, 60, 66–**67**, 178, 179
Reckless 186, 188
The Red Danube 26

Red-Headed Woman 186
The Red House 14, 18
Red Rust 197
Redford, Robert 128
Redgrave, Michael 181
Reed, Donna 21, 70, **114**
Reed, Florence 14, 217n32
The Rejuvenation of Mary 186
Relative Values 71
Rembrandt 93
Remember? 221n235
Remember the Day 164
Remember the Night 46, 48, 154
René, Rose Marie 53
Rennie, James 149
Renoir, Jean 17
The Rescuing Angel 59
The Return of a Man Called Horse 202
The Return of October 212
Revere, Anne 6, 35, 80, 95, 111, 163–**167**, 181, 204
Revere, Clinton 163
Revere, Paul 167
The Revolt of Mamie Stover 124
Reynolds, Adeline De Walt 5, 185
Reynolds, Debbie 38, 48, 116, 118, 121, 124, 126, 127, 131, 158, 177, 178, 224n380, 224n420
Reynolds, Marjorie 35
Rice, Elmer 43
Richards, Jeff 125
Riders to the Sea 9
Ring Round the Moon 208
Ringwald, Molly 84
Risdon, Elisabeth 6, 33, 43, 44, 47, 50, 67, 68, 69, 76, 110, 167–**170**, 174, 190, 202
Risdon, John Jenkins 167
Risdon, Martha Harrop 167
Ritter, Charles 171
Ritter, Lucy Hale 171
Ritter, Thelma 6, 95, 118, 121, 170–**178**, 215
The Rivals 28, 42
The Road to Rio 201
The Road to Rome 159
The Road to Singapore 194
The Roaring Twenties 87, 170
Roberts, Allene 18
Robertson, Dale 176
Robeson, Paul 102, 183
Robinson, Edward G. 18, 120
Robinson, Jackie 36
Robinson, Jay **97**
Robinson, Shari 166
Robison, Henry 185
Robison, Julia 185
Robson, David Mather 182–183
Robson, Eliza McKenzie 182
Robson, Flora 5, 10, 35, 69, 83, 93, 125, 132, 167, 178–**184**, 189, 217n34
Robson, May 3–4, 5, 6, 7, 45,

72, 85, 127, 145, 159, 161, 163, 172, 174, 184–**189**, 190, 202, 208, 210
Rogers, Ginger 12, 29, 34, 37, 51, 64, 69, **130**, 140, 147, 177, 225n453
Rogers, Jean 22
Rogers, Kasey 225n442
Rogers, Will 55, 57, 192
The Rogues 71
Roland, Gilbert 18
Romberg, Sigmund 125
Romeo and Juliet (film) 139
Romeo and Juliet (play) 23, 185, 212
Rooney, Mickey 21, 62, 65, **122**, 123, 169
Rope 189
Rose Marie 114, 115
Rosen, Samuel 164
Rossitto, Angelo **200**
Routledge, Patricia 41
Rox, John 159
Roxie Hart 12, 64
A Royal Divorce 14
The Royal Family of Broadway 185, 205, 220n162
Royle, Selena 21, 62, 65, 118, 122, 123, 149, 217n3
Ruggles, Charles 39–**40**, 42, 59
Ruggles, Wesley 19
Ruggles of Red Gap **40**, 44
Runyon, Damon 110, 111, 187
Rush, Barbara 61
Russell, Gail **169**
Russell, Hattie 191
Russell, Jane **216**
Russell, Rosalind 39, 54, 60, 125, 139, 150, 160, 163, 170, 172, 191, 205, 206, 210, 219n124, 220n190, 221n237
Rutherford, Ann 30, 42, 46
Rutherford, Margaret 94, 190
Ryan, Irene 32
Ryder, Wynona 137

Sabotage 9
Sail Away 157
Saint, Eva Marie 120
Sakall, S.Z. "Cuddles" 32, 65
Salome 16
San Antonio 32
San Francisco 147, **162**
Sanders, George 13
Santa Barbara 13, 16, 127
Santley, Joseph 153
Saraband for Dead Lovers 183
Saratoga Trunk 31–**32**, 179, 181, **182**, 227n594
Sargent, John Singer 229n658
Saroyan, William 21
Satan Met a Lady 149, 193–194
The Saturday Night Kid 138
Saturday's Children 43
Savage Intruder (aka *Hollywood*

Horror House/The Comeback) 201
Save Me the Waltz 76
Saville, Victor 70
Scacchi, Greta 202
Scandal at Scourie 123
Scaramouche 167, 170
Scarface 18
The Scarlet Empress 78, 180
Schafer, Natalie 127, 164
Schildkraut, Joseph 198
The School for Scandal 185
Scorsese, Martin 16
Scott, Martha 46, 170
Scott, Randolph 85, 156
The Sea Hawk 135, 136, 179, 180–181
Seaton, George 6, 170, 172
Seaton, Phyllis 6, 170
Second Fiddle 140
The Second Mrs. Tanqueray 23, 68, 209
The Second Time Around 177
The Second Woman 32
The Secret Fury 169
The Secret Garden 71, 91–92, 190
The Secret Life of Walter Mitty 22, 30
Segal, George 83, 146, 151
Seitz, J.F.R. 96
Selznick, David O. 25, 26, 33, 35, 66, 69, 76, 90, 103, 105, 107, 108, 138, 160, 178
Separate Tables 71
Sergeant Rutledge 61
Sergeant York 190
Sessions, Almira 76, 134, 221n236
7 Faces of Dr. Lao 151
Seven Women 83, 184
The Seventh Cross 124, 190
70, Girls, 70 128
Shadow of a Doubt 190
The Shadow of the Thin Man 37, 185
Shanghai 195
The Shanghai Gesture (film) 145
The Shanghai Gesture (play) 217n32
Shaw, George Bernard 43
She Done Him Wrong 36
She Stoops to Conquer 19
She Wore a Yellow Ribbon 130
Shearer, Norma 5, 49–50, 85, 87, 93, 115, 125, 131, 132, 134, 139, 142, 155, 157, 186, 205, 214, 218n71
The Shelf 171
The Shepherd of the Hills 45, 48, 113
Shepherd, Cybill 132
Sheridan, Ann 36, 125, 133, 146, 206
Sherman, Lowell 219n114
Sherman, Vincent 206

Index

The Shewing-Up of Blanco Posnet 9, 133
The Shining Hour (film) 21, 63
The Shining Hour (play) 68
Shipman, Louis Evan 205
Shirley, Anne **153**
The Shocking Miss Pilgrim 155, 165, 170
Showboat (musical) 137, 138, 139
Show Boat (1929) 184, 190
Show Boat (1936) 102
Show Boat (1951) 120, 175
The Show-Off 178, 191
Sidney, Sylvia 44, 113
Sifton, Claire 214
Sifton, Paul 214
The Sign of the Ram **211**
The Sign on the Door 72
The Silver Cord (film) 22, 74, 83, 207
The Silver Cord (play) 72, 73–74
Simmons, Jean 123
Simon, Neil 131
Simpson, Russell 79
Sinatra, Frank 157
Since You Went Away 103, 107, 118, 124
The Singing Nun 123–124
Sister Act 158
The Sisters 74–75, 147, 221n230
Six of a Kind 40, 193
Skelton, Red 109
Skinner, Cornelia Otis 222n300
Skipworth, Alison 6, 29, 40, 56, 75, 76, 78, 127, 168, 174, 189–**196**, 202, 208
Skipworth, Frank Markham 191
Slaves 202
Small Town Girl 59
Smith, Alexis 32, **119**, 123
Smith, C. Aubrey 65, 211
Smith, Rex 96, 144
Smith, Winn Revere 167
The Snake Pit **47**, 150
The Snoop Sisters 127, 129
Snow White and the Seven Dwarfs 197
Solid South 96, 152
Somewhere I'll Find You 149
A Son Comes Home **41**
Sondergaard, Gale 12, 44, 53, 69, 117, 118, 142, 150, 154, 163, 181, 196–**202**
The Song of Bernadette 28, 69, 164, 204
The Song of Songs 75, 194, **195**
Song of the South 106, **207**
Sorry, Wrong Number 123, 125, 129
Sothern, Ann 30
Sparks, Ned 34
The Spider Woman 196, 199, **200**
The Spider Woman Strikes Back **199**, 200
The Spiral Staircase 25

Spoto, Donald 56
Spreading the News 9
Spring Freshet 153
Springer, John 42, 100, 159, 160, 213
The Southerner **45**
Stage Door 50, 189, 190
Stage Door Canteen 211
Staggs, Sam 176
Stanislavsky, Konstantin 141, 142, 144
Stanley, Kim 17, 38
Stanwyck, Barbara 17, 18, 46, 48, 63, 111, 115, 116, 123, 133, 154, 178, 201, 218n37
Stapleton, Jean 82
Stapleton, Maureen 80, 132
Star for a Night **77**, 78
A Star Is Born (1937) 3–4, 5
A Star Is Born (1954) 7
Star Trek III: The Quest for Spock 13, 18
Starling, Lynn 140
Station West 124
Steele, Tommy 71
Steen, Mike 224n420
Steiger, Rod 48
Stein, Gertrude 163
Stella Dallas 102, 113
Stephens, Harvey 197
Stephenson, Patricia Ziegfeld 55, 61
Sterling, Robert 149
Stevens, Ashton 23
Stevens, George 20
Stevens, Risë 32
Stewart, James 35, 43, 44, 46, 63, 69, 79, 94, 120, 128, 145, 150, **173**, 219n140
Stickney, Dorothy 160
Stine, Whitney 187, 193, 226n510
Stingaree 132, 133
Stompanato, Johnny 221n234
Stone, Lewis 62, 186
Storm, Rafael 64
Storm in a Teacup 11
The Story of Alexander Graham Bell 62–63, 154
The Story of Irene and Vernon Castle 140
The Story of Mankind 124
The Story of Temple Drake 154
The Story on Page One 83, 175
Straight Is the Way 85
The Strange Affair of Uncle Harry 12–13
Strange Cargo 147
The Strange Death of Adolf Hitler **198**
The Strange Love of Martha Ivers 218n37
Strasberg, Lee 81, 197
The Stratton Story 120
The Strawberry Blonde 225n462

Street Scene (film) 44
Street Scene (play) 43
A Streetcar Named Desire 81, 176
Strictly Unconventional 191
Strode, Woody 61
Strongheart 39
Stuart, Gloria 51
Sullavan, Margaret 21, 44, 60, 128, 145, 185, 221n237
Sullivan, James 89
Sul-Te-Wan, Madame 105
Summer Holiday 62, 122–**123**
Summer and Smoke 151
Summer Stock 114
Summertime 218n84
Sunday 23, 28
Sunset Boulevard 202
Susan and God 115
Suspicion 211
Suzy 133
The Swan 95, 99, 125, 127
Swanson, Gloria 74, 112, 115, 195
Sweet Bird of Youth 83
Sweethearts 206, 207
Swift, Clive 41
Swindell, Larry 196
Swingin' the Dream 108
Switzer, Carl "Alfalfa" 48, 220n144
Synge, J.M. 10, 11

A Tale of Two Cities 139, 190
Tall Story 156
Talmadge, Norma 74, 202
The Taming of the Shrew 111
Tamiroff, Akim 141
Tammy and the Bachelor 37, 131
Tammy and the Doctor 48, 157–**158**
Tammy Tell Me True 49
Tandy, Jessica 165
Tarkington, Booth 39, 152
Tarnished Lady 154, 214, 216
Tartuffe 84
Tarzan and the Amazons 146
Tashman, Lilyan 35
Taylor, Clarice 110
Taylor, Elizabeth 17, 59, 65, 83, 120, 163, 181
Taylor, Laurette 14, 96, 97
Taylor, Libby 34, 100, 107
Taylor, Robert 44, 64, 142, 144, 160, 170, 221n235
Taylor, Rod 120, 158, 184
Taylor, Vaughn 16
Teenage Rebel 37, **130**, 225n453
Tell Me That You Love Me, Junie Moon 166–167
The Tempest 93
Temple, Shirley 63, 74, 78, 95, 103, 161, 201
The Ten Commandments 18, 185
Terry, Ellen 209
Test Pilot 115

Index

Thalberg, Irving 49, 93, 138
Thank Your Lucky Stars 103
That Hamilton Woman (aka Lady Hamilton) **10**, 11, 69
That Midnight Kiss 26
Thatcher, Leora 154
Theatre 96–97
Theodora Goes Wild 63, 168, 170
There's Always Juliet 209
Therese 212
These Three 22, 164
They All Kissed the Bride 58, 59
They Gave Him a Gun 85
They Made Me a Criminal 186
They Met in Bombay 163
The Thin Man 86
The Thin Man Goes Home 165, 206
The Thirteenth Chair (1929) 190
The Thirteenth Chair (1937) **210**
Thirty Minutes in a Street 89
39 East 228n625
This Land Is Mine 136
This Side of Heaven 19
Thomas, Bill 97
Thomson, David 172
Thorpe, Richard 161, 205
Those Redheads from Seattle 121
3 Godfathers 130
The Three Lights 186
Three Men on a Horse 110
The Three Sisters 14, 164
Three Smart Girls **51, 203**, 206
Three Strangers 190
The Thrill of It All 158
Tierney, Gene 37, 64, 115, 145, 154, 165, 176, 178, 216
Tiffin, Pamela 151
Tilbury, Zeffie 189
Till We Meet Again 203
Tillie and Gus 193
The Time of the Cuckoo 218n84, 225n423
Titanic 172
To Catch a Thief 98, 99
To Each His Own 60
Tobacco Road 154, 189
Tobias, George 156, 158, 174, 197
Tom Sawyer 78
Tomlinson, Jennie McGaughey 111
Tomlinson, Samuel Joseph 111
Tone, Franchot 44, 62, 85, 186, 193
Tonight or Never 195
Too Hot to Handle 115
Topper (film) 59
Topper (TV) 151
Topper Returns **58**, 59, 177
Topper Takes a Trip 59
The Torch Bearers 39, 40, 41, 56, 191–192
Torch Song 86
Torn, Rip 17, 167

Tortilla Flat 172
Toys in the Attic 166
Track of the Cat 44, 48
Tracy, Spencer 11, 20, 124, 147, 162
Tranberg, Charles 225
Travers, Henry 119, 147, 221n237
Tree, Dorothy 163
Tree, Herbert Beerbohm 72, 73
Trelawny of the Wells 185
Trevor, Claire 18, 53, **77**, 86, 113, 123, 148, 150
The Trojan Women 212
The Trouble with Harry 128, 129
The True Story of Jesse James 121
Tucker, George Loane 167
Tucker, Sophie 103
Turner, Lana 70, 113, 116, 149, 221n234
Twain, Mark 23
The Twelve Pound Look 23, 24
Two-Faced Woman 190
The Two Orphans 186
Two Wise Maids 196

Uncle Tom's Cabin 19, 168
Undercurrent 115
The Unholy Wife 48
The Unseen **169**
Urecal, Minerva 134
Urmy, Keith 84
UTBU 171

Valente, Alfredo 142
Valiant Is the Word for Carrie 84, **85**, 102
The Valley of Decision **70**
Valli, Alida 25
Van Cleef, Lee 125
Van Dyke, W.S. 113, 161, 205
Van Fleet, Jo 86
Varden, Evelyn 26, 29
Varden, Norma 136, 190
Veiller, Bayard 189, 210
Velez, Lupe 169
Venable, Reginald S.H. 21, 22
Vera-Ellen 32, 115, 157
Verdon, Gwen 171
Vertigo 150
Vidor, Charles 164
The Visit 201
Vivacious Lady 20, 44, 46, 219n140
von Sternberg, Joseph 180, 204

Wagner, Jack 38
Walker, Patricia 82
Walker, Stuart 43, 152, 220n196
Wallach, Eli 82
Walpole, Hugh 27
Walsh, Raoul 16
The Waltons 49, 127
Waltz of the Toreadors 128
The War Against Mrs. Hadley **20**, 21, 22, 64

Warburton, John **31**
Warner, Jack 179
Warren, Lesley Ann 71
Warrick, Ruth **207**
Warwick, Dionne 202
Washbourne, Mona 95, 190
Watch on the Rhine 46, 204, 205, 207
Waterloo Bridge 144–145, 206, 207
Waterman, Willard 150
Waters, Ethel 25, 26, 92, 100, 107
Watson, Leila Morlet 204
Watson, Lucile 28, 46, 50, 65, 69, 75, 76, 125, 127, 133, 139, 168, 202–**208**, 210, 212
Watson, Minor 36
Watson, Thomas Charles 204
Watts, Jill 34, 100, 222n305, 223n311, 223n337
Waugh, Evelyn 89
The Way of All Flesh 88
Wayne, John 47, 125, 128, 130
We Are Not Alone 134, 179, 190
We Were Dancing 115
Webb, Clifton 13, 18, 95
Webster, Annie 209
Webster, Ben 209, 210, 212, 229n678
Webster, Margaret 209, 212
Webster, "Old Ben" 209
Wedgeworth, Ann 167
Weissmuller, Johnny 146
Welles, Orson 12, 118, 125, 141
Wells, H.G. 89
West, Mae 16, 33, 36, 38, 56, 78, 85, 102, 111, 116, 123, 155, 192, 193, 219n114
West Side Story 22
Westley, Helen 45, 61, 120, 168, 197
Westman, Nydia 154, 199
Westmore, Perc 193
Whale, James 88, 89, 128, 134, 144, 225n461
What a Life 108
What Ever Happened to Baby Jane? 201
What Price Hollywood? 35, 36, 37, 219n114
Whatever Happened to Aunt Alice? 83, 202
What's the Matter With Helen? 123
Wheeler, Bert 139, 140
When Ladies Meet (1933) 41, 50, 52, 64
When Ladies Meet (1941) 64
White Banners 22, 65
The White Cliffs of Dover 70, 181, 185, 190, 211
White Heat 190
Whiteoaks 24
Whitty, Alfred 208
Whitty, Mary Ashton 208

Index

Whitty, May 6, 10, 53, 68, 69, 122, 143, 145, 159, 162, 163, 189, 202, 208–**212**
Who's Minding the Store? 127
The Wicked Age 111
Wickes, Mary 139, 158
Wife in Name Only 140
Wife vs. Secretary 186
Wilde, Oscar 16, 62, 137, 183, 209
Wilder, Billy 93, 205
Wilder, Thornton 21, 46
Wilding, Michael 91
Will Shakespeare 181
Willard, John 199
William, Warren 34, 85, 87, 149, 194, 214
Williams, Bert 103
Williams, Emlyn 80, 81, 209
Williams, Esther 121
Williams, Larry 223
Williams, Rhys 80
Williams, Tennessee 80, 81, 83, 84, 151, 175, 213
The Willow Tree 19
Wills, Chill 155
Wilson, Marie 149
The Wind and the Rain 128
The Wings of the Dove 82
Winninger, Charles **51**
Winter Meeting 32
Winters, Shelley 227n573
Winwood, Estelle 5, 19, 20, 94–95, 99, 125, 185, 225n423
The Wistful Widow of Wagon Gap 115
With a Song in My Heart 172, 176

Witherspoon, Cora 33, 56, 58, 69, 162, 176, 212–216
Witherspoon, Maude 216
Witness for the Prosecution 90, 93, 136
Wives Never Know 41–42
The Wiz 110
The Wizard of Oz 3, 58, 161, 197, 215, 221n235
Wodehouse, P.G. 137
The Wolf Man 141, 145
The Woman in White 119, 125
Woman of the Year 20
A Woman's Face 115
The Women 39, 42, 100, 107, 108, 110, 112, 113, 115, 125, 139, 157, 205–206
Wood, Natalie 28
Wood, Sam 29, 31, 86, 87, 181
Wood, Tom 152
Woodard, W.R. 78
Woods, Donald 204
Woodward, Joanne 174
Woolley, Monty 174
Woolsey, Robert 139, 140
Wray, Fay 37
Wright, Teresa 69, 122, 211, 212
Written on the Wind 82
Wuthering Heights 178–179, **180**, 183
Wycherly, Margaret 74, 154, 168, 189–190, 210
Wyler, William 22, 113, 179, 199
Wylie, Philip 74
Wyman, Jane 28, 118, 123, 124, 146, 178
Wynn, Keenan 28, 32

Wynyard, Diana 132
Wyoming 113, 146

Yarbo, Lillian 34, 100, 107
The Yearling 190
Yeats, William Butler 10
Yes, My Darling Daughter 21, 203
Yolanda and the Thief 129, 131, 175
York, Dick 156
You Can't Beat Love 147
You Can't Take It with You 22, 41, 63, 65, 69, 190
Young, Gig 83
Young, Jordan R. 43, 219n141
Young, Loretta 25, 70, 78, **91**, 92, 133, 195
Young, Mary 204
Young, Robert 21, 32, 64, 170
Young, Roland 40, 58, 59, 62, 149, 151, 153, **194**
Young Cassidy 184
The Young in Heart 59
Young Mr. Lincoln 53
The Young Philadelphians 61
Young Tom Edison 21, 65
Young Widow **216**
You're My Everything 164, **166**
Yurka, Blanche 12, 43, 67, 139

Zander the Great 50
Zanuck, Darryl F. 45, 170, 172
Ziegfeld, Florenz 39, 54, 55, 61, 192
Zukor, Adolph 47

www.ingramcontent.com/pod-product-compliance
Ingram Content Group UK Ltd.
Pitfield, Milton Keynes, MK11 3LW, UK
UKHW050535150426
5217IPUK00026B/1945